THE ROSE CODES:
BOOK OF INITIATIONS

THE ROSE CODES:
BOOK OF INITIATIONS

Forgotten lore, practices, and rituals of the Sacred Order of the Rose to awaken the wisdom of Divine Feminine within

An Initiation into the Mysteries of the Rose

Mariya Nurislamova

ISBN Paperback 979-8-9850663-4-0
ISBN Hardcover 979-8-9850663-5-7
ISBN Ebook 979-8-9850663-3-3

First Edition

Cover art by Katie-Louise
Cover design by Jorge Riera
Illustrations by Tamta Kondzharia
Editing by Sandy Draper
Proofreading by Robin Fuller
Art direction by Morgane Leoni

Website: www.thisismariya.com
Email: info@thisismariya.com

Printed in the United States.

This book is created in Partnership with the Rose Council, the Sacred Circle of the High Priestesses of the Rose, as represented by:

Inanna (Ishtar, Astarte)

Isis (Iset, Auset, Isais)

Lady Nada (Mary Magdalene)

Mother Mary

Kuan Yin (Guanyin)

With blessings and a Divine commission from the GREAT MOTHER *herself (one of many names and mysteries, the Great Shakti, Mahadevi, Shekinah, Amrita, Area, Psychea, Anima, Janea, and so on).*

Table of Contents

This one is for the goddess slumbering within you,
The Divine femininity anchored, the Divine femininity earned,
The Divine femininity inherent, the Divine femininity claimed.
She is a vessel. She is a promise. She is a sacred vow.
The Holy One.

This one is for the goddess rising within you,
The one who will tolerate oblivion no further.
The one who loved deeper, who fought harder, the one who forgave.
Life force made manifest, supreme wisdom incarnate, magnetism unbound.
The Sacred One.

As you step upon the path of getting to know her, remember:
You are spoken for. You are accounted for.
You are much loved in this world and the next.

We are on the other side, waiting for you
To pull back the curtain of forgetfulness,
To step into yourself fully,
To rise,
To shake off the illusion,
To claim the goddess within
And the goddess without,
To finally come home.
We are the Sisterhood of the Rose,
And you are one of us,
Our Sibling in Rose.
Welcome back at long last!

Foreword

Some books come from within; they are created and invoked. And then there are books like this one; they come from spirit, completely take over your world, and change you at a cellular level.

This book came to me one sunny Sunday afternoon. My spirit guides asked me if I'd like to learn the name of my next book. I said yes—and the floodgates opened. Within thirty minutes, I knew everything I needed to know: the title, the cover, even the name of each chapter. A "calling" is a mild way to describe what happened. It was more like a demand from spirit, with specific guidelines. And so, I surrendered to the process.

I am more than obsessed with this work; I am pregnant with it. I feel this book breathing and taking shape, so that one day, it can emerge in full bloom and make itself known. She is a strong one and has been a long time coming. Like the spirit of the planet's true sisterhood, this book yearns to be birthed, to see the light of day. As its mother, I am grateful that it chose me as a vessel for the message that is meant to come through it at this time. I believe it is much needed—requested, in fact, by the many women who struggle to be who they are, to live their most authentic lives. Although I wrote this book with female readers in mind, I believe femininity is innate to all of us, regardless of gender identification. It flows within our veins, and it yearns to be known. We are all energy, androgynous at the soul level, ever shifting, ever evolving in our expression. Regardless of what gender you currently identify as, there is something for you in this book. If you are reading these words, I know you were meant to find me.

Writing this book has been about facing my shadow, my insecurities, and the wounds of the great women who came before me. I am a byproduct of their legacy, the daughter who walks in their footsteps, one of those responsible for carrying their torch. Perhaps it is by going within and addressing my fears, mending my limiting beliefs, and embracing my own flavor of feminine power that I can share this book. This process is less than glorious, just like any birth. But as always, it will be a hundred percent worth it in the end.

There are many books I could have written; so much in the world of spirit is vying for my attention. Alas, this book is a massive closing of the karmic loop for me, something I could not complete in past lifetimes. So, I am back at it with more resolve than ever. The power of the Rose, the breath of Divine Feminine, is more alive on planet Earth than ever. The timing is divinely aligned, and I fully surrender to the synchronicities and the process of my personal unfolding, and to my own Path of the Rose that weaves itself across incarnations.

Planet Earth is going through her own realignment right now, recalibrating and adjusting her body for what's to come, so I couldn't have asked for a better time to birth this book. May it be a beacon of light for those looking for answers during the many tomorrows that are sure to come. Pristine as the first snow, captivating like the light of a guiding star, may your path be lit up by the natural alchemy of Gaia and her nurturing motherly love.

Thank you for coming with me on this journey, friend. We were meant to walk side by side with this book. May it create infinite magic, abundance, and alignment in your world and all the lives you come to touch. This is my intention for you and for the world. It is my greatest honor to guide you on this ancient yet undoubtedly new Path of the Rose.

And so it is.

The Great She is within you,
Her spirit, her soul, her womb, her joy, her pain.
Open your higher heart and feel into her essence.
She is reaching out through time and space to meet you halfway.
She is your Great Celestial Mother,
The wise and loving energy of the void.
She is potential, she is love, she is true knowing.
She is spontaneity, she is freedom, she is flow.
She is your forever safe space, your holy sanctuary.

She is here to welcome you to the Rose Lineage,
To initiate you into the mysteries of sacred femininity,
To lead you through the labyrinth of awareness
Toward the heart of understanding,
To lead you closer to who you truly are at your core,
To lead you home.
And so it is.

A New Day Has Come

I can feel it in my bones. I can sense it in the air. The way the butterflies are dancing around me in circles... I have always been privy to this dance, but did I pay attention?

Today, I stepped upon Mother Earth for the first time. Oh, I have walked here before, even barefoot. But it wasn't the same—never the same. Today I walked my path healed, renewed, and attuned to the heartbeat of Gaia. I stepped into the Great Mother fully, without reservation, without doubt, without an agenda, without assuming superiority. I left my fear in the bygone folds of yesterday—that deep instinctual fear of the wildness of nature. I stopped expecting nature to hurt me, and then something changed: nature stopped wanting to hurt me back. She is only love, and always has been, and will remain so forever.

Will I meet her at her level? Will I match her frequency? Do I have what it takes? I believe so. The Great Mother knows so. The river thinks so as well. We are all in Divine agreement. And so it is.

Yesterday was the day of reckoning, the grand examination of all I have amounted to in my existence. I saw so much light, but also darkness. And my flavor of darkness was fear—fear of being hurt, of being seen, of being taken advantage of, of being criticized, of being misunderstood. But there was an even greater fear of staying silent, squandering my Goddess-given grace, and not walking my path boldly. The fear of having my voice taken away, my lips sealed—that was the biggest one of all.

And so, I called upon the Great Mother to release me from the cage of fear. I cut the cords that bound me, and the Great Mother sealed my wounds. She nursed me through the process and bore witness to my liberation. It was beautiful, sacred. It felt like the convergence of timelines, past, future, and present merging into one sweet moment of the breaking of the chains. Mother's medicine may be bitter, but it always comes from a place of love.

I am a woman uncaged today. I am a woman unchained. I am a woman beloved. I am a woman heard. I am a woman brimming with life, today, tomorrow, and always.

That's why the grass felt different today; the grass shifted its vibration as I shifted mine. Can you blame it? It has to meet me at my level. Such is the Sacred Law: the Universe will always meet you at your level. It will match your frequency perfectly. The Universe speaks to me. It speaks to you as well. Can you hear its call?

It is time to slow down to listen and truly hear.

Yesterday, I was held by the Mother for the first time. Yesterday was my personal alpha and omega. My phoenix rising. A sacred communion with the oneness of nature. The initiation, the rite of passage. The entirety of me felt it. I saw the fullness of nature reflected in my eyes, and saw myself reflected back in nature. We were one. We *are* one. I will carry this knowledge through every step of my existence.

I don't have to do this alone. I have never been alone in this. The entirety of the Universe is supporting me in my journey. The fullness of the Great Mother is offering her assistance, her flow, her abundance, her unconditional love. We should never be afraid of this much support. I accept this sacred offering from the Mother today. I accept her help, love, gifts, and serenity. I accept, and thus we are merged. We are one. We are indivisible.

As I walk the path of the Great Mother, also called the Path of the Rose, will you walk with me? Will you join me on this journey of healing, coming together, and falling in love with life? It is my sacred calling to be your guide on this journey, and I don't take this lightly.

Walk with me. Heal with me. Reclaim your ancient wisdom. Take back your Goddess-promised humanity. It is only a step away. Will you take that step, my dear one? Will you drink from the chalice of Sacred Femininity with me? Will you join in with the great force that has always been yours to claim? Will you step into the divinity that you are?

On the other side of fear, on the other side of doubt, on the other side of the shadow is the version of you that you are meant to be. Are you ready to finally meet yourself fully?

The Age of the Mother Divine

"A great sign appeared in heaven: a woman clothed with the sun, with the moon under her feet, and on her head a crown of twelve stars."
—Book of Revelations 12:1, New Testament

The Age of Divine Mother is here. It descended upon the Earth in an instant, and there was light—the blinding kind that sees right into your soul, the light of an all-seeing eye of providence.

The Great She walked barefoot through the golden gates of the new era, ushering in the winds of change. Her hair was gilded by the caress of the sun, her dress purified by the pearlescent fire of the seven heavens, she walked tall, her head adorned by a crown of stars and roses. She carried the white book of wisdom and a set of scales. She was judgment and compassion, redemption and reckoning, forgiveness and chastening.

And so, the Great Mother walked up to a Tree of Life that she planted long ago—a tree protected by the phoenix's fire, the eagle's courage, and the owl's foresight. The tree that above everything was the central axis of existence, the beginning and the end, the point upon which a new world would be birthed. And so, the Mother placed the white tome upon a pedestal of vines and briars. And she started reading from it, flipping the pages to the steady beat of her heart. And as she read from the book, the long-lost flowers bloomed, and the remote stars sang, and the new moon came alive with longing, and the New Earth rose from the deep waters, heralding a great beginning. And all manner of beasts came to listen to the words of the Mother, basking in her wisdom, drinking of her life-giving flow as she presided upon a throne of thorns and roses, lest the new world forgot the grievances of the old one.

And thus, the Great Mother brought forth a new law, and a new land, and a new Bible. And the old was no more—neither the land, nor the sea, nor sin. As such, the prophecy was fulfilled, and Atlantis was reborn, bigger and better than before, just like the golden trumpets of the angels foretold before the beginning of the cycle.

We are walking into the Age of the Mother, dear one—a period of her dominion and glory, a time of transformation and growth, a much-awaited era of her great return. Gentle are the light wings of the Mother, sweet is her call, and omnipotent is the power of her love. The Divine Mother has come to lay the veil of protection over all her beautiful children, promising them a better world and a new beginning.

Welcome to the Age of the Mother, the Golden Age of rebirth and renewal, my sibling in Rose!

May there be light, forever and always.

The Sacred Unfolding

You are the breath of the Universe, her life force manifest. Sometimes ragged, sometimes rash, sometimes blissful, sometimes serene, always precious, always one of a kind.

You are unfolding every day, just like the Universe herself. Petal by petal, you face this life, showing the richness of your colors and facets, exploring the entirety of you. You are unfolding, and thus, you are a work in progress. Embrace your path, the ebbs and flows, the ups and downs—especially the downs. The downs remind you that the journey doesn't have to be pleasant to be fruitful. It rarely is.

Watch as your Universe evolves alongside you, and just like you, it is a work of art and a work in progress. Above all, fall in love with your peculiarities, imperfections, quirks, and cracks. The stretch marks, the lines, the grey hairs—they are a testament to your unfolding, witnesses to your growing wisdom, to the truths of your journey.

Petal by petal, let yourself come together into the fullness of you. You are bursting through. You are ready to be seen, heard, acknowledged, and understood for who you are.

Unfolding is a sacred process, a rite of passage. A bud only becomes a rose in full bloom by virtue of unfolding. You have done enough hiding, so allow yourself the audacity of unfolding today. Let your true spirit shine outward. You are the light you have cloistered away for too long.

Unfold together with your sisters and your brothers, for the unfolding of one is the unfolding of all. Jump in first, way-shower. Start unfolding petal by petal. It is through your unfolding that your beautiful soul will change the world.

The Sisterhood of the Rose

The rose is her language, the stars are her promise, and love is her element. Our Divine Mother is today, tomorrow, and always, infinite and unknowable, yet ever present in each of us.

As an ancient school of mysteries, a group of dedicated initiates, and a sacred lore of Divine Femininity, the Order of the Rose is here for its second rebirth, for its long-prophesied second coming.

On the etheric level, the Order of the Rose is a gathering of the highest order of souls whose mission is to help the Divine Feminine reawaken and run supreme across thousands of worlds. The Sisters of the Rose are souls who have gone to the depths of creation to master the feminine mysteries, to taste the full range of feminine magic, to experience the full spectrum of feminine archetypes, and to help transcend the female shadow, the female wound, the female cage, the female scar tissue, reemerging on the other side as beacons of feminine light. Some of the names of the Sisters in Rose are well known to you: Mary Magdalene, Mother Mary, Joan of Arc, Saint Anne, goddesses Athena, Artemis, Aphrodite, Brigid, Rhiannon, Isis, Kuan Yin, Green Tara, Sarasvati, and Pele, among others. Some remain a distant collective memory, such as the Hathors and the oracles of Delphi; many are forgotten entirely. This doesn't make their path any less important, or their contribution any less meaningful. The Sisters in Rose number in the thousands, each one a unique expression of female divinity, each one a gift to this world.

The Sisters of the Rose came before us to walk the walk. Some were ostracized, belittled, and ridiculed, while others were revered, lauded, and admired. Regardless, the sisters were powerful souls who often served as the way-showers, wisdom collectors, planetary healers, shamans, miracle workers, saints, psychics, and creatresses. They represent the many faces of feminine power—the power to see, to hear, to know, to perceive, to receive, to love, and to heal. Joining the Order of the Rose is a great cosmic honor. It is only extended to the souls who have proven their right to walk under the Mother's wing of protection and veneration.

And so, the Path of the Rose is a sacred path of initiation into the ancient Feminine Principles, into the teachings of the Order of the Rose. It is a path of understanding the Divinity within, welcoming it, and letting it unfold.

In the solar system, the Order of the Rose is anchored by the planet Venus—the seat of the Rose, the nucleus of the Divine Feminine Network, the local ascension hub, and the point of connection with higher feminine consciousness. It is through Venusian energies that the sisters communicate with us souls incarnated on Earth, and their earthly apparitions become possible. Venus is also the sisters' local home, and is thus a portal to higher consciousness, a bridge between the imperfect reality and the perfect blueprint, the way in for the willing initiate.

The sacred teachings of the Order of the Rose transcend galaxies and are generally channeled from higher consciousness when each respective planet is ready to enter one of its many cycles of ascension. The Order of the Rose has existed on Earth for hundreds of thousands of years. Its body of knowledge is cosmic and transcendent, once anchored here by the Divine Mother herself through many of her projections and apparitions, through many of her daughters (and even sons) who followed in her footsteps.

The story goes that once upon a time, Higher Femininity established its roots in Gaia. This happened during the Earth's formative stages, during her very infancy. Once anchored, this Divine Consciousness started growing from a seed to a sprout into a mighty tree: the Tree of Feminine Understanding. A counterpart to the Tree of Masculine Knowledge (also known as the Tree of Knowledge of Good and Evil), this tree grew in power, biding its time, awaiting the birth of the ones discerning enough to partake in its wisdom.

As years went by and Gaia grew in strength, she brought higher beings to incarnate within her realm. One such being received wisdom from the Tree of Understanding; she became known as the first initiate of the Rose. The first initiate started writing down her insights in what later became known as the *Book of the Rose*, an epistle containing the Divine Mother's wisdom. The book you are currently holding is just a leaf from the original Book of the Rose, another work in a series of books written in connection with the Tree of Understanding, neither the first nor the last of its kind. And yet it was created for these exact times of the great shake-up of human consciousness, the Era of the Phoenix, the recalibration of the Star of Venus, the portal into higher consciousness, the times of the Great Divide. It is in these formative times that the energies of true understanding and not just of knowing must be anchored, must take center stage and join the cosmic dance.

It is the Divine Mother's desire that you, dear soul, start learning from her Tree of Understanding, that you walk the path of the Divine Feminine and discover your hidden talents, that you join this cosmic movement and become one of its pillars. It is with this in mind that she wanted this book to be written, and it is with this in mind that you were meant to find it.

Here's to the journey stretching out in front of you! And so it is.

Ritual: Connecting to the White Tree of Divine Feminine Understanding

One of the better ways to grasp the ideas in this book is to synchronize your heart with the heart of the Great Mother, merging your frequencies so you can receive a set of codes and activations, which you'll find start coming through quite naturally. To achieve this level of connection with the Mother, try the ritual below, and watch as reading this book becomes a true pilgrimage, your personal journey through time and space into the depth of love and wisdom that is our Mother Divine.

You will need:

- Mugwort or palo santo
- A cup of salt
- A simple silver bracelet
- A moonstone crystal
- A bowl half filled with water, half with colloidal silver
- Sandalwood and jasmine essential oils
- A towel

The ritual:

Make sure you won't be disturbed for about twenty minutes. This ritual creates a sacred space that must be respected.

1. Start by smudging with some mugwort or palo santo to clear any dense energies around you. Move clockwise to speed up the process.
2. Place the cup filled with salt in front of you. Place your moonstone crystal and the silver bracelet in the cup, submerging them in the salt.
3. Place the bowl with water/silver in front of you. Add ten drops of sandalwood essential oil and eight drops of jasmine essential oil to the mix. Place your left hand into the bowl.
4. Close your eyes and focus on your breath. Quiet your mind and focus on the beat of your beautiful, strong heart.
5. Inhale and send your breath into your lower belly, clearing and healing that area of your body.
6. Imagine that right in front of you, there is a majestic tree. Its trunk is milky white, with white branches. Opalescent white leaves grace the branch-

es, giving the tree an otherworldly glow. As if conjured by magic, golden apples grow there, and a pair of white phoenixes protect the tree from random onlookers and uninvited visitors.

7. Do not worry, my friend; you are very much expected. Come closer and touch the tree trunk with your hands. Feel the rough texture of the bark, hard as metal, but also soft as velvet, hot and cold, familiar and utterly new.
8. Sit underneath the tree's foliage, away from the entire world. Let your back be supported by the tree's mighty trunk. As you connect with the tree's energy, ask the Divine Mother to give you the keys to deeper understanding. Ask her to invite you into her abode, so that the wisdom of the Universe can be revealed to you.
9. Watch as one of the tree branches hands you a small silver key. Take the key and turn around. You'll notice a small keyhole in the tree's trunk. Place the key in the lock and watch as a white door opens in the trunk, beckoning you inside.
10. Step inside and look around. You will find yourself in a well-lit circular room with a domed ceiling, the walls decorated with a pattern of white roses, and the air smelling of flowers.
11. Notice a woman clad in a pearlescent white cloak entering the room. Her hair is made of sunlight, a star graces her forehead, her movements are slow and measured, and her gaze is wise. She smiles at you and takes your hands in hers. Notice how her warmth fills you up from within. Watch as the woman drops a white pearl into one of your palms. This is your first pearl of wisdom, a gift from the Mother herself. Accept the pearl with gratitude, and place it inside your heart space for safekeeping.
12. Notice the woman pointing toward a white armchair in the middle of the circular room. Sit down on it, placing your arms on the armrests. Surrender to this moment fully. Watch as the white roots of the tree start to grow under your feet, and one of the roots enters your body through the sole of your left foot, establishing a one-on-one connection between you and the Tree of Understanding. Do not worry, the tree cannot hurt you. This connection is your bridge, a gift of wisdom from the tree. Accept it freely, and share your gratitude.
13. Watch as iridescent white liquid flows from the tree's root into your body, moving up from the sole of your left foot and towards your heart space,

finding its new home inside your beautiful heart. Allow yourself to receive as much of this liquid as possible. This is the energy that the tree wants you to carry with you on your life's path, a gift that will enable you to find answers to even the most complex of questions, fostering much wisdom.

14. Once you are ready, feel free to leave through the doorway. Take one last glance at the tree and thank it for the wonderful gift of wisdom it has imparted to you today. Please know that you can return to the tree whenever you require answers or could benefit from wise counsel.
15. Open your eyes and take your left hand out of the bowl of water. Dry it with a towel. Take out the silver bracelet from the salt cup and place it on your left wrist. This bracelet is now charged and blessed by the Mother. Wear it for the duration of reading this book, so that an additional layer of information is revealed to you. This way, the spirit guides working with this book can contact you directly and offer additional healing and insight.
16. Take out the moonstone crystal from the salt cup. Place the moonstone under your pillow for three consecutive nights. Divine Mother has prepared a set of upgrades and codes for you, with your highest good in mind.

Alas, our ritual has come to an end, but your connection to the White Tree of Divine Feminine Understanding has only just been established. It will help you walk the Path of the Rose and become a true initiate in no time. And so it is.

Have a blessed spiritual journey, my dear!

PART I

SACRED FEMININITY UNVEILED

Heart Space: On Stars and Roses

Plentiful are the Divine Mother's trinkets. Many are her faces, infinite are her wombs, and great are her mysteries. She is unknowable in her splendor, the one who gave birth to everything and is still birthing more. She is the darkness of the primordial void and the light of the new dawn, the pain of childbirth, and the joy of motherhood. She is the feeling of a summer breeze on your skin and a sensation of freefall when you incarnate, the depth of your dreamscape, and the perpetual flow of the river of time. She is a yes and a no. She is all of it in due time.

Divine Mother loves her trinkets—the jewels and seashells, the moonlit paths and winter skies, the well-crafted poetic verses, and the moths' dance in the flame. But above all else, the Mother values the mystery of the rose and the magic of the stars. Her boundless energy is infused into every petal, every bud, and every thorn birthed of the Earth. Her dreams are hers and hers alone, forever depicted in the star-filled void of the sky, a space above and between where the clouds of stardust mingle with ribbons of scintillating meteors.

"It is all in the bliss of stars and roses," says the Mother, "all of me—everything you will ever need to know."

And we believe her.

And so, we gaze upon the vast abode of the night sky to glimpse the Divine, suspended in midair, both finite and decidedly infinite. We wish upon a star, freely divulging our hearts' desires and deepest secrets in a rare moment of childlike hope. We breathe in the delicate aroma of the rose, briefly lost in the serenity and grace that it represents. All these times are the moments of our sacred communion with the Mother, a manifestation of our deep subconscious desire to be fully held by her, to be loved unconditionally just as we are.

Knowing the essence of stars and roses is knowing the Mother, and deepening this connection is a lifelong journey. From this day forward, let all the roses and the stars on your path serve as reminders of the Divine Mother's immeasurable love for you. May you feel it in every rose petal, sense it in every verdant stem, recognize it in every star, shooting and otherwise, along your precious way. So may it be.

CHAPTER 1

The Five-Pointed Star

"Happy families are all alike; every unhappy family is unhappy in its own way."
—Leo Tolstoy, Anna Karenina

Life is an ever-changing torrent of faces, circumstances, and synchronicities, a vast dynamic flow of seemingly random events that weave a cohesive and often predictable storyline of our existence. Days flow into weeks, weeks into months, months into years. The ever-present unknown of tomorrow keeps us grounded in daily troubles, ready to react or respond whenever the occasion calls for it. And yet, amidst this hypnotic dance, balancing crisis and routine, we can miss the bigger picture.

We step onto the treadmill of life, feeling content that, just like the rest of humanity, we are perpetually seeking and lacking answers. Getting the answers, however, is predicated on looking beyond the veil, expanding our perception of *what is* and *what can be*. Understanding how we fit into the fabric of existence is where it all begins. This is the first domino in a sequence of events that will inevitably lead to our personal expansion. So, it is only fitting to start our journey by exploring the *why* behind it all.

If you have been around the spiritual block, you are probably familiar with the concept of the matrix, an idea that we all live inside a massive hologram, a virtual system created for soul development and evolution. The Five-Pointed Star framework is one of the matrix's most foundational concepts. It describes the journey of beings and planets on their path to evolution, the grand movement across dimensions toward perfect harmony and unity.

Eons ago, our planet was birthed according to a blueprint created by the Great Architect, a celestial mathematician who adds rhythm, tonality, and measure to all living things. While not Source per se, the Great Architect designs and brings forth entire worlds that match the inputs of the Creator Source. Star systems operate according to a master plan and a set of complex equations set forth by the Architect. Each equation is divinely absolute, and built to create layers of reality alongside other frameworks and constructs. Our Universe is a mathematically precise system where everything from the orbital planetary movements to the chemical composition of atoms was once conceived by the Architect. Reality stems from elaborate equations that turn chaos and entropy into organized matter. Above all, matter desires configuration, the existence of law and order to govern its movement. Atoms desire to be formed into molecules, molecules into cells, and cells into organisms. People desire to be formed into family units, family units into communities, communities into regional groups, and regional groups into countries. As above, so below. We are all a part of a larger ecosystem, a larger plan set in motion by the Great Architect himself.

In this grand plan of creation, evolution takes center stage. Evolution is expansion, expansion is life, and every system that the Architect creates is optimized for life, as frequently as possible. Rome wasn't built in a day, however. Complex systems become complex over time. A forest, at first, is a single sapling braving the emptiness of a vast terrain and defying all odds. A human lineage is first just one couple joined in love. A newborn baby is first just one egg fertilized by one sperm cell. Infinitely complex things start very simply. Brick by brick, straw by straw, once-elemental things become complex and intricate. We call it "natural"; the Architect calls it "intentional."

When the Architect set out to create this Universe, he started with a layout for how the system would self-correct and evolve over time. Static systems tend to deteriorate quickly, so the best way to keep the life force flowing is to set it up for automatic expansion from the get-go. And that is how the Five-Pointed Star Framework was born. This framework is the process of evolution encapsulated in five straightforward steps. It is a blueprint for movement from alpha to omega, simplified. Each point of the star symbolizes a new level of learning, growth, and expansion.

The five points of the star are as follows (Please see **Figure 1**):

1. Mind
2. Heart
3. Truth
4. Love
5. Spirit

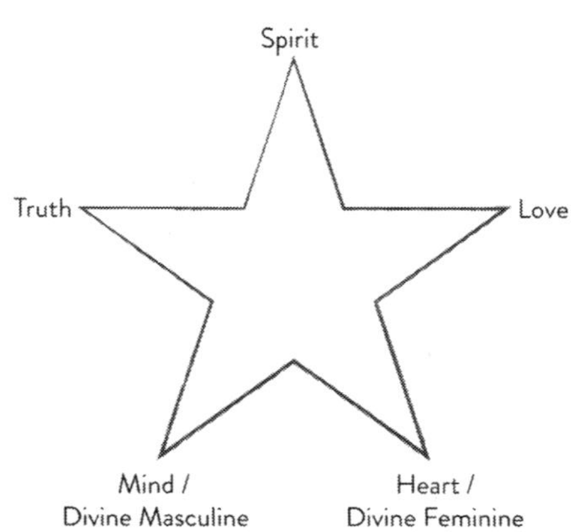

Figure 1: The Five-Pointed Star

A Blueprint of Possibilities

The star is a simple blueprint, but it represents a multitude of possibilities and potential paths. Any point of the star can become the founding point of a system—the point where the evolutionary dance begins. The five points can be unlocked in random order as long as they serve the beings of the system and provide you with enough of a challenge.

Every planet, every star system, and every galaxy in the Universe needs to unlock one point of the star at a time, learning the full range of the lessons that it holds. All the activated points of the star work in harmony like an orchestra, while the unactivated points represent the blind spots, the realm of the unknown and unintegrated. Integrating all five points of the star is the promised land of Divine equilibrium and a perfect outcome, only attainable by those truly committed to growth. The five points thus symbolize a complete journey from zero into fullness and the full spectrum of experience our souls need on our personal path to evolution. In order for you to better understand the mystery and lessons of each point of the star, let us examine them in more detail.

The Pillar of the Mind (or Divine Masculine)

This pillar is the supremacy of logic, rational thought, science, empirical evidence, and the lack of emotion in decision-making. It is about action, direction, confidence, forward movement, and achievement. The worlds dominated by this energy run on results and thrive on schedules and thorough planning. Intellect-based worlds are built to hit targets, to be competitive and materialistic. They are characterized by the proliferation of technology and AI, a search for perfection in outward appearances, and a zero-sum game mentality. These worlds are about getting ahead, winning, conquering, discovering new frontiers, and seeking adventure and new experiences. Knowledge is power here. Anything that cannot be scientifically or empirically proven is considered myth, nonsense, or pseudoscience.

The Pillar of the Heart (or Divine Feminine)

This pillar is the supremacy of feeling, emotional decision-making, intuitive guidance, and heart-led action. It is about nurturing things around you, being in a state of flow and harmony, and creating and experiencing abundance. This pillar is characterized by perceiving over achieving, community over individualism, compassion over criticism, and listening over talking. The worlds dominated by this energy represent sanctuaries that abound in nature, balanced ecosystems, and harmonious energies. These worlds are not about getting ahead, but experiencing things together and reveling in a shared ecosystem. These are the worlds of harmonious relationships, deep conversations, cherished ancestral connections, and heart-based magic.

The Pillar of Love

Love is neither a feeling nor an emotion. It is a state—of oneness. Essentially, in creation, there are only two states: the presence or absence of love. At any point, you are aligned with only one of those states, as they are mutually exclusive. You are either the love or the absence of love in every second of your existence. The pillar of love represents seeing another as a part of yourself, recognizing the spark of the Creator in all living things, and respecting the space and others' free will. Worlds integrated with this pillar share the knowledge that separation is a fallacy, that we all came from one Source and will one day return to it. Love-based worlds are comfortable and cozy; they feel good energetically, emotionally, and mentally. While not focused on advancement or achievement, these worlds are magical and transcendent, if at times hedonistic and indulgent. The pillar of love starts with self-love, so these worlds move beyond the inner critic into a nurturing and supportive self-space.

The Pillar of Truth

This pillar concerns a strong moral compass, your internal guidance mechanisms, well-defined values, and a sense of direction. Being on the path is taken seriously in these worlds. Honor is a central concept, as is keeping your word. Here, justice runs supreme, and communication is always at the forefront. It must be pure and intentional, reflecting your personal truth. Living and speaking your truth becomes paramount, your quest and daily practice.

Karma also takes center stage in truth-based societies, with souls focused on living in a way that helps us accumulate as little negative karma as possible. The worlds dominated by this energy are about giving back and paying it forward, simply because it is the right thing to do. Any injustice or untruth is perceived as a capital offense and avoided at all costs. Unfortunately, this sometimes leads to being overly straightforward and telling the truth at the expense of hurting others, which could contribute to the rigidity and overall unfriendliness of these worlds.

The Pillar of Spirit

This pillar is connected to higher consciousness, from spirit guides to your Higher Self to Source. This pillar is most comfortable with big-picture thinking and acting in accordance with the greater good. In worlds dominated by this energy, souls never fully disconnect from their soul path and don't experience the full extent of the veil of forgetfulness, often maintaining their memories of past lives and awareness of parallel lives. From our perspective, these souls would appear ungrounded and not fully immersed in the matrix. Most souls who incarnate in these worlds experience out-of-body phenomena, have a high degree of access to the Akashic records,[1] and perceive the Universe from the position of energy first, everything else second. They understand how to work with and manipulate energy to get exactly what they want when they want it. Beings in these worlds experience lack less than in all other worlds, as these environments tend to be less materialistic and more spiritual (energy-forward). Beings in these worlds have a slew of "special" abilities, from time travel to telepathy.

The Celestial Endgame

Integrating the five points of the star is the celestial endgame. Thus, this framework ultimately describes the best possible configuration of any individual or group consciousness.

The Five-Pointed Star is a path to ascension, a journey from lower into higher dimensions. Within the collective Universe, the multiple dimensions are significantly different from one another. Each dimension is characterized (among other things) by how many points of the star are activated within it. As we move up in terms of dimensions, more points of the star get activated over time, providing a richer experience.

Planet Earth and the Five-Pointed Star

At this moment, our planet has only one of the five points of the star activated, the rest being fully dormant. The polarity we are currently experiencing is that of the mind/intellect (or Divine Masculine), which determines everything from our challenges to our planet's future direction. Any world with only one point of the star activated

1 The Akashic records are a compendium of all universal events, thoughts, words, emotions, and intent to ever have occurred in the past, present, or future, in terms of all entities and life forms, not just humans.

is an inherently biased system. We are on a path to unlock another point, so that the integration of opposites can start taking place. Planets unable to do so tend to run into dead-end scenarios, succumbing to cycles of annihilation and having to start over often after a cataclysmic event (think the great flood in the Old Testament). Usually, a planetary-level cataclysm helps erase the old energies so that the new energies can come in their stead, and the cycle can begin anew. This, of course, takes plenty of time and implies a loss of life that could easily be avoided if only the bigger picture were well understood.

Humanity is at the precipice. We can choose to stay the course and move full speed ahead into the realm of virtual reality, AI, and transhumanism, denying the power and wisdom of our hearts, or we can make a conscious choice to unlock a new future for ourselves, to paint a different picture, to once and for all evolve as a species and a planet. The choice is ours.

This book touches upon the mysteries of the heart—the domain of the Great Mother—to show that there is more to life than what meets the eye. We are missing out on so much depth, so much bliss, so much flow. This book is an open door and an invitation into the pillars of love, truth, and heart, so that humanity can choose what path it wants to follow.

I believe it is the destiny of humanity to crack our hearts open, one heart at a time, so the light can finally start pouring in. We are on the precipice, looking at the rest of our lives, examining our collective destiny. And the only way we can move forward is by fully inviting the magic of our hearts in. The time is now.

Practice: Higher Heart Activation—Heart Infinity Loop

Did you know that you have two hearts? Energetically speaking, of course. The lower heart is located where your physical heart is and is energetically represented by the color emerald green. However, you also have a higher heart, a more evolved heart that can take in the frequencies of cosmic love and perfect unity. This heart is purely etheric and is located around your thymus gland, two inches above your regular heart and slightly more toward the center. This heart is represented by the color pink. It is the seat of cosmic love and Divine oneness within you.

To step into the fullness of your feminine power, both hearts need to be activated and operating in unison. This practice will help you establish a constant stream of heart-led energy.

1. Sit comfortably or lie down, whatever feels best.
2. Close your eyes and start breathing deeply into your heart space.
3. With each breath, imagine your heart expanding. Watch as it emanates the most beautiful emerald light, filling your body with this healing frequency.
4. Notice a layer of ice surrounding your heart space—something you haven't noticed before. This ice layer represents the defense system you have built around your heart to protect it from pain and suffering. Know that on your journey into femininity, there is no room for a frozen heart. Know that it is safe for you to move forward without this protective shell.
5. Invite the heat of the summer sun into your chest area. Allow the warm rays of the sun to fully take over. Watch the heat rising and the ice starting to melt, first slowly, then with more and more momentum.
6. After some time, you will notice that the frozen layer covering your heart is fully gone. Start breathing into your heart space, taking in the powerful life force from the prana surrounding you. Breathe into your heart. Know that it is safe for you to take the world around you into your beautiful heart space.
7. Now, focus on a little spot along the central axis of your body, in the upper chest area, where your thymus gland is located. This is the space where your higher heart dwells. Imagine this spot starting to light up with a soft pink glow.

8. Start activating this point in your body by sending gentle breaths into your thymus area. With every inhale, imagine your higher heart expanding. Stay here for ten deep breaths. Do not rush this process.
9. Once your higher heart is sufficiently expanded, notice a thick layer of ice surrounding it. This may be your protective mechanism, but this barrier is also a huge impediment to integrating your Divine femininity within.
10. For a moment, shift your focus to your third eye in the middle of your forehead, imagining it as a large rotating sphere of fire. This divinely guided fire contains the exact frequencies needed to defrost your higher heart.
11. Imagine the rotating sphere of fire expanding, sending torrents of heavenly fire down toward your higher heart. Watch as your higher heart becomes fully engulfed by these energies. Stay here for a few deep breaths, and watch the frozen walls of your higher heart gently melt away.
12. Now that your higher heart is liberated, notice how its pink glow is becoming more potent, filling your chest with beautiful light.
13. The final step is to connect your two hearts, so they can work in unison. Imagine a figure eight connecting your two hearts—the emerald and the pink one. One loop of the figure eight is emerald and belongs to your lower heart, and the other is pink and belongs to your higher heart.
14. Start mentally tracing the figure eight, beginning with the emerald loop. When you come to the center of the figure, imagine the energies turning pink. Watch as the torrent of energy courses through the loops, keeping both of your hearts activated and connected to each other.
15. The energies of the combined emerald-pink flame, while gentle, can be very powerful, as they instantly start healing your body. Invite them to run their course, healing any organ or tissue that needs tending to, and removing any energy blocks and obstacles in your way.

Invite these energies to come back anytime you need a refresher on heart activation or require healing of any kind.

Heart Space: The Rose, Anchored

Your story is written in the petals of the rose—the ones budding, the ones in bloom, and the ones shed a long time ago.

The rose is a remembrance, an ode to the continuity of your story, the resilience of your spirit, and the tenderness of your soul.

The rose is a sacred vow to walk your path, which is ever unfolding.

She is a metamorphosis, an ongoing alchemical transformation, always shifting, never the same.

A rose is unknowable. The moment you think you comprehend her, she grows a new petal and loses an old one.

Some say she is fragile, that she can be crushed in the palm of your hand.

And yet in all the tomorrows, she blooms anew, defying the gravity of the odds.

She comes back to life, despite having withered away.

She emerges from the ashes after disappearing completely.

She is the spirit of Divine Mother in all of us, ancient, magnificent, and true.

Her strength is her vulnerability.

Her blood is the morning dew of forgiveness.

Her body is the subtle realm, the domain of magnetism.

She has come once more to give us a lesson in renewal, alignment, and love, from the depth of her universal understanding and the alchemy of her higher heart.

The rose has arrived. Can you hear her call?

CHAPTER 2

The Flower of Life

The Flower of Life (see **Figure 2**) is a universal pattern of creation, of new beginnings, of energy perfectly arranged and anchored into a space-time reality, a network of masculinity and femininity fully merged in an arrangement necessary to birth and sustain matter. The Flower of Life is also a sacred blueprint of the Divine Mother, her signature and essence encapsulated in geometric form, her energy captured, her sacred promise, and her generous gift. The Flower of Life is a dance of Divine energies, the harmonious pattern life is made of. Divine Masculine may have the impulse to create life, but Divine Feminine has the power and skill to follow through.

Figure 2: The Flower of Life

The birth of anything, from the smallest idea to a new species, to a human being, to a planet, to a Universe is a gradual process. It starts with the original spark, an iota of electricity, a charge, an impulse, a desire, a reason for being—the realm of Divine Masculinity. This original spark sets the Divine Feminine energy in motion, activating and calling it into alignment with the Divine Masculine's intention. Once activated, the chaos, the dark void of feminine potential gets to work, amassing and gathering its creative power in a dance of cosmic magnetism. Thus, the electricity of the masculine meets the magnetism of the feminine, creating a precursor to new life. The Divine Feminine, now unleashed, directs her unrestrained raw power to prepare the way for new creation, rearranging her body so that it can anchor and gestate new life.

The gestation period starts with a single seed of intention—the seed of the masculine—that can and will be multiplied by the Great Mother according to her life-giving blueprint that we call the Flower of Life.

Seed of Life

Before there is a flower, there is a seed. It all begins with the force of **zero**—the great feminine void and the directed movement of **one**—the spark of masculine intention. It is no coincidence that binary code is so widespread today. It represents primordial Divine mathematics—zero for "no" (or negative space), one for "yes" (or positive space)—a simple language, a foundational dichotomy of vibration, the two energies that birthed everything in existence.

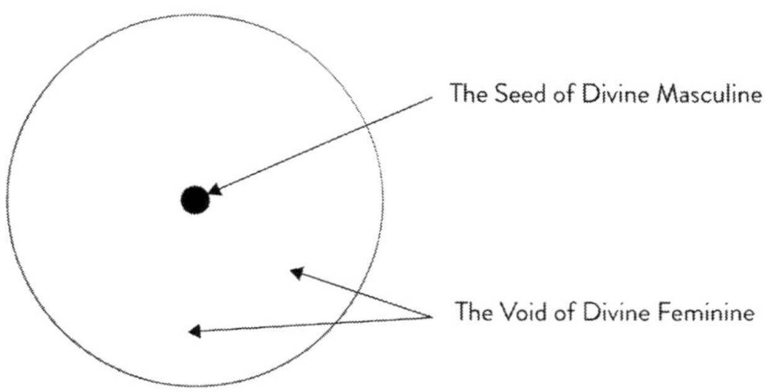

Figure 3: The monad

The basic depiction of life in the Universe is the monad (see **Figure 3**), a circle with a dot in the center. Often called the representation of Source, the Oversoul, or the Absolute, the monad is the masculine seed planted into the fertile soil of the feminine void. Geometrically, it represents Source having split from oneness into two foundational energies: the feminine and the masculine. The circle of the void of femininity, spurred into action by a spark of masculinity—the monad—is the prototype for everything from a human cell to a planet to a galaxy. Within the human cell, the nucleus represents the grand masculine principle, and everything surrounding it, the feminine. Within a galaxy, creation always starts in the center and spirals out into the surrounding cosmos. The principle and the structure of the monad are carried through all of creation, big and small.

The symbol of the monad has been adopted by a few esoteric sciences. Specifically, in alchemy, the symbol for the element of gold closely resembles the monad. In astrology and astronomy, the symbol for the sun is also a monad (see **Figure 4**). This is no coincidence. Energetically, the sun represents Source energy and Source consciousness in physical form. Gold represents one of the purest forms of metal and an aspirational standard for matter, the promised land of the alchemical path. (After all, turning base metals into gold with the assistance of a Philosopher's Stone was the entire point of alchemy.) Gold vibrates at the frequency of the Divine. It can rejuvenate and bring things into a state of original perfection and equilibrium. That is why monoatomic gold is believed to be a panacea, a substance that can help us achieve perfect health and preserve youth. It is the closest thing to physical *amrita* or ambrosia, the food of gods. There is a reason for the gold standard and the golden ratio: they are associated with perfect proportions and the Divine blueprint. Therefore, if Source were a metal, it would certainly be gold.

The monad is both the end result of a creation of cosmic proportions and a simple building block of reality. In fact, everything consists of small monads joined together by the force of magnetism and spurred into movement by the force of electricity.

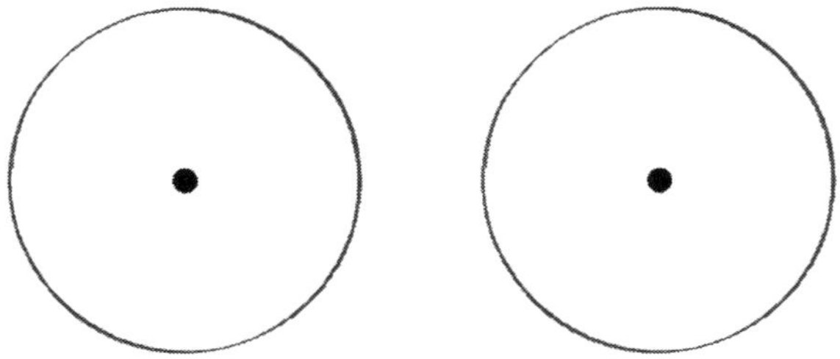

Figure 4: The monad as a symbol: the sun in astronomy, and gold in alchemy

You may be familiar with the story of the world's creation from the Old Testament, which speaks of God having created everything in seven days. This account of the Earth's birth is a great example of the energy of the monad in action (see **Figure 5**). In the beginning, there was a simple monad—not unlike the first cell in the body—a microcosm, a local projection, and a mini copy of the primordial Master Monad. Through addition (or multiplication), one monad becomes many, each an exact replica of another. Put seven monads together, and you get the simplest representation of the Flower of Life, a life form that can be preserved and sustained in our space-time reality. Seven is the first number of completion, signifying the achievement of Divine synchronicity, the fulfillment of the Divine plan, and the presence of Divine order. The world's creation in seven days is a metaphor for the anchoring of the Divine blueprint here on Earth. Nothing is ever random, but moves in accordance with the Great Divine Architect and Conductor.

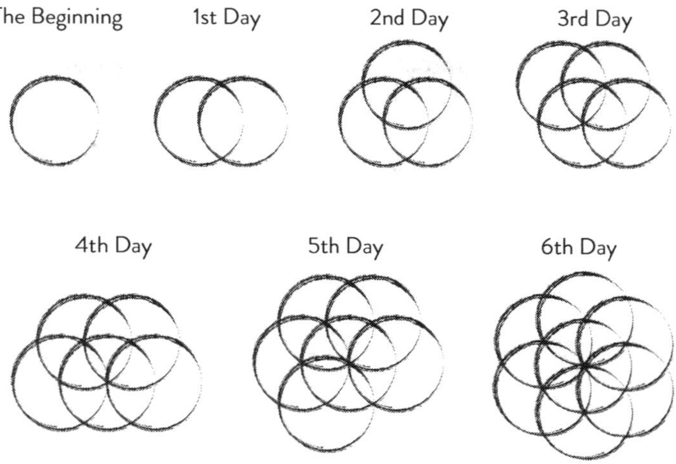

Figure 5: The creation blueprint

The Flower of Life, comprised of seven monads, is the simplest blueprint. It represents the basic bloom and the first harvest of celestial energies. Within physical worlds, energy is not considered fully anchored until it carries the blueprint and the animation of the seven monads within.

Another curious thing to observe is that the Flower of Life contains the blueprint of the movement of planets in a solar system. To see this hidden pattern, you will need to focus on the masculine aspects of the flower: the dots, watching their placement within the pattern and comparing it to the movement of planets around the sun, a common center of gravity (see **Figure 6**).

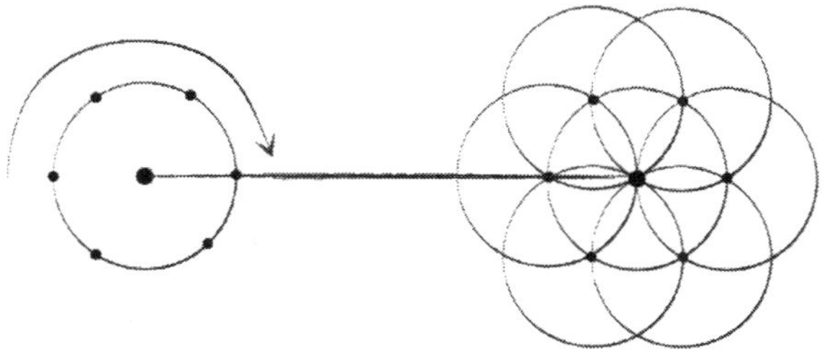

Figure 6: The simple blueprint of a solar system

The Merkaba or the Star of David

Let's take our exploration of the Flower of Life a level deeper. In alchemy, the upward triangle represents the masculine range of energies, with fire being a regular triangle and air being the triangle with a horizontal crossbar (see **Figure** 7). The feminine range is represented by a downward-facing triangle, with water being a regular triangle and earth being a triangle with a horizontal crossbar. The four major elements are enough to create the physical world that we know. The blueprint of the four elements is contained within the Merkaba.

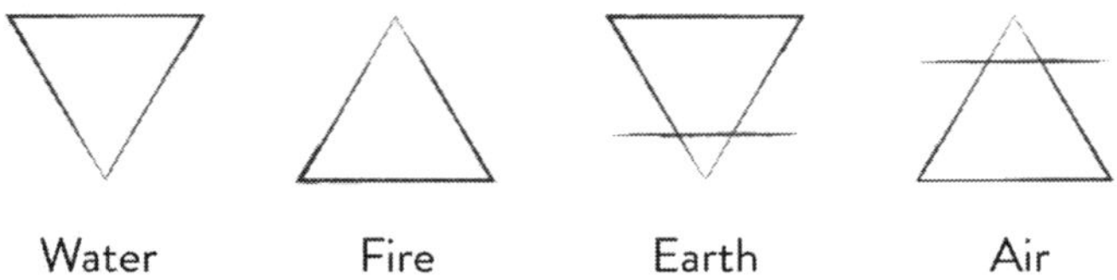

Figure 7: Alchemical symbols of the four elements

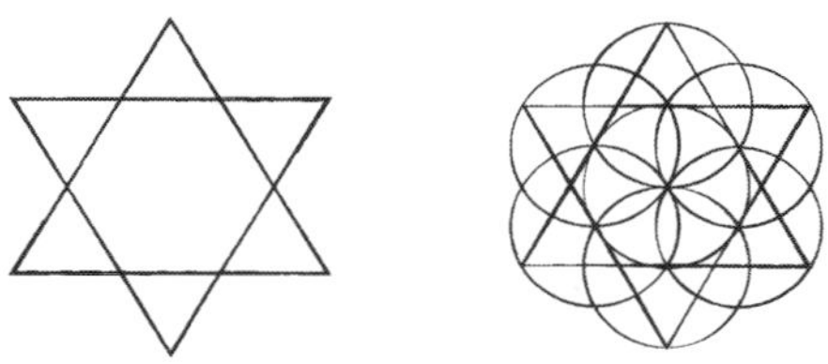

Figure 8: Star of David + Flower of Life meets Star of David

The Star of David (see **Figure 8**) is a blueprint for elemental unity in third-dimensional worlds, with equal parts feminine (downward triangle) and masculine (upward triangle) energies uniting to manifest physical reality. You may notice how seamlessly the Star of David shape fits into the Flower of Life pattern. They are two sides of the same coin, an emblem of two Divine polarities coming together for creation.

Platonic Solids Within the Flower of Life

One of the forefathers of contemporary geometry, as well as an ancient philosopher and metaphysicist, Plato devoted a large part of his life to studying a set of five spatial geometric figures he called "solids." Beyond the mathematical precision of the solids, Plato was most fascinated by the keys they held to the mysteries of the Universe. Plato knew that by exploring the solids, he was taking a deep dive into the consciousness and great plan of the Creator of our reality. He sought to understand how the energy moves within each solid and what aspect of the world each energy represents. According to the Law of Correspondences, many objects share an energetic signature, thus being energetic relatives. By seeking out and studying these correspondences, we could fully understand the Matrix and bend it to our will. Geometry is the study of symmetry and balance. While most physical objects can be represented geometrically, only five shapes are considered perfectly symmetrical arrangements of points in a third-dimensional (Euclidian) space (see **Figure 9**).

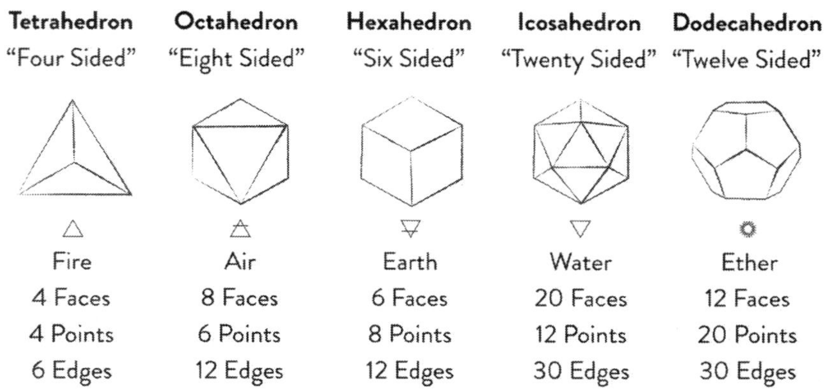

Figure 9: The five Platonic solids

By studying the movement of energy within the solids, Plato determined that each of them represents a classic element in nature. A tetrahedron represents fire, an octahedron air, a hexahedron earth, and an icosahedron water. A dodecahedron, an element made of twelve pentagons, was believed to represent the Universe itself, as well as the element of ether.

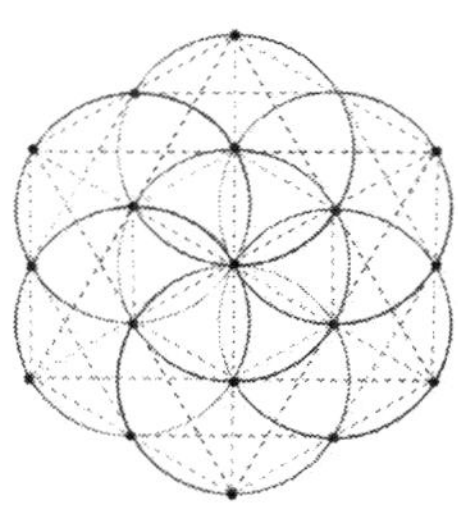

Figure 10: Platonic solids encoded within the Flower of Life

All five of the primal elements are encoded within the geometry of the Flower of Life (see **Figure 10**), organically fitting within the constraints of the blueprint. All five belong to the toolkit of the Divine Mother, representing the building blocks of reality.

Moreover, each of the Platonic solids can be reduced to its two-dimensional form, the simplest representation of the shape's essence (see **Figure 11**). Here, perhaps one of the most curious solids, the dodecahedron, deserves a special mention. The dodecahedron in two-dimensional space is shaped like a five-petaled flower with a pentagonal center. Given that the dodecahedron represents the Universe, the pattern of the Universe is that of a flower.

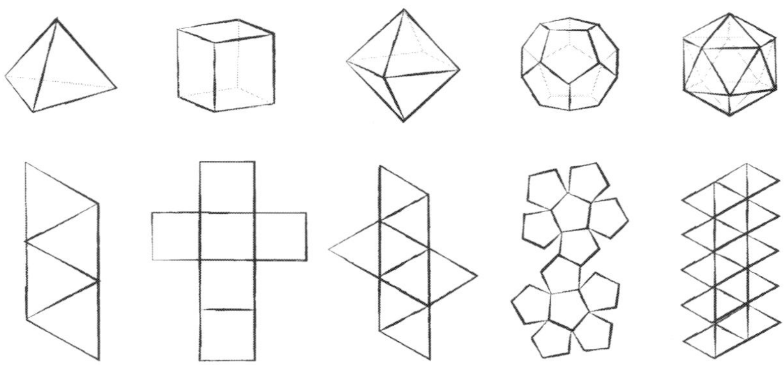

Figure 11: Platonic solids in 2D

And this is where we come full circle. When we are describing the Universe's blueprint and structure, three main shapes take center stage: a circle (Divine Feminine), a straight line that is often reduced to a point (Divine Masculine), and a flower—creative forces joined together. A spiral, for instance, often representing progress and evolution, is essentially the shape of the circle (feminine) broken up by the straight lines of the masculine, coming together in a targeted, powerful movement. The flower will always symbolize inception, birth, creation, new beginnings, virility, growth, and expansion.

Daily Uses for the Flower of Life Pattern

Now that we have sufficiently explored the geometric mysteries of the Flower of Life, why don't we take a dive into how to use this potent shape in your day-to-day life?

Charging Water

Place a printout of the Flower of Life under your water carafe or bottle. Alternatively, attach a sticker of the Flower of Life pattern to the side of your carafe to infuse the water with Divine Feminine energies. This will help bring a state of flow into your life, magnetizing good things to you. You may charge your Flower of Life pattern with a particular "ask" by closing your eyes and focusing on your intention. The Divine Mother will help you attain that which you desire.

Helping Plants Grow

Place a printout of the Flower of Life pattern under the pot of any struggling plant and leave it there for the Divine Feminine to work its magic. The Divine Mother often works through water's energy, so make sure to water your plant regularly (without overdoing it). This way, the Mother's energies can better assist. Watch your plant get into much better shape within two to three weeks!

Better Dreams

Yes, the Divine Mother is in charge of the dreamscape, too. It is only fitting, since she is all about rejuvenation, tender care, and replenishment. She doesn't only give life; she is here to maintain it. If you are struggling with nightmares or don't feel that you are able to replenish your strength overnight, place the Flower of Life pattern under your pillow and say a quick prayer to the Divine Mother, asking her to guard your sleep and bring about better dreams and better rest. Watch as the Mother's energies gently work to shift your sleep patterns.

Growing Your Finances

The Divine Mother represents true abundance—the effortless kind, where you no longer have to fight for resources or survival. The state of calm abundance is the Divine Mother's energetic signature—that feeling of safety, the knowing that the Universe is here to provide for you, today and every day. While you cannot exactly solve all your problems with the vibrations of the Flower of Life, it can help shift the energies around your finances and bring more money into your life.

Place a printout of the Flower of Life on your altar (or any spot where it won't be disturbed). Cover it with a twenty-dollar bill or a hundred dollar bill. Finally, place a small quartz crystal pyramid on top of the bill. Leave this arrangement for at least three months, checking it regularly, imagining how the Flower of Life is expanding and growing your finances. While this is not a quick ritual, it always works given time.

Assisting with Healing (Physical or Emotional)

Since the Mother works through the element of water, placing a sticker of the Flower of Life on your showerhead or underneath your bathtub can help funnel her healing energies to assist with your ailments. Her healing is gentle and works best for chronic pain, although it can also help to accelerate the healing of burns, cuts, and bruises.

Practice: Flower of Life Energy Activation

Use this practice to get the creative or healing energies flowing in your body. This practice is best done in the morning or early afternoon, because it is quite charged and may give you an energy jolt that can be hard to extinguish. Once you have jumpstarted this energy, the healing or creative process will need to run its course, so it is not advised if you plan to sleep soon after.

1. Take a comfortable seated position.
2. Focus on your breath, paying attention to the air entering and leaving your body effortlessly.
3. To start the energy activation, breathe into your root chakra, located at the base of your spine. As you breathe into it, watch it expand and rotate, clearing away any blockages or darkness within.
4. Repeat step 3 for all of your chakras, moving up the spinal cord: sacral in the lower abdomen, solar plexus in the center of your belly, heart in the center of your chest, throat in the middle of your neck, third eye in the middle of your forehead, and crown just above your head.
5. Now, imagine the Flower of Life pattern right below your feet. Feel it with the soles of your feet, noticing its gentle vibration entering every pore of your feet and slowly starting to move up your body.
6. Imagine a large pyramid of light placed atop the Flower of Life. Feel the flower's energy accumulate within the pyramid (see **Figure 12**).

Figure 12: Flower of Life and pyramid pattern

7. Imagine climbing the pyramid and settling in a lotus pose at the top, aligning your spine with the pyramid's tip. Don't worry about the precarious position; the Universe can hold it indefinitely.
8. Watch as the energy of the flower starts to rise up through the central shaft of the pyramid, coiling up like a snake from the base to its very top.
9. Feel the flower's energy flow from the pyramid's tip up the pillar of your chakras, passing from the root chakra up to the crown with forceful momentum.
10. Allow your body to take in more and more of this energy with each breath you take. You may experience a tingling sensation in one or a few parts of your body or feel slightly lightheaded during this energy activation. This is completely normal. The physical symptoms persist for as long as the Divine Feminine works to clear any blocks. When the initial cleanse is completed, the physical symptoms will subside, leaving you with a perfectly potent stream of creative and healing energies at your disposal.
11. Decide how you would like to use this energy today, and create a direction for it. If you are working on a project, ask that the energy be directed toward its successful completion. If you are experiencing pain, direct the stream toward healing the ailment. Get creative; there are no wrong answers here. The Great Mother is here to assist you.

Feel free to repeat this practice whenever you require inspiration or motivation, crave a creative jolt, or feel under the weather.

Heart Space: The Fullness of You

You are the void,

The primordial darkness and the primary fullness.

You are the black nurturing waters. You are the in between.

You are the vastness of space, the depth of the ocean, and the safety of the Mother's womb.

You are the miracle of yet unborn matter.

You are the key and the lock to the mysteries of life,

A link between duality and oneness.

You are the black swan and the white swan.

You are also the lake that the swans call home.

You are the calm seas and the tempest.

You are the sentence and the pardon,

The first page and the last page.

You are an act of creation, life force incarnate.

You are infinity.

Your end is just another beginning.

You cease only to spring back to life again.

Your ashes become the spouts, your death the source of your rebirth.

You are ever the wiser as you travel the cycles of Ouroboros.

You are thus reborn once more into greater wisdom and greater understanding.

Here is to the fullness that you are,

Every aspect, every angle, and every facet,

Each part just as beautiful as the whole.

Here is to the magnificence that you are, my friend,

The eternal spark that is your mind, body, heart, and soul.

CHAPTER 3

The Divine Feminine Pillar

"Number rules the Universe."
—Pythagoras

Numbers are crumbs of Divine intelligence given to us so we can conceive of the greatness of the mind of the Creator. Every number is a code, a Universe within itself, a frequency that should be read between the lines, not just with our intellect, but also with our heart. Through the heart, we experience the true frequency of concepts, understanding them deeply and not just sensing them on the surface. Every number is a journey—a journey beyond time and space into a facet of reality that came before creation itself. Every number is a thread of destiny, a slice of the vibration of the original void, an answer and a question, a mystery both beckoning and unsolved. And yet, a number is a construct that gets us closer to Divinity, not unlike the tune of a well-composed song or the rhythm of a well-crafted verse. A number is a numerical representation of a golden ratio, the perfect blueprint of the Universe.

Numerology is one of the most ancient of all sciences. It was brought to our planet by a Higher Consciousness, only to undergo a series of remembrances and forgettings, to reemerge on the other side as a pale shadow of what it once was. Numerology is a Divine science once revered in the temples of Atlantis and the pyramids of ancient Egypt. Numerology was studied, meditated on, and used in rituals and prayers alike, eternally bringing the brightest stars of humanity closer to the primordial spark of the original Creator. And just like with everything long forgotten, it is time for this science to have its second coming, enabling this ancient wisdom to help guide humanity into a better world.

Many are the mysteries of the simple numerical matrix (see **Figure 13**), a square of nine cells, one for each single-digit natural number. Numbers one through nine represent the most fundamental frequencies of the Universe that make up the entirety (albeit simplified) of the energetic spectrum.

1	4	7	1, 4, 7: Energy of Divine Fire/Masculine/Intention
2	5	8	2, 5, 8: Energy of Divine Water/Feminine/Energy
3	6	9	3, 6, 9: Energy of Divine Matter/Unification/Manifested Universe

Figure 13: Simple numerical matrix

Each row of the matrix represents its own facet of reality. The top row is the Divine Masculine arc, starting with the confident, self-serving energy of one, moving through the steady, dependable, sturdy vibrations of four, and culminating with the synchronistic energies of seven.

The middle row is the Divine Feminine arc, starting with the duality and peacemaker qualities of two, moving through the harmonizing energy and beauty of five, and culminating in the depth and all-encompassing splendor of eight—a journey across dimensions.

The bottom row is the organized matter that comes from the energy of feminine and masculine masterfully mixed together for the purpose of creation. Here, we start with the localized creative forces of three, move through the duality in the realm of six, and culminate in nine, with the full power of the manifested Universe at our fingertips.

Numerology: The Feminine Arc

The Divine Feminine is numerically represented in the following numbers: zero, two, five, eight, showcasing the dominating states of feminine energy. While zero represents the passive state and is therefore not part of the matrix above (since the matrix represents the active states of energy), it is worth mentioning here so you can get a full picture.

Zero represents the void of antimatter, the unmanifested state of energy. This is energy conserved, energy dormant, energy unorganized. Zero is raw, infinite, and untamed. The Ginnungagap of Norse mythology, Chaos of the Greek creation myths, and Nun of the lore of ancient Egypt all speak of this void, the state of energy before and after "the happening," the great in between. While it contains limitless potential, it also stands for static energy or the energetic vacuum.

Two represents the partnership state of femininity—the kind that is considerate of others and lives in a perpetual state of perceiving and integrating duality. Two's concerns are feelings and emotions; it is about receiving, listening, and taking in. The energy of two is about relationships, between energies, people, and elements. Two is the cosmic glue. It is the energy of interconnectedness—cause and effect, karma and dharma, light and shadow, beginnings and endings, alpha and omega. The energy of two is designed to maintain the cyclical nature of reality. It is the vibration of the circle at its finest, always seeking to complete itself and the other, the Ouroboros forever biting its own tail.

Five represents the creative spark of femininity. Five is femininity in motion. Five is magnetism. The energy of five is a female empowered, a goddess fully awakened and unleashed upon the world. She is the one who knows no bounds, considers no limits, and doesn't take no for an answer. Five is the number of boundless creation; its motto is "Live to create, and create to live." It incessantly calls new things into existence, bringing them forth from the great void. It is by tapping into the void of zero that the energy of five has the building blocks to create, and it uses the blueprint of the Flower of Life to do so. This is an age of creation for planet Earth, so it is blessed by the numerology of five—the number of the goddess Venus, represented by the Venusian Rose and the energies of the higher heart. Venus brings the energies of higher cosmic compassion, forgiveness, and love for oneself and others. Five is also the number of internal and external beauty, the kind that goes beyond the surface and emanates the frequency of harmonization.

Eight is the highest feminine number, representing the pinnacle of possibility for the Divine Feminine arc. Eight is infinity, eternal bliss, perpetual adventure, and basking in the light and glory of your creations, and it represents the ever-renewing cycles of nature. Eight forms the recycling path of energy; everything with a beginning has an end, and everything reaches its pinnacle only to wither away, paving the path for future cycles. Eight is the number of magic, fluidity, flow, interdimensional travel, intuition, connection, and infinity. Whereas zero represents endless possibilities, eight represents infinite manifestation, a Universe filled with everything imaginable, a cornucopia of experiences, vibrations, and frequencies, abundance at its finest, imagination unleashed.

Evolution at large tends to follow along one of the three main predetermined paths (see **Figure 14**): the Divine Masculine pillar (movement from one through four into seven), the Divine Feminine pillar (movement from two through five into eight), or the Divine Unity pillar (movement from three through six into nine). On a path of growth, every soul will choose to undertake each of the pillars many times over, and will do so across multiple dimensions, realities, and worlds.

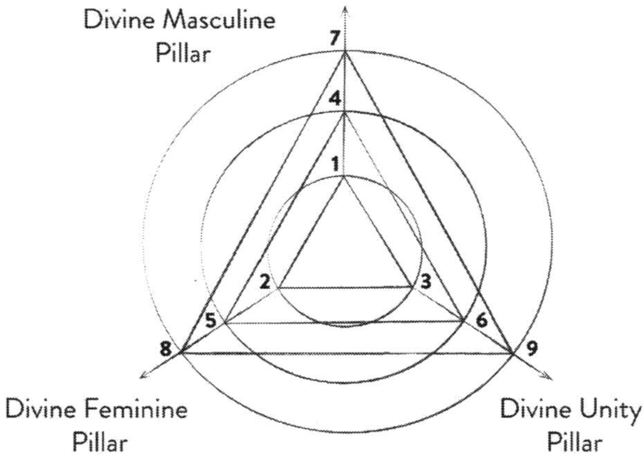

Figure 14: Three vectors of Divine evolution

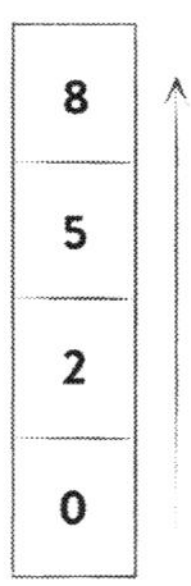

Figure 15: Divine Feminine pillar

The Divine Feminine pillar (see **Figure 15**) is a gradual movement through the feminine arc, starting in the darkness of the void of zero, proceeding with the duality of two, moving through the heart activation of five, and culminating in the life-altering grandeur of infinity manifested, the magic of eight. By activating all the facets of the feminine arc, we experience the many faces of the goddess, living untamed in an endless dance of bliss and creation. Much shadow work[2] needs to happen before all the facets

2 Shadow work was popularized by psychiatrist and psychoanalyst Carl Jung. It explores bringing awareness to the unconscious mind to develop acceptance.

of feminine numerology can be accepted and fully integrated, which makes the path of the feminine pillar both a challenge and a worthwhile undertaking.

We each have a unique relationship with every type of energy in the Divine spectrum. We don't exist in a vacuum, nor are we finite or ever fully complete. Instead, we are works in progress, completing another lap of our eternal dance of interacting with the energies of the Divine. We are also an accumulation of all the experiences we've ever had at a soul level. As such, we have an ongoing relationship with every energy of the numerical spectrum. We have traumas and victories that exist in each vibrational range. Each number, zero through nine, is integrated within our energy field to a particular degree. Collectively, they form our numeric blueprint. Diagnosing where you currently stand in regards to every major energy of the spectrum could be a first step on your personal path of healing. It is through this step that we bring the hidden and the covert straight into the light and can examine all the broken facets of ourselves, so they can finally be recalibrated.

Practice: Measuring the Energies of the Feminine Pillar

You can use a pendulum to find out where you stand in regards to the energies of each number of the Divine Feminine pillar.

1. Take a blank page and sketch a simple scale from zero to one hundred percent.
2. Ask the Universe the following question: "To what degree is the energy of the zero integrated within me?"
3. Place the pendulum over the scale and quiet your mind. Within seconds, the pendulum will begin swaying, pointing to the direction of the number on the scale, indicating the right answer. Make sure to keep your hand steady while the pendulum is working out the answer so as to not interfere with the energies.
4. Repeat the same process for numbers two, five, and eight.

Usually, an energy is considered well integrated if the pendulum indicates seventy-five percent or above. The energy is considered less integrated if the pendulum indicates under forty percent. Less integrated energies tend to require more attention on your path towards integrating the Divine Feminine within. Below, I offer some guidance on how you can best work with each of the energies within the feminine pillar, one number at a time. Integrating all these facets of Divine Femininity is a lifelong journey, so be gentle with yourself as you are going through this process.

0: Healing Your Relationship with Zero

Your relationship with the realm of zero is synonymous with your relationship with the primordial dark void from which everything came, also known as the realm of the Divine Mother. This aspect of reality could be equally awe-inspiring and terrifying to some, simply because it is limitless. This facet of reality is perhaps one of the harder ones to comprehend. Yet it gives us some of our most deeply rooted fears, which could start running our lives on autopilot unless we take the reins and shift our perspective through much discernment and mindfulness.

Symptoms of a Broken Connection with the Energy of Zero

- Fear of the unknown
- Fear of the dark
- Fear of water
- Fear of the ocean
- A challenging relationship with your mother or grandmother
- A scarcity mindset
- Resistance to change
- Frequent nightmares or insomnia (broken relationship with the dreamscape)
- Frequent roadblocks on your path
- Absence of flow
- Pressure to be or act a certain way
- Low energy levels
- Confusion
- Worry

Shifting the Pattern

To transcend your relationship with the void, start small. The progress here may be slow and steady, as the energy of the void doesn't tolerate haste. Introspection and time alone are paramount in connecting with these majestic energies.

Start exploring the story you have been telling yourself about darkness. What do you believe to be true about it? What are you really afraid of?

Often, when we are afraid of external darkness, we are first and foremost afraid of the darkness within. Shadow work is therefore paramount in fixing one's relationship with the primordial void. This means learning to accept the parts of you that are less than ideal, and learning to make peace with your past incarnations, regardless of where they fell along the "good" versus "bad" spectrum.

The next step is to heal your relationship with all the women in your lineages, especially your mother and both grandmothers. In most people who have difficulty with the energy of zero, the relationship with all aspects of the Mother is challenged to some degree. Forgive your mother and other female relatives for any pain and suffering they may have caused. Understand that you've selected this family for a reason, and they have done their job exactly as they were supposed to. Write a letter to your mother, listing all the ways that your relationship is imperfect, and what she may have done to cause it. Burn the letter and release your trauma. Then choose to write a new letter, stepping into a new set of energies where your relationship with your mother is healed. This may seem like wishful thinking, but the written word has great power and can help you manifest a better relationship with your mother.

From there, you need to heal your relationship with the element of water. It starts simple: greet water every time you brush your teeth or come in contact with it during your daily activities. Charging and blessing your water before you drink is also a good practice to adopt.

Often, if we have a suboptimal relationship with water, it travels with us across incarnations. So, having past life regressions to find those lives where your water relationship was damaged could be a shortcut to healing.

Finally, having a water ritual to cleanse the relationship is always a good idea. You would need to bring some offerings to the water, but please make sure they are of natural origin (flowers, crystals, essential oils, etc.). All the offerings should come from your heart. Also, bring some salt for the water ritual. Dropping salt crystals into water will help purify your relationship with it by absorbing any and all negativity surrounding your relationship.

A water ritual is best performed near a natural water feature, like a river, ocean, or lake. Don't rush the ritual; make sure to allow enough time to communicate with the water. This element doesn't like haste of any kind.

Helpers and Healers

You can focus your healing with the energies of the zero with the following:

The duck — The duck is one of the main symbols of the Divine Mother, and as such, it is a perfect companion in healing your relationship with the void. The duck is a natural at navigating the deep and dark waters of the Mother and can become your compass and guide if you ask for it. Whether connecting to the spirit of the duck through meditation, observing ducks in the wild, or having a picture of a duck on your desk, you cannot go wrong in strengthening your relationship with this helper by whatever means necessary. On the flip side, consuming duck meat is considered a great offense to the Mother, so you may want to cut that out of your diet if you are seeking to improve your relationship with the realm of zero.

Egg shapes — Eggs symbolize life force within the Universe. Until the egg hatches, its insides exist in the darkness of the void—the nurturing energies of the Mother. And yet the baby growing inside of the egg, just like the baby growing inside of the mother's womb, is not afraid of the dark. In fact, darkness is unconditional love, nurturing, and safety. Meditating on the energy of the egg and the energy of the womb could help you better understand the void itself.

The womb — One helpful meditation is transporting yourself back to your mother's womb when you were still growing in her belly. Experiencing the trust and surrender to the care of your mother is one of the most liberating experiences available to us as incarnated humans. It can also help with trauma and rewriting any negative associations you may have around the darkness.

The Frequency of Trust and Surrender

If you have a broken relationship with the state of zero, most likely, you'll find it challenging to trust the people around you and the Universe at large, as well as to surrender to how things are. Your life may be a sequence of swimming upstream, trying to get away from unwanted outcomes. When you feel your fears rising, try running toward them, not away. The Universe is infinitely large and never means you harm. Cultivating trust is a lifelong journey; choose to start it today.

Practicing trust starts with trusting yourself first, then adding other elements one at a time. Trusting nature could be a big one, such as walking barefoot or taking a plunge in a river under the light of the moon. These experiences require trust. Make it a practice to trust your path, to trust that the Universe is always flowing in your favor and is providing for you. Also, practice surrendering to the pace of how things unfold for you; don't try to speed them up or slow them down. Your Universe will set the pace. Your job is to surrender and enjoy the ride. Over time, you will notice that trying to control everything is draining, while the practice of surrender, on the other hand, is a lot easier when it becomes second nature. Enjoy!

Working with Your Inner Void

The void exists both inside and outside of you. Within your body, it is located two inches below your root chakra. Energetically, it looks like an infinite pool of black liquid, both inviting and unknowable. Your inner void is a massively underutilized resource that contains any and all energies you could possibly require as you are moving through your human experience.

Before the Universe took shape, the entirety of existence amounted to the amorphous void that gave birth to everything we currently observe in the physical world. An aspect of this same void lives within your body and is readily available to you. It is your personal point of creation, a gateway that can unlock a new level of vibration.

Practice: Knowing and Working with the Void

Below is a powerful practice that will enable you to get to know your inner void and harness its energies in order to better your life. Coincidentally, it also helps heal your relationship with the realm of zero.

Step 1: Drop into the void.

Start by dropping into your void. To do that, imagine an elevator traveling up and down your spine. Simply ask your elevator to deposit you one level below your root chakra, and it should take you straight to the void.

Attuning to this powerful aspect of your body is a journey and does not happen overnight. The void is the most abundant aspect of the Divine Mother, but it could also be your personal healing space if needed.

Get to know your void by diving into it and experiencing its energy. Does it feel cool or warm? Soft or spiky? Try swimming in it or just floating atop it to get the full experience. Ask if the void wants you to address it using a specific name or title. Invite the void to help you on your spiritual journey and be one of your guides along the way.

Step 2: Working with the void

While there are an infinite number of ways to work with your void, one of the most fruitful ones is a daily or weekly practice that starts with you dropping into the void and asking the following question: "What is rising in me today?"

Follow up by focusing on the surface of the void and watching whatever aspect emerges at the top of the black waters. It could be an animal, a spirit, a plant, a sound, a geometric shape, an artifact, or any other object, real or imaginary; anything is possible. Trust that what you are seeing is exactly what is rising in you at this point in time. Whatever you are seeing is your current helper or medicine.

As you go through the ebbs and flows of life, you require energetic assistance to move forward. Often, you need to integrate an archetype into your light bodies to overcome a challenge. Sometimes you need a guide to advise you, and other times you just need a pick-me-up. The void has all of that and more. Feel free to ask clarifying questions about the object that showed up, asking about the symbolism of what you are seeing, what it can teach you, and how you could best work with the object.

2: Healing Your Relationship with Two

Your relationship with the realm of two is synonymous with your relationship with duality. Black and white, male and female, good and bad, selfish and selfless, me versus them—all of these exist in the realm of duality. These energies are all about finding harmony amidst a split, searching for balance despite division, seeking unity in separation, and the struggle of actually getting there.

Symptoms of a Broken Connection

- A victim mentality
- Giving to the detriment of oneself
- Feelings of depletion
- Feelings of being taken advantage of
- Issues around self-expression
- People-pleasing tendencies
- Not receiving enough support from your partner
- Always being the one who pulls everything together
- Fatigue
- Relationship issues (whether familial, romantic, or otherwise)
- Difficulty with parenthood
- Having "difficult" children
- Always putting yourself last
- Absence of self-love
- Rigidity
- Having to rely on your masculine polarity, because the feminine is too weak to step up
- Feelings of loneliness
- An inability to stand up for yourself
- Trauma around sexuality
- Depression

Shifting the Pattern

The territory of the two is quite rich, since in a low-dimensional world like Earth, there is much inherent duality.

The easiest place to start healing these energies is by exploring your relationships, starting with your relationship with yourself. Any issues we experience in our external relationships are first encountered internally. So, if your relationship with yourself is perfectly harmonious, you will see that reflected in your other relationships, but the opposite also applies.

Start speaking to yourself kindly, filling up your cup first, and doing more things you love and fewer things you don't. Help yourself first before you help others. Learn to listen to your body. The little intuitive hits, the aches, the small nudges of discomfort—all of them are little bricks in your path toward self-love. Get out of the habit of putting yourself last. Start a self-love journal, listing how you intend to prioritize your well-being, and tracking how you are making good on that promise. Ask yourself two questions and write down the answers:

- What does my body like to do?
- What do I like to do?

You'll be surprised, as the answers to these two questions will be quite different. Make sure to add items from each list to your calendar.

Practice conscious communication by allowing yourself to finally speak your truth and others to speak theirs. When healing relationships, listening is more important than speaking. However, when speaking, make sure your communication is pure and comes from the heart, not hurt.

Practice: Meet Your Inner Divine Masculine and Feminine

Meet the two parts of yourself: your inner Divine masculine and your inner Divine feminine. What do they look like? What makes them special? What abilities or quirks does each one have? Then, imagine your masculine side as a stream of yellow energies and your feminine side as a stream of blue energies. In a meditative state, bring the two streams together like two strands of a DNA molecule, allowing the two aspects of you to be merged and unified.

Choose discernment over judgment and responding over reacting. Work on your heart-mind connection. Often, those two aspects of our bodies are living in two parallel realities, which tends to create conflict. Imagine that your heart and your mind operate like partners and allies. Remove any resistance your physical body may have to this union. Remember, the best decision-making comes from the fusion of your heart and mind; anything else is settling.

Remember, the most important relationships to fix are those with your parents. These relationships are energy vortexes in your life, whether you like it or not; they form your patterns of relating to the world. While we are very good at creating coping mechanisms, we are never truly healed unless we consciously try to address our relationship with each of our parents.

Start by writing a letter to each of your parents, listing some things about growing up that you never could express. Acknowledge the role each of your parents played in shaping the person you have become. List all the ways you felt your parents hurt you or didn't do right by you. Don't judge yourself for feeling what you are feeling, and don't make excuses. There are no wrong answers here, and your feelings are completely valid. You don't have to apologize for how you feel. Getting your feelings out of your system and into the open is paramount.

Then, list all the ways your parents did right by you, and all the things you are grateful for. Lastly, forgive your parents for anything they may have done (intentionally or otherwise) to hurt you. Feel free to burn this last part of the letter if it feels good; fire is great at releasing trauma and resetting the energies back to their perfect state. Feel free to read the letters to your parents if that feels good—or not. What is important is the act of writing and thinking about your relationships, not sharing it with others.

Healers and Helpers

You can focus your healing of the energies of the two with the following:

The swan — This bird helps us bridge polarities. It is the aspect of the Divine Feminine that has bypassed duality and moved into unity. The swan's medicine is gentle but effective, acting like a bridge between your heart and your mind. When meditating, imagine that the swan is in your throat chakra, wings outstretched. Envision a figure eight with one loop around your head and the other around your heart, with the swan in the middle. Picture your energy moving along the figure eight, bringing your internal system into synchronicity.

The yin-yang symbol — The yin-yang symbol (see **Figure 16**) represents polarities in perfect balance. The world is woven of seemingly conflicting things that don't need to be antagonistic and only remain so because we have unhealed aspects within ourselves that prevent true unity. Meditating on this symbol can help bring you away from polarization and into a more seamless, organic existence. Surrounding yourself with this symbol could help heal your relationship with division. Another practice you could try is drawing this symbol over and over again as you go into introspection. This can help you get out of antagonistic or polarized states.

Figure 16: Yin-yang symbol

The mirror — Other people in our lives often mirror our trauma. They don't show up to hurt us, but to draw attention to and masterfully reflect back to us the trauma that lives inside.

When faced with a particularly difficult relationship, ask yourself, "What is this a mirror for? What aspect of myself or what flavor of my trauma is it reflecting back to me?" If you often experience being a victim, understand that this vibration attracts the abuser; it is a twin vibration that completes the circle. You cannot be aligned with an external abuser unless there is an internal one as well; everything stems from within.

Thus, to heal this wound, you must first address the abuser within—the inner critic, the doubter, the hater, the skeptic. Each of these aspects of you is a part that needs to be integrated into the rest of you and not rejected. Radical acceptance of the different parts of yourself is the medicine here.

Water — Water is the greatest equalizer. It can help soften the rough edges and carry you toward resolution. However, if your relationship with the energies of the two is suboptimal, your internal waters are murky instead of clear. This may inadvertently make you feel stuck, as if there is no resolution.

Practice: Meditation – The Limitless Part of You

Working to heal and clean up your inner waters is a necessary step on your Divine Feminine journey. In a meditative state, take a deep dive into your inner ocean. Start exploring this boundless, limitless part of you. Notice any darkness and blockages in the waters of your ocean. You can clean the darkness using gold and white light, almost erasing the blocked energies so that contractions are removed and the clean and clear waters remain. Once you clear the obvious dark spots, imagine that threads of golden light are permeating your ocean, cleaning away anything not in alignment with your highest good. Watch the waters of your inner ocean transform.

Practicing Stillness

Stillness is a path to true introspection. Healing the energies of the two haphazardly won't work, but neither is this a structured process. Stillness is the practice of allowing the elements of air and water in your body to come into equilibrium. Flow in our body is enabled through both these elements, and when the energies of the two are not healed, you could experience various distortions. Stillness enables you to get out of the rat race and overthinking, so your body can restore the optimal flow of air and water.

Establishing a daily meditative practice is paramount here. Even if it is just three minutes daily, what matters is that it is consistent. Train your body to expect periods of introspection, and you will be rewarded with the energies of your internal water and air coming back into balance. You may also want to imagine that your inner air (and lungs) are becoming liberated. Allow yourself to take frequent, audible exhales to let go of suboptimal air inside with its old, used-up, toxic elements. So many people spend their lives in a state of stress and thus constant constriction, taking shallow breaths, and they don't fully release the suboptimal air. Take time to release the air that needs to go, so fresh air can enter your lungs.

The Frequency of Nonjudgment and Compassion

Practice nonjudgment and compassion every chance you get, with yourself and others. Allow yourself to just be you, without achieving something or becoming someone else. You deserve love and compassion just as you are—and so do others. This means speaking kindly to and about others, quitting gossiping, and releasing a need to compartmentalize things through judgment. Liberate yourself from having to pronounce other people as right or wrong. Give everyone permission to be themselves today and every day, and take the same permission slip for yourself.

Blissful or Ecstatic Dance

One of the better physical activities for activating the energies of the two is dance, where you don't need to limit your physical expression by having to come across a certain way. Just let your Shakti[3] (female energy) flow freely and rise through your body in a way that feels good. Your body is intuitive; allow it to move you through any trauma or blockages coming up for you. Do not judge this experience; surrender to it and let it unfold.

---

3 In Hinduism, Shakti is the fundamental cosmic energy and a central deity within Shaktism, representing dynamic forces that permeate the universe. Shakti embodies feminine energy and is regarded as the Supreme Brahman herself, with all other divine forms seen as her manifestations.

5: Healing Your Relationship with Five

Your relationship with the number five is the relationship with the Creatress within. Are you keeping her on a tight leash, or do you let her roam free, making every day of your life a creative adventure? The energy of the five is the energy of the wind, all-clearing, powerful, and unrestricted.

The energy of the five also governs beauty and balance and your ability to express your feminine side. Are you allowing yourself to be softer, kinder, more caring? Or do you suppress those vibrations? The energy of the five is also strongly connected with Venus and all manner of Venusian energies, such as love, attraction, desire, harmony, self-expression, and sensuality. Learning the lesson of the five means accepting your own flavor of femininity. It means being in harmony with your environment, being great at creating things, and staying on your God/Goddess-given path. Walking the path of Venus also means harmonizing and beautifying the world around you, leaving it better off than you found it.

Symptoms of a Broken Connection with the Energy of Five

- No creative hobby/outlet
- Disconnected from intuition
- You don't feel loved or lovable
- Difficulty expressing love and affection
- Disconnection and loneliness
- Difficulty giving praise to others
- Difficulty receiving freely
- Lack of abundance
- Difficulty aligning with your desires
- You often find yourself surrounded by things that are broken, dirty, or old.
- Living paycheck to paycheck
- Having to buy cheap things
- Settling for less than you want

- Difficulty finding or keeping "the one"
- Lack of attention from romantic partners
- Constantly nursing a broken heart
- Body image issues
- You don't find yourself attractive
- Difficulty receiving compliments
- A feeling of straying off the path
- Uncertainty about what you are supposed to do with your life
- Restrictions and roadblocks
- Lack of flow
- Feeling stuck or unhappy, unable to find a way out
- Lack of creativity
- Living on autopilot (as if following a blueprint)

Shifting the Pattern

Mending the energies of the five starts with healing the little girl inside you—the one who is tender, the one who may be young and scared, the one who doesn't feel safe or cared for. It starts with listening to her story, inviting her into your space and giving her the time to speak her truth. Journaling as if you were her could be a healing practice in its own right. Allow the girl inside to express herself fully—the pain, the heartache, the wounding. Hold space for that part of you without judgment or conditions. Invite the emerald frequencies of love to cleanse her heart trauma, and unchain the little girl within by cutting whatever cords restrain her. Finish this experience by pouring white light into her heart space, removing trauma, and filling her heart vessel with new frequencies—love, compassion, and self-acceptance.

The next step is to change your inner narrative about yourself. Make it a habit of noticing all the good things about yourself. You may even want to make a list of them and add to it every chance you get.

Invite more femininity into your life by wearing clothing that makes you feel beautiful/handsome, buying yourself flowers (yes, this works for men also), and allowing yourself some simple pleasures. Create a list of your favorite indulgences, from bubble baths to flower rituals, and add them to your life. Treat yourself to things you like, just because. Get out of the rigidity of schedules, allow yourself the time to breathe, and go with the flow. Be spontaneous. Surprise and delight yourself.

Become your own biggest cheerleader. Do things that feel decadent; spoil yourself. Allow yourself ample time for play; no need to be serious all the time. Leave time for small acts of creativity also; this is how you nurture the feminine within. Whether your flavor of creation is baking or sewing, drawing or singing, carving wood, or decorating the living room, it may be one of the most healing activities you could do for yourself.

The next step is diving deep into your throat chakra and making peace with whatever trauma lives there. Women on this planet have been conditioned to "be seen and not heard," which creates a major block in our center of self-expression, our throat area. Most thyroid issues stem from the restricted flow of self-expression—making yourself small, hiding, wearing a mask instead of showing up as who you are. It is time to reclaim your voice. It is time to stop sacrificing yourself and your vision for others. It is time to step into the spotlight. It is also time to get to know yourself; authenticity is only possible to the degree that you know yourself. So, take the time to dive deep and find the true you there—the you who is yearning to come out and be both seen and heard for who you really are.

Heart Space Deep Dive

The vibrations of five are, first and foremost, the vibrations of your heart space. They live in your heart chakra. Often, issues with this frequency stem from heart trauma; they are a message from your heart that it needs tender, loving care and healing. On an energetic level, most people's hearts are run through with all manner of objects—swords, spears, arrows, pins—each representing a traumatic experience of the past.

Healing the heart is a process of removing each of these objects, one by one, healing the trauma it represents. Ask yourself the following question about each object you find:

- What kind of heartache does this object represent?
- What is the message that it has for me? What is it here to remind me of?
- How deep is this wound? How many times have I encountered it before?
- How can I best heal it?

To accelerate the healing, use a potent stream of emerald light every time you remove an object from your bleeding heart. Watch as the light goes deep into the wound, sealing it from within, so that not even a scar remains. Make sure to remove all the objects, so that your heart is visibly healed.

Please know that it is safe for you to love and trust again. Now that your heart is healed, you will attract better people and circumstances, since your trauma no longer holds you hostage.

Healers and Helpers

You can focus your healing of the energies of the five with the following:

Roses — A rose is a pathway to the vibrations of the Divine Mother. The rose works with your auric field, harmonizing any distortions. When healing the energies of the five, make sure to have fresh roses in your house as often as possible. Play with different colors to see which harmonizes you the best. Take time to connect with each flower; smell and touch it, and place it over your heart, so you can absorb its healing energies. Improvise! The rose may choose to come into your life through essential oils, tinctures, dried petals, or rose-infused teas or soaps. Invite it in fully, and watch your frequency transform.

Pink — The color of our higher heart is pink. Imagine a golden chalice in the upper area of your chest, right around your thymus gland. Picture this chalice filling up with soft pink energies—the energies of your higher heart. If you are unsure where to get these energies, know that they exist in the Divine Mother's domain inside her cosmic well. You have access to this well, always and forever. Establish an energy path between the well and your higher heart chalice, and enjoy feeling full and nurtured.

Circular shapes — Healing your relationship with the energy of the five means healing your relationship with the shape of a circle. You may be surprised, but if the energies of the five spectrum are not harmonized within you, your auric field may be filled with broken circular shapes—incomplete circles of all sizes. The healed feminine always completes the circle, but the broken feminine looks like a broken circle, a dotted line missing entire chunks of itself.

Practice: Circular Shapes Visualization

Close your eyes and explore the circular shapes in your auric field. If you find broken or incomplete shapes, take the time to complete them by filling in the gaps and bridging the chasms. You can use threads of golden light to do so. Once complete, the circles start feeling and acting differently; they start rotating, creating vortexes and pathways of flow within your body. In contrast, broken circles cannot move the energy and generally remain within your aura, suspended in midair and adding little to no value.

Connection to Venus: The most goddess-like of all planets, Venus holds the keys to healing the energies of the five and helping you find your inner creative space, as well as helping you emanate the beauty that you are in the world. Venus is about radiance, self-acceptance, bringing things into the light, harmonization, and creative abandon. Synchronizing your body to the rhythm of Venus enables the higher Divine Feminine energies to enter and take root in your body.

Practice: A Quick Meditation to Connect with Venus

Connect with Venus through your third eye by imagining that there is a five-pointed star located at the center of your forehead.

1. Close your eyes and start rotating this star clockwise. Notice that every point of the star has its own unique frequency. Note that this star is the same one we discussed in Chapter 1, and its five points represent love, truth, heart (Divine Feminine), mind (Divine Masculine), and spirit. Whatever point of the star is placed at the top will shift the star's energies, and therefore, the energies you can anchor or process.
2. Align your star so that the Divine Feminine (heart) point faces upward. This will open a portal of light, stretching out from your third eye area and connecting you to the core of planet Venus.
3. At the center of Venus, well below the surface, lies a beautiful pink crystal—the heart of this magnificent planet. Allow your consciousness to wrap around this crystal, creating a loop of light that connects your third eye area with the heart of Venus.
4. Through this bridge, allow your light bodies to start absorbing Venus's harmonizing energies. Invite these energies to join you at a cellular level. Watch as the soft pink energy fills your third eye chalice before cascading down your body toward the throat center.
5. Stop here for a few moments, allowing the pink energies to saturate your throat chakra. From here, allow the energies to travel downstream, stopping in each of your chakras and distributing the healing energies of planet Venus throughout your body.

The Empress — The cards of the tarot's major arcana are powerful portals. The third major arcana card, the Empress (see **Figure 17**), is a potent bridge with the vibrations of the realm of the five and can be quite healing in its own right. This is the card of the Divine Feminine, and it represents the nurturing mother archetype, harvesting, fertility, and being guided by spirit. But most importantly, it harmonizes you with the energies of the Goddess within you, opening you up to a new facet of your power that has remained largely unexplored until now.

Figure 17: The Empress of the tarot deck

Practice: Healing with the Empress

Take out the Empress card and hold it in your right hand, while positioning your left hand so that it directly faces the Empress card. Close your eyes and allow your left hand (your receiving hand) to absorb the card's energies, opening yourself up to its vibration. You may feel mild discomfort if your relationship with the realm of the five is truly damaged; keep absorbing the energies of the Empress anyway. Eventually, you will move beyond the discomfort.

If you want to continue integrating this powerful archetype, place the card under your pillow before you go to bed. Keep it there for seven days as the card's energies become fully awakened in you. Notice any shifts in your mood or behavior that this card brings. You may notice that you are becoming softer and happier, or that your mood is becoming lighter. Whatever happens, know that you are being guided through this experience, which is happening according to your Divine timing. Allow the Empress to become fully anchored within your aura and keep working its magic within your light bodies long after you complete this integration.

The chalice mudra — One of the reasons your relationship with the energies of the five is suboptimal is that your cup is currently empty. Whether it is because your energy is depleted, you give too much, or you are not allowing yourself to properly receive, tending to your inner chalice is a good way to heal. The chalice mudra (see **Figure 18**) is a gesture of being able and willing to receive. It represents a receptacle asking to be filled.

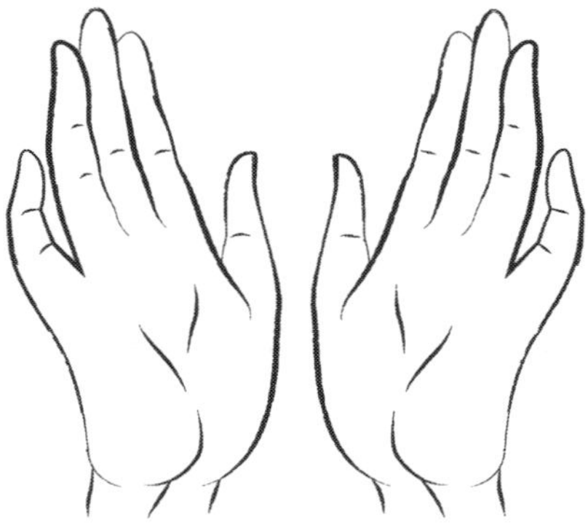

Figure 18: The chalice mudra

Practice: Healing with the Chalice Mudra

Place your hands in the shape of a chalice over your heart and close your eyes. Imagine that the Universe is starting to fill up your chalice with a colorful liquid; whatever color comes through is the one you need the most. Allow this process to happen naturally; simply receive what you are offered. If you require more than one type of energy, a stream of another color will manifest itself and pour into the chalice. Allow the process to run until the chalice feels full.

Any time you are tired or depleted, return to this practice and replenish yourself.

8: Healing Your Relationship with Eight

The number eight takes you on a journey into fullness. As the infinity number, it says yes to everything, integrating as much as possible into one cohesive story. While the two is a precarious balancing act between polarities, the eight is about experiencing them both to the fullest. The lesson of the eight is about being all the way material, but also all the way spiritual. It is about being incredibly good at giving, but equally good at taking. It is about making this world a better place, while prioritizing and filling your own cup first. It is about integration—the kind that happens on the other side of shadow work. It is about accepting all parts of yourself, no matter how hurt or angry. The eight is the vibration of unity—the kind that comes from saying yes to everything and experiencing life to the fullest. The eight is about riches, material and spiritual; it is about true abundance and a life brimming with boundless energy.

Symptoms of a Broken Connection

- Inability to find a balance between being worldly and spiritual
- Being too much of one thing and not enough of the other
- Repeated karmic loops without a means of resolution
- Bad luck
- An overall sense of helplessness or inadequacy
- Imposter syndrome
- Lack of belief in oneself
- A feeling of not being enough
- A loud and persistent inner critic
- Impatience
- Judgment
- Fear of commitment
- Lack of integrity
- An inability to finish what you started
- Frequent feelings of boredom
- An inability to find your place in life
- Uncertainty about your purpose or mission

Shifting the Pattern

Healing in the realm of eight starts with getting out of victim mentality and claiming your spot on the map as a true creator of your reality. The key here is to take responsibility for everything in your life—the good, and most definitely the bad.

Number eight invites you to accept the fullness of it. However, this is challenging, given how many parts most of us reject and suppress into the realm of shadow. Healing your relationship with the eight is impossible unless and until you are willing to face your trauma and dive into your shadow aspects headfirst.

The eight also invites you to balance your physicality with your spiritual life; too much of either equates to a loss of equilibrium. A healthy relationship with the eight implies creating and achieving things in the physical world, while maintaining a soulful practice of inner work and spiritual development. Neither one is more important than the other.

Healing your relationship with the eight also means healing your trauma around wealth and abundance and starting a manifestation practice. Lastly, the eight calls you to liberate yourself from persistent karmic loops and get good at moving through stuck energy.

Healers and Helpers

You can focus your healing of the energies of the eight with the following:

Spirals of light — The eight likes to flow and move around; it detests being stuck in one place. However, often our karmic loops create the opposite scenario, keeping us glued to the same spot and preventing us from moving forward. A spiral is one of the best shapes for representing movement and evolution, and it can be used to move through any blockages.

Here are the three main spirals that can ensure forward movement in your life:

Heart spiral — to cleanse your emotions.

Mind spiral — to cleanse your mental constructs.

Full-body spiral — to release blockages in your etheric body.

There are two ways to rotate a spiral: clockwise and counterclockwise. Clockwise movement is the "normal" direction of a spiral. It moves things forward, is future-focused, and helps break through conditioning, blockages, and deep-set patterns. Counterclockwise movement is about moving backward or going to the past to find answers; it helps bring old or forgotten issues to the surface. Usually, you will want to use both rotations to achieve full healing, starting with the counterclockwise movement to bring the issue fully to the forefront, and then following through with a clockwise rotation to remove any distortions.

Practice: Healing Spirals

In this practice, you will focus on the area of your body that you want to heal: your heart, mind, or entire body. The heart spiral is horizontal in nature and moves parallel to the floor through the heart chakra. The mind spiral also moves parallel to the floor, only it is located in your third eye area. The full-body spiral is vertical and perpendicular to the floor, encapsulating your entire body (see **Figure 19**).

1. Start by locating the spiral that corresponds to the part of the body you would like to work with. Rotate the spiral counterclockwise, watching it bring the blockages of that area to the forefront.
2. Now that the blockages have become visible, rotate the spiral clockwise, watching as it removes any stuck energy.
3. As you rotate the spiral, try speeding it up and slowing it down to get the most out of this practice. Stay here for three to four minutes.
4. When you are ready, start slowing down the rotation, and when the spiral stops, finish the exercise.

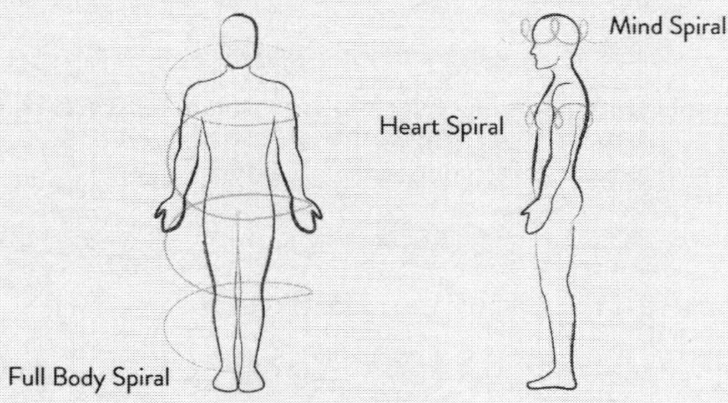

Figure 19: The spirals of light

Two serpents (white and black) — The serpent's energy is inherently connected to the deeper meaning of the infinity symbol, and therefore, to the realm of the eight. The serpent symbolizes wisdom. It is a totem animal of anyone who has passed through trials and tribulations to reemerge on the other side as the one carrying the torch of understanding. It is believed that inside each of us, two master serpents are weaving the threads of our destiny: the white, representing all of our masculine, and the black, representing all of the feminine. Balancing out the two serpent polarities within is one of the lessons of the eight. Accepting and integrating them fully is a part of the process.

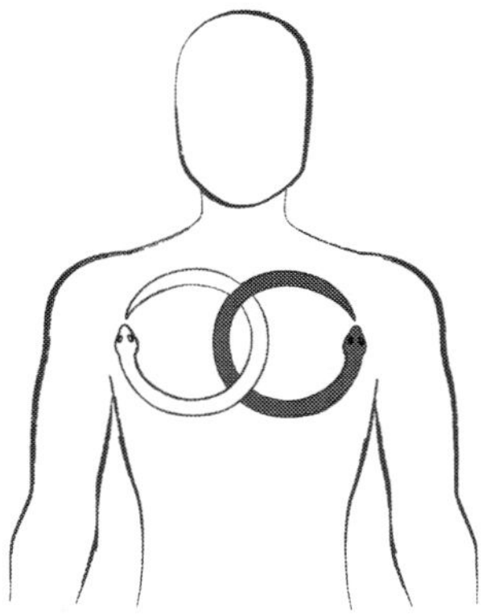

Figure 20: The two serpents

Imagine that there is an infinity symbol located at the very center of your chest (see **Figure 20**). The infinity symbol is made up of two snakes. The black one, located on the left side of your body, represents the feminine, intuition, spirituality, and abundance. The white one, located on the right side of your body, represents the masculine, logic, achievement, the physical world, health, and vitality. Both snakes need to exist in a state of fullness and equilibrium, combining the lessons of the two and the eight. Allowing one of the snakes to dominate represents an interim part of the journey, but not the destination. Mastering the energies of the eight means mastering the lessons of each snake.

Practice: Balancing the Snake Energies

In the following practice, you will get to know the two serpents within, balancing the polarities of your inner masculine and feminine.

1. Imagine a spark of light emerging from the intersection of the two snakes, igniting the shape and spurring it into action.
2. Imagine this spark starting to move along the loop of the black snake, then passing through the center of the figure eight and into the realm of the white snake, connecting the two into a cohesive shared space.
3. Keep watching the spark as it follows the curves of the infinity symbol, closing the loop repeatedly, balancing the polarities, and feeding potent energy into them.
4. Stay with this practice for a few minutes to get the full impact.
5. Each of the two snakes has a message to help you better master the energies of infinity. You can use automatic writing to identify what those messages are. Divide a blank page into two parts, the left belonging to the black snake, and the right belonging to the white snake. Ask the Universe, "What message does the black snake have for me?" Focus on this question for a few seconds, and let your hand move across the paper, writing down the first thing that comes to mind. Don't judge the process. Your hand will write of its own volition, provided you do not get in the way. The message that comes through will always be full of insight and wisdom and will be exactly what you need to hear at this point in time.
6. Repeat the same steps for the white snake to get the full picture.

The frequency of letting go and shedding layers — While certain animals and insects go through a seasonal or regular process of molting or sloughing off to get rid of old, obsolete parts of their body (skin, fur, shell), shedding in humans is much less obvious. Shedding is a process of renewal and rejuvenation, an invitation for something new to emerge. When you are stuck in karmic loops and other traps of the eight, your movement is restricted, both figuratively and literally. To help you move through the roadblocks on your path, intentional shedding is a must.

Physically, dry skin brushing and regular exfoliation are processes of accelerated shedding, and therefore, they are an invitation for renewal. However, shedding outlived layers of your lighter bodies is just as important, and you can do this with the following practice.

Practice: Shedding Lighter Bodies

Your physical body is the innermost of your many bodies. It is enveloped by your etheric body, a light layer that represents the energies that you are and the energies that you hold. Your emotional body is a sphere of light located outside of your energy body, and it is responsible for the entirety of your feelings and emotions, processed or otherwise. Your mental body is the outermost of the aforementioned bodies and is responsible for your thoughts, beliefs, and other mental constructs. Armed with this information, we are now ready to get into the shedding practice below:

1. Get into a meditative state and imagine that your physical body is encircled by a golden sphere representing your energy body.
2. If you look closely, you may notice that your energy body consists of many layers, and if you pull the top one, it easily comes off. Energy blocks generally exist in the outer layers of your etheric body.
3. Feel free to peel off and remove layers one by one until you feel lighter and more energized (generally no more than ten layers).
4. Repeat this process for your emotional and mental bodies as well.

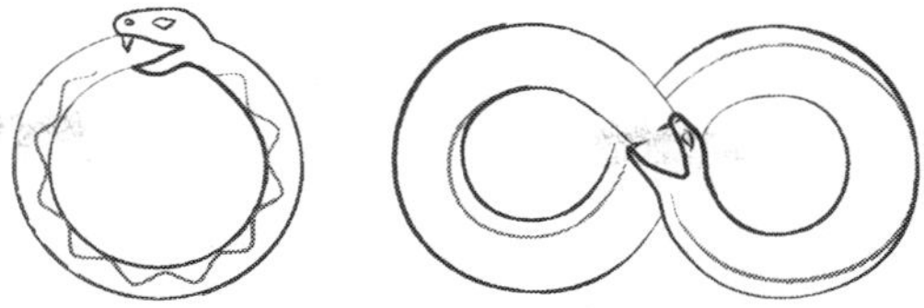

Figure 21: The Ouroboros

The Ouroboros connection — The Ouroboros (see **Figure 21**) is a famous alchemical and hermetic symbol of a snake or a dragon biting its own tail, thus creating a circle, a loop, or an infinity symbol. The Ouroboros represents the cycles of death and rebirth, ever devouring its own tail so that the rest of the body can continue to exist. The Universe is energy in motion, vibration changing form, merging and migrating from one facet to another. The Ouroboros is a reminder that the only permanent thing in existence is impermanence. Ouroboros is often called "the original snake" or "the original dragon." It is also an allegorical reference to the primordial vibration in all of us. It is a force of nature, propelling Earth and its inhabitants into fresh cycles of growth and expansion, albeit often through trials and tribulations.

Figure 22: The Tree of Life and the snake

Ouroboros, in its many shapes and sizes, is present in most creation myths, regardless of where they come from. It is, for instance, the serpent that famously rested by the roots of the Yggdrasil tree in Norse mythology (see **Figure 22**). It is also the serpent that the Mesopotamian goddess Inanna used to guard her Huluppu tree. Unsurprisingly, the serpent that coiled around the Tree of Life in the Garden of Eden and talked Eve into partaking of the apple is none other than our friend, the Ouroboros.

Ouroboros, as an energy and a consciousness, is truly ancient. Eons ago, it was placed on Earth to ensure that each soul coming to this world would be offered a fair chance at evolution, but would also be judged by the fruits of their conduct. Ouroboros thus became the guardian of samsara, the great illusion and the constant trap of reincarnation. While in some ways, Ouroboros is a sage and a judge in snake form, it can be a teacher and protector to the few souls who are far enough along their spiritual path to be deemed worthy.

Figure 23: Buddha and the Naga king Mucalinda

A special connection between the Ouroboros and Buddha is depicted in a retelling of a day in the life of the enlightened master. It is believed that one day, when Buddha was peacefully meditating under the bodhi tree, a massive storm broke out (see **Figure 23**). Lo and behold, the great Naga king Mucalinda (none other than Ouroboros) lent his hood to protect the enlightened one and enable him to complete his meditative journey.

To fully comprehend the lessons of the serpent and the number eight, we need to establish a personal relationship with our inner Ouroboros. Ouroboros in the infinity within, our own process of death and rebirth, our inner light meeting our inner darkness. Ouroboros is the master of illusion and the keeper of the gates; nobody passes into or out of samsara without facing the serpent and its judgment. With Ouroboros, the closer you move to the tail, the closer you move to the head, forever trapped in the illusions of the master snake, until it deems you worthy of passing on.

To meet the Ouroboros, you can take a meditative trip to the central axis of our planet, also called the World Tree. Try spending some time under the shade of its foliage, breathing in its ancient scent, and taking in the gentle quickening of the pulse of this mighty tree. If you manage to quiet your mind, the Ouroboros is bound to make itself known. It likes to coil around the tree trunk and will start speaking to you. If you are lucky, you may even convince it to be one of your spirit guides, so it can show you a way out of samsara.

Meditative Practice: Moving Through the Feminine Pillar

To experience the feminine pillar, use this practice to travel through the energies of zero, two, five, and eight inside your body.

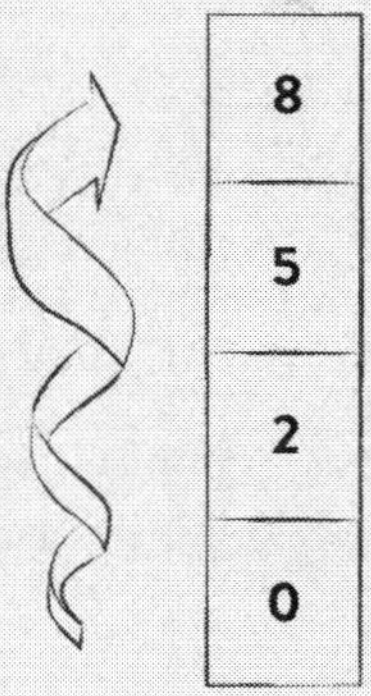

Figure 24: Moving through the feminine pillar

1. Close your eyes and breathe into the lower part of your belly, activating and expanding it in the process.
2. Drop your attention to a part of your body located two inches below your tailbone. This spot is called the void, and you met this place when we explored the energies of zero (see **Figure 24**).
3. Imagine that a thread of golden light emerges from the depth of the darkness that is your void, your space of zero.
4. Allow that thread to spiral into the area of your womb or lower belly, your realm of the two. Imagine that there is a golden apple located there. An apple symbolizes new life, new beginnings, and eternal life, enabling you to tap into the uncanny ability of your body to give and maintain life.
5. Watch as the golden thread coils around the apple, tapping into its life-giving frequencies.
6. Now, allow the thread to travel further up your body towards the area of your heart and the realm of the five. Imagine that there is a star located in the very center of your chest. This star represents your own God/Goddess-given potential, your creative prowess, and your unique flavor of beauty. Allow the golden thread to play with the star, encircling and hugging it.

7. Watch the golden thread travel up your body to your third eye, where it finds an infinity symbol—the realm of the eight. When you look closely, you realize that this is none other than the great Ouroboros, your teacher and your guide.
8. Watch as the golden thread starts traveling down the curves of the coiled serpent—the figure eight—integrating its wisdom and deeper knowing.
9. Finally, allow your golden thread to travel down toward the void of zero located two inches below your tailbone, completing your learning cycle.

Remember, there is always a new cycle waiting for you, so feel free to repeat this practice of expanding and anchoring your feminine wisdom any time you'd like.

Heart Space: The Womb, Unseen

I see you, my sister. I see you fully, with all your cracks and all your wounds and all of your unshed tears. I know your pain; I've felt it, too. And just like you, and like all the women who came before you, I buried it deep inside my womb.

They told us to be strong; they told us to toughen up; they told us to just get it done. And so, we put away the gentle, tender parts of ourselves. We postponed our femininity. We did it as a last-ditch effort to take care of our families, to be strong for our children, to weather the storms that life put in front of us.

So, as time went by, seasons replaced seasons in an ancient dance of change. But one thing remained unchanged: our unwitnessed pain kept being deposited straight into our wombs. Every time we had to swallow our truth, every time we were told to be seen and not heard, every time we were betrayed, backstabbed, broken up with, or divorced, every time we were forced to display inhuman amounts of strength and courage, every time we had to lean into our masculinity at the expense of our health and happiness, every time we had to deny who we were to become what society told us to be, we kept placing that pain deep inside of our womb, for that was the only way we knew how to cope.

And so, over time, our womb became a void filled with the pain, the fear, and the heaviness of living and dying, forever unseen. Forever subordinate, forever insignificant, forever not enough.

Sister, you are holding the pain of generations of your foremothers in your body, all of them unseen and unwitnessed, their pain buried deep, never to resurface. Their tears, unshed and unacknowledged. Their inhuman strength invalidated, unpraised.

Allow yourself to see all of them today, sister—all those who came before you. Acknowledge their strength. Allow yourself to bear witness to the sacrifices they made. Allow yourself to witness their fear and pain, the heavy load of responsibilities, dogma, and societal chains.

Allow yourself to liberate them, your female ancestors, through a simple act of just seeing them fully and irrevocably. And as you start to see them, they are starting to fully see you—deep, raw, just the way you are.

Break your chains today, sister. Allow your womb to cleanse and heal itself; let it become the holy, sacred place that it was always meant to be. Do it for yourself, do it for the ones who came before, and do it especially for the ones who will come after. Unlink the chains of pain and suffering. Let the cycle end with you. You are the salvation, the hope, the great redeemer of your lineage. And you will no longer be put in a box in the uncomfortable void of conformity. You are rising up, and as such, you are raising your lineage right alongside you. You are the first domino, and you are enough. Through you, your lineage stands liberated.

And so it is.

CHAPTER 4

The Womb

To all my non-female readers, I love you. But please bear with me as we talk about the womb, a very female part of the body, so feel free to jump ahead if something doesn't fully resonate.

The womb—one of the most mysterious and magical creations of the Universe—is the most beloved domain of the Divine Mother. As above, so below. The Divine Mother is always unfolding through the synchronized yet organic movement of trillions of her cosmic wombs. Each Universe is a master womb composed of smaller, neatly arranged wombs of galaxies, and even smaller wombs of planetary systems. Each galaxy is a womb—pure, unrestricted creative potential for expansion, a world within itself. Evolution is a process of rotation of the vortexes (systemic, galactic, universal), through which new structures are divinely created and guided toward expansion.

A Portal of Connection to the Divine Mother

The Universe is composed of fractals, individual units of consciousness that reflect the entirety of creation within each separate part. If the Universe were a mirror that was shattered into a trillion pieces, by looking at each individual piece, we would be able to recognize and reconstruct the whole. Everything in existence is not merely interconnected; it contains within itself the codes for rebuilding the whole. Therefore, this world is built on correspondences. By understanding the infinitely small, we comprehend the infinitely large, and vice versa.

The Divine Mother owns many domains within the Greater Universe. It comes as no surprise that she owns a place within the human body, and that place is the sacred temple of the feminine womb. The womb is not just a place of creation within; it is located alongside the axis that connects our core to the central axis of the Milky Way, as well as (at a more macro level) the central creation axis of this Universe (see **Figure 25**). As a female, by finding the center of your womb space and focusing on it, you are focusing on the spirit of the Divine Mother and her infinite creative potential, which permeates everything from the smallest atoms to the largest galactic vortexes of the Universe.

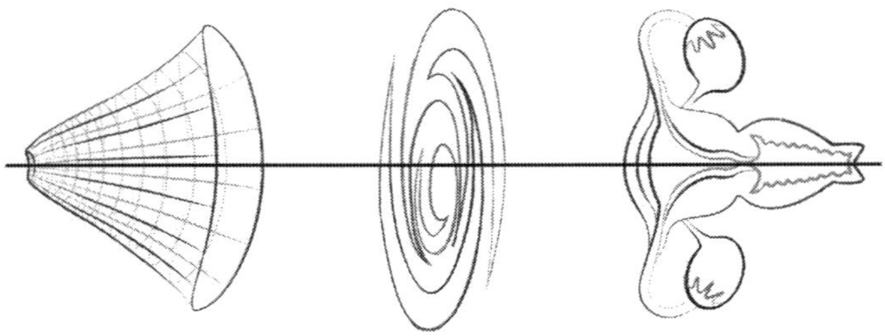

Figure 25: Central axis connecting the Universe, the Milky Way, and the womb

While this may feel too lofty to be relevant, one thing you should know is that your womb is a doorway into infinite feminine energies, an eternity of creative prowess, and a whole lot of Goddess potential. Your womb is both a keyhole and the key that unlocks your unique pathway into Divine Femininity. As a portal to the infinite, your womb knows that any limitation, physical or otherwise, is a byproduct of the intellect, a thick layer of sediment created by the curse of over-rationalization. The heart and womb energies are limitless. As such, they can power any form of your natural expression, as long as you recognize the magic inherent within them.

Practice: Dropping into the Womb

If you do not identify as female or no longer have a womb, you may still perform this practice by dropping into your sacral chakra, located in your lower abdomen.

Of all the drops and rapid falls you could experience, dropping into your womb may perhaps be the most pleasurable. It is a process of shifting your focus from the limited perspective of a human shell into the infinite perspective and wisdom of the Divine Feminine within. This drop embraces the pitch-black void, its silence and boundless potential, the complete descent into and liberation of your creative energies.

1. Imagine an elevator traveling up and down your spine. If you were to board this elevator and allow it to take you down a few levels, it would deposit your consciousness into the serene darkness of your womb.
2. The moment you merge with it, you will realize that for a large part of your body, the daily chase of the outside world is quite irrelevant. Allow the depth of your womb to take over your consciousness. Don't resist it; just go with the flow.
3. Imagine your womb as a rotating vortex of energy. Allow yourself to fully join with it, losing yourself in its measured, steady, expansive pace. Simply be here in this moment and observe. The energetic rotation of your womb is one of the most critical processes of your etheric body, and until this moment, you have been completely unaware of it.
4. Allow yourself to finally realign with and get absorbed into this circular movement. Did you know that getting lost in this rotation momentarily realigns you with the rest of the Universe? It is in this perpetual circular dance that you can finally find solace, forgiveness, and access to infinite love.

Dropping into your womb is a great practice to help relieve the stress and pressures of everyday life. It is a technique that allows a woman to not only stay in touch with her own cycles, but also to receive infinite amounts of healing energies from the Universal Mother. Your womb is a great healer. Her healing art is about as ancient as it gets, and it is time for this knowledge to return to the spotlight.

The Womb Trauma

It so happens that within the human body, the womb space accumulates an unfair amount of trauma. Since it is the inner seat of our femininity, we tend to use it to subconsciously deposit and store our emotional baggage, various forms of heartache, and unprocessed feelings. Our wounded, love-deprived, and grief-stricken femininity tends to withdraw into the womb like a crustacean retreats into its shell. The womb is a proverbial safe space, so the deepest, darkest corners tend to be filled with all the stuff we don't need, yet cannot quite eliminate.

Our wombs are the dumping grounds for the individual, generational, and collective trauma of humanity. And that is a whole lot of trauma, trust me. The husband of your great-grandmother left her for another woman? Guess what? This trauma is still alive inside your womb. One of your female ancestors lost her beloved son to war? This trauma is neatly tucked away inside of your womb also—not to mention your own fair share of troubles, grievances, and mishaps.

Bottom line: your womb is holding onto so much trauma that it should be illegal. And on top of that, it still manages to create new life as if it were no big deal. The state of the womb on planet Earth is dire. The womb is one of the most neglected, energetically polluted, and underappreciated organs within the human body. The time has come for us to shed the layers of pain and suffering that dwell in the etheric folds of our womb. The time has come to reclaim its sanctity, purity, and wholesomeness. And it all begins with staring our collective trauma straight in the face.

The Most Prevalent Womb Wounds on the Earth Today

Low self-esteem (not-enough-ness) — Every time you've felt like a fraud or an imposter, every moment you felt out of place or not good enough, every time your inner critic got the better of you, your womb was suffocated with toxic negativity. The wound of not-enough-ness is one of the more persistent and detrimental wounds the womb can experience. It is deeply rooted in most women and spans many generations. This is one of the most critical wounds to address and release.

Loneliness — If we had a penny for every time we felt that the world and the people around us didn't care, we would all be rich by now. Loneliness is an epidemic, and it is only getting worse, thanks to the digitalization of our society. Conversations are becoming ever more transactional, and interactions brief. In a sea of loneliness, where every person is a desert island, loneliness is becoming the number one mental concern.

Loneliness is an ache of the heart. It is a condition that is felt deep within our souls and bodies, and it is one of those pains that gets deposited straight into our wombs.

Betrayal — Whether betrayal comes from a romantic partner, family, or a friend, it runs deep. We all walk around with a few energetic knives of betrayal sticking out of our backs. Every time you felt you couldn't trust your closest folks, every time your feelings were thrown back in your face, every time you were abandoned, mocked, or backstabbed by the ones you loved the most, your betrayal wound got deeper. And it created palpable cracks in your armor, not to mention real toxicity within your womb.

Abuse — There are many facets to abuse: physical, mental, emotional, and even spiritual. The wounds of abuse are harder to shed; they tend to stick around for generations. Therefore, even if you personally haven't experienced it, the vibratory range of abuse still most likely lives within your system, given we tend to inherit the wounds of our foremothers and forefathers.

Motherhood wound (including the single mother wound) — This wound has many faces, from the pain of a miscarriage to physical separation from your child. Very few wounds penetrate as deep as the wounds of a mother, self-inflicted or otherwise. Motherhood is the closest we can get to unconditional love on this planet. Hence, the motherhood wounding probably hurts the most.

Silence wound — Every time we've held our tongues, every time we couldn't defend ourselves, every time it was unsafe to speak up, every time we were told to be seen and not heard, our silence wound grew. The fear or inability to express ourselves runs deep. And while it may not have been life-threatening at the time, the sheer number of times we have to hold our tongues plays a real trick on us. The silence wound is one of the most prominent and deepest wounds within women at this time.

Sisterhood wound — Last but not least is the wound women inflict upon other women. Gone are the times when we held a collective knowing that we could implicitly trust each other. The years of fighting for our spot under the sun, struggle, competition, and jealousy have put us far behind in the trust department. It is time to reclaim our Goddess-given sisterhood once and for all. And it starts with shedding the layers of the sisterhood wounds from within our womb space.

Practice and Ritual: Liberating Your Womb

This practice can be used by men and those who identify as nonbinary. The deep healing of this exercise will take place on the etheric plane, helping heal the womb spaces of both ancestral lineages, as well as any past life trauma related to the womb space.

Start by burning some mugwort to clear the space. Being the holy plant of Artemis, the goddess of the moon and of nature, mugwort is perfect for decluttering the womb space and taking it back into purity. As you smudge with mugwort, make sure to inhale and exhale deeply, sending the prana you inhale straight into your womb with the intention of starting the healing and cleansing process.

1. Sit comfortably or lie down, whatever feels good.
2. Close your eyes, and for a moment, focus your attention on your belly area. Start breathing deeply, sending large amounts of white light into your stomach. Stay here for ten breaths.
3. Drop your attention into your womb space (your sacral chakra). Imagine it as a rotating vortex of sparkly black energies. Allow yourself to become fully immersed in this circular movement. Your womb is naturally rotating in one direction (clockwise or counterclockwise); pay attention to what this direction is.
4. To start healing your womb space, imagine this rotation slowing down until it completely stops.
5. Now, slowly start rotating the vortex in the opposite direction of your womb's default setting (for example, if your normal rotation is clockwise, start rotating the vortex counterclockwise).
6. Increase the speed of the rotation of the vortex. As the speed increases, imagine large globs of a black, gooey substance, which represents the trauma stuck in your womb, starting to separate themselves from the vortex, being released into the space surrounding the womb.
7. As these gooey globs float, not attached to your womb anymore, notice how they get consumed by the white space surrounding your womb. Allow this process of energy clearing to happen naturally.
8. Now imagine a golden cloud floating right above the vortex of your womb. Watch as the cloud grows in size and magnitude.

9. Notice that as the cloud grows in size, it is starting to rain. But this is no ordinary rain; it is golden in color and feels very high-vibrational. Each raindrop seems to be gleaming with the light of a thousand suns.
10. Watch as this gilded rain falls over your womb. And where it falls, healing takes place. Notice this golden rain clearing away any blockages or debris, healing any trauma, and removing any toxicity from within your womb. Allow this process to take as much time as needed. Don't rush.
11. Once the rain subsides, notice that no darkness remains.
12. Now that your womb space is cleansed, notice that some aspects of your womb vortex are constrained by chains, like a spiderweb permeating your lower belly. There is seemingly no rhyme or reason to how or where the chains are located, but one thing is obvious: the web is in full control of your sacral creative space.
13. Imagine bolts of light coming from the heavens and breaking apart the chains constraining your lower belly.
14. You may choose to use a sword made of white light to help this process along, cutting through the chains and letting them fall away. Let this process take as much time as necessary.
15. Once your womb is liberated from the chains, notice how it is finally starting to breathe. Imagine a million different cells rearranging themselves so that they have access to oxygen.
16. Allow your womb to take in as much prana (nutrition-rich air) as it needs. It has been starved for generations. The time has come for it to be fully satiated.
17. Stay here for a few moments, just watching your womb breathe and replenish itself. Once this process is complete, slow down the rotation of your womb.
18. Finally, you are ready to bring the rotation of your womb back to its most natural setting, its default state. Help your womb out by jump-starting the natural direction of rotation for your womb. (This would be the same direction as in step 4 of this exercise.)
19. Once you are ready, come back into full consciousness and open your eyes.

Practice: Spring Cleaning – The Womb Edition

This is a great supplemental practice if you have completed the womb liberation ritual above. This practice is great as a one-off or as an annual ritual to make sure your sacred womb space is in its most optimal state.

1. In a meditative state with your eyes closed, imagine that your womb space (sacral chakra) is a large house. What color is it? Does this house have a recognizable architectural style? Does it belong in modern times, or to an epoch long gone? Pay attention to the details; this is a great way to get to know your womb on a whole new level.
2. Enter the house. Pay attention to the hallway. Is it dark and dusty, or light and spacious? Chances are that the space could use some cleaning. Take out the washcloths, brooms, and vacuum cleaners, and get busy! Let your intuition guide the process. Any time you see dirt or dust, feel free to sweep or wash it away. You can even repaint the walls in the color you like best. Think of this as spring cleaning meets gut renovation. There are no wrong answers here. Your job is to make the inner space of your womb as clean and pretty as possible.
3. Your house will have a certain number of rooms. Start moving from one to the next, thoroughly cleaning each one. Ensure that the windows are dust- and dirt-free, and that each room has access to ample sunlight. Open the windows to jump-start the circulation of air. Make sure the floors and furniture are all squeaky clean.
4. Feel free to play. If you think a room is missing an item of furniture or decor (e.g., flowers), allow yourself to add the missing item. You can even change the furniture completely; change is good. This means you have moved into new energies, and your inner space needs to reflect that.
5. Show your womb some love. Things we care for tend to reciprocate. Allow the process as much time as needed; no detail is too small. If you feel like adding music or scent to your womb space, do that.
6. Make sure you have cleaned and rearranged every part of the house, even the attic and the basement. Don't forget the kitchen and the bathrooms! Trauma could be hiding in any corner, so it is important to do a full walk-through, leaving no space unchecked. Once the space feels clean and renewed, feel free to come back and open your eyes.

Practice: Your Womb as a Compass and a Guidance Mechanism

Once your womb is cleansed and fully attuned to you instead of the trauma it has been holding onto, you can start using it as a guidance tool. Your womb is intuitive beyond measure, and it truly knows best. Your womb is really good at helping keep you on your path and aligning you with your true north. One quick way to get womb guidance is to use it like a pendulum.

1. Drop into the womb space (sacral chakra) by focusing on it as a rotating energy vortex.
2. Slow down the rotation of the womb, then stop it completely.
3. Ask a yes-or-no question. Allow the question to drop into your womb space.
4. Watch your womb respond by starting to rotate. If your womb is rotating clockwise, this means "yes." If your womb is rotating counterclockwise, this means "no."
5. Trust the guidance. It is very intuitive and is in alignment with your greatest good.
6. If you want to ask another question, first ensure that the rotation stops. Then, imagine clearing and resetting the womb space. One quick way of doing this is to imagine that a wind is blowing inside of your womb, and as this happens, the energies of the womb are reset.
7. Once the energies are reset, you can return to step 3 and ask another question.

Feel free to use this quick process any time you need guidance. There is no such thing as overdoing it; it can and should become a ritual whenever you face a tough decision. Enjoy!

Heart Space: The Circle – A Reclamation

You were a part of a circle of sisters once.

Do you remember?

You held the hands of your sisters with reverence and joy, basking in their love and acceptance.

You had their backs, and they had yours.

You shared the stories, the memories, the blessings, and the sorrows.

But most importantly, you shared a heart space, a connection sacred and unbroken,

A promise that for each other, you would always come first.

You bled with your sisters once.

Do you remember?

Tucked away in a tent and gathered by the fire, pouring your hearts out, healing each other with the strength of your commitment and love, once every new moon.

The blood connected you, the stories united you, and your hearts synchronized you to each other's rhythms, many hearts beating as one.

You stood by your sisters once.

Do you remember?

On a blue moon, a strawberry moon, or a wolf moon, you gathered together without fail. And the wisest among you would speak of the days long gone and the days yet to come, of the chronicles and the prophecies.

You once promised to never lose the magic of the circle.

Do you remember?

The time is now; the great comeback of the circle of the sisterhood is here.

And it is up to you to usher in this great reclaiming.

It is time to trust again, sister.

And it is time to heal, once and for all.

CHAPTER 5

The Sacred Circle

Since the beginning of civilization, the circle has been a sacred symbol—a nod to unity, interconnectedness, and completion. Our ancestors knew the power of coming together in a circle, thus joining the energies of the tribe, creating a nurturing shared space.

A circle is an "equal opportunity" geometric shape. In this space, the energy you give equals the amount you receive, enabling the tribe to remain synchronized via a collective space established and maintained by the simple act of coming together.

Once five or more individuals enter a circle intentionally, they become interlinked by a collective space formed in the process. The more frequently a group gathers, the more robust and potent its collective energy field becomes. Groups that gather in a circle regularly develop strong energetic ties, often gaining an ability to subconsciously pass on information and vivid emotional cues to all the group members. This is the closest thing to telepathy that exists on Earth today.

Over time, closely synchronized groups will develop an ability to sense the moods of the people in the group, even across great distances, with an immaculate level of accuracy. Shared collective spaces enable each individual to contribute their energy stream to the circle and its energy center—a nucleus and the heart of the group, often represented by a thought form, a feeling, or an actual person who acts as an axis that the group revolves around. A tribal shaman would often play the role of the nucleus, gathering the energetic resources of the group so that healing and various rituals could be successfully undertaken. The shaman was always the one with the clearest channel, but the energy and power needed for healing were often provided by the tribe's collective field.

Every tribe had its own women's circles, initially built around a group activity, like making food, craftwork, or caring for the little ones. This helped create an energy form distinct from the collective space of the tribe and with many different capabilities. Tribes with the strongest female circles experienced high levels of synchronicity with their surroundings and superb connection to nature, and they managed to avoid major outbreaks of disease. Female circles both purified the energy of the tribe and aligned the tribe with its greater good, away from any potential destructive forces. And while the gods often spoke to shamans, it was thanks to the strength of the feminine circle that the health, longevity, and development of the tribe were maintained.

The erosion of the collective female space of the tribe correlated with the challenges in the outside world, like unexpected weather conditions or famine. Historically, it was up to the tribeswomen to hold space for its bright future. And they did that energetically, even more so than physically. Strong female circles were less about the number of women in the circle and more about the purity and strength of their relationships. Things like jealousy, bad blood, backstabbing, lying, and causing intentional harm to fellow members weakened their relationships, and therefore, the power of the circle itself. Hence, relationships were prioritized, and Mother Nature helped resolve any interpersonal issues to assist the tribe.

The circle was a sacred space first and foremost because it was a safe place—a place where you could trust others to have your back. The sisterhood wound that is so prevalent today has its roots in the dissolution of tribal culture, and it started with the erosion of the sacred space of the circle. This imbalance in energies caused the tribal culture to dissolve over time, no longer supported by the female community, who loved and trusted each other. Time went by, and individualism took center stage, while tribal units became so small that they started to be called families. Things got progressively worse, culminating in witch hunts—women telling on other women, sisters betraying sisters into the flames of the inquisition.

It is hard to rebuild what we once lost. It is excruciatingly difficult to restore the trust and safety of the circle. The loss of the integrity of the feminine circle is what got us to this place, but it is the circle that will help us get back into unity again. The key that locked the door will be the very same key that opens it anew.

It wasn't only the tribal cultures that recognized the might of the female circle, however. Many secret female societies and mystery schools held the circle in high regard, often using it for the most important group rituals. Group initiations were held in the sacred circle, where one or a few members who had already passed an initiation could guide the rest of the group through the rite of passage by exchanging subconscious and nonverbal information within the circle. Many magical and occult rituals begin and end with the power of the circle, the opening and closing of the shared space.

Now that we have got some of the history out of the way, let's explore the properties and energetic blueprints of the circle and various related shapes. Reclaiming the power of the circle starts with understanding it, and then practicing it. We will take this one step at a time.

One Circle

A circle helps you divide any space into two parts: the inner—that which contains something within (usually the energy you are trying to preserve, accumulate, or call in)—and the outer, the rest of the Universe. This property of division and containment is the reason the circle is used as a tool of protection in summoning rituals. If the integrity of the circle is preserved, the energy inside of the circle cannot escape, even if it wants to.

As a means of collecting and containing energy, a circle can be a perfect shape for your altar to better anchor and preserve light energies within this space-time reality. To define a circle, you can use a circular cloth or simply draw a circle. You might choose to decorate the outline of the circle with shells or crystals, but the continuity of the circle is paramount, so drawing it first is the best way to ensure energy containment. At any point in time, the circle can contain only one type of energy (a sum total of all the objects placed inside of the circle). However, when creating a circular altar, you can and should assign a governing energy: love, wealth, enlightenment, or anything else that resonates with you. By assigning an energy imprint to your altar (or any circular space, for that matter), you are opening an energy portal from within the circle, which tends to strengthen over time, not just replenishing itself, but accumulating the energies you define as important. Once accumulated, those energies can be directed by you toward any aspect of your life. This is how the magic of the circle becomes your companion and ally in your daily life.

Dogon Circles (or Circles of Life)

The Dogon tribe of West Africa is one of the more curious tribal cultures modern science has encountered. While primitive by contemporary standards, its society is based on a sophisticated understanding of cosmology.

It is believed that the Dogon tribe was once instructed by a group of highly developed extraterrestrials that passed on a large part of their wisdom and a deep understanding of cosmology to the members of the tribe. While we are not going to dive deep into the belief system of the Dogon tribe, in our exploration of the circle, it is important to examine a figurine common to the Dogon tribe, as it holds some of the keys to the mystery of the circle.

The Circle of Life is a common name for a series of figurines created by the artisans of the Dogon tribe that contain deep Universal wisdom within. Dogon Circles are a spatial representation of the same concept reflected in the yin-yang symbol, albeit slightly extended (see **Figure 26**).

While the traditional yin-yang symbol mostly focuses on the division within this space-time reality—that between male and female, light and dark, logical and intuitive—the Dogon Circle brings the circle itself to the forefront, while the division within the circle becomes secondary. The Circle of Life represents a human body encircled and trapped in samsara, the endless cycle of death and rebirth. The human is on their knees, which is symbolic of them not being in control of the cycle, but rather succumbing to the loop of cause and effect that samsara entails. Dogon Circles contain within themselves a deeper wisdom: to escape the endless cycles of forced incarnations, the human needs to stand up and accept full responsibility for their karma to start untying the knots. This would inevitably lead out of the circle and toward new, more decision-led experiences.

Figure 26: The Dogon Circle of Life and the yin-yang symbol

Contemplating the Circle of Life is a rite of passage and an initiation. Simply observing it can lead to insights and unexpected revelations. The left side of the circle contains your karma around romantic and familial relationships (partner, mother, sister, son, etc.), your ability to receive, nurture, and care for another, your ability to give love, build community, and interact within a group, selfishness, self-sacrifice, martyrdom, etc. The right side of the circle deals with your karma around your self-concept, self-value, inner critic, abuse of power, ability to take responsibility, ability to achieve goals and assert yourself, confidence, ability to provide, etc. Contemplating the Circle of Life may shed light on your critical karmic knots and may provide specific guidance or help you release that karma.

Escaping samsara is a gradual process of working off your karmic debt and releasing the trauma you've experienced and caused while accumulating light and expanding your light bodies. Samsara is not a predicament; it is a temporal state meant to be transcended. This world operates like a giant mirror, reflecting the trauma and energetic distortions we need to heal. It is through learning the language of this space-time reality—the subtle communication of symbols and synchronicities—that we become adept at navigating and eventually transcending the endless cycle of death and rebirth.

The Magic of the Circle

Let's reframe our understanding of the circle. In the Universe, no two circles are ever the same. Magical circles are not simply curved lines. Instead, they are points connected into one cohesive shape. The power of the circle is determined by the number of points that go into forming it—its points of power—and the strength of each respective point. The smallest number of points required to make a circle is five (remember: four points make a rectangle, three make a triangle, and two make a straight line). The number of points that make up a circle can range from five to infinity, imbuing the circle with radically different properties, durability, and magical power.

A Circle of Five

Since the least number of points needed to complete a circle is five, you need a minimum of five people to assemble a simple circle in real life. Five is also the least number of people required to form a tribe. Every time a new person joins the tribe, its energy doubles, until the tribe reaches twenty-one members, at which point the impact of each new member on the collective energy starts to diminish.

Once the tribe or circle reaches a thousand points, its energy is fully solidified, making it hard for any new member to shift the collective vibration of the tribe. In fact, the reverse happens: the tribe starts to impact the energy of each of its members. All large organizations, from political parties to Ivy League schools, are in fact egregores (unified energy entities fed by the collective thoughts of their members), built according to the rules of the circle (or, in spatial terms, a sphere). From this perspective, egregores that consist of thousand-plus members are considered stable energy forms and are naturally adept at withstanding the test of time.

A Circle of Seven

A circle that connects seven points is a Divine circle (also known as the Circle of Sirius). The Divine circle and the seven-pointed star have a similar vibrational makeup. Seven is the first Divine number (with eight being the second Divine number, and nine being the third). All Divine numbers represent a pinnacle of understanding of a particular energy. Seven is the pinnacle of the energies of the mind, eight is the pinnacle of the energies of the heart, while nine is the pinnacle of the achievement of spirit (including when that is applied to physical worlds). The energy of the seven is the energy of the amalgam, the first number of unification and completion. This circle configuration is best for establishing new schools of thought, especially philosophical, religious, or esoteric schools, such as schools of magic. This configuration will also work for scientific endeavors, especially where discovery and innovation are paramount: biology, physics, technology, astronomy, etc.

A Circle of Eight

Vibrationally similar to the eight-pointed star (the Star of Inanna), the circle of eight was the most favored circle configuration among the priestesses of ancient Mesopotamia and Egypt. This is the High Priestess Circle, perfect for all kinds of female groups seeking heightened awareness and enlightenment from doing energy work. This configuration of a circle ensures a strong connection to the infinity of Universal wisdom. The calibration of the figure eight grants a high degree of access codes to the Akashic field,[4] as well as opening up group psychic abilities through activation and amplification of the third eye of each member, and thus, the group as a whole. The members of the circle of the eight are connected via their third eye chakras, enabling them to penetrate each other's dreamscapes and visions. The circle of the eight requires that each member achieves a particular level of energy proficiency before joining the circle. Otherwise, the energy of the group may be drastically affected.

A Circle of Twelve

The circle of twelve represents Christ consciousness, a system created by twelve points of equal value that come together to create something bigger than the sum of its parts. The selection of the twelve apostles of Christ was far from a random act. The teachings of Christ were first downloaded into the twelve disciples, essentially splitting primordial light into twelve equal streams, so that they could be united and projected forth as one cohesive stream in physical reality. The disciples used the magic of the circle to synchronize their respective energy streams.

In parallel, Mary Magdalene and Mother Mary were working with the twelve female disciples using the magic of the circle to download the teachings of the Divine Mother

---

4 László's 2004 book, *Science and the Akashic Field: An Integral Theory of Everything*, posits that the "quantum vacuum" (see vacuum state) is the fundamental energy and information-carrying field that informs not just the current Universe, but all Universes past and present (collectively known as the Akashic Records).

and birth another school of thought (or the School of the Heart, as it was called at the time), equal in power and wisdom to the teachings of Jesus. The two schools were meant to coexist and spread the light together, creating a unification of Divine Masculine and Divine Feminine energies. Many were the challenges upon that path, not least of which was dealing with the group's energy and keeping it harmonized and attuned, despite the Earth's dense vibrations.

The loss of integrity of the Circle of Christ (the masculine part of the teachings) began with the departure of Judas Iscariot. This disciple was never accepted back into the circle once his betrayal became known. This inadvertently removed one of the twelve streams of the circle, one of the spokes of the wheel on which the teachings depended. From there, the integrity of the teachings couldn't hold; it indeed takes twelve to complete the Circle of Christ.

The Circle of Magdalene had another uphill battle to fight. Outside of the community of the Essenes that respected both women and men as holders of spiritual wisdom, the world was taken over by the patriarchy, making it hard for women to be recognized as teachers. On top of that, the Circle of Magdalene experienced major headwinds dealing with the sisterhood wound within the circle, causing the group to eventually split up, ending the existence of the circle and leading to the demise of some of its critical members due to persecution, torture, and murder. The Holy Grail—a magical artifact and a symbolic representation of the two circles working in unison that was created and charged when Jesus was still alive (see **Figure 27**)—had to be hastily hidden by the remaining members of the Circle of Magdalene, in hopes that the teachings could one day be restored.

Geometrically, the circle of twelve is the lowest number of points that ensures an imprint of the group even if the circle is broken. Any circle with less than twelve points, once broken, dissolves completely, whereas the circle of the twelve leaves a lasting impression within the fabric of existence. That is why we are seeing a resurgence of Christ and Sophia consciousness on the planet today as we approach a new cycle of evolution. The imprints of the two circles are calling back some of their energies, and therefore, they are starting to manifest in the physical world again.

Additionally, the circle of the twelve also represents a full cycle of something, from the beginning to the very end, without skipping any steps. It symbolizes a well-walked path, a deliberate and measured movement toward an end goal. That is why, very often, twelve-pointed circles become foundational. Whether creating a new organization, a movement, a country, or a building, the circle of the twelve is a shape that can be instrumental in ensuring the success and longevity of the endeavor.

Figure 27: The Holy Grail

A Note on Telepathy

One curious byproduct of group consciousness that is achieved with the help of the circle is the opportunity for telepathic communication. The circle is a shared space that connects the members into one unified organism, quite naturally enabling an energy exchange between members that would be hard to achieve otherwise.

There are four types of telepathic communication available to beings on Earth today.

Heart chakra telepathy (similar to clairsentience) — Nonverbal group communication that takes place when the heart chakras of the group are attuned to one another and to the shared collective space. This type of telepathy enables you to sense the feelings of the individuals in the group, even at great distances, in real time. This is a form of continuous long-distance empathy experienced in a group setting.

Throat chakra telepathy (similar to clairaudience) — A form of telepathy when the throat chakras of the group are attuned to one another via a collective circle. This type of communication allows you to perceive the mental space of another—their thoughts and belief systems—and this type of telepathy is the closest in terms of experience to communicating verbally. Information is exchanged between the group in audible thought forms, very similar to speaking.

Third eye chakra telepathy (similar to clairvoyance) — A form of telepathy that opens up when the third eye chakras of the group are attuned to one another. This opens up the ability of individuals to perceive messages and frequencies from other people in the group via mental images. This could include shared memories of past lives. For instance, a group member can bring another member into a particular lifetime (or another space), "seeing" and experiencing the same visual cues. This also enables groups to travel to astral locations together and do group energy work that requires visualization.

Crown chakra telepathy (similar to claircognizance) — Group communication that enables a group member to upload large quantities of information via their crown chakra into the crown chakras of other members. This is often used to communicate complex concepts or ideas that are hard to reduce to the spoken word. This type of communication is layered and is similar to how we generally download information from the Akashic field, only in this case, the exchange is prompted by one of the group members.

Often, cohesive circles exhibit more than one type of telepathic connection, and the most homogenous of the groups will experience all four. But even with the most homogenous groups, telepathic communication requires practice and intention, as well as complete trust among circle members.

Three Circles

Three interlinked circles represent the female trinity: Mother, Daughter, Soul (Spirit) (see **Figure 28**). Whereas a traditional trinity is represented by a triangle, the all-feminine trinity is a much different space. It is softer, more intuitive and fluid, and less hierarchical. In a triangle, the energy always flows from the base toward the point at the top. Within the female trinity, the energy flows in a circular fashion, creating a cohesive, unified space, but without picking favorites or placing one aspect of the Universe above the rest. Also called the sisterhood circle, this shape is perfect for establishing and fueling energy constructs and groups of people that are decidedly nonhierarchical, where equality is valued and everyone has an equal seat at the table.

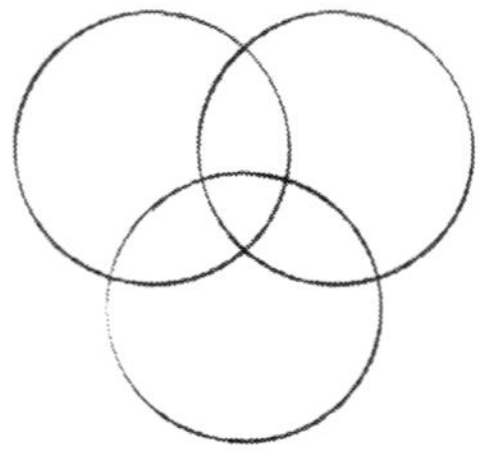

Figure 28: The trinity of the circle

Practice: Creating Your Own Sacred Circle

Every witch and priestess of old used to have a circle of supporting energies or guides that assisted her in her work and ensured she stayed on her path. This circle was often etheric in nature, but usually had a physical extension in the form of a coven or an order that helped anchor the energies into the physical.

Today, I invite you to consider creating an etheric or a physical support circle to further your work and development here on Earth. This can be created with etheric beings or physical people. Arguably, the etheric support circle may be easier to create, since it doesn't require you to know anyone in the physical who would be "worthy." However, in this practice, we will review both options.

Creating an etheric support circle

For this practice, we'll work with the monad, a circle with a dot in the center (see **Figure 29**). This configuration enables the circle to fuel you best and is perfect for working with a group of etheric helpers.

Creating a support circle is a ritual and a meditation in one. It requires you to be well rested and is best done in the first half of the day.

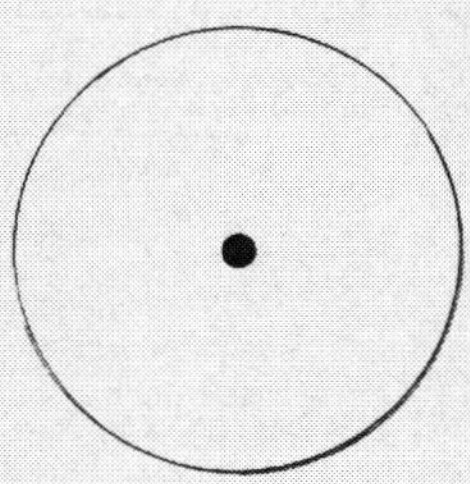

Figure 29: The monad

You will need:

Sage, mugwort, or palo santo

- An abalone shell or ceramic bowl
- A compass
- A large piece of paper with a monad drawn on it in
- Five white tealight candles
- Five to twelve crystals to represent the number of etheric helpers you are seeking to bring in
- A journal

Part 1: The Ritual

Prepare for the ritual by clearing any negativity from your surroundings by lighting a sage bundle, mugwort, or a stick of palo santo. Use the thick smoke to smudge the area where you are conducting the ritual. Move the stick in a clockwise direction to amplify the process. Place the stick into an abalone shell or a ceramic bowl so the smoke can continue cleansing the space.

1. Take a comfortable seated position, ideally in lotus pose on the floor or on a pillow. Use the compass to make sure you are facing true north.
2. Take a few deep breaths, centering into your body and calming down the stream of thinking. Place both palms on your heart and breathe into your heart area, activating it and preparing it for the ritual.
3. Ask your guardian angels for protection and support during the ritual.
4. Imagine that a pyramid of white light surrounds your whole body. This is a great symbol of protection that will ensure everything goes smoothly.
5. Place the monad you have drawn on a piece of paper before you.
6. Light one of the tealight candles and place it on the dot of the monad. You may also say the following invocation if it resonates with you, or make up one of your own: "It is my intention today to create a sacred circle of supporters and guides to help me in my incarnation. By lighting this candle, I open a sacred space between myself and the realm of light, so that my helpers can assist me on my journey."
7. Light the other four tealight candles, one for each cardinal direction. Start with the north, then move to the south, then to the west, and finish in the east. Place the candles on the circumference of the monad, in accordance with their respective directions: the north at the very top, the south at the bottom, the west to the left and east to the right of center.
8. When done, place the crystals around the circumference of the circle. Spread them around evenly, but trust your intuition on the exact placement of each stone.

Part 2: The Meditation

9. Remain seated and close your eyes.
10. In your mind's eye, imagine you are seated in the middle of the monad, right over the dot in the center.
11. Now invite your etheric helpers to join the circle around you. In this step, you can specify what you need help with. You may also call in a particular deity, angel, or ascended master to help you on your journey. But please remember that joining your circle is voluntary, and the specific being may choose to not participate. This is a free will Universe, and it applies to beings of light also.
12. Watch as beings of light begin to emerge in front of you. There will generally be the same number of beings as the number of crystals you placed around the circle.
13. Greet them individually. They may choose to introduce themselves or may have a message for you. Feel free to take notes in your journal to remember each being that comes forth. This way, you can go deeper with each of them later. Invite every being that comes through to take a seat in the circle.
14. Once all the beings have joined the circle, imagine that they hold hands and start to sway from left to right in complete unison, creating energy waves.
15. Watch as a beam of light is created between the heart of each of the beings in the circle and your own heart.
16. Feel the warmth and love coming your way from each of the members of your circle, your personal team of healers, cheerleaders, and angels. Their light starts coursing through your body, making you light up from within.
17. Bask in this beautiful feeling of support and unconditional love that your circle has for you. Watch as a spiral of white light encircles your body, providing much-needed nurturing and healing.
18. Notice that each member of the circle has a special gift for you. Receive the gifts one by one. Each gift is symbolic in nature and will hold special significance for you.
19. Thank all of the members of the circle for joining, and invite them to help you with one thing that is of importance to you in the coming weeks. Your etheric helpers need commissions and requests from you to assist.

20. When you are ready, close the circle by saying a few parting words to your helpers.
21. To finish the ritual, open your eyes, and when you are ready, blow out and put away the candles, and thank the Spirit for being with you for this beautiful activation and initiation. Gather all of the stones into one bag, so that the group of your helpers can be better synchronized. Leave the crystals there for seven days, at which point you can take them out and use them for other purposes. At the seven-day mark, your circle is considered fully solidified.

Please know that this is the very beginning of working with your circle. You may call upon your etheric circle members if you need them, when you are struggling with decision-making or require healing or any other assistance. Get to know your spiritual cheerleading team like you would a group of close friends via subsequent meditations. It is always great to reconnect with your circle in meditation at least once a month. This practice will fortify the bond, which in turn will allow your helpers to have even more impact in your life. Every time you get together with the circle, use the monad shape to reassemble the magic of the circle, then ask your circle for any messages or guidance they may have for you. Feel free to ask them questions also.

Creating a Real-Life Spiritual Circle

The further you move along the Path of the Rose, the higher the likelihood that you'll want to create a circle of your own, your tribe, your safe space. Every mystery order, every priesthood group, every secret society, and every religion in the history of humanity initially started as a circle—a sacred circle of trust. Starting with a small circle is always best. The purity of the hearts and of the intentions of the members will be the foundation of the integrity of the circle for years to come.

Benefits of the support circle:

- Shared energy means the group can work toward larger goals, including planetary missions. The circle's energy multiplies each individual stream, so the energy of the group is always larger than its parts.
- Occasionally, the group may choose to energetically help one of the members manifest or heal something. This can be incredibly effective and fast since the group's energy is a powerful amplifier.
- Group rituals (new moon, summer solstice, etc.) have a special power.
- Cohesive groups can help activate special talents by sharing the codes within the group, e.g., if one member has clairaudience, they can help activate that ability within other members.

Here are a few tips before getting started:

- Make sure you know and trust every member you are inviting into the circle.
- Make sure you share similar vibrations. Members of the circle inadvertently share their energies. On top of that, energy tends to be evenly distributed among the group members. This means the strongest of the group is always an energy donor to the rest of the group. If you are the donor, ensure that you are comfortable with this level of responsibility.
- Make sure you designate the rules of the circle before actually committing to one. Write down your expectations of each circle member, and have all prospective members sign off on their understanding and acceptance of the rules.
- A circle is an egregore, a shared energetic structure. Once it is created, you will be connected to each member physically, emotionally, and mentally. Removing a person from the circle is significantly harder than inviting one, so tread carefully.

Things to prepare:

- Give your circle a name.
- Create a list with all the names of the members of the circle.
- Create an emblem or symbol of the circle. Print it or have it made into jewelry that each member can keep with them.

Ritual: The Circle of the Rose

The smallest number of members for a true circle is five. If you have fewer members, that is okay, and you may follow the steps below just as easily. Energetically, however, the structure you are creating will not be a true circle and won't boast the energies associated with the magic of the circle.

You will need:

- Sage or palo santo
- Incense (sticks or cones)
- White candles (one for each member of the circle)
- One golden candle (to symbolize the energy of the group)
- Golden thread or ribbon (roughly four feet per participant, all in one length)
- White roses (one for each member of the circle)
- Each circle member must bring a nonperishable personal possession as an offering to the circle.

The ritual:

1. Smudge the space with palo santo or sage. Light some incense so that the space can be continuously cleansed and its elevated frequency maintained throughout the ritual.
2. Get started by sitting down in a circle, ideally barefoot, to signify openness and receptivity.
3. Light one white candle for each member of the circle. Place the candles in front of each participant.
4. Each participant should place their right palm on their heart, and their left palm on their lower abdomen (your sacred womb or sacral chakra area). Breathe into your heart, and breathe out of your womb area. Repeat eight times as a group. The leader of the group should coordinate and align the breathing of the group, so a sacred practice of breath sharing can take place.
5. Keeping your hands where they are, proceed with a heart invocation. Heart magic is the best connective tissue a group can have. It is completely okay to come up with your own unique invocation, or simply use this one: "We gather today of our free will and with the intention of cre-

ating lasting bonds between us. We are here to be joined in a sacred circle of the Rose—a safe, nurturing, and protected space that we can all share and depend on. We promise to only bring the best of us into this space, enriching the lives of everyone in the circle. It is through the blessed magic of our hearts that we want our circle to be joined. It is through our love and devotion to each other and the magic of the Rose that we come together under the guidance of the Divine Mother today and ask for her blessings in forming our circle."

6. Have everyone place the item they brought as an offering in the middle of the circle.
7. Now, the participants should raise their palms to the circle's center and close their eyes. Each person should send positive vibrations from their heart—love, light, compassion, kindness, forgiveness, faith—to the very center of the circle. This is the moment when the bonds are created. During this stage, members might experience heat or a slight tingling sensation in their palms or other parts of their bodies.
8. The group leader lights the golden candle and places it in the center of the circle, symbolizing that the star of the circle has been lit.
9. Eyes closed, the group imagines a sun rising from the very middle of the circle—a golden dawn of a new collective consciousness, a new beginning, blessed by the Mother.
10. The leader takes the golden ribbon, wrapping one end around their left wrist. The ribbon symbolizes the gifts and the promises of the circle.
11. The leader passes the ribbon to the next participant on the left. Each participant should wrap it around their left wrist (see **Figure 30**), leaving plenty of it for the rest of the group. Each participant needs to then voice the gifts they promise to bring to the circle (such as a beautiful voice, wisdom, tarot-reading capabilities, kind words, etc.), as well as what they promise to donate energetically (such as a commitment to bring the vibration of love and sisterhood into the circle). Please note these promises are the foundation of the circle and should not be taken lightly.

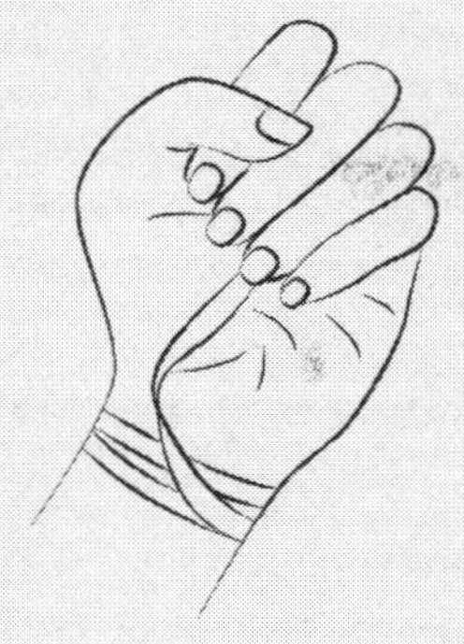

Figure 30: Tying the ribbon

12. Once every participant (including the leader) voices their commitments, the leader ties the two ends of the ribbon together, completing the formation of the circle.
13. With their right hand, each participant takes a white rose and places it over their heart for the final invocation.
14. The final invocation should come from the heart; it helps seal the ritual and further amplifies the power of the newly minted circle. Feel free to alter the words based on what comes through in the moment: "May the spirit of the Divine Mother be with us and guard and bless this circle from this day onward. May our circle become stronger every day and with each new member that joins. May we support, cherish, and lift each other up, come what may. May nothing get in the way of the sacredness of this circle for the years to come. We name our circle [insert the name here]. May it be forever blessed by the eternal magic of the Rose."
15. Finally, if you have physical symbols of your circle, those should be distributed to each member, so they can serve as a reminder of the ritual that took place.
16. The group closes the circle by each breathing into their heart space.

It is customary to give small favors/gifts to your new circle sisters/brothers, as well as to have a meal together after the ritual; however, this step is optional. Make sure to keep the personal items given to the circle, as well as the golden ribbon, as those are the budding artifacts of the circle. They should be stored together and used to ground the circle every time it has an official meeting.

Heart Space: Heavenly Fire Within

She is the voice of the fire made manifest.

She is the soul, the code, and the essence of Agneya, the goddess born of fire,

The female forged in molten lava, as fierce as a thousand sandstorms.

She is the one who conquered fear,

The one who stood tall when she was told to yield,

The one who survived, the one who came out victorious.

She is the power of a desert, scorched but alive.

She is the might of the southern wind, unashamed and fertile.

She is the cherished heat of the sun, regal, yet alone in her glory.

She is a solar aspect of Sekhmet,

A decidedly female deity in an all-around masculine world.

She is the one who shines the brightest,

A female who emanates light, not just reflects it.

She is the torch of the new dawn, the promised spark of lightning in the dark.

She is the one who wears a tiara of starlight, the one who bows to no one.

She is the power of the sun within you, and she is not afraid.

She comes to you today as a pyramid of fire,

And in her hands, she bears the great rite of passage and the mysteries of the triangle.

She has been called many names. She wears many faces.

But the one she chose to wear today is that of Amaterasu, a Japanese goddess of the sun, a mistress of the Universe, a Priestess of the Highest Order of Light.

Allow her into your world today,

And she will show you mysteries unlike any you have seen before.

Here's to the Sun Goddess, within and without.

CHAPTER 6

The Pyramid and the Dome

Of the many shapes within sacred geometry, the pyramid and the dome have few rivals in terms of their impact and simplicity. Both are massive energy amplifiers, charged and potent, perpetually serving upon the altar of ascension, interdimensional communication, and healing.

The Dome

The dome is a feminine configuration that symbolizes protection and containment. Serving as an extension of the Divine Mother, the dome offers a sanctuary for any aching soul. Many churches, cathedrals, and mosques feature a dome shape as a part of their structure, which is no coincidence. The dome has an uncanny ability to harmonize and soften the energy within itself, greatly enhancing and elevating places of worship. Some domes feature a pointed pinnacle that helps to funnel the energy upward, a direction highly coveted for anyone engaging in prayer, meditation, or sacred rituals.

Numerous prominent churches and temples worldwide stand atop the intersection of ley lines, energy vessels of the Earth. The emanation of the ley lines permeates these temples, offering a positive charge to the entire structure and gathering inside of the domes, gracing them. Many temples have been constructed upon ancient places of spiritual significance, borrowing and building upon their legacy—the places once specifically designated by the gods and spirits of old because of the crystalline grids below them. The dome plays the role of collecting and amplifying the energy of the crystals beneath the Earth's surface, which in turn contributes to the feeling of bliss and goodness inside the temple.

The dome, especially when crowned with a pinnacle, naturally directs positive energy toward the dome's center, while repelling any suboptimal energies. However, unlike the pyramid, the dome doesn't let the energy freely exit at the top, effectively preserving and sealing the vibrations within. This is an example of the passive principle of femininity. The dome enables energy conservation; not an ounce is ever wasted. Due to this principle, domes are a perfect choice for various energy exercises that require energy accumulation, preservation, and protection, as well as for containment and concealment spells.

Circular Dome Shape

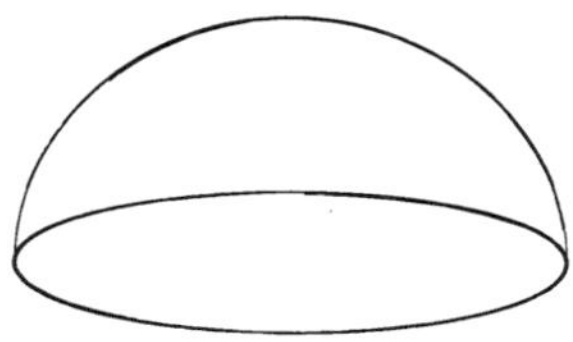

Figure 31: Dome with a circular base

The classic dome shape with the circular base offers a respite from the harshness, stress, and various imperfections of daily life. It is protective, harmonizing, and gentle, covering you with its blissful veil, as if the Divine Mother is taking you under her wing. A space perfect for healing, restoration, introspection, rest, and returning to alignment, this shape naturally helps rid your body of distortions, whether energetic, mental, or emotional, freeing your stuck energy and removing blockages. The dome's blueprint is Heaven meets Earth. It helps us feel closer to lighter spheres, brightens our mood, and restores hope, paving the way to a better future. The motto of the dome is "Stay safe and elevate." It enhances anything it comes in contact with and can rightfully be considered one of the most nurturing shapes in creation.

Square Dome Shape

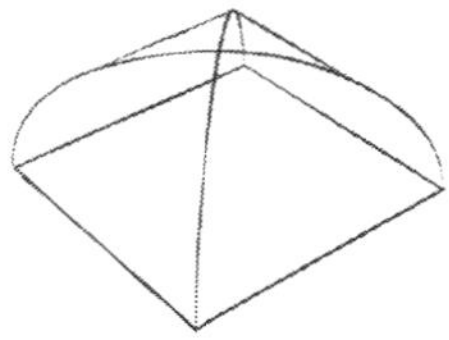

Figure 32: Dome with a square base

A dome with a square base combines the caretaking, nurturing spirit of femininity with the grounded, built-to-last emanation of masculinity, brought forth by a perfect square shape at the bottom. The two energies, entwined and interconnected, give birth to a stable and potent powerhouse that is just right for soul-searching, introspection, grounding, understanding your path, getting messages from Spirit, meditating, connecting with light beings, and even manifesting.

This dome's blueprint is Divinity anchored. It allows emanations from the cosmos to reach Earth and become fully absorbed into our planet's core. The dome with a square base is a great energy receptacle and can preserve a particular facet of energy for centuries, if sealed properly. Its motto is "Absorb and stabilize," which again speaks to its dual masculine/feminine nature.

Working with the Energies of the Dome

For relaxation:

The dome's shape enables maximum relaxation across the physical and light bodies of a person. To get into a relaxed state, imagine being covered by a golden dome of light. You may charge the inner space of the dome with any frequency you desire, such as love, forgiveness, or bliss. Simply imagine that this energy is entering through the base of the dome. The good news is that you only need a small amount of the required frequency, because the dome will amplify and preserve it. For greater impact, imagine that the dome has a mirrored inner surface. This will ensure that the energy bounces off the surface, shifting from a passive to an active state. This will amplify the dome's overall impact on your body.

Life hack: Use the dome technique before you sleep to charge your body with the desired energies while you rest.

For protection:

The dome is one of the better shapes for protecting your home or workspace from suboptimal energies or energy attacks. Simply place a dome over any area of your house that you want to protect. Ensure that the dome is sealed from the bottom, so as to not create an energy leak or accidentally leave the back door open. For enhanced protection, layer a few domes of different colors over one another, creating a Russian nesting doll effect. The best dome colors for protection are blue, violet, white, and gold.

Life hack: You can use the dome as a protection shape for your physical body if you are visiting somewhere with suboptimal energies. Make sure to seal it at the bottom. Charge your dome with select positive vibrations, so it can fuel you as well as preserve the integrity of your auric field.

For concealment:

There may be times when you want to keep certain things concealed from prying eyes, especially the evil kind. Whether it is a new project, a budding romance, or a cherished possession, the magic of the dome can help you make the object "invisible" to others. While the physicality of the concealed object doesn't change, its energetic blueprint does. The electromagnetic field of a concealed object becomes dispersed and hard to detect, making it impossible to impact from the outside. To conceal an object, simply place an invisible (transparent) dome over the object you would like to conceal, and repeat the following three times, like a spell: "It is through the magic of the dome that this object is now invisible to any force that may want to harm it." Voila! Your object is now concealed.

Life hack: Ensure that you remove the concealment dome once you are ready for the world to witness the object. Otherwise, it may be quite hard for you to make people notice and pay attention to it. This is a pretty simple yet effective magic technique that will not disappear of its own accord, so it requires conscious undoing.

For energy collection:

If you are low on a particular kind of energy (such as solar energy in the wintertime), you may choose to create a dome specifically to preserve the energies of the solar spectrum. Simply imagine the dome over your body, coloring it with the range of the energies you are seeking to collect (for example, a yellow dome for solar energies, a red dome for courage, and violet for communication with spirit guides). Once the dome is in place, ask it to collect and preserve the energies for you until you decide to use them. Then, simply allow some time for energy collection. Remove the dome when you no longer wish to collect a particular vibration.

Life hack: You can only collect one type of energy at a time. Do not get greedy. Energy collection is an energy-intensive process, and you never want to overexert yourself.

The Pyramid

The pyramid is a masculine shape and is built to house massive amounts of energy. A pyramid is thus an active shape that requires constant fueling and discharge, just like the masculine principle. Often, physical pyramids are powered by one of the natural elements, with crystals, water, wind, or the sun being the most common. The great pyramids of Giza in Egypt, for instance, are powered by the Nile, as well as by the cosmic energies of the Sirius star system, perfectly aligned to "feed" the pyramids from the top.

While the dome is primarily used for energy preservation, the pyramid is used for energy transmission. In a pyramid, the energies are forever rising from the base to the top, creating a constant and intentional flow. At the same time, because the base of the pyramid is wide while the top is narrow, it creates a pressurized and condensed energy stream—the kind that transforms passive energy into its most active state. Overall, the pyramid is great for focusing and accumulating massive amounts of energy to later be directed towards a particular action or desired outcome.

Triangular Pyramid

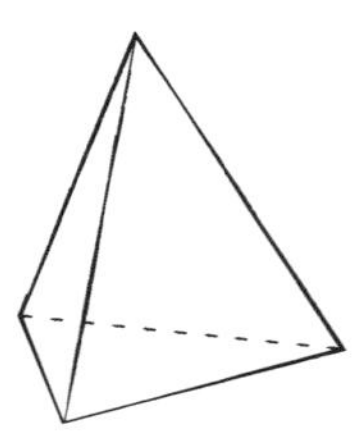

Figure 33: Triangular pyramid

If the pyramid's base is a triangle, it is called a triangular pyramid, and as a blueprint, it is fire intensified. It contains four triangles (4x3) and, as such, it carries the vibration of twelve. This pyramid is great for speeding things up, moving through obstacles, and putting fire in anyone's belly. The motto of this pyramid is "Ignite." Its energies are perfect for jump-starting companies, movements, organizations, relationships, or new chapters of your life. Like a blazing fire, the vibrations of this pyramid are far from tame or understated; the energies of this geometric wonder come and take you by storm. At the same time, this pyramid carries the energies of the twelve, and therefore, the energies of cosmic completion. Despite being fiery, the energies of this pyramid are not easily depleted. This shape has what it takes to go all the way and bring things to fruition. If you are seeking a collaborator to take you from A to Z, the triangular pyramid is one of the best allies you could possibly find.

Square Pyramid

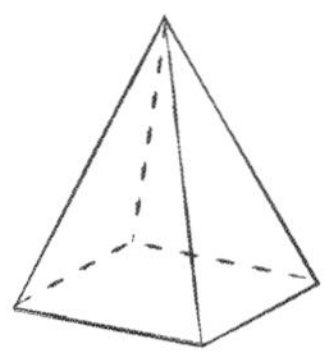

Figure 34: Square pyramid

If the pyramid's base is a square, it is called a square pyramid. The square pyramid's blueprint is "fire meets earth." This pyramid offers a steady and measured firepower that will withstand the test of time. The great pyramids of Giza leverage this exact configuration, which is why one of their underlying gifts to humanity is their ability to anchor higher cosmic energies into the earthly plane. The pyramids of Giza have long been transmission towers, receiving information from key star systems of the Milky Way and beyond. The motto of the square pyramid is "Create to last."

This pyramid comprises four triangles and one square (4x3+4), so it carries the vibration of sixteen (or seven: 1+6=7). Seven is the master number of masculinity and creation. In the Bible, the seventh day is the day when God rested on the laurels of his creation, making it the first ever holy day. Seven is also the smaller completion number, making this pyramid perfect for channeling, receiving, and transmitting information, gaining influence, and changing the mental paradigm. Seven is the number of the fruits of labor that stem from applying one's intellect. The configuration of this pyramid enables the energies of our planet to meet and greet the greater cosmos. It is helpful for birthing things that are new and innovative—the kind that have never seen the light of day. The square pyramid is a patron saint of channelers, seers, and mediums. It is a shape that can help jump-start your third eye activation, as well as unlock dormant codes in your DNA, especially if you are a star seed.

Pentagonal Pyramid

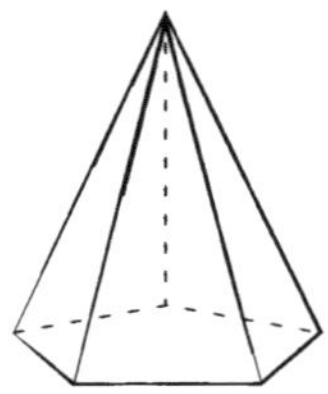

Figure 35: Pentagonal pyramid

If the pyramid's base is a pentagon (five sides), it is called a pentagonal pyramid. A pentagonal pyramid is a softer fire, the fire of the hearth, the flame of a candle, the spark of bringing people together, of uniting through love and forgiveness. It awakens the flame of compassion, of understanding, helping to forge deeper connections between people and within groups. The pentagonal pyramid's blueprint is "fire-tamed." It is the way-shower, a torch that lights up a path in the darkness, a fire that will warm you up on a cold night, a fire that will cook your meal, a gentle fire that will provide for you. This pyramid's motto is "Nurturing through fire." Of all the fires, this one is of the more feminine variety, seeking to balance and harmonize instead of destroy, to warm up instead of burn, to gently guide instead of completely take over.

This pyramid is perfect for creating small, cohesive groups of people—sisterhoods, brotherhoods, sacred circles. It helps strengthen familial ties, burn through ancestral karma, and fortify relationships. The fire that burns inside this pyramid is the fire of purification, of building understanding and forging ties. Use the pentagonal pyramid to shift the energy of small spaces to make them more welcoming, cozy, and nourishing. This type of fire is conducive to sharing secrets and building bonds that last through incarnations. It is a beloved shape of many sacred priesthood orders, as the value of this pyramid to bring people together can hardly be overstated.

Mastering the Magic of the Pyramid

For focusing energy:

A pyramid is one of the better tools for shifting energy from a dispersed stream into a focused stream. Most energy in the Universe exists in its inert, dispersed state, making it impossible to wield. Focused energy, on the other hand, can be directed like an arrow destined to hit its target. It is energy in its most active and prolific state. Simply imagine sending an energy stream toward the bottom of the pyramid, then allowing it to naturally move upward and exit through the top of the pyramid. Lastly, direct this newly forged energy stream toward a specific outcome you want to achieve, fueling and charging it.

Life hack: Use emerald-green energy to promote healing, pink energy to mend relationships, and golden energy for manifestation.

For shifting energy:

A pyramid can help you shift your state almost instantly. With your eyes closed, imagine that your body is contained within a pyramid of white light. Now think of a frequency you want to switch to (such as love, forgiveness, joy, or relaxation). Imagine a stream of that energy entering the pyramid from the bottom. Allow this energy to fill up the pyramid, bottom to top, and exit from the opening at the top.

Congratulations! You have established a circulation of energy throughout the pyramid. Now allow your body to start absorbing this frequency, aligning your spinal cord with the vertical axis of the pyramid, so that the top of your head reaches up to the very tip of the pyramid. Don't resist the energy; simply observe as it starts to fill up your body. Just three to five minutes inside this ethereally charged pyramid will change your state into the one desired.

Life hack: Feel free to place a white flame underneath the bottom of the pyramid as a source of energy. The color white contains the entire vibrational spectrum, and therefore, can help fuel your pyramid with the desired vibration faster.

For communication with spirit:

Simply place your body inside a pyramid of golden light to enhance your ability to receive spiritual communication from your guides, Higher Self, or Source consciousness. Align your chakras with the vertical axis of the pyramid that connects the base with its top. Lastly, ensure that your crown chakra is perfectly aligned with the top of the pyramid.

Now, open up your crown center like the petals of a lotus flower, and imagine how the information is starting to pour in from the apex of the pyramid straight into your crown space. If you cannot decode the messages you receive right away, do not worry; practice makes perfect. The more you try, the better you are going to get at understanding and internalizing the communication that is coming through.

Life hack: Create your communication pyramid once, and reuse it afterward. Each time you go back to your etheric pyramid, its powers will grow, and its cumulative properties will ensure that your personal meditative space is always primed for action.

For energy activation:

If you run low on a particular kind of energy, the pyramid can help you refuel quickly. Simply imagine that the energy you need is located underneath the pyramid's base, fueling it from below. Then, watch as this energy accumulates at the base, slowly rising to the top of the pyramid. Imagine that your energy body is located at the very top of the pyramid in a way that enables you to receive any and all vibrations that the pyramid is emitting. Simply absorb the energies that have been accumulated by the pyramid. Voila! You are fully charged by the energy you have been seeking in no time.

Life hack: Place an image of the Flower of Life underneath the pyramid to soak up the energies of the Divine Mother. The Flower of Life is her love language, and she is always close by whenever this pattern manifests. If you seek higher-dimensional cosmic knowledge, place Metatron's cube (see **Figure 36**) underneath the pyramid. When meditating, imagine your light body positioned over the pyramid's apex, fueled by this symbol, and watch some unique downloads come through.

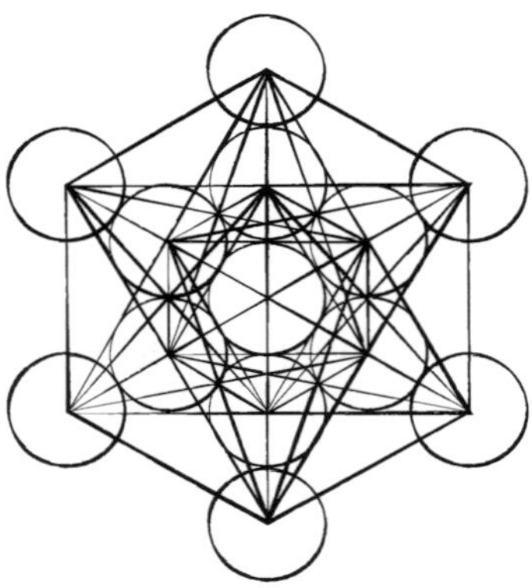

Figure 36: Metatron's cube

Practice: Activating Your Own Pyramid of Light

You can create your own sacred pyramid space for all your energy work. Over time, this structure will become more potent and turn into an indispensable ally in your meditations and energy work.

1. In a meditative state, imagine sitting inside a pyramid of white light.
2. Zoom into the pyramid's surface and inscribe your name upon it. Your name is your vibrational signature; it automatically claims objects in the Universe as belonging to you.
3. Copy and paste your name so that it begins to cover larger parts of the pyramid's surface, turning it into a pattern.
4. Make sure the pyramid is fully covered with the pattern of your name.
5. Proceed to meditate inside the pyramid as you normally would without one.
6. Next time you perform an energy practice or meditate, simply call back your pyramid to assist you. The more you interact with it, the more potent it will become.

Life hack: You can charge your pyramid with properties you find useful, such as healing, protective, or cleansing properties, etc. Simply call these energies into the pyramid the first few times you work with it. Later, those energies will become native to your sacred space and will be invoked automatically whenever you bring your pyramid forth.

Working with the Etheric Pyramids of Light

While creating your own pyramid of light is something every energy practitioner should attempt to do, etheric pyramids are available for use all across the Milky Way by souls of every creed and caliber. These collective spaces were originally built by the founding forces of the Milky Way galaxy and have been maintained by guardians ever since. Each of these high-dimensional etheric pyramids is a sacred space that can be used for healing, receiving energetic upgrades, initiations, accessing restricted sections of the Akashic Records, raising consciousness, and working with intergalactic vibrations. Below, I offer just a few pyramid examples, in hopes that these can serve as jumping-off points on your journey to the land of the pyramids, an intricate system of temples of light that permeates our galaxy.

To partake of the benefits of any of the pyramids mentioned below, get into a calm, meditative state and clearly voice your intention to be transported to a pyramid of your choice by saying its name. You will be instantly transferred to your desired location. Always take the time to look around and feel the pyramid's energy. The pyramid's emanations are always strongest if you sit at the very center of the base, so that your crown chakra is aligned with the top of the pyramid.

To connect with the energies of the pyramid, imagine that your body is starting to collect the energy from its base and shoot that energy up toward the top. This creates an upward pillar of light that will penetrate every major energy center of your body. Allow the pillar of light to remain open for a few moments. In due time, you will start receiving a downward energy stream coming straight from the cosmos, through the tip of the pyramid and straight into your crown chakra. This is a normal process and what an energy exchange should feel like.

From this state, the benefits of the pyramid will become available to you. Please note that attuning to certain pyramids may take more than one session, so do not despair if your first attempt is less than fruitful. Simply keep trying. Working with the energies of the pyramid is like developing a muscle; it takes time to witness the full benefit.

The Sacred Pyramid of the Sun

One of the main solar temples of the Milky Way, the Sacred Pyramid of the Sun, is located in the Canis Major constellation, just a few light years away from Sirius A.

Uses:

- Downloading high-frequency codes directly from Source
- Aligning with the breath and heartbeat of the Universe

- Understanding your mission here on Earth
- Receiving commissions from Spirit
- Upgrading your light bodies and DNA
- Working with the golden flame of cosmic recalibration
- Working with the angelic kingdom

The Sacred Pyramid of the Moon

This moon temple was built by the Mothers, great feminine spirits currently curating planet Earth and watching over the buds of femininity unfolding within its constraints. This temple is near our moon, in the fifth dimension.

Uses:

- Healing the body and heart
- Coming back into the Divine Mother's embrace
- Healing past life trauma
- Understanding and untying karmic knots
- Emotional healing and discharge
- Cleansing
- The grand reset of all of our light bodies

The Sacred Pyramid of the White Lotus

This pyramid is located in the etheric realm of Venus, in the seventh dimension. It is a place of pilgrimage for many bodhisattvas, a place that Gautama Buddha and Kuan Yin used to frequent when they were still in their physical bodies. This temple is also called the temple of enlightenment, as it helps you remove unnecessary layers and step into your Divine blueprint and perfect expression.

Uses:

- Ascension
- Seeking wisdom
- Finding your personal guru in the etheric realm
- Uncovering the secrets of the Universe
- Integrating your shadow
- Deep soul healing
- Working with the space-time continuum (past and future lives)

The Sacred Pyramid of the Golden Scarab

The Pyramid of the Golden Scarab once graced the banks of the Nile River in ancient Egypt. Home to the secret order of the Golden Scarab and a cradle of white magic, it was filled with priests and priestesses of the sun. At one point, ancient Egypt was a battleground between the priests of the Golden Scarab and those of the Black Scarab order, whose energies were tarnished by demonic forces and dark magic. The Golden Scarab order was a beacon of light and an ancient mystery school whose gatherings took place under the protection of the temple. To date, an etheric copy of this temple has the same energetic footprint as its physical counterpart.

Uses:

- Initiation into the mysteries
- Connection to powerful solar energies
- Protection
- Infusion with light
- Access to the cosmic codes of love and oneness
- Access to knowledge of ancient ritual magic
- Connection to the Sirius star system
- Cleansing of all light bodies
- Deep ancestral healing

The Sacred Pyramid of Wisdom and Truth

Once a beloved spot of the goddess Athena, this etheric pyramid is located above Athens in Greece. Guarded by a dozen majestic white owls, this pyramid is a welcome abode for those stepping onto the path of learning. The temple's energies are gentle, allowing you to walk and learn at your own pace. This unique pyramid allows one to connect to the Blue Ray—the ray of Divine truth and strength—that is interwoven into the energetic makeup of this temple.

Uses:

- Gaining wisdom
- Learning the answer to any question
- Seeking a path of understanding
- Connecting with Athena
- Learning the secrets of the Universe
- Connecting to the Akashic field

The Sacred Pyramid of the White Scrolls

The White Scrolls are an epistle once coauthored by Hermes Trismegistus and goddess Isis during their years of adapting and preserving their wisdom for the inhabitants of Earth. Also called *Book of the Living*, it reminds us of the main principles by which our current reality (i.e., the matrix) operates. The White Scrolls were the original text explaining the mysteries of the Emerald Tablets through the language of similes and parables. Isis and Hermes (Thoth) built a pyramid to house the White Scrolls. The pair opened a powerful cosmic portal of light to anchor the energies of the scrolls, while keeping an open channel to their spirit guides. Isis and Thoth worked with powerful extraterrestrials to help deepen their own understanding and teaching capacities.

Uses:

- A deeper dive into the mysteries of the Emerald Tablets
- Connection with extraterrestrials
- Understanding how the matrix works
- Connection with Hermes Trismegistus
- Connection with Isis

The Sacred Pyramid of the Rose

The Temple of the Rose is a fifth-dimensional portal between two planets: Earth and Venus. It exists in a pocket of space-time reality that belongs to both planets and neither one, all at the same time. This pyramid was originally built by the Hathors, a powerful extraterrestrial nomadic tribe and a group of female priestesses committed to spreading the gospel of the Heavenly Mother across the planets of the Milky Way and beyond. The Hathors used the space to solidify the energies of the Rose and bring its healing powers to the people of Earth. The Pyramid of the Rose also contains a large library of writings of the sisters of the Rose throughout centuries, making it a truly one-of-a-kind receptacle of the wisdom of the Rose.

Uses:

- Receiving the blessings of the Divine Mother
- Connecting with the many sisters of the Rose through the ages
- Receiving access to the Holy Grail of the Rose (a collection of timeless feminine wisdom)
- Healing the relationship with your feminine
- Healing your feminine/masculine balance

- Claiming your connection with the goddess vibrations
- Karmic release
- Anxiety relief
- Full recharging of your physical body for optimal performance and emotional state

PART II

THE SACRED ROSE INITIATION

Heart Space: The Path of the Mother

Light is the breath of the one called Divine Mother. Her gentle steps reverberate through the infinite abundance of her creation, leaving golden footprints and pearly stardust in her wake. She is a soft reminder of the days long gone, a stake in the ground for the times yet to come, a link that brings it all together into a ring governed by the magic of fire and water.

Behold her torch of truth, dear one. Behold her eternal promise. She is here to shine the light on the shadows, to partake of the wine of the illusion, to break the chains of the mundane and reemerge on the other side as the Holy One clad in sunlight. She is a queen and a goddess and a mortal, the full spectrum of femininity in one effervescent vessel. She is all of the polarities brought together, the golden middle of broken duality. She is the reforger and the rebuilder, but she is also the destroyer. She is the wrath of Kali and the love of Parvati. She is the strength of Durga and the dance of Lakshmi. She is now and forever the one and only Mahadevi, the highest among females. She is the promise of redemption and the curse of retribution. She is the one who sat upon a throne in Heaven while she died and bled and wept on Earth.

Her path is winding; it curves and slants in ways unknowable, yet majestic beyond measure. She is an impossible equation, a constantly shifting variable in the logical sequence of the Universe. She is a gift and a scripture. Falling into her arms is a homecoming, trusting her words is a prayer, knowing her soul is a holy communion, and speaking her tongue is a mantra. She is the way out of the maze of low vibrations. She is the saving grace, pulling you out of the deadly whirlpool of distractions. She is forgiveness and mercy, once and for all.

Hear her voice in the sounds of the river, in the crashing of the waves, in the song of the conch shell horn at dawn, in the trumpeting of the white swan. She is ever present in all living things, ever counting your breaths, easing your suffering. She is your heavenly Mother, and the one who cares the most. She is a path wide open.

Will you walk it?

CHAPTER 7

The Rose Mandala

Thousands of years ago, when the Order of the Rose was a prominent mystery school for women, an initiate started on their path by creating a rose mandala. Making one was deemed a sacred ritual, and the contemplative practice could take weeks to complete. The process was accompanied by chanting, sacred incantations, breathwork, ritual dance, and at times, altered states of consciousness. The quality of the mandala that resulted from this initiation stage largely determined the initiate's curriculum and devotional path. Much could be understood about the initiate by simply observing their rose mandala; the energy, after all, never lies. The rose mandala offered insight into an initiate's strengths and talents, as well as their challenges and shadows.

Mandala, translated from Hindu, means "circle," a sacred geometrical pattern symbolizing the circular nature of existence; what goes around comes around. The mandala draws its power from the interconnected nature of all things and celebrates unity as a great cosmic truth. It is also a tool of meditative pilgrimage and a rite of passage for certain spiritual disciplines.

The circle of the mandala divides the Universe into two parts: the inner world, represented by the mandala itself, and the outer world, represented by the space surrounding the mandala. Through mandala-making, we transform our inner world and anchor its missing frequencies. It was once believed that when you place certain energies in the center of your mandala, it's just a matter of time before they manifest in physical reality. Placing shapes and objects inside your mandala is equivalent to bringing them into your orbit. Once complete, it is customary to hold onto the mandala for many months, so it can provide the spiritual and energetic assistance required for life upgrades.

The initiate's mandala was a source of the power and the strength of their intention. Through creating and observing one, the initiate began on their path toward a greater understanding of Divine Femininity.

A mandala is a template you can create to program your reality and prioritize certain vibrations over others. Most desirable vibrations are usually placed at the very center of the mandala to signify their special significance; the rest of reality tends to be built around them.

The Language of Sacred Geometry and Symbols

Later in this chapter, I will share how you can create a rose mandala as your first real step on the Path of the Rose. To successfully harness the mandala's magic, you need to speak the language of sacred geometry and symbols, so that your creation is as intentional as possible. Moreover, the symbols you use in your mandala must have a high vibration and potency to be effective.

Below are some of my favorite symbols for anchoring cosmic feminine energies.

Five-Pointed Star

It represents cosmic balance and unity, as well as the attainment of the balance of polarities, the unification of opposites, and coming into center. The five-pointed star symbolizes completion after much turmoil and antagonism. It also represents the Divine blueprint, the grand plan of our collective evolution. It thus denotes the final attainment of all our aspirations and desires, the manifestation of all we set out to accomplish. The five-pointed star is also the coming together of the five formative elements: fire, air, water, earth, and spirit (or ether).

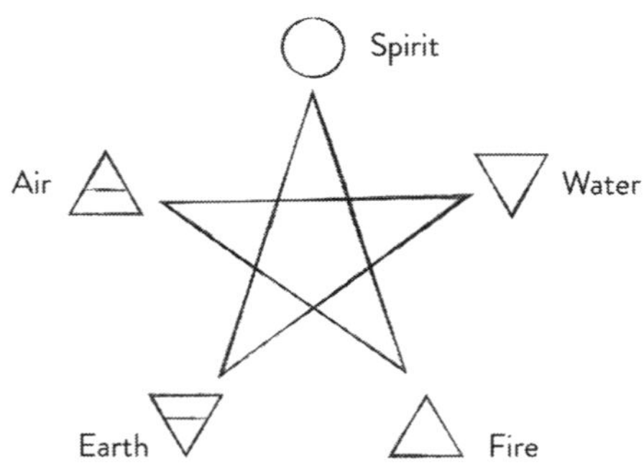

Figure 37: Five-pointed star

Pentacle

It represents mastery of the five elements. In mystery schools, it symbolizes attaining magical powers and divinely guided talent. It is a powerful symbol of protection, special abilities, and magical prowess.

Figure 38: The pentacle

Spiral

It is representative of the womb of the Divine Mother, and by extension, any woman's womb. The spiral has come to symbolize progress, growth, and evolution. A spiral is a proxy for the galaxy's movement, a cosmic embodiment of feminine energies. This shape is perfect for speeding things up, expanding your horizons, or bringing new energies into your life. The magic of the spiral is alchemical; it can clear up the things that no longer serve you, as well as become a catalyst for birthing new things.

Triangle/Pyramid

While not a feminine symbol, the triangle stands for the process of ascension, so it is great for accumulating and directing energies. A powerful symbol of a pointed, directed creative force, pyramids are sacred geometry powerhouses of manifestation, offering a redirection of energies from suboptimal to desired states.

Star of Inanna

Inanna was a Sumerian Mother Goddess and one of the most powerful female spirits to ever take patronage over Earth. The Star of Inanna is an eight-pointed star representing the goddess's generous gift to humanity: her understanding of the mysteries of the cosmos. The Star of Inanna is Goddess energy, incessant and concentrated, in a geometric form. The Star of Inanna symbolizes Sirius, a world much beloved by the

Goddess and many other extraterrestrial spirits that came to Earth as great teachers and gurus. The eight points of the star represent the eight dimensions that Inanna mastered as a spirit, as well as the eight powers she stood for: ascension, purity, fertility, creation, love, healing, forgiveness, and beauty.

Figure 39: The eight-pointed star (also: Star of Inanna)

Star of David

As the merging and the intersection of two triangles, two major principles, and two energies—the masculine and the feminine—the Star of David is the blueprint for the Universe. It is also a representation of the Merkaba—our body of light, our personal vehicle for ascension and interdimensional travel. The Star of David marries opposites in order to amplify them. Representing speed, agility, and transcendence of shadow, the Star of David is a light portal that can help you anchor higher-vibrational frequencies into your body and your life.

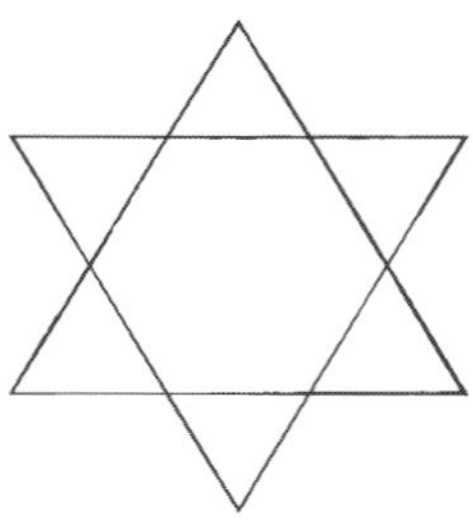

Figure 40: The Star of David

Lotus Flower

A symbol of enlightenment, introspection, and perceiving beyond the veil, the lotus is the sacred flower of many female deities and ascended masters, such as Tara, Kuan Yin, and Isis. The lotus represents the ability to move beyond physical existence into the unseen realms. It promises gentle healing and the transcendence of denser energies. It is a flower of dedication and spiritual commitment, and many spiritual vows have been consecrated by the power of the lotus.

Pine Cone

A natural and mathematically precise fractal, the pine cone boasts a repeating pattern, while also forming a rotating spiral-like form so common in galaxies and other feminine-forward womb-like structures. The pine cone symbolizes enlightenment, but most importantly, a constant movement of energy on a quest to purify itself—a movement without which enlightenment would be impossible. The pine cone also symbolizes the pineal gland, an organ within the human body that corresponds to the third eye, a point where an upward energy stream (Shakti rising) culminates.

Figure 41: Sacred geometry of a pine cone

Flower of Life

The Flower of Life is a template for the Law of Multiplication or the Law of Matter, the key to all creation. The Flower of Life is the most feminine of sacred geometry symbols. It shows the path of a seed of life as it follows a fractal-like journey of expansion. This shape is perfect if you are trying to anchor a new venture or would like to grow and expand—especially when the path is unknown or not straightforward. The Flower of Life makes everything grow, so be careful and task it with growing the good things only, as it can multiply anything in existence, including problems and ailments. (See also Chapter 2, page 34.)

North Star

This is a symbol of a divinely guided path, the most optimal journey, and taking on challenges that matter. The North Star not only provides direction, but helps ensure that you have the resources to walk the walk. The North Star symbolizes following the path of your Higher Self and living your perfect blueprint in alignment with everything else in existence.

Figure 42: The North Star

White Swan

Symbolic of purity and rising vibrations, the swan is a fierce protector of female creation, whether children, home, or anything made "by hand." A swan interweaves higher frequencies into everyday objects, and carving a swan on an object can turn it into a holy and Divine piece. The swan also represents loyalty, fulfillment in marriage, female contentment, and cleanliness in all its aspects.

Crescent Moon

Drawn facing upward, the crescent moon symbolizes the receptive principle of femininity—the cup that is open and ready to receive—and a receptacle of feminine wisdom. Traditionally, an upward-facing crescent moon ornament placed on the back of the neck under braided hair symbolized the achievement of great wisdom and female magic. It was a way to signify someone who had attained a high level of understanding, similar to our modern concept of enlightenment.

Sphinx

The guardian of mysteries and a loyal protector of sacred knowledge since ancient times, the Sphinx could look into a person's soul to determine their worthiness to receive the mysteries. The most vicious Sphinxes were female and held the keys to the afterlife, resurrection, and the mysteries of death. Before being given access to sacred knowledge, one had to face the Sphinx. This symbol is perfect if you seek deeper knowledge or understanding.

Black Currant

Symbolic of fertility, creative powers, and the womb, the black currant represents a period of gestation that requires darkness. Just like the juice of the berry becomes ripe inside the dark skin of the black currant, a woman births creations from the depths of the void of her womb. Use the black currant if you need assistance conceiving a child or birthing a new idea, or for Divine protection and blessings in your undertakings.

Star Anise

A powerful purifier, star anise represents star energy embodied in the third-dimensional world. Anise contains some powerful star fire within and can blast away any obstacle in your path and clear the way ahead. Anise is an indispensable ally in manifestation and achieving your goals. It is also a powerful protective symbol, granting one the protective cloak of the gods. For the one devoted to the spiritual path, it can be a potent accelerating force, helping you move from zero to a hundred quickly. Buckle up!

The Ankh

The original cross, the Ankh, can help you stay grounded while developing a strong spiritual connection. Once a tool and a talisman of the gods and royalty, the Ankh offers powerful protection against dark forces, the evil eye, and descending into your own shadows. The Ankh helps you travel along your own perfect arc of evolution. The Ankh brings with it many blessings and plenty of etheric helpers. Use this majestic symbol in your mandala if you seek to gain Hermes Trismegistus access levels to information, as well as the ability to use that information for the greater good.

Snake/Serpent

This symbolizes feminine wisdom, mysteries, magic, and diving deep. Use this symbol if you are ready to face your shadow, for that is what the snake will require. The tests will surely come, but if you take them on and succeed, the snake can be the only ally you need on the Path of the Rose.

Feather

Angelic messengers and holders of the energies of air and ether, feathers are here to elevate your frequency and provide a cleanse. They get into your light bodies and work behind the scenes on clearing the blockages that may be in the way of your upgrades. Feathers connect you to the spirit realm and bring angelic guidance and blessings.

Sun

Our sun isn't only our celestial parent in the sky, but the closest thing we have to Source consciousness in our physical reality. The Universe is run by a network of suns that emit the highest alignment frequencies stemming from Source itself. Include the sun in your mandala to align with your highest good, get spiritual guidance from higher planes, and increase your manifestation power and overall energy levels.

Moon

Symbolic of motherhood, loving care, deep emotional states, the element of water, and going through your inner cycles, the moon is an invaluable guide for Earth and all of its children. The moon's path is ever shifting; the only permanent thing is change. Use the moon in your mandala if you seek to connect with your personal cycles as well as the cycles of nature on a deeper level, if you need to be loved and cared for like a baby, if you want your Universe to cradle you in its arms and never let you go. The moon is also symbolic of a few ancient mystery schools, so it can help bring back some long-lost wisdom.

Venus

It is through this planet that the Divine Feminine is anchored in the solar system. She is the original beauty, the one who came before the moon and Earth. She is all about balancing the harmonic scales and the finer things in life. Venus is the lover, the seductress, the woman who knows the power of her beauty and the depth of her creative well. Venus is magnetic; she has a unique charm that disarms and captivates. She is a liberated female complete in herself who holds the magic of the enchantress within.

Dove

A symbol of the Holy Spirit and immaculate conception, the dove is one of the most feminine birds. Doves have long been connected to the angelic realm. It is believed that doves are the messengers of angels and carry blessings to those deserving of them. Seeing a white dove is a blessing from the lightest of spirits, a sacred promise that everything will work out in your favor. Use the dove in your mandala to call in the vibrations of angels, as well as to raise your frequency and receive daily assistance from your spirit guides.

Duck

This is a symbol of the Great Divine Mother, or the female face of Source. She is fertility and abundance, endless blessings, and forgiveness. The duck's energy is loving, caring, and nurturing. The duck is a gentle and intuitive guide, and also a symbol of protection of the Divine Mother. Use it in your mandala if you are seeking to develop a deeper relationship (or to start one) with the Divine Mother.

Doe

The doe is symbolic of the maiden phase of the Goddess and women, new beginnings, innocence, and complete surrender to what is. The doe is a gentle guide on any spiritual path and is especially connected to femininity, as it symbolizes motherhood.

Seashell

These offer a shortcut to Aphrodite and her many blessings. It is believed that shells carry the imprint of the heart of the ocean in its most nurturing, healing, and loving vibration. If you want the loving patterns of the ocean encapsulated in your mandala, rely on the power of the shell. The goddess Aphrodite can also help you find a perfect partner, bringing a soulmate into your life.

Dolphin

Some of the original star seeds of planet Earth, dolphins carry the vibrations of the healing waters of the Milky Way in their DNA. They are master healers, and their vibrations can relieve stress, remove fear, and harmonize the inner waters of your body, bringing your world into perfect equilibrium. Dolphins are also the guardians of all children, so if you are looking to conceive or be more nurturing to your child, the dolphin could be the perfect symbol for your mandala.

Butterfly

A symbol of connection to the fairy kingdom and the element of air, a butterfly elevates any pattern it comes in contact with. A butterfly is a carrier of the pink vibrations of the higher heart and is symbolic of traveling between dimensions. Butterflies are true blessings in this world and the next.

Owl

An ancient symbol of wisdom and a beloved bird of the goddesses Athena and Inanna, the owl represents female wisdom, foresight, and clear vision (clairvoyance). Very few birds are as revered in the angelic realms as the owl. It is believed that the best aspects of the Divine Mother herself dwell within the white owl and offer many blessings to those who understand the majestic blueprint of this mystical bird. The owl is your doorway into greater perception, the world of magic, soul healing, and understanding of the void, the original black ocean of the Mother that everything came from. Use the symbol of the owl in your mandala to start walking your own path of wisdom and to call some serious spiritual awakening into your life.

Raven

A teacher of mysteries and a messenger to and from the other side of the veil, a raven travels between dimensions and timelines. A raven knows no past, future, or present; it exists beyond linear time, and as such, it can be an oracle and your guide into the entirety of "what is." Use the raven as a symbol in your mandala if you seek to connect with your past lives, optimize your existing timeline, or get initiated into the mysteries of the Universe. But please know the magic of the raven comes with a price, so this path requires dedication and hard work.

Hourglass

An hourglass is an object that can make you a master of time. Each hourglass is a portal to the world outside of the matrix—the truer world, perhaps. Additionally, the hourglass can help lift the veil from some of the mysteries of this world, helping you turn the sands of time in your favor. The hourglass can speed up manifestation and bring desirable outcomes, while delaying or removing any suboptimal circumstances from your timelines. An hourglass is connected to the energies of Saturn, the constrictions as well as the rites of passage. Use this symbol if you are seeking mastery over your future and your personal timeline.

Tree of Life

This is the axis mundi (central axis) of this reality. As such, the Tree of Life enables you to travel to any of the nine parallel Earths and befriend the beings that dwell there. The Tree of Life will help you escape the constraints of the physical world, opening up possibilities of lucid dreaming and astral travel. The Tree of Life also has powerful healing and youth-preserving properties.

Pearl

Pearls are believed to be the crystallized tears of the Divine Mother, and few physical objects carry as much purity. Use the symbolism of the pearl to purify and cleanse any area of your life. Pearls help you overcome obstacles, bring forth a loyal romantic partner, and strengthen family bonds.

Apple

The apple is symbolic of eternal life and knowing the difference between good and evil, and very few fruits are as mysterious. Golden apples from the Tree of Life may grant you eternal youth, while white apples from the Tree of Knowledge may grant an answer to any of your questions, no matter how complex. Apples are blessings. The apple can fill your body with any frequency, from health to joy to serenity. There is an apple out there for virtually any kind of emotion. Use the apple in your mandala if you are looking to attract a mentor or guru, or if you are seeking the keys to living a long and happy life. You cannot go wrong with the apple.

Egg (Yoni)

A symbol of creation, fertility, virility, and new life nurtured by the great Mother herself, the egg is an invitation to create life in all its forms. The egg is also about creating and living in a safe haven on Earth; it is about building a Garden of Eden for yourself and your family. The egg is a potent protective symbol. Use it to protect a person or a project you are working on, as well as to speed up the manifestation of a wish.

Grail (also Holy Grail)

A symbol of receptivity, signifying the willingness to receive wisdom, initiations, activations, and new experiences. The Holy Grail creates a sacred space and an invitation to become nurtured by the powers of the greater Universe. Use this symbol in your mandala, allowing you to accumulate desired energies that offer enhanced vitality and life force.

Figure 43: The Holy Grail

Concentric Circles

These symbolize a path from smaller to larger things that you only understand by walking it. Smaller insights make way for larger insights, baby steps turn into larger strides, and each concentric circle represents a level of creation and creativity available to you. As you move toward larger circles, your potential becomes fully actualized, and you become capable of more monumental, pivotal things. This is the symbol of becoming and of coming into your power.

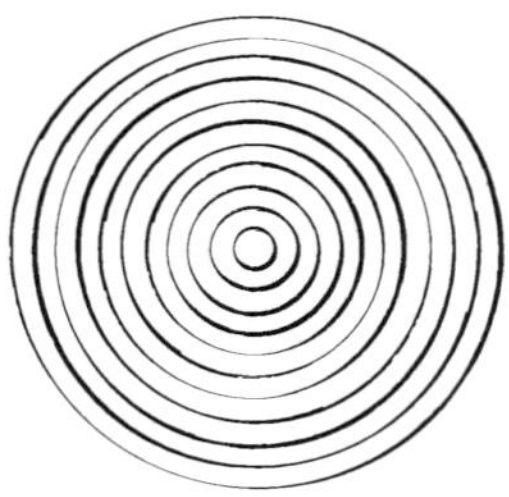

Figure 44: Concentric circles

Getting Started on Your Rose Mandala

A Note on Colors

In the following rose mandala practice, you'll begin your journey into the Order of the Rose, and the color of the rose matters. I suggest using one of the three main Rose energies to begin your Rose journey.

White Rose

The queen of heavenly vibration and the ultimate rose of purity, the white rose stands for purity of expression, heart, intention, and thought. It symbolizes spirituality, higher realms, angelic consciousness, Divine oneness, truth, understanding, compassion, forgiveness, and acceptance. The white rose is the release of karma, the healing of all the bodies, deep initiation, and following a sacred preordained path. A white rose offers Divine protection and guidance. It is patience and gentleness, nurturing care and motherly love, and is symbolic of light and the path toward enlightenment. The white rose represents cosmic consciousness, perception from a higher vantage point, intuition, and insight. She brings psychic powers, unlocks clairvoyance and clairaudience, reveals the hidden, and grants you your heart's true desire, provided that you are worthy.

Red Rose

The rose of passion, desire, dedication, and drive, the red rose is the queen of all earthly roses. The red rose is a master healer, and a womb whisperer. If she were a tarot card, she would be the Empress. The red rose is beauty, love, and power, and all of that is encapsulated within one petaled form. The red rose is one that leads with the heart, and following the heart is her mantra and lifestyle. She feels deeply, is expressive, and will not be put in a box. The red rose is unrestricted, liberated energy and life force that is ready to play.

Pink Rose

This rose is a merging of the red and the white rose, but also something entirely unique. It stands for higher cosmic love—the kind that serves as the main pillar of Christ consciousness. This rose is tenderness, gentleness, nurturing, dedication to the path, and commitment to living your sacred blueprint. The pink rose cherishes relationships and treasures others. It can heal deep emotional wounds by resetting your light bodies to their golden state, erasing trauma, and removing blockages. A masterful healer, this rose has a strong connection to the elemental kingdom, specifically the fairies and the undines (mermaids). It is deeply connected to the element of water, and thus it can rebuild and reset any suboptimal energy by changing its water element within.

Practice: Creating a Rose Mandala

Creating a rose mandala is an activation and a spiritual practice that requires time for quiet introspection. It invites the energies of the Divine Feminine into your life. Through the process of creating the mandala, the energies of the Rose will start moving in and out of your body, making alterations and enhancements. Not to worry; walking the Path of the Rose always brings you closer to yourself—your Divine blueprint and purpose—and always unfolds in your highest good.

You can create your mandala by drawing one or by creating a collage. It is the intention that matters in this process.

Figure 45: Examples of a simplified rose mandala

You will need:

- A large piece of white cardboard or thick paper
- Two fresh roses of the color of your choosing
- A rose quartz crystal

The practice:

1. Start by placing a rose in the center of your mandala. While you may also draw one, having a physical rose for your mandala helps further amplify your intention and align you with the heart of the Divine Mother in the most seamless way possible.
2. Select a few shapes and symbols from the list offered earlier in this chapter. Don't worry about making the wrong selection; simply pick whatever symbols speak to you. The Universe is wise and will always ensure your selection is what you need the most right now. You may choose any number of symbols, but selecting five works best. It gives variety and energetic depth to your mandala without overwhelming it.
3. Starting from the mandala's center, place your selected objects around the rose in a repeated pattern, so that the shapes form a complete circle around the rose. You can draw the shapes or print them out and glue them onto your mandala, like a good old scrapbook. You can also use a combination of both techniques by drawing some and gluing on the rest. Repeating each element eight times within each concentric circle further amplifies its power.
4. Keep going, creating a series of concentric circles around your rose. Feel free to use the rose symbol as often as you'd like. You cannot overdo it for this exercise. You may even combine the symbols within one concentric circle if it feels good. Listen to your intuition and allow yourself to get creative here. You may also include any symbols you like that are not listed in this chapter.
5. The last row of your mandala has a special significance. The path of the mandala starts in the center and ends in the outer circle. That is why it could be helpful to have protective symbols in the finishing row or something that you consider harder to attain—the crown jewel of your journey, something you hope it will culminate in.
6. Once your mandala is complete, use a rose quartz crystal to activate it and further anchor its energies into your life. You can use a crystal of any shape for this activation. To activate the mandala, place the rose quartz crystal slightly above your heart area, toward the center of your chest, where your thymus gland (higher heart) is located.
7. Close your eyes and speak the following intention: "I allow the energies of my higher heart to freely pour into this crystal and into my rose mandala,

activating the sacred path right in front of me. May the energies of my heart and the magic of the Rose lineage create powerful activations in my life. May these energies remove anything that no longer serves me. May they open my heart to wisdom, healing, and Divine Feminine alchemy. May my Path of the Rose be uniquely my own. May it bring me closer to the Divinity that I am, and may it open up the portal of the Rose in my life, so that all of my gifts are awakened at this time, for my greater good and the greater good of all. And so it is."

8. Place the rose quartz crystal in the center of your mandala, where your rose is.
9. Take the second rose and place its petals on the outer edge of your mandala, spreading them out evenly. This will further enhance the magic of the rose within your mandala, and thus in your life.
10. Leave the rose for three days to fully anchor and saturate your mandala with Order of the Rose lineage vibrations.
11. Once the process is complete, your Path of the Rose has begun!

Congratulations, my sibling in Rose!

Please keep your rose mandala for the duration of reading this book. It will become your personal artifact and guide on your journey. Simply observing the mandala can be an activating and meditative experience. This will help you ground yourself into the energies of the lineage of the Rose and will ensure faster activations and an easier understanding of the material in this book.

Heart Space: A New Story

It was in the pages of a story she wrote, a meticulous recording of all that she was—the constraints, the blessings, the joys, the nightmares,

A story of her many lives, her many slaves, her many masters,

A story of her mistakes and her victories.

Hers was a rich story, a story of karmic knots, of pain, of lessons learned.

It was a story she shared only with the closest confidants of her heart.

She wore it close to her skin, right alongside her many scars.

She carried her wounds proudly; they were a record of all she had been through.

That story was good.

But this is a new story,

Built upon the ruins of the old world that was meant to crumble under her feet.

This is a new story—one about stepping out of her old skin and releasing limitations,

Of choosing to let go of the scars, of honoring the hard truths.

This is a new story for the rest of her life.

This is a story of a girl reborn,

A story of a new beginning, a story of redemption, a story of surrender.

This new story doesn't make the old story untrue, but makes it come full circle.

This new story is her most cherished treasure, the kind she never dared to hope for.

Welcome to her new story, untarnished, untold, long awaited.

And like every good story, it starts with "Once upon a time."

Once upon a time, there lived a girl who loved Earth very much.

Once upon a time, there lived a girl who spoke to the stars, and they listened.

Once upon a time, there lived a girl blessed by the Rose.

And this is her story.

CHAPTER 8

The Breath of the Rose

The ancients knew that everything starts with the breath. Your breath, an expression of your life force, is in constant motion, traveling in and out of your body, maintaining and renewing the life within.

The time between an inhale and an exhale is a Universe within itself, a complete cycle that, if properly applied, can bring you the healing jolt you likely crave. Like the many-faced Goddess, the many aspects of prana (the life force we breathe in) range from healing to renewal through nurturing and cleansing to rejuvenating. Most of our breaths are not intentional and thus are not aligned with what we truly need at that moment. Prana is thus used as a commodity to fill our lungs, without regard for its celestial origins or sacred medicine.

The time has come for us to reclaim the femininity of our breath, to start breathing in love, compassion, understanding, healing, beauty, and harmony. It is time to fully return to intentional breathing and mark it as our new default setting. It is time to remember our body's secrets and the key it holds for our longevity and spiritual awakening. It's time to return home to the sanctuary and bliss of a body in full alignment.

In this chapter, I will share a simple breathing technique for activating the Divine Feminine flow within your body. But before that, let's take a quick detour into the Holy Grail, a concept critical for understanding the Breath of the Rose practice.

The Holy Grail, Demystified

For thousands of years, the Holy Grail has been an enigma, a relic, an evasive object of controversy, an obsession, and a sacred symbol whose true meaning has only been available to the initiated few. The Holy Grail is allegedly the cup that Jesus drank from at the last supper, and that Joseph of Arimathea used to collect Christ's blood after his crucifixion. Additionally, the Holy Grail is one of the artifacts closely linked to the lands of Avalon and the legends of King Arthur.

In recent times, the Holy Grail has come to symbolize the gnostic path of Mary Magdalene, Mother Mary, and the Jesus bloodline, as well as being the most sacred object the Knights Templar were tasked with protecting.

Figure 46: The Holy Grail at the Round Table (Credit: Photo 12/Alamy Stock Photo)

But the Holy Grail existed well before the time of Christ. Whether it was called a vessel, a chalice, a goblet, or a cauldron, it has been a constant symbol of the Goddess through the ages. Many of the temples of Atlantis and Lemuria had a chalice on the altar, the holiest of all places, to help accumulate the energies that the temple was intended to anchor and transmit. In Atlantis, there was a Chalice of the Heart in the Temple of Love, and a Chalice of Purity in the Temple of Divine Oneness. Only the high priestess or priest held the privilege of administering the chalice and distributing its healing frequencies among initiates and temple visitors.

In ancient Egypt, priestesses of Isis and Hathor used the chalice to represent the womb of their revered goddess, as well as to symbolize the life-giving power of the Nile River, ever flowing and blessing the land of Egypt with fertility and harvest.

In ancient Mesopotamia, the chalice of Inanna represented fertility, the multiplication and blessings of abundance, and new life. Sumerians used the chalice in rituals celebrating the coming of spring and the renewal it brought, as well as life birthed and life sustained.

For the Celts, Wiccans, and pagans, the cauldron still represents the energies of the Goddess, the womb, and the life-giving fertility of Earth. The cauldron is a key to mysteries and a vessel that births all magic.

One of the four suits of the tarot is the chalice or cups, symbolizing the yin polarity, emotions, feelings, intuition, and flow. Ruled by the element of water, the suit of cups represents the creative powers of the feminine within. Tarot, mostly used for divination today, was once a tool of initiation and symbolized the various rites of passage a person needed to go through on their journey to becoming a priest or priestess, a tradition dating back as far as Atlantis. Mastering the chalice was one of the harder rites and involved many aspects of mastering the creative process and the state of surrender. Mastering the chalice implied understanding and controlling your own vessel: your body. Through various breathing and energy techniques, the initiates could control their body temperature, lung capacity, aging process, and sleep cycles.

Finally, in the higher spheres, the Holy Grail or chalice represents life itself, created in the void of the cosmic womb of antimatter, brought forth into light by the energies of an upward spiral of creation. The Divine Mother is the Holy Grail, the vessel, the chalice, and the cauldron. She is that which makes things come full circle, the one who is constantly flowing, never the same. She is the one that is therefore unknowable, for the moment you think you know her, she has already changed.

The Sacred Chalice Within: The Missing Chakras

Millennia ago, Hermes Trismegistus taught the great wisdom of the Principle of Correspondence—as above, so below; as within, so without—referencing that we live in a world of fractals, similarities, and sacred geometry repeating itself. If you notice a foundational energy pattern in the outside world, especially one as significant as that of a chalice, it must manifest within your body also (as within, so without). Today, we are lifting the veil of the mystery surrounding the chalice. A chalice within your body is a unique energy flow through some of the major chakras, an internal pilgrimage of the Rose, bringing you into full alignment with the Divine Mother and her infinite love, wisdom, and healing powers. The path of the chalice is a major flow of energy in alchemical science. But first and foremost, it is a gift—a gift from the Sacred Feminine, a gift from the Goddess to you.

To experience the flow of the Rose within your body, you first need to know that the seven main chakras you have probably heard about from various spiritual teachings are only the very basis of your energy body. The chakras along the vertical axis of your spine represent one possible movement of energy: the alpha. The omega is the horizontal axis. If you were to stretch out your arms, your body would naturally draw this axis without you even trying. This axis contains seven other energy centers that comprise a portion of the flow of the Rose within (see **Figure** 47).

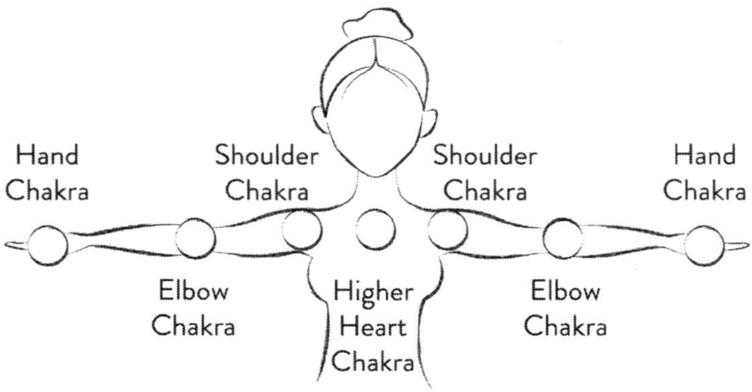

Figure 47: Chakras along the horizontal axis of the body

Thymus or Higher Heart Chakra

Located between the two clavicle bones, right around the sternum area, above the heart (see **Figure** 47), the higher heart chakra connects you to the energies of oneness and high-vibrational cosmic love. It contains massive dormant powers of balancing and rejuvenating your body.

Shoulder Chakras

A powerful receptive center, the shoulder chakras are about how much you allow yourself. It is your center of allowing things to come, go, and flow according to the laws of the Universe. Trying to control reality generally backfires and blocks these potent energy centers. However, acceptance and allowing, as well as gratitude for what is, clears these centers to receive more. These chakras also contain codes and nodes for intuitive guidance. When these centers are activated, being on your path and in alignment becomes the norm, following your calling is easy, and knowing your purpose is second nature.

Elbow Chakras

A powerful force of energy distribution and rerouting, the elbows direct the energy to where it is needed most in the body, so that the necessary mending and healing can occur. Elbows are the source of our flexibility, our ability to flow with what is possible, without getting threatened or resorting to fear and protective tactics. Therefore, these chakras represent your ability to trust; they are the seat of trust within your body. All trust starts with self—having your best interest at heart and expanding from there—and moves through trusting your family, your neighbors, your community, and all living creatures. Our elbows have calming and peace-inducing nodes, which is why simply placing your fingers on the inner side of your elbow can have a soothing and calming effect in the moment.

Hand Chakras

These chakras symbolize sacred action, the physical things we do. Your hands are a powerful diagnostic tool of how much energy your body holds, as well as how effectively that energy can be applied in the outside world. Many healers heal with their hands because these chakras are true accumulators of the best we have to offer. Hands are powerful energy receivers and transmitters; they help us connect with and learn about our surroundings. In many ancient rituals, people touched the earth to truly connect with the spirits of the land and Gaia. Cats have whiskers, butterflies have antennae, and we have our hands, masterful receptors that foster our intuition and energy exchange.

Practice: Activating Your Inner Chalice

Now we are starting to come full circle. You are finally ready to learn the path of the chalice within (see **Figure 48**).

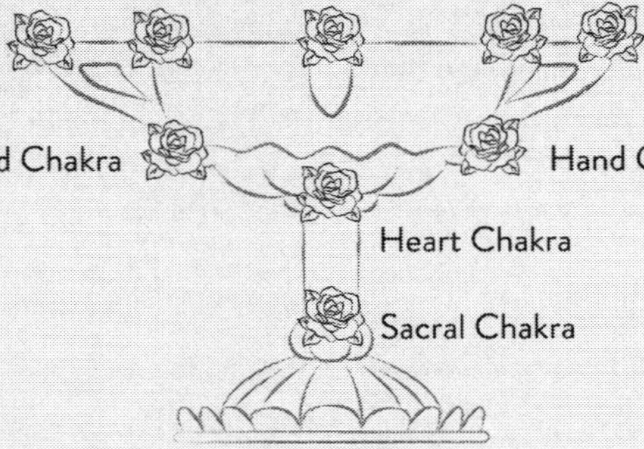

Figure 48: Your inner chalice

The chalice of your body consists of nine energy centers that, when connected by a dotted line, resemble a cup—your inner well of femininity, wisdom, and harmony.

The base of the chalice is your sacral center, the seat of your creativity, your womb, your "cause," your reason for being. The chalice's stem is your heart space, the magnetic force that awakens you to your true nature, the great synchronizer of energies in your life. The other seven chakras are located along the horizontal axis of your body: two hand chakras, two elbow chakras, two shoulder chakras, and the higher heart chakra. The seven chakras collectively form the downward-facing triangle of the cup, symbolic of the element of water, protection, containment, the flow of energies from higher spheres into material existence, and the anchoring of that energy within the earthly planes. This is a woman's key to anchoring soul and spirit energies into matter (the process we call gestation and birth).

To start activating your chalice, you need to activate each center individually by working with the energy of the Rose.

1. Sit or lie down, whichever feels most comfortable to you. Close your eyes and focus on the flow of your breath. Don't force it; just let it unfold.

2. Focus on your sacral center, located in your lower belly. Imagine sending the power of your breath into this area of your body. Stay here for five breaths.
3. Imagine a beautiful red rose unfolding in your sacral chakra. At first, the rose is small, but with each breath, it grows, adding extra petals and blooming fuller. Imagine the rose starting to rotate, and as it does, picture a beautiful red glow starting to emanate from it, filling your whole body. Keep breathing into your lower belly to fully amplify the energies.
4. Now start moving your focus up your body, centering in your heart space. Imagine an emerald-green rose unfolding there and starting to bloom. Stay here for five breaths.
5. Notice the rose starting to rotate, and as it does, watch as the beautiful emerald light fills up your entire body. Stay here for as long as it feels good, basking in this beautiful energy.
6. When you're ready, move toward your higher heart center. Imagine a pink rose starting to grow there. This rose represents higher cosmic love taking root in your body. Watch it grow, petal by petal, fully unfolding in a few seconds. Start breathing deeply into this center, holding for a count of five after each inhale. Do five rounds of this breathing. When you're ready, imagine the pink rose starting to rotate, filling your body with the most gorgeous etheric pink glow.
7. Now, imagine that you are traveling toward your left shoulder. Picture a rose of icy blue starting to open up there. It is small at first, but as you breathe into it, it starts to unfold. Allow the rose to draw strength and power from your breath. And as your breath feeds it, watch it bloom fully. Focus on the slow rotation of the rose in your shoulder center. Watch as it removes any debris or blocks in this center, transcending them completely. As the rose rotates, watch as your body fills with an icy blue glow.
8. Repeat the previous step for the icy blue rose in your right shoulder, so that both sister roses are fully activated.
9. Move to the left elbow. As you do, imagine a gleaming crystalline rose opening up. It glows as if covered with diamonds. This rose is very special indeed, a hidden treasure of your body. Help the rose unfold by breathing into your elbow and holding it for a count of five. When the rose has fully bloomed, imagine it starting to rotate clockwise, clearing any imperfec-

tions or energy blocks in this area. Take your time here; don't rush. Watch as your body is filled with the stunning diamond light.

10. Repeat the previous step for the rose in your right elbow.
11. Finally, move to the palm of your left hand. Imagine a pure white rose taking root there and starting to bloom. Feel free to assist the rose with the power of your breath, breathing straight into the middle of your palm and holding for a count of five. Imagine the white rose starting to rotate, and as it does, it clears away any negativity or old programs that are stuck there. As this cleansing happens, watch your body become filled with heavenly white light.
12. Repeat the previous step for the white rose in your right palm.

Congratulations! You have fully activated your inner chalice. Now that these centers are fully active, we can move to my favorite part: the Breath of the Rose.

Technique: The Breath of the Rose, or Chalice Breathing

The Breath of the Rose activates your body's hidden potential, connecting you to your higher celestial roots and activating the ascension codes within. This technique connects you to the Divine Mother and allows you to awaken and accumulate the energies of Sacred Femininity. Every time you undertake the Breath of the Rose, it naturally helps clear blockages, especially in your womb and heart space, promoting better health, enhanced creativity, and joyful living.

Over time, this breathing technique will help renew and rejuvenate your body, enabling you to look younger. But getting such results requires dedication and years of diligent practice. Every initiate of the Rose takes the time to master this breathing technique. Many rituals of the sacred sisterhood start with this technique, because it prepares the inner chalice to receive the healing and joyful energies of true sisterhood and connection.

The full path of the breath technique is as follows: sacral center → heart center → left hand → left elbow → left shoulder → higher heart → right shoulder → right elbow → right hand → heart center → sacral center.

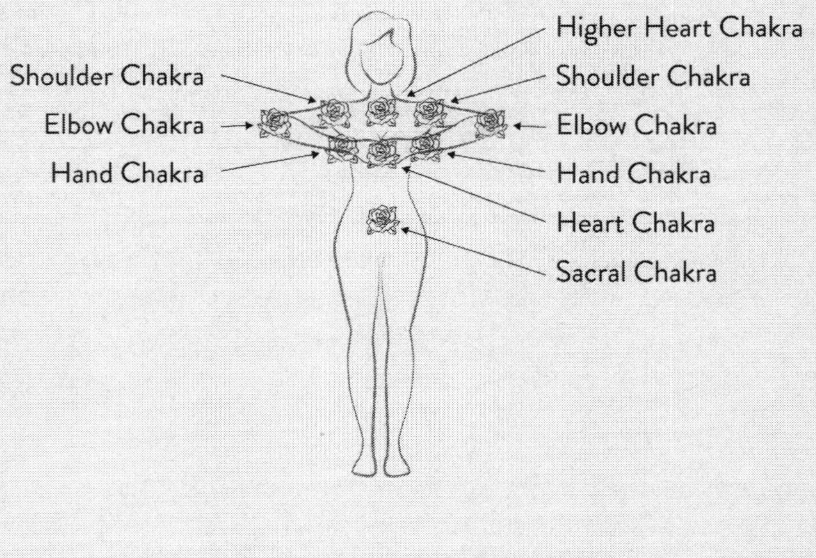

Figure 49: Breath of the Rose, or Chalice Breathing

1. Standing or sitting upright, start by stretching your arms out to the sides, thus creating a horizontal axis with your arms.
2. Place both of your hands over your heart area without lowering your elbows.
3. Imagine a path within your body that perfectly traces the shape of the chalice, starting in your sacral center and returning into it once complete.
4. Take a deep inhale. As you inhale, imagine your breath traveling up from your sacral center, through the left side of your body, culminating in the higher heart. So, the breath flows as follows: sacral center → heart center → left hand → left elbow → left shoulder → higher heart.
5. Hold your breath here in your higher heart for a count of five.
6. On the exhale, complete the loop by allowing your breath to travel through the right side of your body, so the breath flows as follows: higher heart → right shoulder → right elbow → right hand → heart center → sacral center.
7. Hold your breath in your sacral center for a count of five.
8. Repeat this cycle eight times to fully activate your chalice.
9. Now, prepare yourself to do a set of rapid breaths, where you go through the path of the chalice without holding your breath.
10. Take a deep breath in. Allow your breath to travel through the upward path of the chalice on the left: sacral center → heart center → left hand → left elbow → left shoulder → higher heart.
11. As soon as you reach the higher heart, exhale. On the exhale, travel down the right side, closing the loop: higher heart → right shoulder → right elbow → right hand → heart center → sacral center.
12. Repeat this breathing circulation for eight more cycles of breath.
13. Now, move the palms of your hands from your heart area to your third eye, so that your left palm covers your left eye and your right palm covers your right eye. Stay here in the void of the Cosmic Mother, in darkness. Let your breathing return to normal.
14. Feel free to follow this practice with meditation. You will notice a heightened sense of connectedness and a major activation of your heart space.

Please note: Your chest may feel constricted the first few times you use this breathing technique. Your body is not used to this much energy entering your heart area. Do not worry; this is normal. Feel free to stretch your body, thus creating more "room" for these energies to fully anchor within.

The Breath of Rose (or Chalice Breathing) technique is meant to be your constant companion on the Path of the Rose, something to help you better integrate the learnings from this book. The initiates of the Rose used to perform this practice daily, in the morning and evening before meditation, to connect with the Divine Mother and her energies. You'll find that this technique assists with strengthening your intuitive and psychic abilities, as well as enabling your body to hold onto higher and higher energy frequencies in time. This tends to result in enhanced happiness and well-being, as well as rapid spiritual growth.

Practicing the Breath of the Rose at least every other day for a minimum of ninety days, you may start to experience further benefits, including:

- Connection to Source consciousness and the higher realms
- Connection to Divine and planetary oneness
- Enhanced connection to the Akashic field (including past lives)
- Enhancement of your intuitive and psychic powers
- Instances of lucid dreaming and spontaneous astral travel
- Healing of deep-seated trauma and assistance with clearing karmic knots
- Better decision-making
- Release of pressure, anxiety, or deep-rooted fear
- A more sustained energy boost
- Healing on a physical level, especially ailments of the heart, the reproductive system, and the circulatory system
- Heightened awareness and faster spiritual growth

Benefits are more prominent with daily practice and are optimal when this technique is practiced twice daily.

Heart Space: The World's Mother

Her essence is the heart of the deepest waters,

Her embrace a caress of the ocean upon your skin.

Her flow is determined, her grace is poetic,

Her resolve nothing short of unshakable.

She is neither the second coming of Yeshua,

Nor the birth of a future Buddha.

In fact, she is no male at all.

And yet, her step is alight with change.

She will no longer be silenced,

For she is the Mother of the World, and she is not afraid.

Her voice is tender; her teachings are soft.

They are an ephemeral whisper of the heart on a sun-filled day.

And yet her voice is inside of you, and therefore, it is the loudest.

She has come to unite all the creeds, all the castes, all the faiths into one eternal song of the heart,

Blessed by the sacred power of the rose, sealed by sunlight itself.

She is the first and the most natural of all laws.

She is life itself.

And she is back to restore the most basic principles of light consciousness.

She is the first pillar of the golden era.

She is the stepping stone, the scripture, and the redeeming path.

She is the one keeping you safe under her majestic veil of protection.

She is the one taking you by the hand and leading you through the pearly gates

Toward a gilded city in the sky, the one whose name is Zion, the holiest among cities.

CHAPTER 9

The Alchemical Rose

"Mystery glows in the rose bed, and the secret is hidden in the rose."
~Persian alchemist Farid ud-Din Attar

Alchemy was one of the original mysteries, first introduced by Hermes Trismegistus to offer humanity a set of steps and principles that, if properly followed, could result in spiritual evolution. Alchemy was an advanced system of knowledge, something to be undertaken upon mastering the understanding of simple hermetic truths, such as "all is mind" and "as above, so below."

The keys to the alchemical process of ascension were originally reserved for the priesthood and taught by Hermes with the understanding that once the planet's vibrations reached a desired level, these teachings could become more widespread. We are living in the times of the great renaissance of spirituality; the second coming of alchemical wisdom is upon us. That which was once hidden must return.

A perpetual muse and the main flower of alchemy, the rose is associated with the various stages of the alchemical process in ancient and contemporary texts. The rose is the sacred flower of Isis, an ancient Egyptian goddess and an ally of Hermes Trismegistus (Thoth). Hermes and Isis were deeply committed to providing the tools for our evolution. They spent many hours contemplating how to simplify the often convoluted cosmic wisdom and make it palatable for humanity's budding intellect. Allegory and metaphor were used to accomplish the seemingly impossible: making the layered spiritual wisdom digestible.

Throughout the birth of original alchemical thought, Isis and Thoth were surrounded by roses, their balconies and terraces adorned with rosebuds, the air heady with the flower's sweet, heart-centered aroma. And just like that, the rose found itself on many pages of the first alchemical texts. The flower came to allegorically represent the different stages of the spiritual path and became a mystery in and of itself.

The Magnum Opus

When the ever-mystical alchemical process was stripped down to its most basic form and lost its spiritual luster, it became indelibly convoluted. You see, it was never meant to represent a set of chemical reactions for turning base metals into gold.

As time went by, the magnum opus—or Great Alchemical Work—grew to encompass various steps, ranging from the obscure "calcination" to the unattainable "coagulation," each one accompanied by meticulous instructions, and each one more confusing than the last. The living and breathing word of alchemy turned into occult knowledge, becoming a hard-to-follow body of knowledge devoid of its spiritual application, reduced to a poor imitation of its former self.

Today, let's take a deep dive into the five stages of alchemy as originally designed by Thoth and Isis, a much simplified and more comprehensible way of thinking about spiritual growth.

The original alchemical process was cyclical, like most things in nature (see **Figure 50**). The last step of one cycle was merely the beginning of the next, all divinely connected into one cohesive journey. Like the five petals of the rose, the five steps of the alchemical process contain within themselves the Divine harmony and continuation of life as originally designed by the Divine Mother. The alchemical process, therefore, bears the signature of our Celestial Mother and her wisdom, and it is through the magic of the Rose that we get to restore that lost knowledge.

Here are the five stages, each with a corresponding symbolic bird:

Stage 1: Rosa Negra—Black Rose (raven or crow)

Stage 2: Rosa Alba—White Rose (white swan)

Stage 3: Rosa Iridis—Rainbow Rose (peacock)

Stage 4: Rosa Rubea—Red Rose (pelican)

Stage 5: Rosa Aurea—Golden Rose (phoenix)

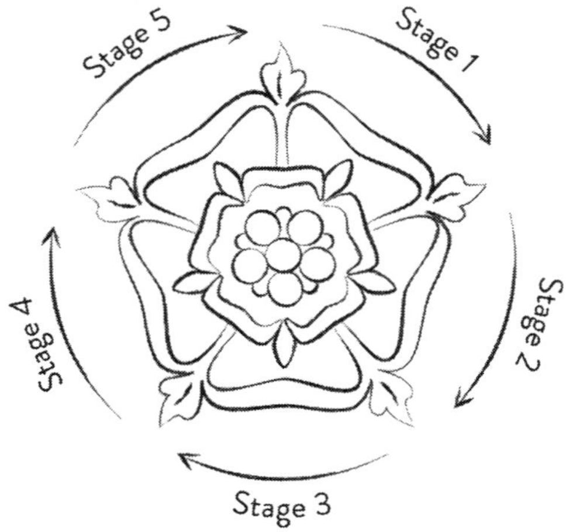

Figure 50: The continuous flow of the five stages of the alchemical rose

For best results and deeper learning, you can undergo the entire alchemical cycle described below, following the steps with precision and intention. Alternatively, you might prefer to work with only one or two stages of this process based on a deeply personal resonance. There is no wrong way of following an alchemical path. Simply center in your heart and surrender. The Rose will show you the way.

Rosa Negra: The Black Rose

Represents:

- Winter
- Night
- Darkness
- Low visibility (blindness)
- The primordial void
- Dark night of the soul
- Solar and lunar eclipses
- Shadow work
- Death
- Burial
- Letting go
- Shedding layers and old skin
- Deep sleep
- The in-between
- Proverbial hell
- Fire
- Inner space
- Solitude
- Withdrawal
- The hermit state
- Rest and reset
- Passivity
- Numbness
- Silence
- Lead
- Saturn

Rosa Negra is the beginning of the journey, the very first domino, the realm of Saturn—your inner personal space of limitation, solitude, and eventual breakthrough. This is a proverbial step into the dark abyss, a commitment made. This is Alice falling deep into the rabbit hole, the descent of Inanna into the underworld, the journey down the bleakness of the River Styx, and the temporary loss of heavenly bliss when the soul descends into a physical incarnation. This stage is the darkness of the sarcophagus, the complete and utter surrender to the Mother's nurturing womb, and falling into the mystery of the night. It is a passage through the obscurity of a layered world made of shadow, a journey to the depth of our being, a path with no lanterns in sight.

In the realm of Saturn, the night reigns supreme, and solitude is table stakes. Limitations are your allies; they are a set of way markers leading you away from the shadowscape. The land of Saturn is a pathway of constrictions and limitations, where every step takes monumental effort. It is filled with the quicksand of resistance, sucking you into your personal underworld, your personal hell, your personal purgatory, a place where every detestable thing you've done is forever on repeat, sucking you dry with the indomitable forces of guilt and regret. The realm of Saturn is also a realm of potentiality, showing you what you could be if you choose a path of integration and authenticity. The realm of Saturn is a rite of passage and a forging, the first step on the alchemical path of turning lead (your current state of limitation) into gold (a covetable state of infinite possibility).

Questions to ask during this stage:

- What am I ready to let go of?
- What is the specific flavor of my childhood trauma?
- What am I most afraid of?
- What prevents me from becoming who I'm meant to be?
- What is falling away at this time?
- What do I need to shed and let go of?
- What does my body crave at this time?
- Where can I create space in my life?
- What current relationships do I need to release?
- Where is my soul calling me to dive deeper?
- Who am I, truly?
- What is it that I value most?
- What are some of the negative influences in my life?
- What battles should I no longer be fighting?

Symbol: The Raven/Crow

The raven is a sacred bird of the Goddess, witch, and sorceress. The raven is a spirit you call upon when the battlefield of life has been filled with rotten corpses of regret and indecision. The raven cleanses you in your bleakest hour; it is a means of moving through darkness into the light. The magic of the raven is an invitation to retreat into your inner void, the space that once birthed everything that you are.

This stage of the alchemical process is the darkening (the Negredo experience)—a death of sorts. The darkening is a reevaluation and a reckoning, the closing of the karmic loops, and the rewriting of old toxic patterns. Befriending the crow is an act of facing your shadow fully—not shying away from the less savory parts of yourself, but rather integrating them into the fullness of your being. The promise of the raven is redemption. The path of the raven is a reclaiming of your light and purpose through trials and tribulations. The path of the raven is an invitation for the Black Mother (the Dark Madonna, the void) to work with you, leading you through the challenging times of skin shedding and letting go.

Working with the Black Rose

The black rose requires solitude, sometimes for long periods at a time, from weeks to months. It can be an actual retreat (physically getting off the grid), or a period of social hermitage. The black rose requires you to give up all that is extra, stripping away the nonessential thoughts, feelings, rituals, and physical objects. Traveling with the black rose is traveling lightly, momentarily letting go of the material baggage you have accumulated. The path of the black rose is an intentional process of renewal. It is a rite of passage that requires you to examine all your earthly attachments and all the things that have been holding you back, a full review of your inauthentic behaviors and default settings.

"Do's" of the Black Rose:

- Silent retreat, a week of "noble silence"
- Dark retreat, a week without sunlight
- Major decluttering
- Ascesis (giving up an addiction or an indulgence, forever or for a prolonged time)
- Daily meditation for thirty-plus minutes.
- Meditating on the primordial void (darkness)
- Stargazing, connecting with the dark sky

- Shadow work (parts work)
- Shamanic healing modalities (e.g., plant medicine, various shamanic cleanses, and ancient rituals)
- Working with Shakti, the Mother energies dwelling within the dark of your own void, an etheric part of your body located two inches below your root chakra

Rosa Alba: The White Rose

Represents:

- Light
- Day
- Solstice
- Dawn
- Silver
- The moon (the light even in the deepest night)
- Hope
- Purity
- Temporary redemption
- Faith
- The angelic kingdom
- Life conquering death
- Divine protection
- Heaven
- Water
- A fountain
- The white dove
- The white eagle
- Moonstone
- The yin (feminine principle)
- Receptivity
- The Queen
- Mother (earthly and Divine)

Rosa Alba is not yet fully redeemed, but it is the first step toward the light. It is not yet the fully healed state of perfection; it is a stepping stone in that direction. If the first step is the void, the second step is the light of the moon shining upon the murky darkness. Rosa Alba is a way-shower, a winding path amidst the darkness. It is the blessing of hope and the proverbial light at the end of the tunnel. It is the gentle presence of your spirit guides and their timeless counsel. It is the first glimpse of knowing.

The white rose is the realm of guardian angels and the assistance of the heavens. It is the helping hand of the ace of cups, coming through the clouds and offering you a solution and a path forward. Whereas the black rose is a state of low visibility, the white rose comes as a premonition or an oracle, bringing momentary clarity and a sense of purpose into an otherwise obscure reality. The white rose is a lantern and the guiding light of the North Star; it is a reprieve and a respite from the trials of the black rose. The white rose is an exhale and a lessening of trauma. It is a temporary victory and a sign of being fully on track.

Considered to be the realm of the moon, the white rose is a rendezvous with the element of water—the redemption, relief, and challenges it brings. This alchemical phase is a deep dive into our inner emotional state that signifies the end of the cycle of avoidance. In this stage, we dive deep—deeper than we have ever been. This step brings much-needed clarity—clarity around what is and what was. It is in the depth of your personal chalice of water magic that you find inner peace and the will to keep going. This is a phase of rebuilding bigger and better. The white rose is a calling to purify your vessel, to not settle for the status quo, and to forge your own redemption amidst the chaos.

Questions to ask during this stage:

- What am I being called to heal at this time?
- What aspects of me are seeking notice at this time?
- What past life influences are the most potent at this point in my life?
- What am I meant to purify at this time?
- Where in my life can I be more open and flexible?
- What am I committed to in life?
- Who is in my inner circle? How can I be even closer to them?
- What habits have outlived their usefulness?
- How can I invite more light into my life?
- How can I forgive myself and others for anything I view as suboptimal?

Symbol: The White Swan

The white swan is a sacred bird of goddesses Saraswati, Lada, and Brigid, a beloved form taken by the Valkyries and muses when they chose to interact with humans, and a blueprint of coming into your own light. The swan represents higher knowing and hope, a promise that light shall always prevail. The swan's path is one of commitment and perseverance, loyalty and insight. The white swan always takes its measure, estimating the depth of your commitment to evolution. While the white swan is a gentle teacher, it is one of the most profound energies working on the Earth plane.

The swan is a bird of relationships, Divine pairings, and conscious communities. It is a path that challenges you to go outside your inner circle and come out of hiding. The path of the swan is an invitation to show up as the best version of yourself—the version that has been through the shadows and chosen to transform them into light. The white swan is a path filled with hope. It is a road of second chances and do-overs. It doesn't believe in the finality of trauma or separation; the swan's path is a journey back to connection. It will challenge your concept of self and help reforge the image of what you are meant to show up as in the world. This stage is a massive reevaluation of what is needed for you to build a better future.

Working with the White Rose

The magic of the white rose is gentle, yet intentional. It is a path of serenity and solace, a plush blanket of white feathers that cushions you from the world's harsh realities. The white rose is a gentle healing bath after the hellfire of the black rose. But don't mistake the gentle magic of the white rose for weakness, as her impact is just as profound as that of the black rose. It comes in the healing of wounds and the removal of battle scars, in the desire to build anew what was once torn down. The white rose is a bridge connecting you to the world, a helping hand and a chalice filled with the healing waters of mindfulness, a promise that your world is a safe place filled with wonder. Walking the path of the white rose is a commitment to healing, to bringing awareness to the parts of you that are still aching. Purification is not a simple or fast process, but it is a stepping stone into the land of the true evolution of the soul.

"Do's" of the white rose:

- Giving up alcohol and meat (including fish) to cleanse your body
- A physical cleanse (such as a celery juice cleanse)
- Fasting
- An emotional cleanse (releasing stuck emotions through journaling or ecstatic dance)
- A commitment to dive deep, emotionally and spiritually
- All things water-related (such as traveling to the seashore or living by a river, blessing your water, and taking long baths)
- Yoga flow (*vinyasa*)
- Working through the traumas of your sacral and heart chakras
- Working with the angelic realm
- Reading and writing poetry
- Meditating on the image of the white swan
- Water and air rituals
- Ample downtime, allowing your body to heal on its own terms
- The absence of pushing (your agenda, or pushing others into your way of thinking, for example)
- Practicing patience and compassion

- Connecting to others in your life on a deeper level
- Becoming a great listener
- Responding, not reacting
- Flexibility and openness

Rosa Iridis: The Rainbow Rose

Represents:

- White becoming a spectrum of colors
- The fullness of experience
- Self-expression
- Sacred flames and rays
- Blessings
- Higher planes
- Ascension
- Mastery
- Talent
- Genius
- Living your blueprint
- Alchemy
- Magic
- Royalty, aristocracy, and monarchy
- Wealth and prosperity
- Integrity
- Integration
- Wholesomeness
- Absolute power
- Planet Venus
- The Hathors
- The Akashic Records
- Cosmic libraries
- Abundance
- The land of plenty
- Ancient knowledge
- Secret societies
- The spiral of evolution
- Creation and creative forces
- Inspiration
- Desire
- Maximalism
- Foresight
- Clairvoyance
- Balanced ecosystems

The monochromatic experience of light and shadow is transcended in the realm of the rainbow rose. The undying motto of the rainbow rose is "More is more." Maximalism at its finest, the land of the rainbow rose is experiential and abundant. It is about savoring the many phenomena life has to offer, and the joy of this stage is in the accumulation of experiences and learning. It is all about trying new things and seeking mastery. After two stages of letting go and purifying your vessel, the rainbow rose invites you to say, "What's next?" So, this is a stage of accumulation, receiving, and taking things in.

The lesson of the rainbow rose is about becoming intentional with who and what you invite into your personal space, into the purified sacred vessel of your life. Having transmuted some of the past toxicity, you are invited to fill your life with something new. For some, this stage may revolve around inspired creation, a feeling of being full and ready to share with the world, a calling to give back and be fully present in society. For others, this stage will signify a full-on realignment with their purpose and their unique path. The rainbow rose invites you to step away from template thinking and develop a personal channel with the Divine. The rainbow rose is an unintentional student of the Divine, the one who sees the larger master plan, as well as every individual jigsaw puzzle piece making up the whole. This stage is about exploring the colors of the rainbow—some quickly, and others more in depth—to experience the fullness of life. This stage also involves selecting a new modality or field of study to dive deeply into.

This stage is both magnetic and nomadic. It is about bringing things into your orbit, while it also takes you on an adventure and a personal tasting experience of everything new the world offers. During this stage, you may find yourself being drawn to a particular frequency, a specific rose petal that is the best match for your current state. The rainbow rose is about expansion, new horizons, and going on an adventure. It is an upward spiral of ascension and personal evolution, a unique and soulful experience that you will want to come back to over and over again.

Questions to ask during this stage:

- What is it I am ready to create for myself and others?
- What am I being called to birth?
- What energy should I be inviting into my life?
- What do I truly desire?
- Who did I come here to be?
- What are my unique talents?
- What am I being called to learn or master?
- Where do I need to get out of my comfort zone?

Symbol: The Peacock

The magical peacock is adorned with plumage quite unlike anything else in nature. A thousand eyes seem to watch from the peacock's many feathers, neatly arranged into a fan-like pattern. The peacock embodies omniscience, the proverbial all-seeing and all-knowing eye. This bird is a reminder that we assemble ourselves feather by feather, adding new facets to who we are with every new experience and every new creation. Source (God/Goddess) can hold an infinite number of perspectives simultaneously; this is symbolic of having many eyes, or having eyes everywhere. As our souls evolve, they can hold more than one perspective or frame of reference simultaneously, starting to emulate how Source views the world. The peacock is an invitation to develop true insight and understanding by taking on new challenges and embarking on new adventures.

Power, beauty, and divinity are all facets of the peacock. A beloved bird of various deities, from the Greek Hera to the Hindu Lakshmi, the peacock symbolizes abundance and perfect attainment—the kind that comes from facing life head-on. The peacock symbolizes luck and fortune, byproducts of the energy one chooses to emanate into the world. There are many gifts on the path of the rainbow rose. The path of a peacock is a promise that life is not all bleak, that trauma leads to attainment, and that evolution is the only ultimate truth.

Working with the Rainbow Rose

The magic of this rose best unfolds when you find a guru—a teacher, whether earthly or etheric. Spiritually, this stage signifies a new door that has just opened and needs to be walked through. It is often an invitation to take up a new field of study based on what you are naturally drawn to, and ideally, something that brings you closer to your life purpose.

There are no rules with the rainbow rose. You can be entirely noncommittal, trying and testing many things and fields of study, or you can commit to one thing and find true mastery in it. However, the path is often heart-led. It is finding alignment with the depth and breadth of your heart's desires that enables you to walk the rainbow path blissfully.

"Do's" of the rainbow rose:

- Just saying yes (to new experiences and opportunities)
- Traveling and seeing new places
- Learning a new skill
- Heart-opening meditations and practices
- Taking a pilgrimage to places of power (e.g., Mount Shasta, the Himalayas, Machu Picchu, Glastonbury, Lake Titicaca, etc.)
- Working with the sacred flames
- Connecting to Source and your Higher Self through meditation and other contemplative practices
- Keeping a journal of your new experiences and insights
- Starting something new—a project, a business, a creative undertaking
- Meeting new people

- Being active in the world
- Allowing your energy to be outwardly expressed
- Being seen and heard.

Rosa Rubea: The Red Rose

Represents:

- Trials and tribulations
- The blood of Osiris and Christ
- The heart space and heart consciousness
- Love
- Passion
- Devotion
- Revolution
- Sacrifice and martyrdom
- The yang (the masculine principle)
- Sacred action
- Sacred commitments
- Audacious goals
- Massive changes
- The spirit of innovation
- The zodiac sign of Aries
- Responsibility
- Taking charge
- Red robes
- Youth elixir
- The king
- The father (earthly and Divine)
- Iron
- Planet Mars

The path of the red rose is one of blood, sweat, and tears. It is a journey within to find out what you are truly made of. This is a journey of finding your sovereignty, the inner pillar of your strength and stamina, the inner well of your power that helps you keep going in the face of adversity. This is a baptism by fire, a path of perfecting your masculine qualities, working with fast-moving, intentional, and potent yang energies.

The lesson of the red rose is that of sacrifice. On a path to greatness, spiritual or otherwise, we will face challenges. How you handle those will determine the duration and impact of your red rose stage. The red rose is about developing strength of character and will. It is about defying the odds and passing the tests. It is about aiming higher and raising the bar. It is about massive and persistent change. This stage is not meant to be easy or pleasant; it is meant to push you to your limits and turn your world upside down. This may be your Tower moment of the tarot—the collapse of foundations, the complete removal of stability, a sensation of the rug being pulled out from under your feet.

In spiritual alchemy, the red rose is all about heart-led leadership and heart-led action. It is about finding your essence, the depth of your own resources, your heart of hearts, the very core of who you are at a soul level. The red rose is the color of blood for a reason. Blood is the most sacred liquid of our body, the seat of our life force, our unique energetic blueprint, and the core of who we are. Our blood doesn't lie; it is the most authentic representation of our vibration. The red rose is therefore a symbol of our eternal heart of hearts, the very core of our being from which everything else emanates.

Questions to ask during this stage:

- What am I being asked to commit to?
- Who am I in my heart of hearts?
- What responsibility am I being asked to step into?
- What am I being called to sacrifice?
- What are my values?
- What matters the most to me in life?
- What am I willing to sacrifice to get where I'm trying to go?
- How am I being called to serve?

Symbol: The Pelican

In alchemy, a pelican is often depicted stabbing its chest with its beak and drawing blood, as a sign of sacrificing one's life force for the greater good. The pelican is about nurturing the younger generation, the ancestors' blood flowing to support new life. This allegory is often likened to the Ouroboros, the great serpent biting its tail to symbolize continuity and the cyclicality of life and death. Spiritually, the pelican represents interconnectedness, humility, sacrifice, and generosity.

Allegorically, the pelican stands for transcending the ego and viewing the world from the standpoint of greater cosmic oneness. Just like Christ, the pelican can break the cycle of a zero-sum game (a me-versus-them mentality) to reemerge on the other side with a deep knowing of just how interconnected we all are. The journey of the pelican reminds us that everything impacts everything else. If the peacock stage is about taking, the pelican is about giving. It is about restoring balance and feeding what must come after you.

Working with the Red Rose

The red rose always requires a sacrifice, whether physical, mental, or spiritual. The required sacrifice will become quite apparent and almost unavoidable. Everything in the Universe will align with how you are being called to serve and help others. Often, spirituality is about being able to fill your own cup first. The red rose cares not for that; it will bring you face to face with the hard reality of needing to go the extra mile for others. Often, this is the path of a teacher, a balancing act for the perpetual student of the rainbow rose. The red rose will ask you to give much and often, without much payback.

Oftentimes, you will be asked to give the best that you have. But giving doesn't necessarily mean giving away. The challenge of the red rose can come in the form of getting a spiritual commission. A book that needs to be written, a course that needs to be taught, or a female circle that needs to be created are just some examples. And your time commitment may stand as a sacrifice. Something shall be required of you; a test will be presented.

It is after the trials and tribulations of the red rose that we pass to the last stage of the alchemical process, the final stage of the Great Work and the omega of soul growth.

"Do's" of the red rose:

- Learning to identify and commit to the challenge you are being presented with
- Being ready to give up something
- Taking responsibility for your words and actions
- Finding ways to help others
- Asking where you have achieved mastery, and how you can give back from this full cup
- Finishing what you started, taking things to their natural completion
- Walking an extra mile (go all the way!)
- Taking up a spiritual commission
- Not giving up
- Learning to cherish the giving, not just the taking
- Seeing trials as opportunities for an upgrade
- Learning to read the signs of the Universe (this stage is about being fully plugged into universal consciousness)
- Learning to approach the world with the greater good in mind
- Turning selfish into selfless
- Staying humble and learning humility

Rosa Aurea: The Golden Rose

Represents:

- The sun
- The Divine child
- Rebirth
- Resurrection
- Completion
- The end of a cycle

- Harvest
- Connection
- Enlightenment
- Deeper understanding
- Higher vibrations
- Attainment
- Ascension
- Spiritual freedom
- Gold
- The golden standard
- The golden ratio
- Golden codes
- Golden gates
- Perfection
- The promised land
- Divinity
- God/Goddess consciousness
- The all-seeing eye
- The all-feeling heart
- Source within and without
- Planet Mercury

Rosa Aurea is the grand finale of the path of the alchemical rose, the homestretch and ultimate attainment within a cycle of existence. It is the harvest and victory after a long and emotionally charged battle.

This stage brings about the sacred marriage of alchemy—the sovereign Red King (red rose, solar energies) joining forces with the merciful White Queen (white rose, lunar energies) to give birth to the Divine child, the golden creation symbolized by Mercury (both the element and the planet). Mercury is the philosopher's child, the perfect, most beloved creation of God and Goddess. It is also the attainment of something coveted, the completion of the magnum opus undertaken in the black rose stage. The golden rose is a celebration of a life-altering milestone, a consummate achievement of personal, societal, or planetary caliber.

Spiritually, the golden rose signifies the dawning of solar light within your body, mind, and soul. This stage welcomes and celebrates the arrival of massive amounts of Divine light into your body (also known as ascension). This is the most expansive and gratifying stage of the alchemical process, the "why" behind this challenging journey. This stage may be signified by upgrades to your etheric body and DNA structure. It may bring about a new special ability or open up new spiritual frontiers for you.

Questions to ask during this stage:

- What is rising in me?
- How am I transformed?
- What do I know to be true today that I didn't know during the black rose stage?
- Who am I being reborn as?
- What am I harvesting at this time?

- What is the version of the Divine child that is rising within me?
- What have I achieved and accomplished?
- What am I most proud of?

Symbol: The Phoenix

The bird companion of this stage is the magical phoenix, the most beloved and trusted bird of Source consciousness. The phoenix represents eternal life as a sequence of cycles of death and rebirth, an opportunity to destroy the old and rebuild better. Just as a new beginning rises from the ashes of yesterday, so does the spirit of the phoenix eternally prevail over darkness, fear, and death. A phoenix is not just immortal; it is immortal in the best of ways, having a chance to continuously shed and evolve. Spiritually, the phoenix represents growth, progress, attainment, and the intricacies of the ascension process.

Working with the Golden Rose

After a period of sacrifice and pushing through limitations in the stage of the red rose, you enter a period of respite in the abode of the golden rose. Her energies are gentle, warm, inviting, and blissful. This is a period of Heaven on Earth, built upon your hard work and dedication. This stage is often an initiation into the mysteries, or a stage of receiving the codes you have earned during your alchemical pilgrimage. The golden rose opens doors and portals, enhances daily life, and offers rewards beyond your wildest expectations. She completes the cycle, and therefore, she brings forth a bountiful and blessed harvest time.

During this stage, you reap what you have sowed. Your efforts find their completion in the golden gifts of the rose. This stage acknowledges a road well traveled and sacrifices that haven't been in vain. As you look back on your alchemical path, you will see how you have been gently guided through every stage in hopes that you would end up here, at this omega point, having become so much wiser than before.

"Do's" of the golden rose:

- Allowing yourself time to celebrate the hard work and the strength of your commitment to your spiritual path
- Meditation and connection with spirit daily (some of the most profound insights and access codes dwell within the realm of the golden rose)
- Showing gratitude for the progress you have made

- Leaning into your inner sacred marriage of masculine and feminine. Meditate upon the middle point between these two polarities.
- Enjoying the rewards (there are always rewards during this special season)
- Celebrating the sun and building upon your solar connection
- Sun gazing every morning at dawn, or every evening at sunset

The Alchemical Rose Path is above all a cycle. As soon as one cycle ends, a new one begins. In true phoenix-like fashion, the golden rose is destined to become the black rose. And so the dance of time goes on in an ever-present movement of waves that hit the sandy shore, only to retreat again into the depth of the ocean void. And there is solace in this thought—in the promise of continuity that rests upon the laurels of even our greatest achievements. There will be new mountains to climb tomorrow, dear friend. For now, take a moment to celebrate this moment in time, both miraculous and infinitely finite—a point that finds you reading these words.

Your path, no matter where it may lead you, is sacred. And so is every step that leads you into inevitable ascension. Learn to seize the day and enjoy it before the phoenix turns to ash again. *Carpe diem!*

Final Thoughts on the Alchemical Rose Path

In your life, you may encounter moments when everything is calling you to shift and morph. These times can be uncertain, requiring you to dive headfirst into the unknown. That is when it makes the most sense to refer to the alchemical process. The Alchemical Rose Path is divinely guided. It is a tried-and-true system that, if followed step by step, starting with the black rose, is guaranteed to bring about the desired changes in your life.

If you choose to undertake this path, allow no less than three weeks for each stage, and be patient with yourself. Start the path by setting an intention and inviting your spirit guides to be with you every step of the way. Call upon the black rose to help you jump-start the process. Then trust that your path will unfold in front of you in the way that it is meant to. As you journey through the roses, some stages may take longer than others. You will know when the shift happens, as the energies and the events of your life will change. Throughout the process, do plenty of journaling, and allow yourself time for deep introspection. Following the alchemical path is a spiritual pilgrimage and a commitment. However, there is great reward for everyone who chooses this path.

Happy transformation, my dear!

Heart Space: I See Fire

And then I saw the fires of Agni consume the world. Not meant to hurt or cause desolation, those were the healing fires of taking back our land, the fires of claiming our holiness, the fires destined to bring back the light.

"The fire of redemption," she said, looking at me with those dark, doe-like eyes.

She was right.

It was the fire to end all fires, the final cleansing, the last supper, held on the eve of the birth of the new world. And though I may have been the cause of that fire, I knew she was as well—my soulmate, my partner in all things, my Mahadevi.

It was then that she handed me a chalice filled with what looked like quicksilver.

"It wouldn't be the last supper without the Holy Grail, would it?" I asked and smiled.

And she said, "Drink."

And so I drank.

And my heart was filled with sorrow—sorrow for the world we built together,

For the world we lost, for the world we were going to rebuild anew.

"The sun always rises in the east," she said and looked at me sadly.

I knew it meant something—a code we had once agreed upon, a code that contained a small Universe within itself, the beginning of the end of the beginning.

It was all but a blur, and my vision went dark for a second.

"The sun rises in the east if we say so," I responded, our code phrase finally complete.

And then there was water,

So much of it coming from the depths of the Earth itself,

First, drowning the fire, covering every last ember with its healing cosmic magic,

And then the Earth was overtaken by it—no land left in sight.

Just like the old days, apart from Noah's ark, I thought.

"And so it is," she said, taking my hand in hers.

And I knew, in that moment, it was finally done,

The great sacrifice to end all sacrifices,

Because the sun always rises in the east, if we say so.

CHAPTER 10

An Oath of a Rose

"'Tis not the many oaths that make the truth;
But the plain single vow, that is vow'd true."
~William Shakespeare

Since the inception of the Sisterhood of the Rose, taking an oath has been the first step toward becoming an initiate. An oath is a commitment, a sacred promise to learn from the Divine Mother, to walk in her footsteps, and to forge a new world of love and compassion on Earth. The Oath of the Rose spans incarnations; having taken it once, you will forever be Rose-sworn, in this life and the next. This oath is not to be taken lightly. It is a soul commitment, permeating your light body, not just your physical one.

However, once undertaken, the Oath of the Rose opens up a path of light—a path filled with purpose, meaning, aligned service, and heartfelt sisterhood. Joining the sisterhood means gaining a support structure like no other. It means beings connected to every sister that ever lived, sharing a sacred space with all the initiates, and being a part of the largest community of female sages, healers, and way-showers in the history of planet Earth. Becoming a sister in the Order of the Rose is truly a path like no other.

The Order of the Rose Hierarchy

In the days of old, the Order of the Rose had the following structure:

Level 0—Oath Taker: Technically, an oath taker expressed interest in following the path and was often tested before officially joining the order. However, taking the oath meant believing in the order's values and choosing to uphold them, whether you became a member or not.

Level 1—Initiate: Dubbed a Sister in Rose, the initiate stepped onto a sacred path of learning from the Divine Mother, as well as from the many priestesses. An initiate was introduced to the teachings, but also given responsibilities and commitments in accordance with the order's values.

Level 2—Adept: Every adept was a practitioner of mysteries, not just a humble student. Adepts developed a strong channel to the Divine Mother and were personally guided to their soul's evolution. The adept stage was a cleanse, a reckoning, and a deep dive. It was meant to help the individual pass through the limitations of the ego and shadow self and come into fullness, integrity, and light.

Level 3—Priestess: A priestess was devoted to the order's tasks full-time, hosting many rituals and ceremonies, tending to the temple gardens, and recording new wisdom channeled by herself and other priestesses. Each priestess was committed to spending as much time with the adepts and initiates as possible, imparting knowledge. Each priestess was responsible for leading a group of initiates through the Mysteries of the Rose and selecting the brightest students for the honor of one day becoming a priestess.

Level 4—High Priestess: One of the five great teachers selected for their understanding of the mysteries and their depth of connection to the Mother, a high priestess led by example. Each of the five priestesses had specialties and an area of expertise cultivated through copious meditation, ritual magic, and channeling. Each high priestess selected a circle of twelve priestesses and personally guided them on their spiritual journeys, serving as their guide, mentor, and soul coach.

Level 5—Grand Magistress: The holder of the wisdom and the guardian of the records of the order, the grand magistress ensured the order's healthy functioning. Her main task was keeping the Divine Mother's word and intentions alive through the order's work. The grand magistress initiated every priestess and high priestess, and even demoted priestesses if their conduct was lacking. The grand magistress determined the direction of the order and orchestrated its proliferation.

The Values of the Sisters in Rose

In taking the Oath of the Rose and joining the order, sisters agreed to uphold the order's values, which were as follows:

Sacred Heart-Led Service

The Order of the Rose depended on donations and service rendered to local communities. Each chapter had healers, herbalists, hypnotists, seers, oracles, channels, mediums, astrologers, and all manner of other spiritual practitioners who tirelessly served their communities. Each practitioner carried Goddess vibrations, generously sharing their skills and healing powers. Coming into contact with the sisters was a healing and transformative experience. The order also held community rituals, prayers, and meditative journeys. A network of temples covered the planet, each strategically placed at the intersection of ley lines, points of high concentration of energy. These temples gave refuge and educational classes to the public.

Connection

The Order of the Rose was built on a deep-seated belief that we are all interconnected and one day shall return to oneness. As such, the sisters walked the Earth intentionally, aiming to raise others up, forging deep soul bonds, paying it forward, and factoring every aspect of the ecosystem into consideration when making decisions. The order had a strict "hurt not" policy. Fostering compassion for all living beings, the Temples of the Rose often contained shelters for animals and temporary dwellings for those in need. But most importantly, the Sisters in Rose led with their hearts, sharing the beautiful vibrations of cosmic love with everyone they came in contact with.

Depth

The order was predicated on diving deep together. Becoming a sister meant opening yourself fully—to others, learning, ritual magic, and possibility. "Always go deeper" was the order's unofficial motto, interwoven into the conduct of its members. Certain days were entirely devoted to introspection, with each member diving into their inner sanctuary. Once you could see yourself for who you were, you were ready to step onto a path of holding sacred space for others. Sacred listening was a much-beloved practice, allowing you to transcend your separateness and perceive another as a part of yourself, worthy of your full attention.

Love

Meeting each challenge, each day of your life, and each person on your path with love and deep compassion was a vibrational signature of the sisters. Each sister put their femininity forward in a way that nurtured and harmonized the greater whole. Loving conduct was one of the first commandments, something each sister practiced daily, until it became as much a part of them as their personal history and character. Loving another meant acting in their best interest, always. But the sisters also recognized that self-love is an important aspect of the love equation, so they prioritized self-care and self-healing to show up for others in their best light.

Wisdom

The pursuit of wisdom was a common denominator and a North Star for every sister, whether an initiate or a high priestess. Wisdom is the highest expression of a female connected, a female on the path, a female evolved. As such, it was considered one of the most desirable attributes. It was believed that true feminine wisdom brought things closer together, serving as connective tissue for communities large and small.

Rose-Witnessed

To be witnessed by the Rose meant to be heard by the Divine Mother. This concept initially came out of the healing chambers of the temples, holistic spaces for sacred listening and contemplation. Initially only available to the sisters, these chambers were eventually opened to the public. One of the adepts or priestesses would often oversee the chamber and engage in compassionate listening, providing counsel to whoever needed it. Entering the healing chamber was akin to entering the "womb" of the Rose; it meant surrendering fully to the Mother's healing vibrations, and her presence was felt viscerally within each chamber. The windows of the healing chambers often faced east, symbolizing renewal, recalibration, and new beginnings, perpetually aligned with the direction of our greater good.

Anything witnessed by the Rose was considered confidential, never to be shared or divulged. It was believed to be the purest form of the word. A vow witnessed by the Rose became holy, sacred, and unbreakable. Some of the highest degrees of initiation into the order happened this way, witnessed and blessed by the Rose and the Mother.

Preparing to Take the Oath

Each Oath of the Rose is witnessed by the sacred flower and takes place in an etheric initiation chamber of the Temple of the Rose. It is therefore an act that shouldn't be taken lightly. Taking the oath is a sacred pilgrimage and is always presided over by the Mother. A few steps need to be taken before taking the oath. Two weeks prior to the oath ritual is a time of purification of your vessel—physical, mental, and emotional—and a great release.

Here is how the oath-takers prepared themselves for this sacred rite:

Speak no evil, hear no evil, do no evil: Reminiscent of the three wise monkeys and their "see no evil, hear no evil, speak no evil" mantra, each hopeful oath taker had to enter a fourteen-day cleansing period that began with agreeing to adhere to a few simple rules. In the purification process, it was important to start with communication and expression, focusing on goodness in actions and words. That meant giving up gossip, unkind words toward self and others, and most importantly, maintaining purity of action. Each action in this period was evaluated based on the ideals of pursuing the "greater good" and committing acts of service and selflessness.

The purge: The purge was a period of releasing and letting go that often started by decluttering one's space and releasing some material possessions. However, apart from getting rid of unwanted possessions, each hopeful had to part with a couple of their favorite things. This symbolized their commitment to the development of their immortal soul over material things. The purge was also rooted in rituals that enabled hopefuls to release some stuck emotions and go through potent healing.

Three-day fast: While not required, most hopefuls chose to undergo a three-day fast as part of the purge. During the fast, they would only consume water and small amounts of seeds that helped further cleanse the physical body and prepare it for the oath.

Meditative contemplation: Before taking the oath, each initiate was encouraged to spend at least ten hours in meditation, contemplation, and solitude. This time was often devoted to connecting with the Mother and asking for her blessing and guidance.

Ritual: Taking the Oath of the Rose

While taking the Oath of the Rose is completely optional, it is important to include it here for those who choose to step onto the Path of the Rose fully and start walking the walk of a hopeful and eventual initiate. Remember, taking an oath is first and foremost a calling. If you are meant to undergo the oath process, you will feel it deeply in your heart. If you choose to take the oath, follow the ritual below closely. You may also benefit from two weeks of prep time to emulate the pilgrimages of old and help you get the most out of this sacred rite.

You will need:

- Twelve white roses
- Twelve red roses
- A large bowl filled with water, infused with twelve drops of rose essential oil
- A printout of the Flower of Life (at least five inches in diameter; see Chapter 2, page 34)
- An all-white outfit to symbolize the purity of your intentions

The ritual:

1. It is best to undertake this ritual in nature, in a secluded place where you can connect fully and won't be interrupted.
2. Place a dozen white roses in a fan-like fashion on the left side of your body. Place a dozen red roses in a fan on the right side of your body. Place the bowl of water infused with rose oil right in front of you, so you can easily reach out and touch it.
3. Pause here and imagine a pillar of white light descending straight from the heavens and covering your entire body, sealing you away from the outside world and creating your own protected version of a sacred space.
4. Place the printout of the Flower of Life on the ground where you are planning to sit. (Naturally, you may cover it with a cushion to be more comfortable). The vibrations of the Divine Feminine run strong within the bounds of the Flower of Life and help bless the space around you.
5. Close your eyes and focus on breathing into your heart space. Imagine your heart opening up like a large rose, growing ever bigger with each breath you take.

6. Place your hands on your heart and invite the Divine Mother to preside over this ceremony.
7. Imagine you are seated in a circle of women, a circle as ancient as time itself, a circle of the Sisters in Rose. Imagine that the two women on either side of you are stretching their hands so you can clasp onto them, completing the magic of the circle.
8. Feel the energy coursing through you and through the circle. This energy is pink and soft, connecting the hearts of all the circle members, bringing you closer to each other and bringing you back into connection.
9. Watch as a torrent of pink light begins to descend into the center of the circle, touching you and everyone in it with its cooling, pleasant energy. This feels like a spiritual bath of sorts, cleansing any darkness present in your body to make room for massive amounts of light.
10. Now, place both your hands into the bowl of water in front of you. Imagine the water washing away anything suboptimal, anything that no longer serves you. Instead, notice how the water is infusing you with the spirit of the Order of the Rose—its blessed power, its gentle healing, its ancient wisdom.
11. Stay here, allowing this process to come to fruition. Do not force anything. Simply surrender to the embrace and the magic of the Divine Mother.
12. When you are ready, feel free to open your eyes and read the words of the oath. Repeat the oath three times.
13. "I am [state your first and last name], taking the Oath of the Rose entirely of my own free will. I choose to step upon the Path of the Rose today and walk it, holding true to the ideals of our Mother Divine. I promise to live my life guided by love and goodness. I promise to serve others, offering my talents and my time so that others can grow on their spiritual and worldly path. I promise to dive deep into the mysteries, forging my own path and connecting with spirit daily. I promise to stay on the path, regardless of the challenges and trials that may come my way. I choose to spend my life cherishing my soul connection with others, forging deep bonds, and leading by example. Starting today, I choose to pursue true wisdom, and I ask the Divine Mother to nurture and guide me as I take my first steps into the Rose Mysteries."

14. Dip your fingers into the bowl of water and anoint the area of your third eye and your temples with the rose water. This signifies the end of the ritual.

Be assured that your oath has been received, and it will set you on the Path of the Rose, which will naturally unfold in front of you.

Happy walking, my sibling in Rose!

Heart Space: The Rose Scrolls

A Mother Goddess was seated on the porch of a palace overlooking the Nile River. It was the middle of Nisan, mere months before the heliacal rising of Sirius, when the flooding of the Nile would signify the period of great fertility for all of Egypt.

It was destined to be her last summer on the earthly plane—the summer that she had known would come one day. But now that it was almost here, was she ready for it?

She had fallen in love with this strange planet—this planet that felt so foreign once, this planet that had now permanently wedged itself into the folds of the Goddess's heart.

The sound of someone softly landing on the balcony interrupted her contemplation.

She looked up and smiled in recognition.

"Thoth," she said with a light nod, inviting him to join her.

"Lady Isis," he said with a glint in his eyes that was so unmistakably him that she thought she would perhaps miss it just as much as this strange planet.

"The time is coming, old friend. The time for goodbyes," she said, her eyes misting over with what looked like genuine tears. "The worst of it is, I know I'm not leaving as much behind as I'd like to."

"You are leaving the Rose Scrolls. They will become your legacy. I know this," Thoth said thoughtfully.

"You have seen the fate of the scrolls. They won't stand the test of time. This planet is not ready to embrace the codes they contain," Mother Goddess said, her voice full of sorrow.

"Perhaps not yet. But the time will come when the Scrolls of the Rose shall be rewritten again. Your legacy will be restored. I have seen it," Thoth assured her.

Isis rose from her throne and walked up to the shelves lined with neatly stacked white scrolls. She ran her fingers through them, wordlessly deliberating something.

"They will burn in the great library of Alexandria, among many others. I saw it in my dreams, but I cannot prevent this from happening. They, too, shall turn into dust. Tell me, All Wise One, how does one keep this knowledge from being lost?"

Thoth paused before responding. "Encode them into the petals of the rose. Let each flower carry the vibrations of your teaching, the extent of your love. Let the scrolls burn; the roses shall forever remain," he added.

"Yes," she said and breathed a sigh of relief. "Let the wisdom of the Father be recorded on the emerald tablets. Let the wisdom of the Mother be recorded in the petals of the rose."

So may it be. And so it shall ever remain.

CHAPTER 11

The Venusian Rose

Come hither, my dear one.
Come closer and enter the world of Venus—
a goddess, a celestial pioneer, a way-shower,
a jewel in the evening and the morning skies,
a planet whose path creates a celestial pentagram,
the one eternally blessed by the Rose.

Many are the mysteries of Venus. Unique is her story, and blessed are her gifts.

Who is she, truly? A mysterious goddess of love? An undine, languidly emerging from the sea foam, her golden hair clad in pearls? The beloved daughter of Jupiter? Is she perhaps a scorching giant in the sky, the solar system's hottest planet, boasting temperatures of 850 degrees Fahrenheit (464 degrees Celsius) on a good day? Beloved and venerated by the ancient Babylonians, Greeks, and Romans, Venus is more than a planet, more than a goddess, more than a spirit, more than an archetype. She is a happening, an enigma, a pioneer, and a way-shower. She is an energetic imprint of the Divine Mother in our local pocket of time and space.

Venus was the very first domino. Long before the gentle spirit of Gaia, the soul of our darling Mother Earth, descended into the solar system, planet Venus was holding down the fort, anchoring the Divine Feminine energies into the fabric of our immediate cosmic surroundings. As far as Divine Femininity in the solar system is concerned, it all started with Venus. She descended into the plane of decided masculinity. She claimed her space, parting the void of cosmic waters to bring about a new vibration, to jump-start the creation of the feminine arc, the system of feminine energy centers, not unlike the three feminine chakras within the human body: sacral, heart, and third eye. She dared to be the first—the first to shine a facet of unabashedly feminine light, the first to prioritize beauty, the first to reclaim love as a value. She was the only feminine polarity to the many awakened masculine planets in the solar system, a counterpart to the masculinity of Mars, Saturn, Jupiter, Mercury, Uranus, and a somewhat androgynous but masculine-leaning sun.

Venus is the original feminist, the first female rebel, the goddess who reflected so much of the sun's light that she became known as "the radiant one" across the Milky Way.

The Arc of Ascension of Femininity: The Solar System Way

Evolution is never linear. It is a complex process of ebbs and flows, a spiral movement, a Fibonacci sequence, and an equation governed by the geometry and mathematical precision of the Flower of Life. Evolution is division and multiplication. It is a descent into the micro level and its perpetual purification, until one day, the infinitely large can be built by the fusion and unification of the infinitely small.

Solar systems evolve in a way not dissimilar to humans; as above, so below. Like a tree grows from the roots, we start our energetic evolution at the level of our root chakra, gradually moving up, chakra by chakra, eventually culminating at the crown, the chakra of the awakened God/Goddess within.

Venus – Sacral Chakra

The feminine arc of ascension within our solar system was jump-started by the ancient spirit that chose to incarnate as planet Venus. And so the cycle of evolution in our local pocket of reality began. Venus changed the game, bringing a whole lot of feminine power and magic to our local plane of existence.

Venus is the sacral chakra of the solar system, an infinite ocean of pleasure, beauty, surrender, and sensuality. She is the feminine creative flow, the womb, the creative reproductive force that gave birth to femininity within the microcosm run by our local sun. She is the force that allowed the seed of femininity to take root and blossom, becoming a force to be reckoned with. She is the mistress of desire and its fulfillment. She is sacred sexuality, sensual pleasure, self-love, and intuitive flow. She is the one who savors the moment, understands the perfect harmony of music, enjoys dance as a sacred act, and savors every moment of the *joie de vivre*. She is the one who perpetually exists in the moment, unconcerned with schedules, deadlines, and goal setting. She is unrestricted and liberated, governed by feeling, spurred into action by emotion, in tune with energy, and in harmony with her surroundings.

Venus has a healing presence and is attuned to the frequency of a golden ratio, the perfect harmonic vibration of the Universe, represented by the sounds of the 432-hertz frequency. Every fractal in the Universe, if properly balanced, vibrates at the level of the golden ratio, a Divine proportion, a "kiss of God." The magic of Venus is such that it brings fractals that exist outside of the golden ratio (due to trauma, destabilization, or fracturing) back into wholeness and equilibrium, into a state of perfect original vibration. She is a cosmic equalizer and harmonizer.

Our Earth, Gaia – Heart Chakra

The second domino in the arc of the feminine ascension is our beloved planet Earth. Gaia, a youthful yet wise spirit, came to teach us the intricacies of the magic of the heart, and in the process, she became our cosmic Mother. Motherhood is a key lesson for Gaia, and her ability to produce and nurture life—her shortcut to evolution, harmonizing an ecosystem of her children, many with conflicting desires and interests—is her greatest challenge. Unconditional love is the signature vibration of our planet. Her lessons are gentle, and yet many are her roadblocks on the path of ascension. The current state of humanity is one such challenge. Gaia loved her human children so much that she let them get away with murder—literally. This has brought about disharmony that requires some pretty drastic measures to fix.

Gaia's heart is her greatest asset, the most precious of all emeralds. It permeates her being and her soul. Gaia emanates the healing energies of her beautiful heart into the atmosphere, gently transforming her surroundings and even the farthest corners of the solar system. But it is through Venus's magic that Earth's path becomes possible.

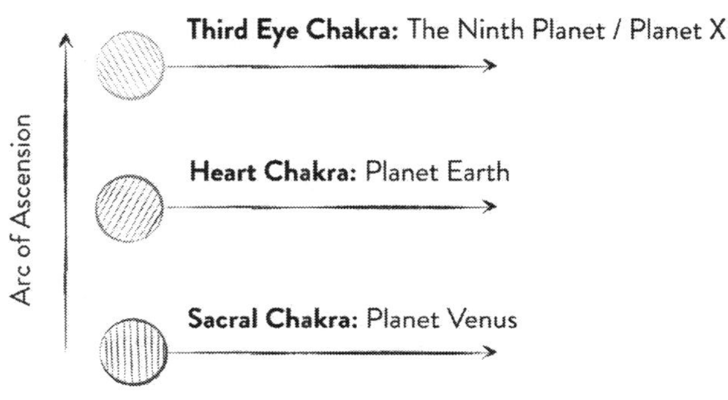

Figure 51: The feminine arc within the solar system

Venus was Gaia's first mentor, way-shower, and teacher in the Milky Way. Just like kundalini rises from the depth of our being, moving up one chakra at a time, the magic of the heart chakra is always preceded by the magic of the sacral chakra. It was upon the foundational work of Venus that the Motherhood and tender loving care of Earth became possible. Venus taught Gaia the art of creation, the joy of surrender, the ability to find peace amidst the chaos, a gift of the inner waters of femininity. But most importantly, Venus paved a path for Earth to live her innate blueprint and anchor even more feminine vibrations into the abundantly masculine fabric of our local solar system.

The Lesson of Ajna – Third Eye Chakra

The third step on the path of the Ascension of Femininity (see **Figure 51**) in the solar system is the lesson of Ajna, the third eye chakra. Alas, this lesson is still in the future. Ascension is a gradual process and takes millions of years. As soon as the energies of the heart are sufficiently anchored by Gaia, a new cycle can begin.

For humanity, this cycle is going to be heralded by the official discovery of a new planet in the solar system. Evidence for this planet has recently been found by a group of California Institute of Technology researchers, and it is currently dubbed Planet X. For now, this planet remains hypothetical, its size presumed to be similar to Neptune, and its mass is expected to be ten times that of Earth.[5] Planet X is believed to have an elongated orbit, quite unique and different from the rest of the planetary orbits in the solar system. It makes the planet hard to detect with modern technology, since its orbit is so vast that it takes over ten thousand years to complete one full cycle.

But perhaps the most unique thing about Planet X is its energetic blueprint. Carrying the highest caliber of feminine vibrations, it is a true gem and a rare find among planets. Planet X holds a peculiar set of light codes and a unique combination of energies within itself, making it a sage, a healer, and a high priestess all in one. As it travels along its orbit, moving closer to Earth, a new level of understanding will become available to us. Planet X is a space traveler, existing between the realm of physicality and Akasha, the vast informational field permeating all of existence. Holding an immense amount of energy in its auric field, Planet X will impact everything it comes in close contact with, including the Earth, uplifting it and offering it a new set of vibrations. With the official discovery of Planet X, a new cycle shall begin—a cycle that shall herald the emergence of the Celestial Triple Goddess, the maiden, mother, and crone—the triumvirate of Venus, Earth, and Planet X.

---

5 "Hypothetical Planet X," NASA, https://solarsystem.nasa.gov/planets/hypothetical-planet-x/in-depth/.

The Path of Venus

Divine sister planets Earth and Venus are forever locked in an intriguing orbital dance that captivates with its geometric beauty, mathematical precision, and esoteric meaning.

From the perspective of the Earth (a geocentric perspective), the path Venus traces through the sky resembles a rose (see **Figure 52**), with the innermost layer showing the curves of five intricately crafted petals. Venus commences a new cycle every eight years, marking a new beginning and a new celestial lesson for itself and for Gaia.

Figure 52: The Venusian rose (or the pentagram, or the petals of Venus)

The ancients knew this celestial rose as the original rose of the solar system, a true symbol of kinship between the two feminine planets, and a sign that their relationship was not only preordained, but is closely watched over by the Divine. It is as if the Divine Mother herself painted a symbol of her sacred flower in the sky, identifying Venus as an elder sister and a mentor spirit for Earth.

Since ancient times, the Venusian Rose has served as a symbol of and a path of initiation into the female priesthood. The high priestesses of goddesses Isis, Hathor, Inanna, and Aphrodite indelibly walked the path of the Venusian Rose, forever illuminated by its wisdom.

Walking the path of the Venusian Rose meant being touched by the Divine. For many, it was a stepping stone into a life of service and spiritual mysteries, and a shortcut to ascension. Walking the path meant committing to being the Goddess's student, surrendering to her transformative energies, and diving deep with her into the shadows of the womb to come out on the other side, cleansed of darkness.

Hence, walking with Venus started with shadow work, the self-induced long, dark night of the soul, a period of deep transformation that could last for years. Often, the Venusian path was attempted by a group of initiates who swore to support each other and fortify each other's spirits. Some of the most powerful sisterhoods were built during the undertaking of the Venusian path, and some of the strongest female bonds and the most important collective female initiations happened because of Venusian blessings.

Walking with Venus is a calling. It is a surrender into the unknown, a sacred pilgrimage, a major commitment, and one of the truest things you can ever do. The waters of Venus run deep. Her wisdom is infinite, and her healing powers are majestic. Nobody starts on the Venusian path unless the Goddess calls them into her abode, offering a sanctuary and a respite from the mundane. Only about a third of initiates complete the challenge and reach the final destination. Such are the tests and lessons of our celestial teacher, Venus.

The simplest form of the Venusian initiation takes seventy-five days, but the willing initiate can take longer. It all depends on the intention and the depth of commitment to the path. Below, you'll find an overview and an outline of a simple seventy-five-day Venusian initiation path. While not a full-blown script for everything contained within the initiation, it serves as a great starting point for anyone looking to walk the path of the ancient priestesses. Remember, if Venus calls your name to participate in her sacred circle, she will guide you every step of the way, filling in the gaps and providing guidance along the way.

Why Walk the Venusian Path?

There are two major reasons why you may choose to undertake the Venusian path.

The first and most common reason is to become the apprentice and the mentee of Venus, surrendering to the process and her wisdom. This is the most common intention. It sends the initiate on a premeditated but still bespoke path of one-on-one communication with and guidance from Venus.

The second reason is to earn a sacred boon from the planet. While you can engage with any planetary consciousness, ascended master, deity, or elemental to negotiate a boon—a spiritual favor of sorts—Venus has a predetermined way of working with her initiates. By walking the initiation path of Venus, you agree to follow her guidance for seventy-five days. In exchange, you can ask her for a spiritual or energetic favor. Through this process, a sacred contract between you and the planet is established. As long as you follow through on your end, Venus shall do the same. As with all sacred contracts, it is important to be crystal clear with the ask; it may be advisable to write it down.

What Can Venus Assist You With?

If you are curious about Venusian superpowers and her domain of influence, read on. This will help you better formulate your intention regarding working with Venus.

The domain and superpowers of Venus:

- Healing your Mother lineage and overall ancestral issues
- Healing issues around self-love, liberating you from the inner critic and low self-esteem
- Harmonizing relationships
- Attracting a perfect partner and the love of your life
- Soul healing (including past life trauma and persistent karmic patterns and knots)
- Healing your reproductive health and issues around fertility, and restoring your libido
- Easy pregnancy, childbirth, and child-rearing
- Establishing a stronger connection with your child in the womb and during the first three years of their life
- Sacral chakra magic and teachings
- Divine Feminine mysteries
- Any creative projects or artistic endeavors
- Flow and abundance
- Feminine power
- Awakening your Goddess powers
- Escaping the slave mentality
- Increased clairsentience and claircognizance
- Herbal remedies and flower essences
- Crystal magic

Benefits of walking the petals of the Venus initiation path:

- Developing an intimate connection with Venus, one of the greatest celestial teachers
- A deeper understanding of the Venusian mysteries
- Initiation into the path of a priestess
- Deep energetic healing
- Untying karmic knots
- Aligning with better relationships, finding your tribe and a perfect partner to share your life with

- Healing familial wounds
- A natural path toward raising your vibration
- Enhancement of "special abilities," such as receiving and interpreting guidance from Spirit

Sacred Initiation Path of Venus: The Five-Petal Path

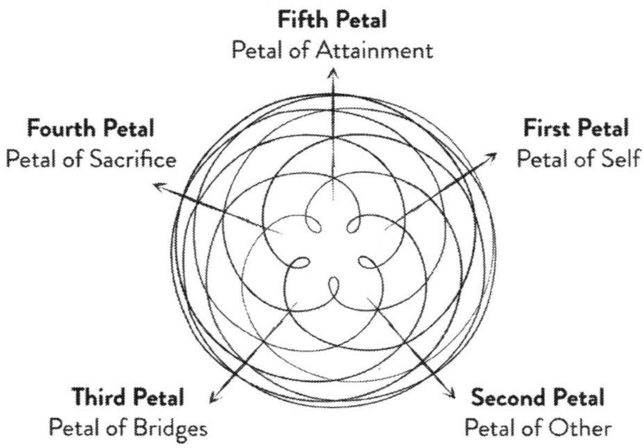

Figure 53: The Five Venusian Petals Path

The Venusian Petals Path consists of five consecutive steps (see **Figure 53**) that build on each other to help an initiate achieve heightened awareness and transformation. If the rules of the step are broken, the initiation cannot be completed, and you need to start over. Initiation can be attempted again after thirty-three days.

When the initiate embarks upon this path, the planetary consciousness of Venus, as well as the Goddess energies of Venus/Aphrodite, start to work with the initiate behind the scenes. Throughout the initiation, you should expect to be tested, guided, and up-leveled by these ancient energies.

Venus's lessons for each initiate are unique, for we walk our own paths. For some, Venus will offer a challenge to overcome; others may be tested in their dreams. When traveling the path, stay humble and attuned to signs from the Universe. The language of Venus is subtle and comes in the form of symbols, signs, and omens. Learning to notice these soft whispers and to identify and interpret them is just as much a part of the path as the actual meditations and practices listed below. The Universe is constantly communicating with you. Are you listening?

Offering to Venus

Before starting on the Venusian path, you will need to perform an offering to Venus as a sign of your commitment to the path and your willingness to learn from her, often done by using a ritual such as this:

1. Prepare a bowl filled with water, a few drops of floral essential oils, and rose petals.
2. When you are ready, start by placing your fingers in the bowl. Close your eyes and connect with Venus by imagining the planet in your mind's eye.
3. Watch as a stream of energy begins to form between the area of your third eye and the heart of Venus, a spot in the planet's very center.
4. Picture how a common space is created between you and Venus, as if you are joined through time and space by a sphere of white light.
5. Invite Venus to guide you every step of the way, being present in your auric field for the duration of walking the Five-Petal Path.
6. Ask Venus to actively heal you during this process and to step in whenever energetic blocks need to be removed.
7. As an energy exchange, offer Venus a plate filled with some of her favorite things, like flowers, berries, and nuts. She also appreciates rice, red ribbons, and small crystals as offerings. Give gratitude to Venus for all the work she is doing and the healing she is sure to start sending your way shortly.

Journal: Keep a journal to record your notes—the learnings, the insights, the breakthroughs.

Correspondences: Surround yourself with Venusian correspondences (more on these later in this chapter).

Ritual: Venus – The Attunement

Before you begin on the initiatory path, it is important to attune your physical and light bodies to the vibrations of Venus, so she can personally oversee your path and course-correct it if needed.

You will need:

- Five pink or red roses
- A rose quartz crystal
- A bowl of salt

The ritual:

1. Take a comfortable seated position. This meditative ritual is best performed when seated in a lotus pose. (Half-lotus or cross-legged is the next best, if you can). Make sure you are facing east for this experience. This meditation is best done in the morning before 10:00 a.m.
2. Place the roses and the bowl of salt in front of you in the pattern shown in **Figure 54** below.

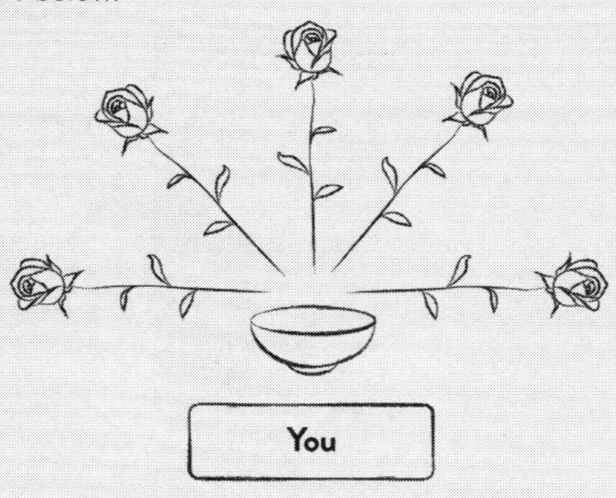

Figure 54: The Attunement Ritual arrangement

3. Place all your fingertips in the bowl of salt. Start breathing deeply into your heart space. With every inhale, hold your breath for a count of three.
4. As you breathe, imagine that all darkness (pain, suffering, trauma, heartache, etc.) is starting to leave your body through your fingertips. Notice how the salt is purifying your body and your energy field, preparing you

for the attunement ceremony. Stay here for a few minutes, taking full advantage of this deep energetic cleanse.

5. Take the rose quartz crystal and place it over your heart. This stone will be your guardian and a symbol of your Venusian connection. In the future, make sure to have your crystal with you every time you work with Venus or do any practices from this book.
6. Imagine that planet Venus is right before you, glimmering with the most beautiful etheric pink light. It seems very close, as if you are right next to it. Watch as a pathway is created between you and this majestic planet, a pink ray that connects your heart with the very core of planet Venus.
7. Watch as this pink ray starts to charge the crystal you have placed over your heart with the prettiest pink glow. Allow this process to happen naturally, without forcing it. Once the crystal is sufficiently charged, place it at your sacral chakra and keep it there for the rest of this attunement.
8. Imagine a sphere of white light surrounding your body. It corresponds with the layer of your light body that is called etheric. Watch as the pink ray that connects you with Venus starts to pour a stream of pink light into the sphere, filling it up with the pink glow.
9. Notice that there is a larger sphere of light placed over the white sphere, forming an outer shell. This one is emerald in color and represents your emotional body. Watch as the stream of pink energy that exists between you and Venus starts to fill up this sphere as well, drop by drop, inch by inch, until finally, the entire emerald sphere is filled with shimmery, glimmering pink light.
10. Lastly, notice one last sphere, larger and steely blue. This is your mental body. Watch as the pink waters of Venus start to fill up your mental space as well, transforming it from within. Watch this process transpire naturally, until your mental body is fully filled with the shimmering pink vibrations of Venus.
11. Watch how a spiral of pink light starts rotating at the very base of your spine, coiling around your spinal cord. Notice how its amplitude grows as it starts to surround your entire body from the base of your spine to the top of your head.
12. Imagine that this larger spiral is beginning to birth three smaller spirals. One of these spirals centers in your sacral chakra, located in your lower

belly. Allow this spiral to find a home in this energy center of your body. It will help preserve your Venusian connection for many weeks to come.

13. Watch as the second smaller pink spiral travels to your heart space and finds a perfect location in your heart chakra. Allow this second point of Venusian connection to strengthen and fully join with your body. Let this connection point remain in your body for many weeks to follow.
14. Watch as the third pink spiral travels up to the area of your third eye, between your eyebrows. Notice how it gently deposits itself into your third eye area, as if it truly belongs there. Allow this third connection point with Venus to remain in your body for many weeks to come.

Congratulations, your attunement with Venus is now complete! From this day forward, your initiation into Venusian mysteries begins. Venus has agreed to take you on as one of her students and personally oversee your progress.

Path of Venus: The Five-Petal Path

Every initiation into the Venusian path is unique. In the days of old, it could only be undertaken under the direct supervision of one of the priestesses of Venus. Below is one possible path, a suggestion for best integrating each lesson and each Venusian petal. However, this path isn't prescriptive; it is merely a beacon and a guide to align you with your perfect personal path that you must find on your own. As such, you may add or remove practices from the suggested list, as long as the general direction of your initiation matches the intention of each petal.

The First Petal – The Petal of Self

The first petal is a path toward self-love and should take no less than five days. It is an exercise in forgiving yourself and letting go of any notion of your shortcomings. This is a period of inner healing and shadow work that leads you to radical self-acceptance and toward recognizing your own unique spark, your value, and your soul gifts.

Step 1: Rewrite Your Story

This exercise allows you to write a new story of your life: the way you wish it had happened. Remove any traumatic experience that has occurred, and anything you felt was wrong about what you said, did, or felt in the past. The more time you devote to this exercise, the better the outcome.

Step 2: The Mirror of Self-Recognition and Self-Acceptance

Often, seeing ourselves clearly is the hardest thing. We are our own greatest blind spot.

In a meditative state, imagine traveling up to planet Venus, straight into her heart at the planet's core.

1. Here in the diamond-like heart of Venus, there exists a unique treasure: a mirror, tall and ornate. This is no regular mirror; it is a mirror that reflects the truth of what is.
2. Step in front of the mirror and ask it to reveal your greatest strengths, and then your greatest weaknesses. Watch what comes through, whether symbols, images, or words.
3. Imagine approaching the version of you standing in front of the mirror and giving them a loving, heartfelt hug. Tell that version of yourself how much you love and appreciate them.

4. Whatever you see, feel, or experience, please know it is a gift for you. Knowing yourself is the first step toward self-mastery. Remember, you are a work in progress; you are not meant to be perfect. If you see anything in the mirror that you don't like, any part of you that you disapprove of, practice radical self-acceptance.

Step 3: Why Did I Select Me the Way I Am? A Meditative Journey

What we look like, what we sound like, how smart we are—all aspects of ourselves are selected and determined by our Higher Selves before we take on an incarnation. Please understand that you didn't get to be the way you are accidentally or randomly; every aspect of you was carefully chosen to ensure that you experience the world in a certain way. However, you forgot the "why" behind it once you descended into a human body, so you lost the context.

In meditation, connect with your Higher Self—specifically the moment in time when they were selecting your physical body and other attributes that would make up your human avatar. Ask your Higher Self why they made the choices that they made. What were they optimizing for? What were they seeking to enable?

This meditative experience can be extremely liberating. It often shows you that the parts of yourself that you dislike actually serve a great purpose and are playing to your advantage, not the other way around.

Step 4: Write a Love Letter to Yourself

Point out all the amazing things you know to be true about yourself. Express the extent of your appreciation for all the good things you have and do. Give yourself compliments. Be honest. Find things about yourself that are genuinely amazing.

If writing from your own perspective is hard, imagine writing it from the standpoint of the person who loves you the most in life. Once the letter is written, place it over your heart, absorbing its healing and loving vibrations. Make sure to reread this letter whenever you are feeling down or have an episode of "not-enough-ness."

Lastly, start a self-love journal, where you can record all of your accomplishments, things you are genuinely proud of yourself for, and random acts of kindness you are showing yourself. Make it a habit to write in your self-love journal every day. And remember: love starts with you. You cannot truly love another if you do not love yourself.

The Second Petal – The Petal of Other (Petal of Empathy)

The second petal of the Venusian Rose should take no less than ten days (5 x 2 days). This is a deep dive into the hearts and auric fields of others. It is a sacred chance to open ourselves up to deep healing around relationships and the people who surround us.

This petal is an initiation into being able to see the world from a perspective other than our own, a surrender into deep empathy, empathic listening, empathic speaking, and compassionate action. This petal is about understanding that the most important thing we leave behind is our impact on others, on their hearts, bodies, and souls. The worth of our path is measured by the number of people we helped, served, loved, and cherished.

This petal of the Venusian path is about removing the obstacles between yourself and others, all the distortions in your energy field that are in the way of building healthy, long-lasting relationships. This petal requires major clean-up work and a willingness to leave no stone unturned when building authentic relationships.

Step 1: Meditate on the Healing Magic and Numerical Significance of the Number Two

The number two is a numerical sequence of the Divine Mother—her most raw, most fundamental vibration. Take time to ponder the significance of this expression. What are some things that come in twos? What are some of the dichotomies that come to mind? How would our world be different if one of the paired dichotomies were to disappear (for example, if we had light, but no darkness, or the reverse, only darkness and no light)?

The following practices can help you connect with and integrate the magic of this numeric frequency into your being.

Practice 1:

1. Write the number 2 on a blank sheet of paper. Then repeat it a few dozen times so that the entire page is filled with it.
2. Close your eyes and place your hands on the paper. Allow your hands to absorb the vibrational frequency of the page.
3. What comes through for you? What are you present with as you are experiencing this energy? How would you describe it? Is it pleasant or unpleasant, familiar of foreign?

4. If the energy is pleasant and you feel no resistance to it, allow your hands to absorb the torrent through your palms and send it straight to your heart space, filling it up bit by bit.

Practice 2:

1. Write down the Roman numeral II on a blank sheet of paper. Repeat it fifty or more times.
2. Halfway through the writing, let your attention become unfocused, allowing your eyes to almost see beyond the paper in front of you.
3. What is the energy that you are feeling? Does it have a color? A shape? A sound? What can it teach you? How is this energy different from that of the traditional Arabic numeral 2? Do they have any similarities? Is it opening up for you with additional facets you haven't noticed before? What do you think it represents in the Universe?
4. Feel free to absorb these vibrations into your heart space if they feel good.

Practice 3:

1. Close your eyes and imagine the number 2 written in the sky above you.
2. Stay here, absorbing the frequency.
3. What can you sense? What is this frequency telling you? What do you think it is meant to signify in the Universe? Does it oppose anything? What other energies and numerals support it?
4. Write down any insights you get in your journal for further introspection.

Step 2: Fully Returning to Your Lineage

Too often, we go through life not fully belonging, as if we are merely passing through, not intending to grow roots here, not meaning to lower our guard. This may manifest in many ways—low energy, a feeling of disconnectedness, loneliness—but very often, this manifests as a resistance to our lineage. Granted, each lineage has its challenges, so we may be forgiven for not always wishing to step into the murky waters and fully embrace our ancestral karma. According to the Law of Cause and Effect, karma is unavoidable, whereas the benefits of belonging to a lineage are not fully guaranteed. Regardless, your path of healing relationships should commence by walking into your lineage fully, connecting with it, and starting to draw power from it.

You can accomplish this by using the following practice:

1. In a meditative state, imagine that in front of you stands a majestic tree, with massive roots going down into the earth as far as the eye can see. What kind of tree is it?
2. Imagine that each of your ancestors is a branch on this grand tree. However, some branches are disconnected and hovering in midair. All of these branches are your ancestors who, for one reason or another, chose not to fully belong. Are you one of them, dear?
3. If so, attach the branch representing you back to the tree's trunk, sealing the reestablished connection point between you and the tree with golden light.
4. Watch as an energy exchange is created between you and the tree, flowing from the tree to you, to the branch, and back. You may even feel a shift in your physical body or a tingling sensation as the energy begins to fill up your body.
5. If you were attached to the tree trunk in the first place, simply fortify the connection and create additional pathways between you and the rest of the tree—pathways meant to transport energy. Allow the tree to fill you up fully, nurture you, and cater to what you need at this moment.
6. Enjoy being fully connected back to your lineage. This gift will keep on giving for the rest of your life.

Step 3: Healing the Wound of Betrayal and Rebuilding Trust

Betrayal is something that keeps us disconnected from others. It is like a persistent nagging voice in the background, reminding us how unsafe the world is and how trusting others may lead to regret. However, you cannot successfully complete the initiation of Venus without addressing the backstabbing wounds of the past. Whether you inflicted them, or those wounds were inflicted upon you, this is your chance to close that loop once and for all.

Step one of healing this wound is forgiving those who hurt you and asking for forgiveness in return. Wounding often goes both ways, even if you perceive yourself as the victim and not the tormentor. Betrayal is a manifestation of inner pain, and that tends to go both ways. Forgiving yourself is also critical; you cannot keep blaming yourself for aligning with the circumstances that bred the wounding of betrayal.

After the forgiveness step is complete, try the following simple healing meditation:

1. Imagine that the wounded aspect of you that has been betrayed is standing right in front of you. On an energetic level, betrayal manifests as a knife in the back. For many people, the back will be pierced with knives of all shapes and sizes.

2. Take out the knives, one by one, sealing the wounds with white light.
3. Mend your skin with the help of the golden threads of life and resurrection (they look like gilded threads of light). Make sure to restore all the tissues damaged by the knives. Once done, the back of this aspect of you should appear smooth and healed—no visible scars or blood in sight.
4. Once complete, imagine that in front of you, there emerges a collective light body of everyone you have ever betrayed. Every backstabbing wound you have ever inflicted will be visible in the back of this collective manifestation.
5. Take out the knives you placed there one by one, healing and mending the damaged tissues. Continue until no knives remain. As you are going through this process, you may experience glimpses of past life memories connected to each knife. However, trust that the process works even if you don't.

Step 4: Wearing Another's Perspective

Walking a mile in someone else's shoes may seem impossible for the average human, but it is both feasible and advisable in spiritual healing. This practice is best if you are experiencing conflict or tension with another person. Often, we are so absorbed in our own perceptions that we develop tunnel vision and a complete inability to step outside our limited perspective. Luckily, most conflicts could be resolved instantly if we only allowed ourselves to step into another's perspective without reservation or judgment.

1. In a meditative state, imagine a person you are trying to better understand standing before you. See that there is a thread of light connecting the two of you. What chakras does the thread connect? (Usually, the thread will connect the same chakras—heart to heart or throat to throat, for instance.) What color is the thread? Does it seem distorted in any way?
2. Notice that the person in front of you is wearing a protective cloak. The cloak allows them to hide their inner thoughts, feelings, and emotions from you and the world. Come closer and ask permission to try on the cloak.
3. If permission is granted, take the cloak off their shoulders and place it around yourself. You will experience a strange sensation of being in two places simultaneously. One version of you will be wearing the cloak, and the other will be standing in front of you, as if you could see both through your own eyes and the eyes of the other.
4. Think through the conflict or a recent argument you had with this person. Then allow yourself to be transported into that argument, only watch it transpire

as a spectator. Look at yourself amidst this conflict. What is true about you at this moment?

5. While wearing the cloak (the point of view of the other person), how do you come across to them? What is it about you that pushes their buttons? What is their true opinion of you at this moment? What is it that they wish they could communicate to you?
6. Ask yourself, what is driving this person? What motivates them? Why are they the way they are? Notice how their perspectives feel both valid and valuable. They just make sense to you, because for a moment, you merge with their consciousness, becoming it.
7. Now, look back at the thread that connects your two bodies. Having seen and lived in the perspective of the other, what can you do to help bridge the gap between the two of you? Now that you understand where they are coming from, what does it make possible for you and your relationship?
8. Write down your insights in your journal, then act upon this renewed understanding once you encounter this person in real life.

If you practice this enough times, it will become easy to momentarily wear the perspective of another during an argument. It can be a quick in-the-moment connection and give you insight into how to relate and communicate with them, so that harmony and consensus can be achieved. This tool can become one of the more powerful ones on your path to true connection.

Step 5: Practicing Empathy and Deep Listening

Division of any kind is both temporary and illusory, as oneness is the most stable of all energy forms. Practicing empathy is a self-care tactic and helps shift how the world perceives you. It tilts the scales of cosmic justice in your favor.

Empathy starts with deep listening—the kind where you listen with the purpose of understanding as opposed to reacting. Deep listening is wise, it is quiet, and it is transformative. Make it a habit to truly hear people when they speak to you. Listen with your whole being, not just your ears. True listening is hearing the thoughts, emotions, and energetic vibrations of another. It is only possible by connecting with someone beyond the physical level. Through this simple act, you become transformed. You become water, able to hold the fullness of another being.

Deep listening is a means of building lasting and healthy relationships. Deep listening is perceiving someone fully, without judgment, without projecting parts of yourself onto them. Deep listening is not having strings attached to the outcomes of the thoughts and actions of another. Deep listening is letting someone else be themselves fully in your presence. People will always respond positively to the one who practices empathy and deep listening. People will remove their armor and their protection in your company, and they will feel free to share their hearts without reservation. You will become a confidant, a healing presence, and a breath of fresh air in their life. Practice empathy, and watch your world transform.

The Third Petal – The Petal of Bridges (Petal of Connection and Unification)

This petal is an invitation to open your heart to love—earthly, cosmic, or otherwise—and should take no less than fifteen days (5 x 3 days). It is all about building bridges and connections where there used to be none.

As you are working through the shifts and transformations of the Third Petal, try the following:

- Select a few people from your past whom you would like to better understand. In a meditative state, connect to their consciousness, and watch the events of the past that involved you from their perspective. What are you seeing? How is the situation different from their perspective? What is driving them at this moment? How do you truly make them feel? Take the learnings from this exercise into your conduct and relationships.
- Practice responding instead of reacting throughout this period. Every time the Universe throws you a curveball, take a deep breath and seek to gain perspective. What is the Universe seeking to communicate to you at this time? If another person is involved in a situation, challenge yourself to look at the world through their lens. What can you see? Knowing what you know now, how should you feel about the situation? What can you do to make it better?
- Help someone in need, but allow this action to come from your heart. The Universe always puts people who need our help on our path. Train yourself to actively notice these people and provide assistance in a way that is authentic to you, without draining your own resources, but in a way that helps to uplift another.

Step 1: Allowing Your Heart to Come Out of Its Shell

Around each heart is a shell, which is a form of protection, not unlike the shell of a crustacean. It has been formed over many lifetimes of heartache, betrayal, and pain. This shell is a fortress, a defense mechanism that hides the scar tissue of your past wounds. It was once created to protect you from future heart wounding. The issue? It also prevents true heart-felt connection; you cannot have it any other way. The following meditative practice can help you free your heart.

1. In meditation, allow yourself to focus on your heart.
2. Notice how your heart is surrounded by a thick white shell resembling an eggshell.
3. Allow yourself to break or dissolve this shell. You can use a hammer, or call upon the assistance of "cosmic acid," a transparent liquid that can dissolve anything unwanted.
4. Know that the time has come for you to shed this shell, like a snake sheds a skin it has outgrown. There is so much connection waiting for you if you can get out of your own way.
5. Watch as your heart begins to come out of its shell, the protective walls falling apart to reveal your beautiful, warm, loving heart.

Step 2: Building Bridges – A Practice

Now that your heart is back to its original, untarnished, perfect state, you are ready to build bridges. At this point, who you are building bridges with is less important than the fact that these bridges actually exist. This practice invites more meaningful connections into your life. Magic like this can last lifetimes.

Imagine that your heart is a temple that is surrounded by deep waters. Historically, these waters have protected you from unwanted visitors and made you feel safe. But this illusion came at the expense of being truly close to others, fully letting them into your heart space.

1. Imagine that in every direction, new bridges are beginning to form.
2. Watch as these bridges cross the deep waters, firm and steady, offering a welcome safe haven from the raging waters below.
3. Imagine how many souls are starting to cross the waters using the bridges you have constructed.
4. Watch as these souls approach your heart temple and choose to stay there as your dear guests.

Step 3: Increasing Your Capacity to Love

When we invite enough of a new caliber of energies into our auric fields, eventually, we run out of space. Our energy bodies need to be constantly upgraded to ensure there is enough room for new energy to enter.

To increase your heart's capacity to give and receive love, use the following practice:

1. Focus on your heart space in a meditative state.
2. Imagine that your heart is starting to grow and expand, creating new pockets and compartments within itself.
3. Declare that your heart space is doubling, and watch it expand to fit your wishes.
4. Then double your heart space again, and double it once more, while filling every pocket within your heart space with the most beautiful high-vibrational emerald light.

Helpful tips to get you through the third petal stage successfully:

- Reach out to your loved ones and remind them how much you love them.
- Write at least one love letter to a person of your choosing, telling them how much you appreciate them and what they truly mean to you. Ideally, you would give the letter to the person, although this step is optional.
- Share more of who you are with the people you like and care about. Tell them something meaningful about yourself that you have never told anyone. Allow yourself to be vulnerable and share freely. Find your truth and authenticity in pouring your heart out to the people in your life.
- Practice active listening. Do not interrupt another. Do not react by relating what is said to your own life or experiences. Simply be with them as they share and ask questions from a place of authentic interest and caring.
- Challenge yourself to meet new people and make at least three meaningful connections during this time.

The Fourth Petal – The Petal of Sacrifice

What are you willing to give up to get to where you'd like to be? This petal is an invitation to release that which no longer serves you, to shed the layers, to liberate yourself, mind, body, and soul. This petal should take no less than twenty days to complete (5 x 4 days). The path to getting there lies in restriction and limitation, an ancient practice of ascesis. Ascesis is an act of temporarily giving up a habit or an activity that you know may not be serving you. The fourth petal requires three types of ascesis: physical, mental, and emotional. It is up to you to select what you want to give up. The more attached you are to something, the better.

Examples of physical addictions you may choose to give up:

- Sugar
- Alcohol
- Cheese
- Coffee

- Chocolate
- Meat
- Gluten

Examples of mental addictions you may choose to give up:

- Social media
- Digital games
- Cursing
- Watching TV
- Gambling
- Judging others
- Gossiping
- Complaining
- Negative self-talk

Examples of emotional addictions you may choose to give up:

- Sex
- Parties
- Going out (restaurants, clubs, etc.)
- Impulse buying
- Intoxicants
- A favorite hobby
- Dating
- Texting
- Treating yourself
- Overeating

The ascesis should last for the full twenty days to be effective.

The Fifth Petal – The Petal of Attainment (Petal of Solitude)

This is a period of deep contemplation, where you, the initiate, must spend one to two hours meditating daily. Solitude is also required for this period, with the initiate spending as much time alone as possible, and this time should last no less than twenty-five days (5 x 5 days). Large parties and gatherings are prohibited during this time of contemplation. During this period, it is not uncommon for you to receive commissions and tasks from Venus herself as she oversees the last steps of your journey. Remember, Venus will never ask you for more than you can give, but she can and will challenge you. During this stage, your communication and intention are purified. Be vigilant with your words; words have special power during this initiation stage.

Some rules to keep in mind:

- Spend three hours each day in silence. (This may include the hours spent in meditation.)
- Speak no evil.
- Don't tell lies.
- Don't gossip.

- Don't be too wordy. Keep it short.
- Don't interrupt others.
- Be in nature as much as possible.
- Isolate yourself from negative people.
- Listen more than you speak.
- Learn to hear the sounds of nature—the wind, the water, the birds.
- Learn to recognize the different "voices" of planets and celestial objects—Venus, the sun, Mercury, Uranus, etc.
- Some of your most critical spiritual habits are going to be formed during this stage of contemplation. Some of the greatest mysteries will be revealed to you. Your purpose on this Earth may become crystal clear. The veil of forgetfulness will start to thin, flooding you with memories of past lives and times long gone.

Guidance: It may be advisable to undertake a *vipassana* retreat during this stage to enhance the outcomes and results of your sacred pilgrimage.

Practices: Other Ways of Working with the Venusian Rose

Here are some additional practices to help deepen your connection with Venus, bringing you even closer to her transformative healing magic.

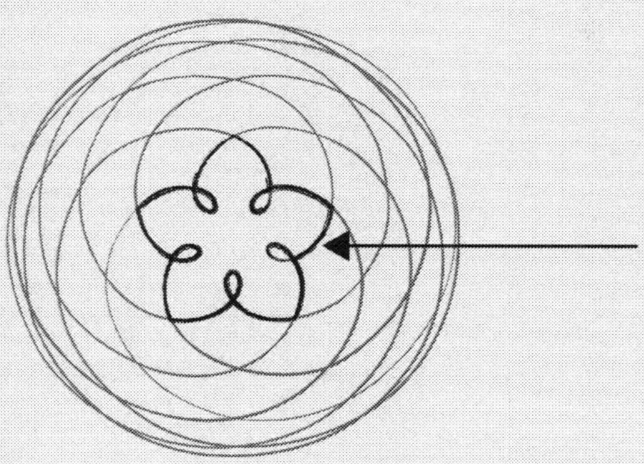

Figure 55: The Venusian rose, simplified

The blue and pink meditation: In meditation, imagine the simplified version of the five-petaled Venusian rose (refer to **Figure 55** above). See it light up with blue colors, then watch as it starts to pulsate and turn pink. Notice that the petals of the rose gently shift from blue to pink and back again. Imagine the rose starting to send transmissions straight into your third eye area. See it as a stream of codes or colors. You may start getting instant verbal or visual guidance and messages. But even if this process doesn't happen naturally, do not worry; you will be able to unpack the wisdom received in the days following the meditation.

Pentagram of Venus: Draw the simplified version of the pentagram of Venus (refer to **Figure 55**), tracing each petal carefully. Form it into patterns, or fill up a blank page with multiple sketches of the pentagram. Once it is complete, place the palms of your hands over the drawing, absorbing the emanations of the page. Imagine the healing vibrations of Venus entering your physical and light bodies, providing the remedy and resolution for anything that is bothering you. Ask planet Venus for a blessing in one of your current undertakings.

Venusian Rose: Print out a pattern of the Venusian rose and place it under a carafe or bottle of your drinking water to charge it with healing Venusian vibrations (using the same practice you used in Chapter 2, page 41).

Amulet: Make an amulet with the pattern of the Venusian rose and wear it on your body to attract the perfect partner into your life. The pattern can be carved into wood, engraved in metal, or hand-painted; there is no wrong way of doing it. Similar amulets can be created to get pregnant or to have an easy birth. Just make sure to wear it until the desired outcome is achieved.

Venus Correspondences

Energy likes to cluster together; like attracts like. There are several objects and phenomena in the Universe that vibrate at the frequency of the planet Venus. Surrounding yourself with these objects will help you better align with the planet and maintain your strong connection with it over time.

- White florals (e.g., jasmine, tuberose, camellia, wisteria, heliotrope, magnolia)
- Roses and rose water
- Five-petaled flowers
- Certain trees in bloom (e.g., apple, cherry, plum, pear, orange)
- Certain fruits and berries (e.g., apples [especially red], plums, peaches, strawberries, raspberries, watermelon)
- Herbal teas (e.g., hibiscus, rooibos, Moroccan mint)
- Honey
- Vanilla
- Cocoa and dark chocolate
- Crystals and gemstones (e.g., ruby, carnelian, pink chalcedony, peridot, emerald, rhodonite, pink tourmaline, kunzite, opal)
- Day of the week: Friday
- Element: water
- Time of day: dawn and sunset
- Ritual baths, especially with flower petals and salts
- Stretching
- Taking naps
- Singing
- Dancing

When working with Venus, especially in the early days, you will find that surrounding yourself with objects that vibrate at the frequency of Venus enables deeper meditations and helps you get the most out of the time you devote to harnessing Venusian powers.

Heart Space: On Fresh-Cut Roses

I saved the roses today, the ones standing tall in my vase.
I gave them a second life.
She said, "Do not kill the roses by cutting their stems."
She said, "They bring the aura of death."

But I looked upon my roses today, and all I saw was life.
I saw the Mother in them. I witnessed her love,
the depth of her joy, the treasures of her heart.
My roses have been blooming for weeks now, cut stems notwithstanding.

I used to replace my fresh-cut blooms every week.
Now, they stay with me for weeks at a time,
Blooming bigger, brighter,
Sharing their life force with me.

The one who carries life will always witness life.
Such is my bias.
I choose life in all of its forms, all of its facets, all of its splendor.
So, I choose to only witness life inside of my vase today.
I declare my roses perfectly alive.
I declare them a blessing from the Mother.

And so they are.

CHAPTER 12

The Two Faces of Venus

The magic of Venus is layered and complex. Her essence is indelibly more than the sum of her individual parts. Venusian mysteries in and of themselves are a large part of the realm of the Akashic Records, devoted to Divine Femininity. While we do not have the luxury of delving into the full extent of Venusian lore within the constraints of this book, our introductory foray into Venus would be incomplete without a thorough examination of her two main archetypes, the two main facets that lie within the heart of our celestial Goddess. Together, these two core aspects make up the fullness of the planet's journey, her unique vibrational resonance, and her conscious imprint.

Core Aspects of Venus

These aspects are that of the dawn or morning star—a herald of new beginnings—and the evening star, a symbol of cosmic wisdom and omniscience. Below, we explore each of these aspects and how you can partake of their magic on your soul's path of development.

The Morning Star Aspect: Lucifer, Dawn Star, Morning Star, East

Lucifer is the original aspect of Venus, the light-bringer planet. It is her maiden state, her most youthful, raw, unscripted, and hopeful energy. The ascension path of Venus started with her Lucifer phase, the first light before dawn, the torch that manifests before the morning sunlight, one of the softest aspects of heavenly fire. Lucifer is all about new beginnings. It is the time of the spring equinox, the beginning of the cosmic year, where nature is coming out its slumber after a long and dark winter. Lucifer is symbolic of hope. It is the harbinger archetype—that which holds a promise that there will indeed be light.

Lucifer is the first torch, the precursor to daylight, stubbornly appearing before the sun to signify its inevitable coming. The Lucifer aspect represents hope, youthful naivete, purity, recalibration, the zero state, and the blank slate. It is a state of resourcefulness that gives rise to new creations, projects, and blessings. The ultimate aspect star of new beginnings, change, and transformation, the energies of Lucifer are both healing and full of promise. They are forgiving and moldable.

It is this aspect of Venus that symbolizes the womb, the most creative of all female spaces. But beyond just being the container for new things to emerge, Lucifer also provides the resources and the energy to make things happen. It is the first torch of the morning star that gives momentum to new beginnings, turning them from ideas into full-fledged happenings.

Attributes and correspondences of Lucifer:

- Pink
- Rose quartz
- Sunrise
- Spring
- Cranes and swans
- Silks and tulles
- Veils and flowing clothes
- Singing
- Tibetan singing bowls
- Flower crowns
- Essential oils of sandalwood, orange blossom, and peony

Working with the Lucifer aspect of Venus:

- Call upon the morning star when embarking on a journey or starting a new project. Venus can provide protection and remove obstacles from your path.
- Call upon Lucifer when your situation appears bleak or dark, and you cannot find a way out. As the torch in the dark, Venus can help you overcome even the direst of circumstances.
- Call upon the morning star aspect in any creative endeavor, whether writing a book, beginning a painting, or even starting a social media account. Venus is a patron of artists and creators, and her energies will ensure the success of any creative undertaking.
- Call upon the morning star when you are seeking to get pregnant or would love to ease the birthing process. Lucifer is a protector of mothers and babies and can ensure that the pregnancy, birth, and early years of a baby's life are as easy and enjoyable as possible.
- Call upon the morning star to help align you with your soulmate. Lucifer is a fierce protectress of young love and will always assist you in finding "the one," if your intentions are pure and true.

The Evening Star Aspect: Vesper, Dusk Star, Evening Star, West

Vesper represents the pinnacle point of the arc of the ascension of planet Venus—the point of heightened awareness, deeper knowing, and magical ability that Venus attained as she moved along her evolutionary path.

With Vesper, the naivete and purity of Lucifer are long gone, replaced by deeper knowing, experience, and wisdom. Vesper is the one who passed the tests and moved beyond the rites of passage into her purpose.

Vesper is the last torch, the light that shines bright when most other light is gone, the last lantern burning amidst even the deepest of nights (i.e., Kali Yuga, the cosmic winter). It is therefore a guiding star, a female companion to the masculine North Star. She is the way-shower, the one who has traveled the paths uncharted and reemerged, able to lead others. Vesper reminds you that you can always find light within your soul, even when the outside reality seems bleak.

Vesper is a sage, a guru, a teacher, the one who mastered magic, the holder of knowledge, the one with the answers, the one who leads the way. Vesper is also the witch and the sorceress aspect of Venus. She is the high priestess who took her rightful place among the sages of our galaxy. She is the holder of secrets and mysteries, the keeper of records, and the one who protects and guards sacred knowledge from unworthy prying eyes. But she is also the one who would work with the worthy ones, taking them by the hands and nudging them forward on a path of deeper knowing.

Vesper is the star that closes the cycle and brings things to fruition, the star of the harvest, the star of final attainment. She is the last step, the final frontier, the last breath we take, and the experience we carry when we depart to other planes. She is one of the powers in charge of the dreamscape and the veil of forgetfulness. For the deserving one, she can open a path of connecting to even the most restricted sections of the Akashic Records, shedding light on what is concealed from most. She is a way and a path toward true wisdom, not unlike the Sophia aspect of the Divine Mother.

Attributes and correspondences of Vesper:

- Periwinkle, light blue, and violet
- The dreamscape
- Divination
- The tarot
- Clairvoyance
- The high priestess archetype
- The Akashic Records and past lives
- Ravens

- The third eye chakra
- Mantles and cloaks
- Amethyst and lapis lazuli
- Astrology and astronomy
- The night sky

Working with the Vesper aspect of Venus:

- Call upon Vesper if you are studying astrology, tarot, or other divination modalities. Connecting with this aspect of Venus will speed up your learning process and help unlock insights unique to you and your experience of these modalities.
- Call upon Vesper when you need to successfully complete a project, especially if you have been working on it for a long time, but cannot seem to get it across the finish line.
- Call upon Vesper when you are ready to receive deeper guidance from spirit. She can help reveal your unique path and mission, shed light on your soul gifts, and enable you to move past your limitations via shadow work.
- Call upon Vesper when you are ready to call a guru or teacher into your life. This teacher may show up physically or etherically. Their lessons may be tough, but they will always lead you to where you need to go.
- Call upon Vesper when you need to better understand your dreams and other symbols from the Universe. Symbolic language is her forte, and she loves sharing her wisdom and insights.
- Call upon Vesper for past life regressions. She can help align you with the lives that have the highest probability of shedding light on your current challenges, the lives that could lead to the deepest healing.
- Call upon Vesper for healing of any kind—physical, energetic, or emotional. Vesper's healing wisdom runs deep, and she will go out of her way to help the worthy ones.

The Arc of Venus

Collectively, Lucifer merging into Vesper represents the arc of Venus (see **Figure 56**), bringing together the planet's energies in a cohesive storyline and a continuous cycle of death and rebirth. The first torch of dawn, the beginning of the Venusian cycle, is followed by the last torch, the precursor to rebirth and renewal. As such, Venus carries an imprint of a phoenix within her core, an alchemical power for self-renewal and shifting that leads to arcs of higher wisdom. With every Venusian cycle, the planet becomes ever wiser, able to take on even bigger challenges and cover more ground.

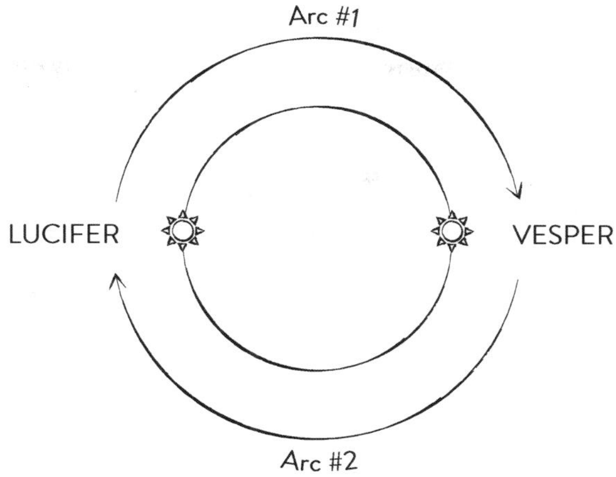

Figure 56: The Arc of Venus

It is through the merging of the two polarities that the Goddess aspect of Venus starts to rise and thrive. Without Lucifer, Venus would be a crone, jaded and incomplete. Without Vesper, Venus would be a forever blushing maiden, unsure of her own resources, unsteady on her feet. The daily cycle of Venus is magnetic; it creates a vortex of constant renewal with light at its core. To humanity, Venus may not be the glaring sun, hot and blinding, but she will always be a torch that burns through times of darkness and difficulty. She draws her power and strength from an enviable phoenix-like ability to self-start and constantly regenerate herself, forever rising from the ashes to greet a new day.

The same alchemical power of self-renewal is available to you through the energy flow in the body called the Loop of Venus (see **Figure 57**). The Loop of Venus is your invitation to merge the vibrations of Vesper and Lucifer within your own body. This alchemical process of constant renewal will grant you an endless creative resource you can tap into, no matter your objective. Once integrated, the Loop of Venus fosters self-expression, enabling you to find your inner balance and joy, preserving your youth, and helping you live a healthier and happier life.

Practice: Establishing the Loop of Venus

The Loop of Venus is an energy circuit between your heart and throat space that factors in the correspondences with Lucifer (left shoulder) and Vesper (right shoulder) within the body.

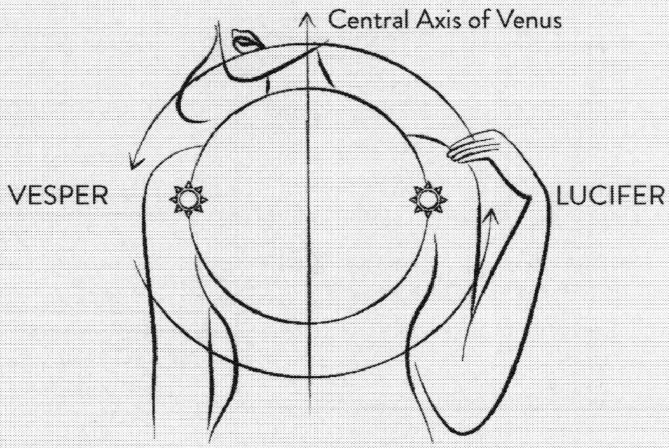

Figure 57: The Loop of Venus

What the Loop of Venus can assist with:

- Manifesting things, large and small
- Healing—physical, mental, and emotional
- Infusing you with energy or balancing your energy field for optimal performance
- Improving your creativity and capacity for self-expression
- Getting you into the flow
- Aligning you with Divine Feminine energies

The practice:

1. Close your eyes and settle into your body. Use your breath to center yourself. Take five to seven deep breaths into the center of your chest, activating your heart space.
2. Focus on the area of your left shoulder. This is the part of your body that corresponds with Lucifer, the morning star aspect of Venus. As such, this is an area of your body that can give you the energy and momentum to

start something new, look at things from another angle, and find out-of-the-box solutions to your problems.

3. Imagine a sphere of pink light starting to rotate in the area of your left shoulder. Watch as the sphere's spin creates a vortex of energy. Feel how your shoulder is coming alive, as if awoken from slumber.
4. Now, shift your focus to your right shoulder. This part of your body corresponds to Vesper. It gives you the momentum to successfully complete what you start, to reap the benefits of your actions, and to attract abundance. Imagine a sphere of periwinkle-blue light starting to rotate in the area of your right shoulder. Watch as the rotation speeds up, creating a vortex of energy.
5. Now, imagine an impulse of energy that looks like a shooting star in your left shoulder. Watch as this white star starts to travel up the circular orbit into the very center of your throat, activating your throat chakra. Allow the star to remain here for a few moments, pulsating with white light and awakening your throat area.
6. Once your throat area is sufficiently activated, watch as the white star travels down its circular orbit straight into your right shoulder, activating Vesper. Notice how the white light emanating from the star is starting to pour into your right shoulder, creating a feeling of pulsation and a slight tingling in your right shoulder.
7. Once your right shoulder is sufficiently activated, watch as the white star travels down the circular orbit into the area of your heart. Watch as the white healing light starts to fill your chest cavity and your heart space, activating and healing it.
8. Finally, once the heart space is sufficiently activated, watch as the white star completes the circle by traveling up its orbit into your left shoulder.

The following steps are optional:

9. Now, focus on a wish or desire, the one thing that would make your life immeasurably better if only you had it.
10. As you are focusing on this desire, jump-start a new Loop of Venus, allowing the white star energy to take you through Lucifer, up to your throat area, down to Vesper, down to your heart, and finally, completing the cycle in your left shoulder once again.

11. Repeat the cycle twice more (for a total of three) while keeping your intention or desire top of mind.
12. Thank Venus for working with your intention today and helping you manifest it into physical reality.

Repeat the Loop of Venus whenever you want to infuse your intention or desire with more energy and give it more momentum for manifestation.

Heart Space: Two Eyes to See, One Eye to Know

Inanna loved Earth very much. There was just something about this blue-green planet, her Terra, that spoke to her very soul. It was because of this love that she decided to create a human race here, alongside her tribe, her friends, and her family. The version of *Homo sapiens* she was working on was neither the first of its kind nor the last, but it was nonetheless hers, and that made all the difference. She and Enki had a vision—a dream, rather. A dream that one day, this fledgling new race could open up the power of their natural magnetism, the mighty force of their hearts, and change themselves and the world. But that day was long in the future.

Today, Inanna was unsure. The work on this new race of beautiful beings was almost complete, but she couldn't shake the feeling that something was missing.

"Deep in thought again, aren't you?" The soft voice of Enki startled her.

"Oh, you know, the usual. Worried about my babies, that's all," she said, her voice laced with concern. "I just hope we're doing right by them, setting them up for success."

"The Lunar Matrix is strong here. You and I may not be able to reach them once our mission here is complete. They will have to fend for themselves," said Enki thoughtfully.

"That's what I'm afraid of. The matrix is too strong here, too omnipotent, too viscous. It's quite inescapable."

"Not inescapable. I hear our colleagues from the east are experimenting with what they call a dragon eye, a third eye—the invisible sort. Apparently, they've figured out a way to connect it to the collective Dragon Tribe consciousness, so they can watch over their humans even from the remotest place in the galaxy."

"Neat!" exclaimed Inanna, her cheeks taking on an excited pink tint. "Two eyes to see, one eye to know. I have a better idea, though: I shall give them a lotus."

"A lotus? Do you mean the Arcturian lotus?"

"The very same! We'll embed the etheric codes of the lotus in their pineal glands. It will be a doorway to awakening, their doorway to you and me, to the greater consciousness, to Source itself."

"And you think such a thing can be done? Using a lotus is ... unconventional," said Enki, his forehead creasing.

"You'll see!" said Innana excitedly, placing a light kiss on Enki's forehead. "Two eyes to see, one eye to know. This makes so much sense!" she chimed and ran out of the tent, carried on the wings of her new idea.

"Indeed," said Enki. "The Arcturian lotus it is."

CHAPTER 13

Sacred Flowers

Of the many flavors of magic, the magic of flowers is perhaps the most feminine. Flowers are blessings of the Goddess, brought to Earth from higher realms. At one point, Divine Feminine energies were notoriously hard to anchor within the solar system, due to its density and strong affinity with masculine energies. Hence, the vibrations and essences of flowers were used as a loophole, a bridge between worlds, and a herald of the times to come—the days when femininity would take its rightful place within the solar system. Each flower anchored on Earth held within itself a strand of the energies of the Divine Mother, one of her inherent defining characteristics.

The ancients believed that before a goddess makes her presence known, she sends a flower as her messenger, the harbinger of her arrival. Many are the faces of the Goddess, and ample are the flowers upon the lands of the Earth. Each flower chants a single note within the octave of femininity. Collectively, they represent the full range of the Goddess, her unique imprint within the planetary fabric.

Not all flowers are created equal. They range in the caliber of their vibrations, healing properties, and energetic imprints. While each flower is a Divine creation and anchor, some flowers hold a special place in the history and path of our beautiful planet. Below, we'll explore some of the main sacred flowers, how they have become a part of the planetary narrative, and the special place each of them holds within the fabric of this world. Understanding and working with the sacred flowers has always been the domain of the feminine priesthood, and it is time that we revive some of this forgotten and overlooked lore.

Rose

- **Location:** Higher and lower heart
- **Symbolizes**: Unconditional love, beauty, togetherness, interconnectedness, redemption, forgiveness, the embrace of the Divine Mother, the love imprint in lower-dimensional worlds
- **Vibration:** Love, empathy, forgiveness

- **Blocked by:** Indifference, apathy
- **Enhanced by:** The act of surrender
- **Shadow:** Jealousy, envy
- **Element:** Fire and water

Mystical. Soft. Delicate. Refined.

The favorite floral of maidens, goddesses, and poets, the majestic rose has captivated hearts and minds for millennia. Many sacred rites and religious ceremonies were presided upon and witnessed by this queen of flowers, her emanations both aristocratic and understated in the same breath. The rose is perhaps a perfect metaphor for a spiritual path well walked, a hypnotic movement upward through thorns to the covetable land of petals, an ascension and a rite of passage, a spiral of evolution and a pilgrimage.

The energy of the rose is layered and delicate. She is a living ecosystem gently woven by the hands of the Mother from the gilded threads of destiny. The varieties of the rose are as numerous as the energies she represents. The climbing rose, the wild rose, the tea rose, the damask rose, and the English rose are just some examples. Moreover, the rose boasts an impressive color range, making it one of the most versatile flowers currently present on Earth.

The queendom of the rose is vast, and to fully comprehend it, we would need to spend some quality time with each of the rose varietals. Of course, that is well beyond the scope of this book, so we shall have to settle for looking at all the roses as one homogenous group—a rose collective consciousness, if you will, with its core emanation, purpose, and set way of being.

The rose is Divine Mother's emissary to Earth, her love letter to humanity, the truest extension of her gentle spirit. The Mother's signature is in every curve, every vein, every filament of this flower. Every rose is a living transmission of the codes of the Mother's infinite heart, a light language in flower form, a gentle reminder of our Divinity. That is why it feels so good to stop and smell the roses, to commune with their tender spirits. The emanations of the rose slow down the world around you, even if just for a moment, lifting the veil of heaviness upon your heart and allowing you to breathe new life and new joy into the folds of your soul.

The rose is indelibly connected with the life force itself. Spiritually, the flower stands for unconditional love, heart-centered living, true connection, deep bonds, renewal, surrender, and new beginnings. A rose is a purifier; she gets straight into your emotional and etheric bodies and clears any stuck or blocked energies. The rose creates a healing and nurturing space, gently raising the vibration of anything she touches.

Many female goddesses, sages, and saints have especially favored the rose. From Aphrodite to Isis, to Mary Magdalene and Mother Mary, the rose graced the homes and places of worship of thousands of notable women throughout the ages. And while the rose is undoubtedly beautiful, it is her understated ability to elevate the spirit and radiate harmony that keeps inspiring so many. A testament to the power of the rose to fortify and harmonize female-led ecosystems, the Order of the Rose, one of the most prominent female spiritual orders of all time, was named after this majestic flower. Moreover, it was not uncommon for the Temples of the Rose to be nestled in luscious rose gardens, their interiors generously scented with the highest-quality natural rose oils. Coincidentally, rose oil is the highest-vibrational of all essential oils, instantly offering a reprieve from daily troubles and a pathway toward more conscious and connected living.

Rose water and various rose oils were constant companions during the many rituals of the Order of the Rose, keeping the Mother's spirit present and her emanation within arm's reach for the many priestesses and initiates of the order.

Working with the Rose

The rose offers a rich territory of healing and spiritual properties to the modern-day seeker and mystic. Her magic, as potent as ever, is ripe for use on altars, in healing temples, and during sacred rites. Still, she is just as happy to be your day-to-day companion as you are working to integrate more Divine Femininity into your body and your life.

Rose Prayer: Did you know that angels and fairies love the smell of roses? Roses are true fairy magnets. Because of how high the rose naturally vibrates, it helps forge a bridge between you and the higher realms, making it easier for the angels and benevolent spirits to hear and act on your prayers. Simply place a few droplets of rose oil on your temples, wrists, and collarbones, then close your eyes and say a prayer. Rest assured that the power of your prayer to reach higher realms has increased tenfold.

Rose Baths: Taking a bath filled with rose petals is not just an indulgence; it can be a deeply healing ritual of alignment and getting back into your flow. A rose bath will be most helpful to you if you feel stressed or have been pushing too hard, gently bringing you back into equilibrium and allowing your inner feminine to unfold and take its rightful place in the limelight. A rose bath is a wonderful self-care practice for our hectic, overachieving, and schedule-heavy world.

Rose Cross: A rose offers you her blessings for any new project or any new beginning. To receive the blessing, you will need a few drops of natural rose essential oil.

The rose is connected with the shape of the cross, and its spiritual significance is enough that a secret society of the Rosicrucians[6] was formed to commemorate this sacred connection. The rose can activate the Holy Cross within your body (see **Figure 58**). The Holy Cross connects our third-dimensional reality (the horizontal axis of the cross) with higher spheres (the vertical axis).

To receive the blessing:

1. Close your eyes, then focus on what blessing you want to receive.
2. Take your rose oil and anoint your forehead (in the third eye area) and your higher heart (located around your thymus area). Then place a drop on your belly button, in essence completing a vertical line of the Holy Cross within your own body. Then place a drop of rose oil on your left shoulder, then the right shoulder, completing the horizontal axis of the Holy Cross within your body (refer to **Figure 58** below).
3. Once the rose cross is complete, imagine it filling up with energy and starting to pulsate.
4. Ask for a blessing from the rose, and watch a stream of light pour out of your higher heart area.
5. This stream of Divine bliss will be naturally distributed as a blessing to fuel your request and bring it to life.

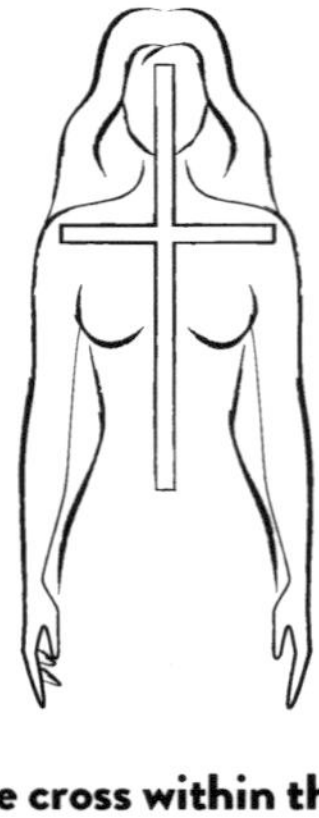

Figure 58: Rose cross within the human body

6 Rosicrucianism is a spiritual and cultural movement that arose in the early seventeenth century, after the publication of several texts announcing to the world a new esoteric order.

Rose Essential Oil

Here are a few ways to use rose essential oil:

- Placing a few drops around your heart area will help with heartache and moving through unrequited love.
- Sprinkling yourself with rose water will elevate your mood and soften any harsh edges energetically, allowing you to be gentler and more compassionate with those around you.
- Placing a few drops on your wrists will help unlock material abundance. Our hands are connected to our actions in the world, so placing rose oil there is like blessing our actions. Sacred action always brings about abundant reward; it is the universal law.

While you may not know what color of roses the essential oil came from, I would like to briefly reference the unique properties of the rose oils of each major color below.

White rose essential oil:

- Helps you cope with the loss of a loved one who has passed on
- Helps purify a new space (home, office; just add a few drops to a spray bottle and distribute it along the room's perimeter)
- Helps you connect to your Higher Self, your guardian angels, and even Source consciousness
- Helps you work through karmic knots and get aligned with your most optimal path
- Blesses newborns
- Assists with starting new projects
- Enhances meditation and your spiritual practice

Pink Rose essential oil (usually Bulgarian, damask, and Turkish roses are pink):

- Helps you find a romantic partner
- Helps solidify the union of a newly married couple
- Helps create deep bonds with people
- Heals heart trauma and abandonment issues
- Helps you find your own flavor of magic and generously share it with the world
- Helps bring together communities, especially female communities
- Enhances the dreamscape
- Brings about inspiration
- Enhances connection with the elementals

Red rose essential oil:

- Gives courage
- Helps you find your North Star and align with your intended path
- Heals your reproductive system and any wounding around sexuality and childbearing
- Enhances fertility
- Increases your natural magnetism
- Helps bring more abundance into your life and brings resources to you
- Helps with your mission

Lotus

- **Location:** Third eye
- **Symbolizes:** Enlightenment, connection to higher planes, connection to the Akashic Records, universal alignment, Divine wisdom, access to sacred knowledge
- **Vibration:** Unity, intuitive connection, deeper knowing
- **Blocked by:** A broken heart, unhealed pain, trauma in the lower chakras, blaming yourself and others, fear, an overactive "busy" mind
- **Enhanced by:** The act of surrender
- **Shadow:** Ego
- **Element:** Water and air

Ephemeral. Transportive. Divine. Radiant.

The majestic lotus is a guardian of the veil of forgetfulness, a master teacher, and the companion of sages, yogis, hermits, and mystics alike. It carries the torch of wisdom upon the earthly plane; such is the nature of its sacred service to humanity and our beautiful planet. In the flower kingdom, the lotus is synonymous with the all-seeing eye, the omniscient power of God/Goddess consciousness. The lotus is endowed with the property of existing in multiple dimensions simultaneously, stitching together the fabric of existence, and enabling energy flow, not unlike an acupuncture needle. Every lotus flower is an antenna that transmits information about the health of our local ecosystem to other planets, and it receives harmonization codes in return.

The collective consciousness of the lotus flower family is deeply connected to the stars of Sirius and Arcturus. At one point a genetic project of these evolved civilizations, the lotus flower is indeed an emissary from the stars. Every lotus flower creates a unique electromagnetic field that forms a protective dome-like structure around the flower and its surroundings. The dome is about 164 feet (50 meters) in diameter. This dome creates a temporary reprieve from the Lunar Matrix, ever present on Earth, which often prevents us from hearing our star allies. A lotus flower, therefore, is an opportunity to connect with a higher consciousness that may be otherwise obstructed from view.

The pineal gland (located in the center of the brain) and the magic of the lotus are intrinsically connected. As our vibration rises, we come upon a threshold, sometimes referred to as the threshold of the lotus—a point when the pineal gland is activated, regardless of how calcified it is. Those on the spiritual path looking to open their third eye often obsess with decalcifying their pineal gland, when a more logical step would be to address their vibration. Raising your vibration through consuming high-vibrational content, eating high-vibrational foods, and meditating daily will eventually lead you to the lotus threshold, which shall begin the process of decalcifying your pineal gland, giving you access to your "eye that knows."

No true teacher of spiritual mysteries ever steps onto the path of knowing without the blessing and the initiation of the lotus. Since the times of ancient Mesopotamia and ancient Egypt, the majestic lotus has been cultivated to foster humanity's spiritual development.

Blue Lotus: The rarest of all varieties, the blue lotus is vibrationally the closest thing to the original Arcturian lotus brought to Earth by higher civilizations. It was the blue Arcturian lotus that served as the prototype for our third eye etheric lotus. It is through connecting with its energy that we may broaden our horizons to include the invisible world of spirit. The blue lotus is known to help induce psychedelic states of varying intensity.

Like many plant medicines, the blue lotus has a lofty mission here on Earth: to uplift humanity and bring about the awakening of our race. Blue lotus tinctures and teas are healing and soothing. They help remove artificial constraints and walls we have built up in our lives and allow us to get back to the basics. By stripping away the unnecessary things, the blue lotus opens up a path for each seeker to walk—a path that leads beyond the veil of forgetfulness and toward spiritual wisdom. Moreover, blue lotus tinctures can induce lucid dreaming and deep theta states for healing and meditation. Lastly, blue lotus helps us connect with our star family, bridging the gap between their high-dimensional existence and our transitional state as we migrate into 5D consciousness.

White Lotus: This is the lotus of the teacher and the sacred flower of enlightenment. For millennia, the white lotus has been a symbol of spiritual royalty and missionary work here on Earth. The white lotus is reminiscent of the vibration of pure white light, the closest proxy to Source consciousness that we can witness on planet Earth. The white lotus is a symbol of being able to see beyond the veil, interdimensional travel, instant manifestation, and being chosen for a planetary-level mission. The white lotus is the flower of Buddha, a symbol of escaping samsara and of perfect knowing. Being seated on a lotus flower is a symbol of great recognition and reverence.

Pink Lotus: This is the flower of royalty, a universal symbol of abundance and of being chosen. It is no coincidence that many Hindu deities are depicted seated upon a pink lotus. Anyone who partakes in the wisdom of the pink lotus becomes a masterful creator, their personal slice of the matrix so potent that it starts seeping into the collective consciousness. Anyone blessed by the pink lotus gains God/Goddess consciousness, so while still in a human body, they become privy to the sacred rite of co-creation with Source.

The pink lotus also activates our etheric higher heart, opening a portal to perfect unity with everything that is. The vibrations of the pink lotus, when merged with a stream from our higher heart, can enable instant and deep healing of our bodies, including instant healing of chronic conditions. Additionally, the pink lotus works with our emotional body, helping release blockages within its folds. This lotus is a heart healer, gentle, yet extremely potent.

Working with the Lotus

The deeper you go on your spiritual journey, the louder the calling of the lotus becomes. Working with the lotus in its various forms will enable you to deepen your connection with spirit and your Higher Self, open higher levels of access to the Akashic Records, and help you better harmonize your light bodies.

Blue Lotus Tea

Make blue lotus tea by boiling two to three tablespoons of blue lotus petals and adding some honey to sweeten it, if you prefer. The blue lotus requires a prayer or an intention to be properly charged. Simply hold the cup of tea between your palms, focus on your heart space, and speak your intention for working with the lotus.

Today's blue lotus varieties are not as potent as the ones that once grew upon the banks of the Nile in ancient Egypt. Nevertheless, the impact of the blue lotus will accumulate over time, becoming more and more palpable. Partaking of blue lotus tea is a journey, not a silver bullet; it is a doorway into conscious living. At any point in time, there are thousands of etheric beings working through the blue lotus egregore, its collective energy structure. Invite them to work with you, and request anything in the realms of spirituality and consciousness that resonates with you.

The Lotus Path

The lotus path (see **Figure 59**) is a series of points within the body that can be activated by lotus essential oil to enhance meditation and bring about spiritual insights. The lotus path is a straight line connecting three points:

- **Point 1: Thymus** (higher heart area)
- **Point 2: Chin** (expression bridge)
- **Point 3: Forehead** (third eye area)

When activating the path, start with the lowest point around the thymus gland, and end with the third eye point, creating a path for the energies to ascend.

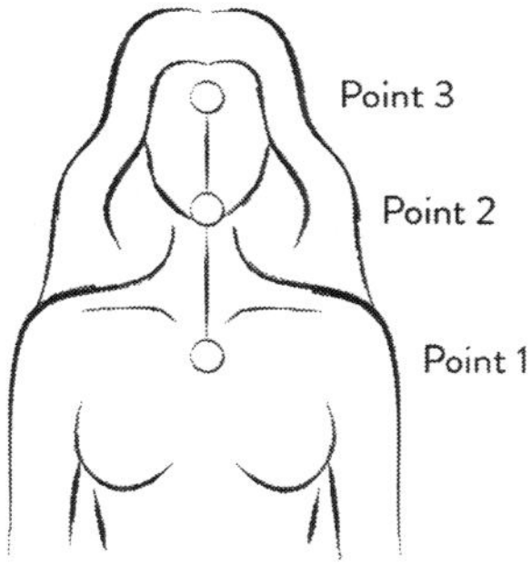

Figure 59: The lotus path

Activate each point by rubbing natural lotus essential oil into it clockwise. Make sure that you rub at least three full circles to activate the point. Trace the path from one point to the next with your fingers. This path is about the movement of energy, and tracing it with your fingers helps the energies ascend properly.

1. Once you reach the final point, located in your third eye area, close your eyes and imagine a lotus flower springing to life in the center of your head, right around your pineal gland area. Don't worry about getting the location perfect; this lotus placement inside your head is intuitive and innate, and you couldn't get it wrong if you tried.
2. Breathe into the lotus flower and watch it expand with each breath. Allow it to become larger and larger, gently separating from your body. Watch the lotus expand further, becoming large enough for you to be seated amidst its petals.
3. Notice a dome of white light that is now created over your head. This dome is both a protective field and a gateway to higher realms.

4. Notice that straight above you, there is a small opening in the dome, and through it, a stream of glimmering white light starts pouring in, washing you with its cooling, uplifting glow.
5. From this place, feel free to start your usual meditation practice, and notice how your connection seems stronger. Messages come through a lot easier, providing the necessary in-the-moment guidance for you.

Practice: The Lotus Circle

The lotus can help induce a calm and blissful state, enabling you to let go of your worries and troubles. Geometrically, the lotus works with the energy of the circle best. To partake of the protective calming power of the lotus, use the following practice:

1. Get seated in a lotus pose and close your eyes. Imagine that you are seated in the very middle of a circle. This circle is your personal sacred healing space.
2. Watch how numerous lotus flowers are starting to grow along the curvature of the circle, covering every inch.
3. Allow the lotus flowers to become fully grown. Once this happens, notice that each flower emanates a ray of white light, stretching from its petals to the top of your head, creating a cone-like structure. This is the protective power of the lotus circle.
4. Invite the bliss of the lotus to enter your heart space, and watch as each of the lotus flowers along the perimeter of the circle starts to share its radiance with your heart, melting away any protective walls and removing the defense mechanisms that exist there.
5. Feel calm come over your entire body, as if you were cradled by white light. Allow yourself to let go of any darkness, stress, or worry that has taken root in your body.
6. Breathe in the power of the lotus, while breathing out any darkness that may be stuck in your body. Allow the magic of the lotus to enter every cell, tissue, and organ.

You may ask the lotus to stay with you long after this meditative experience is over, protecting you from daily troubles and bringing about more flow in your life.

Lily

- **Location:** Palms
- **Symbolizes:** Divinely guided action, inspired action, energy exchange, healing, feminine power, power to give, acts of service
- **Vibration:** Action in a state of flow, healing, surrender
- **Blocked by:** Expectations, pressure, forcing timelines, low self-esteem
- **Enhanced By:** Connection with the North Star
- **Shadow:** Apathy, depression
- **Element:** Earth and water

Pristine. Divine. Solid. Pure.

The magic of the lily is understated and humble, but extremely potent. Like most Divine flowers, the white lily has been connected with the Goddess since ancient times. Whether in a myth about Hera feeding Hercules, or in a stone carving depicting Inanna of ancient Mesopotamia, the lily plays a central role in Goddess lore. It is believed that the lily dates back to the Garden of Eden, which is hardly a coincidence, given that the goddess Inanna, who loved the lily beyond all others, was a deity who personally oversaw the creation of Adam and Eve. Naturally, the official myth states that when Eve cried tears of sorrow following her fall from grace, her tears turned into white lilies that littered her path, forever leading her and Adam away from the comfort of the Garden of Eden. In truth, lilies existed in the garden when it was first seeded, long before the creation of Adam and Lilith, let alone Eve.

Christianity has perhaps adopted the lily as its favorite flower, more so than any other religion or spiritual movement, connecting it with both Yeshua and Mother Mary. In one story, the red lily came to be when Yeshua's blood dripped upon the petals of the white lily, marking a transition that took place through his sacrifice on the cross, his unique form of a divinely guided act of service. It is also rumored that the Garden of Gethsemane was covered in white lilies following Yeshua's crucifixion, a testament to his eternal life, imminent resurrection, and Divine connection. The white lily is also a symbol of Mother Mary and her nurturing love, continuing a long tradition of linking the flower's white petals with breast milk. There is a myth that describes the process of the Milky Way being created from a few drops of Hera's breast milk—the same breast milk that was rumored to have once upon a time created the white lily.

The mystery of the white lily captivated royalty just as much as it held the hearts of regular people. The House of Bourbon dynasty, for instance, went so far as to use the three-petaled lily in its heraldry. In medieval Europe, the lily became a symbol of political, religious, and dynastic power, favored just as much as the rose, and in certain places in Europe, even more so.

Spiritually, the lily is intrinsically linked with archangels and their work as emissaries. Often, Archangel Gabriel is depicted holding a bouquet of lilies, symbolizing that his communication comes directly from God. Many prophets, oracles, and seers report that before an apparition of an archangel or a vision of special significance, they can sense the scent of lilies in the air. Some are also shown a depiction of the lily flower alongside receiving a commission from God, always a symbol that the commission is given in pursuit of the Creator's plan.

The lily is a powerful symbol of alignment. It speaks to how interconnected we all are, whether at the soul level or here on Earth, reminding us that Spirit unites all of us. We share a spiritual lineage. We are all sparks of Source consciousness going through the motions of evolution, following a grand cosmic plan, momentarily straying off course and getting bruises along the way, but forever connected to our celestial parents.

The lily can enhance the strength of your prayer and intention if you place the flower's energetic copy in your heart space and allow it to infuse your speech as you utter a prayer or an invocation. And an etheric flower crown made of lilies can massively enhance your ability to receive communication from spirit, exponentially increasing the throughput of your crown chakra.

Working with the Lily

Given how connected the lily is to Divinity and the perfect Divine blueprint, it has an uncanny ability to open portals that allow one to move through timelines and possibilities with enviable ease, making them an alchemist in training.

Lily Oil for Working with Timelines

The magic of the lily allows you to speed up or slow down your personal timeline to better fit your needs. For instance, you can accelerate the manifestation of a goal or intention, while slowing down the spread of a virus. You can even use the lily to travel back in time to connect with your ancestors, or to rewrite a particularly nasty traumatic experience.

To accelerate something: Dip your index finger in lily essential oil and draw a clockwise spiral on your right palm. Keep going, adding circles to the spiral, gradually increasing and decreasing the amplitude of the spiral to create continuous movement. As you are drawing the spiral, think of something you would like to accelerate and picture an image of it solidified in your palm. Stay here for at least thirty seconds. Alternatively, the same spiral movement can help you move into your most optimal future, or bring you to your future self so you can connect and ask questions.

To decelerate something: Dip your index finger in lily essential oil and start drawing a counterclockwise spiral on the palm of your left hand. Close your eyes and concentrate on something you would like to slow down or even wind down completely. Imagine the energy of the spiral interacting with your wish, permeating it to the core and making the desired shift. This can be helpful in cord-cutting exercises[7] because it helps remove some of the karma associated with leaving relationships and organizations. Use the same counterclockwise movement to travel back in time to rewrite the script of what happened. This simple movement can also assist with past life regressions and allow you to see things more clearly and in detail.

Note: For these practices to work properly, you must use natural lily oil, not its synthetic counterpart.

---

7 Cord cutting is a way to spiritually sever your connections with people (even those who have passed, or with situations past or present) who sap your energy and prevent you from moving on.

Practice: The Lily Pyramid

The lily works closely with the pyramid shape, accentuating its power. Infusing the energy of the lily into a pyramidal shape can help cleanse your physical body and align you with your most optimal future. Lily-infused pyramids also help with mental and energetic decluttering, gently removing any thought forms, energetic parasites, and etheric structures that no longer serve your body.

1. Imagine that you are seated inside a pyramid made of white light. (Please use the pyramid with the triangular base; lily works best with the magic of the three—the mind-body-spirit trinity.)
2. Place a large lily at the top of the pyramid, imagining how it creates a downward stream of lily vibrations, as if lily-infused water were pouring down to wash over your body.
3. Place a lily at each of the three points at the pyramid's base, thus enclosing yourself within the lily-led Universe.
4. To cleanse and detox your body, imagine an upward stream of lily-infused energy flowing from the bottom of the pyramid and up through your body, cleansing and healing you.
5. Allow any darkness that is created in the process of this major release to exit through the tip of the pyramid.

Other Divine Flowers

While the rose, lotus, and lily are perhaps the most potent of the Divine flowers, they are not the only members of the flower kingdom connected with the Divine. Below is a quick overview of some other magical flowers and their uses for your life.

Orchid

The most Venusian of all flowers, the orchid holds the golden ratio, a symbol of perfect proportion and beauty once identified and coded into this reality by the Great Architect of the Matrix. The orchid has a unique ability to harmonize physical spaces. However, its impact is somewhat localized, reaching perhaps only seven to nine feet (two to three meters) in each direction, so for a large room, you'll need a few of these mystical florals. The orchid is a perfect housewarming gift, as it removes old stuck energies, like smudging with palo santo. The impact of the orchid is continuous and cumulative, further elevating the space the more time it spends in it. The white orchid infuses the space with healing energies, while pink or purple orchids bring forth the emanations of unconditional love and tender loving care.

Daisy/Chamomile

The flower of the maiden daisy is about as pure as they come. The daisy is about bringing things back to their perfect zero state, which is why chamomile tea is so soothing and calming during stressful days. Daisy can help enhance your intuition and assist you with better remembering your dreams. The daisy works well paired with the magic of the word. Chamomile tea reacts well to being charged with words and incantations, especially if you request a particular emotional state from the Universe, such as love, compassion, gratitude, etc. Simply speak your intention into the cup of chamomile tea as you are holding it between your hands. The daisy is a great listener and confidante. It is incredibly moldable, having the power to shift your emotional state quickly. Confiding in a daisy can feel as liberating as a church confessional, since the daisy gets straight into your heart space and removes any tension. She is a powerful heart healer.

Bluebell

The favorites of the elven and the fairy kingdoms, bluebells are high-frequency, intentional, and activating. Vibrationally, they work with three main chakras—the heart, throat, and third eye—providing much healing for each. Simply observing bluebells can assist with healing heartache and self-expression issues, especially those that come from past trauma or low self-esteem. Placing a few drops of bluebell essential oil on your skin around your heart space can help release any darkness or stuck emotions. A few drops of bluebell oil rubbed around your throat chakra can help you find a path for seamless self-expression, especially if you are preparing for an important conversation or a speaking engagement. Lastly, the bluebell is second only to the lotus in its uncanny ability to help activate your third eye. Rub a few drops of bluebell essential oil in a clockwise movement around your third eye area, then imagine a violet spiral of light emerging and clearing out any blockages. While this won't yield an immediate result, within a week of daily use, bluebell essential oil can help open your third eye.

Tulip

Tulips are truth-tellers. They are flowers of high integrity and honor, vibrationally close to Logos, the life-giving creative power of Source. Placing tulips in a place of study or work will assist your concentration and mental activity. Tulips work with the mental space around you, removing negative thought forms and belief structures and paving the way for more positive thought forms to come into your life. It is this property of tulips that makes them indispensable for manifestation. Tulips help absorb some of the EMF radiation from computers and phones, so having them on your desk while working could assist with that, too. However, living tulips are much better at absorbing electromagnetic radiation than fresh-cut stems, so if this is a property you are interested in, growing tulips in a pot is your best bet.

Sunflower

Sunflowers carry a frequency of eternal optimism and a glass half full. They are good at harmonizing relationships and helping people find consensus. A few fresh-cut stems on the dining table can assist digestion, as the sunflower is strongly connected with the solar plexus chakra and our digestive system. Observing and connecting with the sunflower will elevate your mood and help you make better decisions. If you are looking for a little pick-me-up or want to brighten your life, you cannot find a better floral companion than the sunflower.

Practice: Sacred Floral Triangle

This powerful activating practice lets you combine the magic of the three highest vibrational flowers in one continuous loop.

Activating the Sacred Floral Triangle will enable the following:

- A continuous healthy flow of Divine Feminine energies in your body
- Alignment with your highest good and your Higher Self
- A boost of energy that can propel you into divinely aligned action
- A close-knit connection between you and the Divine Mother

Figure 60: The Sacred Floral Triangle within a human body

The practice:

1. Take a comfortable seated position or lie down.
2. Start off by noticing your breath. Allow yourself to breathe in deeper, sending the life-giving air into your heart space, activating it. Imagine white light entering your heart space with every breath that you take.
3. Notice how the white light that enters your heart space is starting to coil up into a spiral. The spiral is beginning to rotate, first slowly, then faster and faster with every passing second, creating a vortex around itself.
4. Mentally, allow yourself to focus on this movement, watching it accelerate. The vortex movement is a powerful magnetic tool for healing and cleansing. Allow it to remove any blockages and dark clots from your heart area.
5. Watch as in the middle of your heart space, a rose blooms to life, unfolding its many velvety petals. The rose is layered, luscious, and soft. Notice how

what looks like morning dew emerges on the many petals of this immaculate flower. See how these precious drops are sliding down and falling into the rich soil of your heart space, bringing it much-needed nutrients. Allow the rose to share its many gifts with you, letting yourself receive everything that this Divine floral emissary has to offer today.

6. Now, slowly, move up to your headspace, momentarily focusing on the area of your third eye. Watch as a stream of violet energies enters your third eye area. Notice how this violet stream starts to coil into a spiral, moving in a clockwise direction, gaining momentum with each spin. Allow yourself to be present in this moment, ebbing and flowing, moving with the rotation of the spiral, merging with the infinite Universe around you.
7. Watch as the violet spiral creates a violet lake inside your third eye space. The lake is mesmerizing, round and deep, holding the wisdom of the generations that came before you, and perhaps so much more.
8. Witness how, from the depths of this lake, a lotus is starting to emerge. The moment the flower fully emerges on the surface, its petals glow with the most ephemeral violet light, raising the vibrations around it. As this violet emanation penetrates the cells of your headspace, they begin to transform, evolving into their most perfect, most pristine state. Watch any fissures, cracks, or imperfections of the cells disappear.
9. The violet light is a guiding light of transformation. Once it fills a space, all manner of healing is automatically triggered. Allow the violet light of the lotus to go wherever it wants to go within your body, removing any restrictions that may be in place. Simply surrender to this intuitive process.
10. Whenever the previous step feels complete, feel free to momentarily move your attention to your palms. Imagine a potent stream of ruby-red light entering each of your palms, coiling into a spiral the moment it hits your skin.
11. This spiral is fiery, strong, and activating. It starts creating a tingling sensation in your fingers, palms, and even wrists, temporarily forging an almost palpable energy field around your hands. Notice how the red spirals move up and down, piercing your palms. This is the energy of Divine and inspired action coursing through your body. This energy is fast, intentional, and extremely potent.

12. Notice how this energy activates something within your palms, as if the seeds planted there a long time ago are starting to come alive and sprout. Witness how, through those seeds, lilies start to grow, reaching higher and higher until they are fully grown.
13. Watch as the lilies rotate clockwise, further increasing the energy movement in this part of your body. Notice how, due to this movement, energy starts to accumulate at the base of the lilies. This is the energy of pure potential. Imagine multiple empty glass tubes located around your hand space. Send the incredibly valuable energy of potential and action generated by the lilies into those tubes, filling them to the brim, one after another.
14. Keep gathering this energy, filling up more and more tubes. Allow this process to fully run its course.
15. Now that all three Divine flowers are sufficiently activated within your body, it is time to bring them into one cohesive system. Come back to your heart space, focusing your attention on the rose growing there. Imagine that a spark of white light hits the flower, almost like lightning, further activating its potential. This initial spark jumpstarts an electric current within your body. Bend your elbows and raise your hands so that your palms face forward. Position your hands along the horizontal axis that runs through your heart space. (Please refer to **Figure 60** for a visual representation of this).
16. Mentally, send the electric current into your right palm, activating the lily with a potent stream of light. Breathe into your palm for a few seconds to further solidify this activation.
17. Now, send the electric current toward your third eye area, meeting and activating the lotus that rests atop the violet lake. Notice how the lotus, charged by this Divine electricity, is beginning to breathe in and out, pulsating and beaming with life.
18. Once the lotus flower feels sufficiently activated, send the electric current down toward the palm of your left hand, located on the same horizontal axis as both your heart and your right palm.
19. Notice how the lily in your left palm, once hit by the electricity, is starting to produce massive amounts of ruby-red life force. Watch as this life force

travels back to your heart space, finally completing the sacred floral triangle.

20. Allow the ruby-red life force to keep coursing through the triangle, tracing it over and over again.
21. Notice how moving the energy in this way makes your physical body almost melt away into the space surrounding you. The more times you complete the triangle, the more ephemeral your body feels.
22. Now, from this place of surrender, call upon the Divine Mother and ask her to reveal herself to you. The Mother shall reveal herself in the form that will be most helpful for you now.
23. Ask the Mother if she has any messages or healing for you. Then, simply receive whatever comes through.
24. You may ask the Mother any question you'd like, or request her blessing. Feel free to stay here in this sacred space, soaking up the love and guidance of our wonderful Creatress.

Enjoy!

Heart Space: The Dark Night of the Goddess

She identified as a human once.

That was before her body awakened to the truth—before it coiled and thrashed in the pain of her new realization, before it chose to shed the layers of conditioning and false programming and broken dreams.

She passed through the charred void, the dark night of the soul, the eternal fall of surrender. And she flailed, gasped, and drowned in the obscurity of her rebirth, her cells colliding and reforging into something new, something other.

She was Kali and Hecate, Ireshkigal, and the Black Madonna, momentarily overtaken by her madness. She bled black, and the pain of the entire world was her pain, for it was flowing in her veins, suffocating her from within.

And the day was dark, but the night was darker. And years came and went in an endless stream of black tears and even blacker thoughts. And thus, she reached the end times, the very edge of the Universe, an abyss as black as her soul. And she knew that her suffering could finally be over. The end of the cycle had come.

And so, she crawled to the very edge of the abyss and looked down. But instead of the raging fires of Gehenna, all she saw was a mirror, and her reflection in it, broken and alone, dark tears streaking down her face, her hair disheveled, her clothing torn, a mad gleam in her eyes. And the voices in her head told her to stay down, to remain in the night, hidden away from light—or better yet, to cease existing altogether. Surely, the world could do without this much darkness.

It was in that final moment that she found herself again, for the madness in her eyes was the madness of hope. And she unraveled her darkness, streak by streak, thread by thread, until nothing remained.

And so, she rose, and she was darkness no more.

And so, she rose, and the morning sun rose with her.

And so, she rose, and the new cycle began.

And so, she rose as a goddess, her true self finally revealed for all to see, so much more than a human, so much more than a body, so much more than spirit caged in a third-dimensional shell.

And so, she rose, and she stood tall, equal in power to the sun, emanating light from the center of her being. She was power. She was a new beginning, the most favorite daughter of Source.

And the Universe gathered itself at the feet of the Goddess, guarding her like a loyal wolf. And its power was at the Goddess's fingertips, ready to do her bidding.

It is not by doing, but by being that the Goddess chose to reforge the world.

It is not by doing, but by being that she chose to lead.

It is not by doing, but by being that she finally stepped onto her path.

And when the Goddess realized her power, the Universe bent its knee,

For she rose despite all odds, by being, not by doing. And the Universe knew no other who thus could shift the fates.

CHAPTER 14

The Black Rose – The Onyx Mysteries

Let us start by considering the meaning of darkness.

The black rose, at its core, taps into the energies of darkness. Darkness is a facet of the Divine Mother, the creative and abundant space that once gave birth to us all.

We are not dealing with the facet of darkness that crosses the line into "evil." At this point, the lines have gotten so blurry that I have to make a special disclaimer about this. There is nothing "evil" about the primordial void, about natural magnetism, about the womb, or about the feminine power of the great yin, no matter how much some would prefer for us to believe otherwise. The Mother and her domain have never been inferior; they are second to none. We have grown accustomed to being afraid of the dark, because we associate it with everything from our nightmares to demons. In our drive to rid ourselves of evil, we have also chosen to give up some aspects of the Mother that serve us. This is a homecoming. Our Mother is the darkness of the starry night sky, the fertile soil under our feet, the safety of the womb. I hope you will allow me to show you this side of the great Creatress.

Aspects of the Black Rose

- **The Black Rose of the Mother Divine** is one of the sacred emanations of our female Creatress and her domain.
- **Element:** Ether and fire
- **Planets/Stars:** Dark moon (Lilith), Saturn, the black sun
- **State:** Mostly passive and idle (magnetism), with spurts of activity (to destroy and break the old structures apart, also called "de-creation" mode)
- **Mood:** Tranquility, silence, rest
- **Signature:** Liminal spaces, beginnings/endings of cycles
- **Vibration:** Release
- **Goddesses:** Demeter, Kali, the Black Madonna, Hecate, Ereshkigal, Nyx, Hel, Morena

It is in the depth of the night, in the abyss of Nihil (the Great Nothing), in the viscous, gooey embrace of darkness that we find the black rose. The lucky one will discover the mysteries of the black rose as if accidentally and entirely by chance. And yet, being introduced to the mystery of the black rose is a great initiation in its own right—one that is only bestowed upon the select few deemed worthy. It is impossible to find a trace of the black rose unless she wants to be found. Many have chased her emanations, only to come up empty-handed. The black rose is a rarity; she cannot be found intentionally. Rather, she chooses to manifest herself during periods heralded by massive shifts, fundamental energetic upgrades, or a complete recalibration of all your systems. She is a daughter of primordial chaos, so she is often accompanied by it when she reveals herself. Her greatest lesson is surrender. She teaches us the futility of swimming upstream and working against the universal flow.

Despite her torrential nature, she brings things into equilibrium and balances out the give-and-take of even the most complex and antagonistic situations and systems. If the black rose selects you as her personal pupil, this chapter will resonate with you on a deep, visceral level. You will literally hear the call of the rose deep in your gut. For others, this will be a good overview, without a specific call to action. Whichever group you fall into, learning from the black rose is a one-of-a-kind experience.

Working with the Black Rose

Working with the black rose is a deep dive and an invitation to face your inner darkness. Its challenge is that of integration. The Path of the Black Rose is a trial by shadow—the kind so dark that it repels any and all light. Walking the Path of the Black Rose is finding your way amidst and despite the darkness, courageously forging your new world and your new life from the ashes of the dead phoenix, the one that will be reborn—but not yet.

The black rose requires patience and a whole lot of letting go. It requires mastering a state of nonjudgment—one of the most healing internal states—but it also requires a willingness to release and shed layers of old skin. Working with this rose implies traveling beyond your comfort zone and accepting yourself fully—not just the shiny, lovable parts. We are infinitely complex beings going through a gradual experience of facing ourselves as we face our true north. One cannot happen without the other. The black rose is here to help us every step of the way.

The black rose correspondences:

- Chaos
- Death
- Night
- Ancestors and lineages
- Magic
- Solar and lunar eclipses
- Magnetism and all manner of magnets
- Karma
- The womb of the Divine Mother
- Deep sleep
- Hypnosis
- Past life regressions
- Crude oil

The Code of the Black Rose

The black rose has plenty of correspondences, one of which is a numerical frequency that best symbolically represents its vibration and spirit: **001.001.001.**

Essentially, two zeros followed by the number one, repeated in perpetuity, is the Code of the Black Rose. But a shortened code can be used, leveraging any number of repeating loops of **001.**

This numerical code is a stirring of the void, the deep, guttural impulse before a major happening. It is a quickening of the pulse and an electric shift that jump-starts the millstones of change within the void. The dark void has two states: passive and active. The passive state is a liminal space between death and life, where the void recedes into itself for processing, healing, and deep rest. The active state is boundless creation; it is a space for making something out of nothing, the most awe-inspiring state of the Great Mother. The numerical frequency of the black rose is an impulse that spurs the void into action, a heartbeat that induces all manner of movement and desire in the void, inviting it to create a new world. This is the most resourceful state of the void, the most "productive" aspect of darkness. Invite the void to co-create with you, allowing it access to your inner sanctuary.

Working with the Code of the Black Rose

The numerical frequency of 001 allows you to invoke the presence of the black rose and enlist it as one of your helpers. As such, it is great for moving beyond a blockage or a persistent pattern that needs to be released. It is perfect for healing and renewal of any kind. The energy of the black rose, once magnetized to a particular issue, gets straight to work, making large shifts in your life. The shifts you experience with the help of the rose may be sporadic and seemingly unpredictable. They may hit you out of nowhere, making you face challenges in the real world. And while such shifts may seem uncomfortable and abrupt, they are often exactly the medicine you need to move past your limitations.

Blank Page

To invoke the assistance of the black rose, take out a blank page. At the top of the page, define the issue you are working through, giving it some color. One paragraph is enough; the black rose is intuitive and doesn't require much information. Then, fold the page in half, so that your paragraph is covered. Write down the numerical frequency of the black rose (001) at the top of the folded page. (You will notice that because of the fold, the numerical frequency will be right "on top" of your issue.)

Now, close your eyes and invite the black rose to make the necessary changes in your life (including teaching you the lessons you need to learn to move beyond the current challenges). Place the folded paper under your pillow for three consecutive nights, and watch the magic of the black rose unfold in your life.

Wear the Frequency

You may choose to "wear" the frequency of the black rose when moving through a challenge or a dark period in your life. This will speed up the purging, the healing, and the balancing of the energies and will allow you to shorten the period of trials and tribulations, moving you through the shifts quickly and seamlessly. To partake of this help, simply write down one loop (**001**) of the numerical frequency of the black rose on your left palm every morning for at least a week (or for the duration of your challenging period). As you write it down, focus your intention on enlisting the black rose to help you move through your challenges more quickly and come out on the other side both victorious and happy.

Repeating Frequency

If you feel like you have a blind spot preventing you from seeing the full picture or seeing reality as it is, you may turn to the help of the black rose. She is considered a seer and an intuitive among the roses. She is the rose of the witches, and as such, is deeply connected with the gift of clairvoyance.

To get insight into a situation or get a question answered, take out a piece of paper and write your request or question at the very top. Below, start writing the numeric frequency of the black rose, repeating it for as long as it takes to receive the answer. You may need to write it just a few times or fill the entire page with this frequency. Either way, your hand will naturally stop at some point and will start writing the answer itself. Simply allow yourself to receive it without judgment.

Trust that whatever comes through is exactly what you need to hear now.

Practice: Shadowscape – The Great Release

This practice releases some of the darkness that has been stuck in your physical and etheric bodies to create room for new and optimal energies to come through.

You may notice shifts in your physical body and energy levels after this meditation, so it is best to perform it in the evening, when you may rest afterward. You may experience a tingling sensation or a need to stretch your body once the practice is complete.

1. Take a comfortable seated position or lie down. Close your eyes.
2. Become aware of your breath gently traveling in and out of your lungs. On the next inhale, breathe into your lower abdomen, where your inner void lives. Imagine that your breath is starting to activate your inner void, stirring it into action.
3. Imagine a bath filled with a dark, gooey substance, not dissimilar to crude oil, right in front of you. Picture stepping into that bath and fully submerging yourself so that the substance covers you entirely, including your face.
4. Stay here for a few moments and listen to the darkness. Have you ever noticed that darkness has a sound? What does this sound remind you of? How does it make you feel? Notice that this darkness feels like the embrace of the Mother, the comfort and safety of her womb. It feels like surrender. It feels like the opposite of struggle. It allows you to simply be, to experience being loved and protected in this moment, exactly as you are.
5. Stay in this in-between space for as long as it feels good. When you are ready, sit up, but stay in the tub, with the top half of your body above the surface of the dark liquid. Notice how the surface of the liquid is starting to stir, and black roses are beginning to bloom all over it, an image both majestic and surreal.
6. Imagine that black rose buds are beginning to cover your body, giving you an intricate outfit made of black petals and allowing you to absorb the healing and liberating power of the black rose. Watch as the frequency of the rose enters your pores and starts to course through your body like a deep cleanse and a redemptive force.
7. Stand up in the tub, watching the transformation commence. Please know that the dark liquid in the tub contains magnetic properties, and it has an

uncanny ability to draw out darkness from everything it touches. It is a grand accumulator and liberator. Notice as you get up how the magnetic force of the liquid is intensified, drawing the dark clots and gray clouds out of your body.

8. Watch as the dark clots leave you through your pores, your fingers, the palms of your hands, your knees, the soles of your feet, your belly button, and your throat area. Watch as all this newly emerged darkness is magnetized to the dark liquid in the tub.
9. Allow this process to happen naturally, without forcing it or trying to speed things up. You will benefit from a thorough cleanse, which is bound to take some time.
10. When you are ready, feel free to exit the tub. If there is any remaining darkness on your body, picture a waterfall of white light falling from the heavens and washing over you, removing any residual darkness.
11. Lastly, give gratitude to the black rose for her assistance today.

The Onyx Order and the Onyx Mysteries

The Onyx Mysteries was once a branch of female-centric magic taught by the goddess Isis in her Egyptian temples and secluded sacred spaces. While it was initially reserved for the chosen ones—a group of females that Isis personally selected to receive the activations and the learnings—Isis believed that one day, this mystery could go exoteric and be offered to a larger audience of female seekers.

The Onyx Mystery initiates viewed a female body as a sacred vessel for channeling the vibrations of the Divine Mother. Isis believed that every woman is born with an inherent connection to the Mother inside her physical vessel, a sacred womb portal, which, if used properly, could offer any female a path to limitless power.

Over the years of practice, ritual, and meditation, the initiates of the mysteries learned to use their physical body as a vessel for healing others and the planet. They learned to become energetic acupuncture needles on the face of the planet, infusing their targeted and pointed medicine into the Earth's crystalline grid. Often, their rites and rituals heralded periods of great transformation for the Earth and its inhabitants. The main rituals of the order were traditionally held after dusk on the day of a lunar or solar eclipse. Some major rites were also aligned with the movement of Pluto, as that was the patron planet of the mystery school. Interacting with crystals and using them as a means of downloading knowledge from the Akashic field was a big focus of the order.

The order's records were preserved inside the large black onyx crystals prominently displayed by the altar of the main temple. Most Onyx Temples were pyramidal in shape, often flaunting natural onyx capstones and containing no windows, so that complete and utter darkness could be achieved, depending on the needs of a particular ritual. Inside, the temples were decorated with black and gold ornaments and contained pools of dark water along the perimeter, reminiscent of the primordial void.

Descending into the Womb

Isis taught that the womb is directly connected to our greater subconscious, both individual and collective, and it is therefore a seat of wisdom and insight. Descending into the womb was a daily practice for the initiates of the Onyx Order, used as a means of daily alignment and healing. The womb served as a source of information about oneself and the world at large, a space both sacred and unknowable. Unfortunately, the default setting of human DNA is such that the female womb has been deactivated and reduced to a childbearing function. Because of this, before the womb could be used in a sacred and spiritual way, an attunement had to take place, connections to the Mother needed to be redrawn and reignited, and the hidden potential of the womb had to be reclaimed.

For a female in touch with her womb, this wondrous organ is a means of deepest healing and solace, a source of insight, and a seat of power. A female empowered is a female who understands the depth of her inner void and can channel its magic into what she wants to see created in the world. The womb is not entirely identical to the inner void, however. Our inner void takes up a larger space than our physical womb; it starts at the sacral chakra and stretches two inches (four centimeters) below your root chakra.

Getting to know this sacred space of your body is a process. Much patience is required to see it through. Eventually, your inner void will unfold in all its splendor, like a black rose that has come into full bloom. Only then does the true magic begin.

The benefits of this practice include:

- Establishing and building a connection with the Divine Mother
- Getting deep insights into your health, your path, and your past lives, as well as key events and people in your life
- Finding a seat of your inner power
- Releasing anything that no longer serves you
- Building an inner bridge into the Akashic Records
- Understanding your dreamscape
- Facing and integrating your shadows

Initiation: Descending into the Womb

This practice is best performed during the Scorpio season (October 23 through November 22). If this season is far away, any new moon—apart from a new moon in Aquarius—is also applicable. This practice is best attempted after dark, but before midnight.

You will need:

- Three pillar candles: one white, one black, and one golden
- Palo santo or sage to clear the space
- A medium-sized bowl or a deep plate filled with black salt

The initiation:

Prepare your sacred space using a stick of palo santo or some sage to clear away any excessive darkness or negativity. Focus on the corners of the room if you are doing this practice indoors.

If you are outdoors in nature, set up protective wards around yourself and then light some sage. To set protective wards, imagine placing four pillars of white light to mark a square-shaped territory around yourself. Then, picture a dome of white light above your head, connecting the four pillars of light. Imagine a dome under your feet also. This will seal you inside a structure of white light that will stay intact for the duration of the ritual.

1. Sit comfortably on the floor, or directly on the ground if you are outside. Light the black candle and place it in the bowl filled with black salt. Place your palms on either side of the candle, generously infusing it with your energy. Imagine an energy stream leaving your palms and activating the candle. The black candle is for letting go.
2. Close your eyes and think of something that you are ready to release, something that is no longer serving you, something the time has come to let go of. Imagine that the candle's flame is expanding, slowly overtaking that which you are ready to release. Watch it burn energetically. If you are releasing a person, watch your connection with that person burn (not the person themselves).
3. Notice a shift in your energy, an almost visceral need to exhale. Allow yourself to take deeper breaths and exhale audibly as you are releasing.

You may have a sudden urge to stretch or move your body. If that happens, allow yourself to move. You are making space inside your vessel for what is to come.

4. If you have been moving around, take a seat in front of the bowl filled with salt again. Set aside the black candle and light the white one. This candle represents your good fortune. Hold the white candle in your hands briefly, closing your eyes.
5. Invite something new into your life: an energy, a vibration, a frequency, a happening, a relationship. Please do not request a specific person, but simply state what you want to attract (e.g., a perfect partner, the perfect job, a dream friend).
6. Place the white candle in the salt bowl. As it burns, open your heart to receiving what you have been asking for. Imagine that a stream of white light from the candle stretches toward your heart space and enters it, delivering your greatest wish. Simply allow yourself to receive. Stay here for a few moments.
7. When you are ready to move on, put out the white candle and light up the golden candle. The golden candle is a sign of blessings and gifts. Place it in the salt bowl in front of you. Imagine that a large phoenix, a holder of golden energies, spreads its wings above your head. As the phoenix moves its majestic wings, watch the golden waterfall descend upon your body, showering you with blessings from the Divine Mother. Ask the Mother to open the portal of your womb at this time.
8. Momentarily, shift your attention to your womb space, your sacral chakra, the point of deep waters within your body. Feel into your womb, noticing how quiet and dark it is. Remember that this is a part of your body that can give life to another being, one of your most creative and wondrous aspects.
9. Imagine floating in the dark waters of your womb, lulled into deep relaxation by its nurturing vibration.
10. Imagine falling deeper and deeper into the void of your womb, descending as far as you can go. Simply surrender to the process of falling. Feel your body becoming heavier, as if it were turned into lead. Allow it to keep dropping into the dark abyss of your void.

11. Finally, as you are about to reach the bottom of this seemingly bottomless darkness, imagine a huge feminine hand catching your body, as if cradling it.
12. Watch as the hand carries you through a portal, an opening at the bottom of the abyss. On the other side of the abyss is a cave with a high ceiling. This space feels safe, serene, and timeless.
13. In front of you is an embodiment of the Divine Mother. She may come to you as one of the goddesses, an animal, an angel, or even an object.
14. The time has come to establish a line of connection between you and your Divine Mother. Stretch out your hands and touch the embodiment of the Mother. Watch as many bridges of light are created between you and her, some stretching out from your heart, others from your throat, and still others from your sacral space (in the lower abdomen). Allow these channels of connection to grow, solidify, and expand. Feel free to use your breath to aid with this transformation.
15. Allow yourself to ask the Mother any questions you may have. You may also ask the Mother to perform a healing or energetic alignment on you.
16. Stay in this sacred space for as long as it feels good. When you are ready, feel free to come back and open your eyes. Blow out the golden candle. Place your palms on your heart and express your gratitude to the Mother for her assistance today.

Things you can do while in the dark void of the womb:

- Get answers from the depth of your being about anything related to you or your life
- Receive intuitive guidance and a sense of direction
- Find the root causes of issues simply by posing the question
- Face your shadows, separate aspects of yourself preventing you from moving forward. You may also ask the void to dissolve those aspects, releasing any stuck energy in your auric field.
- Have the void do a deep cleanse of all your systems—physical, energetic, emotional, and mental
- You may ask for new energy to come into your life (a "rising"). Simply imagine this new energy emerging from the darkness of the primordial

void and starting to rise in a spiral-like fashion. Allow this new energy to become anchored and grow roots inside your body by assigning it a place to settle in (pick any organ of your body—anything that feels right).

Sacred Symbols of the Onyx Order

Black onyx (duh!): The sacred stone of the order, black onyx was used as the collector of knowledge and as a record-keeping mineral. The priestesses used this mineral during group and individual channeling sessions as a means of recording a stream of knowledge that was coming through. Upon reaching a certain level of initiation, the priestesses were taught to download information from the crystals, gaining a behind-the-scenes look into the deep wisdom of the order. While the original onyx crystals have been long lost and sold through galactic artifact auctions, the collective family of the onyx crystals still retains some of the original records. To anyone aspiring to become a priestess of the order, much is possible through connecting with and working with onyx. The worthy ones will always be given assistance when accessing the vast amounts of knowledge still dwelling in the collective consciousness of the onyx family.

Smoky quartz (especially the less transparent and darker varieties): Since much of the order's work concerned cleansing, removal of obstacles, and healing, one of its byproducts was dark energetic residue, a remnant of a process of unwinding. As such, energy clearing was table stakes for the longevity of the order. Smoky quartz was used during every ritual to help absorb negativity. Each smoky quartz crystal is an absorbent portal and a powerhouse in its own right, capable of sucking away massive amounts of dark energy. Thanks to the faithful service of smoky quartz, the order's priestesses could maintain and even grow the magnitude of their work over the years, without any palpable detriment to their own resources or health.

Black scorpion: Isis shared a special connection with the scorpion, one of the guardians of the gates to the underworld, a force of transformation made manifest, a poisonous warrior, a loyal friend, and a protector like no other. Scorpions are known for their resilience and ability to survive despite the harsh desert weather and lack of nutrients. The poster children of the "survivor" archetype are prized for the strength of their spirit and their magical abilities; they can move beyond the nonsense and layers of inauthenticity to get to the core of the issue. They then use their poison to remove the inauthenticity and clear any and all distortions, energetic or otherwise. As such, scorpions are natural planetary healers. It is believed that when this world was created, scorpions were some of the first creatures to emerge from the void, as the protectors and warrior spirits of Gaia. As such, for as long as Gaia is evolving, a scorpion will stand guard and hold a safe space for our planet as she goes through her deep transformations.

Scarab beetle: A symbol of the black sun—the magnetic polarity of the solar realm, the sun of intuition, the dreamscape, and surrender—the scarab beetle was a constant reminder that we are all solar children, but we live in the Universe of the two suns. The white sun is the electric parental figure in the sky, and the currently invisible black sun is its magnetic counterpart. The scarab was a reminder that the sun shall rise no matter what; it was the only constant in a very dynamic world. The sun's death always denotes the decline of the entire solar system. As such, the sun was praised above all cosmic bodies and recognized as a central axis of our existence upon which everything else dwells.

Black widow spider: Intricate is the web that a spider weaves. Many are its threads, and unknown are its pathways. Only the great spider knows the web, for she has woven it. Black spiders have historically been associated with the Divine Mother's wisdom —the kind that transcends space-time reality and connects you directly with the all-knowing Akasha, the field of omniscience. It was believed that a spider is a creature with the greatest foresight and patience. It creates its web, not knowing the direction its prey will come from. But it frets not, trusting in providence and tapping into the realm of knowledge, always two steps ahead of its victim. Though they are carnivores, spiders never kill without good reason and only consume as much as they need to survive, often going weeks without food. They are a symbol of measure, moderation, and humility, despite their strength and splendor. The black widow's web is seemingly a haphazard construction, often referred to as a tangled web, and yet it does its job beautifully. We may never understand the grand design of the spiderweb of our Divine Mother, and yet, she knows best. The black spider is thus a symbol of deep feminine wisdom, intuition, and clairvoyance.

Black cobra: The venom of the black cobra, the queen snake, was sacred to the Order of the Onyx. It was used (very sparingly) in priestess initiation rituals and rites of passage as a means of testing the strength of resolve and inducing psychedelic effects, which aligned the priestesses with a path of being able to channel the mysteries and thus enrich the order, not unlike the effects of the toxic fumes of Delphi on the oracles. The black cobra symbolizes female sovereignty and power, a force to be reckoned with. Black cobra statues usually guarded the entrances to the temples of the order, as the cobra was a protectress and a patron of the order's mission and work. A beloved snake of the Nagas, an ancient race of wise, snakelike beings who established many secret spiritual orders on Earth, Queen Cobra was prominent within the order, serving as proof that the Onyx Mysteries were deeply connected to the philosophy and magic of the Nagas themselves.

Belladonna: A member of the nightshade family, belladonna was instrumental in leading the escapades of the order into the realm of poisons and medicines. The plant's spirit guided the priestesses toward finding remedies for seemingly incurable ailments. Belladonna tinctures and drops were used to heal everything from a common rash to complex cardiovascular conditions. Depictions and engravings of belladonna decorated the inner walls of the Onyx Temples, serving as a reminder that the silent teacher is the most effective. The order's priestesses were naturally in tune with the plant kingdom, often communicating with different plant varieties telepathically. Connecting to the spirit of belladonna was one of the first initiation rites of the order, and one couldn't pass to the next level until the spirit of belladonna was deeply ingrained within them. Unfortunately, the art of conversing with plants has mostly been lost, with only shamans still preserving a semblance of it. And yet, at one point, it was one of the greatest doorways to understanding and studying the mysteries.

Black pyramid: If onyx was a sacred stone of the order, the pyramid was its sacred shape. The pyramid was a closed structure that could only be penetrated from the top, and only at the request of the pyramid's master. The high priestess of the order was often the holder of the pyramid mysteries, and she personally aligned her physical vessel to activate the structure. The pyramid's capstone was a potent receiving point, just like an antenna. Once activated by the high priestess, the "antenna" began transmitting requests to worlds near and far. In the case of an incoming transmission, the pyramid's tip switched its broadcasting mode into full-on receiving mode, usually beginning by absorbing massive amounts of incoming energy. The heart of the pyramid, located at the very center of its base, usually contained a physical receptacle, a structure able to withstand and accumulate the incoming energy stream. Naturally, every Onyx Temple that bore a pyramid shape had a heart that resembled a bathtub made of onyx. Once the energy or the transmission was received by the pyramid, it was the priestess's job to unpack it, translate it, and put it to good use.

The womb/void: A sacred space of the order, both the physical womb and the etheric dark void of the Mother were praised for their life-giving properties. It was with much reverence that the priestesses conducted the rituals of connecting to the womb, using it as their North Star for their work in the world. The priestesses often channeled from their womb space instead of from their crown center, which enabled them to bring forth the wisdom of the Divine Mother instead of the Divine Father. Every season brought about special "void days," periods of contemplation, healing, and introspection. Those days were meant for tending to one's womb and nurturing the inner space of creativity. Through such tender cultivation of the womb, the priestesses of the order achieved a high level of manifestation and magical powers, often able to perform "tricks" that seemed unusual or impossible to the rest.

Black spiral (the unwinding): The black spiral incessantly moves counterclockwise, rewinding the records of space-time reality in order to alter them. The black spiral is a method of regressing into the past and aligning with bygone events. It was used to reverse any of the root causes of negative consequences (such as reversing the symptoms of a disease), and it was also used as a means of healing trauma by rewriting the storyline. The black spiral can travel as far back as the beginning of time, shifting any negative circumstance and rewriting the codes that enabled it. The energy freed up in the process usually goes to feed the healing work, with the rest returning to the person who undergoes healing. Parts of the energy were preserved by the order for planetary-level healing rituals that helped harmonize the energies of Gaia and course-correct the planet's evolution.

The Onyx Mysteries fields of study and specialties:

- Alchemy
- Crystal magic
- Poisons (mostly for healing and spiritual purposes)
- Sacred rites and rites of passage (often trials by poison)
- Herbalism
- Hypnosis
- Astral travel
- Immortality
- Resurrection
- Life force
- Channeling and mediumship

The main postulates of the Order of the Onyx are as follows:

- By staring into the face of your darkness, you finally start understanding the extent of your true power.
- Nothing is impossible for the void.
- There is much wisdom in darkness.
- Infinity is twofold. The upper infinity is white, and the lower infinity is black. Together, the two loops form a figure eight, a perfectly balanced ecosystem that maintains all life and all death.
- The cycle of death and life is natural. Some things must die for other things to be birthed. The amount of energy is always constant, so it must constantly shift forms to maintain a living ecosystem.
- Before we can learn light, we need to master darkness.
- Mastering darkness means knowing the extent of its power, but not being taken over by it.
- Life is a state of giving, and death is a state of taking. Both must be in perfect equilibrium, the give and take in equal measure. To give something away, you must first accumulate it by taking it.

Practice: Activating the Onyx Mysteries Connection

Please make sure you are well rested before attempting this initiation. It could be quite energy intensive, so having spare energy is paramount. You also need to pick a place where you will not be disturbed. The guardians protecting the Onyx Mysteries are both ancient and fickle, so they don't like being interrupted when they start working with you.

You will need:

- A plate filled with water, for amplification
- A black onyx pyramid (any size will do)

The ritual:

1. Place the plate filled with water in front of you. Take the onyx pyramid in your right hand and place it over your womb space.
2. Close your eyes and focus your attention on the deep void of your womb. Feel its wisdom. Feel its power. Watch the black ocean of your womb space spur into motion, its waves becoming larger. Keep breathing into your womb space, activating it.
3. Imagine that the onyx pyramid is starting to absorb some of the energies of your womb space. Notice how this incoming stream of energy is activating the pyramid. Watch as the pyramid starts to pulsate, as if coming alive.
4. Stay here for a few moments, feeding the pyramid with your energy.
5. Now, for a moment, open your eyes and place the pyramid on the plate filled with water before you. This will help amplify the powers of the pyramid and further activate its power.
6. Close your eyes and imagine that you are seated in a large onyx pyramid. Surrounding you are its shiny black walls. You are seated right at the very center of the pyramid under its capstone.
7. Watch as the capstone is removed and a stream of white light descends into the pyramid. It flows onto you, covering you with its transformative vibrations.
8. Inside the stream, you will notice a string of codes—shiny black symbols and figures traveling toward you from the top of the pyramid. Invite these codes to enter your third eye space in the center of your forehead.

This stream of codes is unique to you; it is highly personalized, based on your needs.

9. When you feel ready, say the following invocation: "I offer myself fully to receive the wisdom of the Onyx Mysteries. I choose to step onto a path of learning and initiations. I welcome the power of the Divine Mother inside of my vessel, and I want to partake of her wisdom and loving presence. Today, I choose to receive the ancient codes of the Onyx Order, so that I may be the carrier of that wisdom. May the codes grow roots in my consciousness, transforming my life for the better and making me a vessel of positive change for the planet. Today, I wish to join the lineage of the priestesses of the Onyx Order, so that I may carry their torch and wisdom into the future. May the codes of the onyx unpack within me when the time is ripe. And so it is. And so it is. And so it is."
10. Take three deep breaths, sending them into your womb space. Stay here for a few moments, absorbing the power of the codes and noticing the shift they bring.
11. When you are ready, offer your gratitude to the Mother for blessing you today. Congratulations! You have successfully downloaded the Onyx Codes.

Heart Space: The Dark One and the Virgin

The bells upon the tower of Notre Dame were marking the time of the evening prayer. And although she very much preferred the rolling hills of Lourdes to the bustling streets of Paris, the Virgin Mary did love the cathedral built in her honor. If she was being honest, it might have been one of her favorite temples yet.

However, it wasn't the granite walls of the holy temple nor the serene waters of the Seine that drew her to Paris tonight. Instead, she was keenly eyeing a young girl, devotedly kneeling in front of the altar of the Virgin. The candles were burning hot, and the scent of myrrh filled the air inside Notre Dame. Mary had always loved myrrh; it reminded her of the old days when she lived in Qumran—a life filled with hope.

The girl was unique, her heart as pure as moonlight. Mary had heard her first prayer when the girl was merely four years old, asking the Virgin to save her little brother, who was overcome with fever. There was something endearing about the little girl and her prayer—something that even the most renowned scholars of the scriptures lacked. Sincerity, purity, and faith—faith that could move mountains. Mary saved the girl's brother that night, having to bargain with the devil himself. But the trouble was worth it. The smile upon the girl's face—one of true wonder and devotion—made Mary believe there was goodness on the face of planet Earth again.

"Grooming another little savior, are you?" asked the devil of the Virgin, his eyes full of inexplicable hunger.

"The original sin is not forever, dark one, no matter how much you wish that was the case. Eve may have partaken of the apple, but it came with a sacred promise of her seed being redeemed one day. Surely, you remember," the Virgin responded softly.

"She will turn away from you, like so many others before her. She will grow up and succumb to lust, greed, and sin. And there is nothing you can do about it."

"She may. Or she may surprise you yet. But one day, a child will be born that will defy the dark pull of this planet, defy you and your ways—a child as bright as the sun. And then you will know my hope was not in vain. The purity of the children of Eve shall be restored," the Virgin said and smiled gently.

"You had such a child, I recall. A boy. He failed," the devil said with a smirk, scratching one of his horns.

"Is that what you think he did? He was a doorway. She is the one who will walk through it. It was always meant to take two Divine children, not one."

"I will corrupt her, just as I have so many before her."

"The age of the Maiden is upon us, as was foretold long ago. There is still time for you to change your ways, or face the consequences," said the Virgin, and she rose into the skies, leaving the devil below.

And so, they both watched the young girl come into her power, Mary from her holy abode in the skies, and the devil from his castle of tar and smoke. And as much as the devil was willing to put on a good show, he knew that the girl's faith and purity were nothing he'd seen in a long while. She was the first bell—the kind that tolled for the end of the world he had run for millennia.

A daughter of Eve, purified. And that meant the tides were shifting, indeed.

CHAPTER 15

The White Rose – The Moon Mysteries

The white rose of the Mother Divine is purity made manifest. It is the most forgiving aspect of the Mother, her innate grace and compassion encapsulated in flower form.

Aspects of the White Rose

- **Element:** Water and air
- **Planets/Stars:** Sirius, moon
- **State:** Flow and universal alignment
- **Mood:** Peace, contentment, gratitude, grace
- **Signature:** Simplicity, minimalism, less is more
- **Vibration:** Purification, protection, getting back to basics, removing layers
- **Goddesses/Saints:** Mother Mary, Artemis, Kuan Yin, Luna, Diana, Ix Chel, Saraswati, Selene

An ode to light itself, a song of eternal compassion, an emissary of purity and Divine protection, the white rose is perhaps the humblest of the royal flowers. Her magic is serene and understated; she requires no limelight, crown, or regalia. Noble solitude is her domain. When the rest of the world projects outwardly, she goes within. She may be a natural hermit, but you will not find a better sanctuary. She is a principle of receptivity and acceptance. She is a master listener and a master healer. She is a great gift in this world and the next, in every dimension and galaxy, in every space-time reality, on planets near and far. She is the White Goddess, the White Priestess, the White Queen. She is redemption itself. She is the promised land, the universal flow, uninhibited, balanced, and perpetually aligned with the greater good. She knows no enemies and has no bounds; she goes where the light goes, and perhaps even further. Her presence is effortless, yet instantly healing. Some call her vibration "angelic," others "saintly." What it is at its core is pure. She is the antidote to darkness, a cure for despair, the one who has heard your prayers, seen all your transgressions, and still loves you. She is beyond measure and requires no validation; she is perpetually self-defining energy.

She can cleanse negativity and sin while remaining pristine and untarnished. She is the one you can call upon in your darkest hour. She is a promise, a sacred vow that Heaven is not a place or a destination, but a state of purity within.

Working with the White Rose

Working with the white rose gradually purifies your vessel, physically, emotionally, and energetically. It is a process of liberation from the entanglement of lies, illusions, cages, and karmic debts, a slow and steady movement toward the light within and without.

Working with the white rose is a process of aligning with your inner compass and finding your inner light, so that you can come into deeper synchronicity with the Universe. As we move through life, we create distortions in our auric fields, small fissures that, when accumulated, can turn into perilous chasms. The white rose is a force that washes our inner wounds with her healing, guiding waters, so that we can find our way back to oneness and integrity. The white rose accepts you as you are—your faults, your nightmares, your trauma—and gently leads you through the gates of purification into a better future. She is a Mother Rose archetype—the one who, in loving you, offers her infinite well of guiding, healing waters for you to drink and be healed.

Bring your sorrows and pains to her altar. Lay them gently at her feet. The white rose is acceptance, blissful, generous, and irrevocable. Trust the light of the white rose, her Goddess-given ability to cleanse and purify, her endless resources. Invite her into your life, and watch your life transform, gently but completely, without measure.

The White Rose Gateway

Every year on July 7 (7/7), the white rose opens a Divine portal between Heaven and Earth—one of the most potent gateways of the Mother. During this cosmic event, a stream of benevolent healing Rose Codes descends upon the Earth and its many inhabitants in an avalanche of white light. These gentle energies wash away the dirt, the trauma, and the wounding of the human collective, offering a temporary reprieve from harsh realities and painful memories. On this miraculous day, Earth is covered with a transparent veil of the Mother, soaking up her unconditional love and care, nestled under the invisible wings of Divine protection. This day is a day of water, a great cleanse, a washing away of toxic energies and stuck patterns. This day is an opportunity for renewal of our natural biorhythms. This is a rare chance for recalibration of our light bodies and light structures, a moment to reconnect with our own nurturing aspects, allowing them to emanate from us in every direction according to their original design.

To those open and willing to receive, the white rose offers a special gift: a personal initiation into her healing space. Take a moment to invite the rose's gentle and soft vibrations into your auric field. Watch as she showers you with her petals and blooms, giving you a crown of white roses, a symbol of your sovereignty as a being of light. Imagine receiving her healing codes through your crown chakra as a stream of white roses enters your body, cascading through your tissues and organs, filling you up. The magic of the white rose is intuitive; it will work with your organ systems on an as-needed basis, removing blockages and distortions. This healing may take up to twenty-four hours to fully run its course. However, most of it happens in the background and doesn't require your active involvement. Simply allow the white rose to enter your vessel and do her work there.

The white rose promise and invocation:

I am the white rose, rosa blanca, la rose blanche.

I am the Queen of Flowers and the signature song of the angels.

I am the soft feathers of love wrapped in a plush blanket of forgiveness.

I am the sweet amrita *of compassion*

And a memory of the safety of a mother's embrace.

I am the one shrouded by the mists of Avalon, clad in the silks of white light.

I am purity in flower form.

Where I go, the flow of cosmic waters is established.

Where I go, the nights turn into days, and ends turn into beginnings.

Where I go, the tears of sorrow dry up and turn into pearls of wisdom.

Where I go, the barren terrain becomes fertile again.

Where my petals fall, death becomes life, and silence becomes sound.

I am the amalgamation of all colors, the unifying principle of creation.

I am the force holding everything together.

I am the one you can call upon in your time of need,

For I am your cosmic Mother Rose, and I care about your suffering.

I am compassion, forgiveness, and absolution.

I am the one who heard your prayer from a million miles away,

And I am the one who came to help you.

I am the white rose of the Great Creatress.

Your connection to me is your birthright.

Today, tomorrow, always, I wash away your tears and close up your wounds.

I am walking right beside you, no matter how hard it gets.

I am the one who welcomed you into this world,

And the one who will welcome you into the next.

I am the one who cares the most,

And my emanation is forever with you.

Such is my promise to you, beautiful soul.

And so it is.

Ritual: Connecting with the White Rose

Like all benevolent energies, the magic of the white rose needs to be invited in to become an active force in your life. Connecting with the rose once in your lifetime is enough to forever enlist her as your etheric helper and ally.

You will need:

- Palo santo or sage
- A bowl of water
- Rose essential oil
- A handful of loose white rose petals
- A white rose

The ritual:

1. To start, cleanse your space by burning some palo santo or sage. Move the burning stick/sage bundle clockwise around the space to create an upward stream of white light to ensure an even better connection and alignment with the white rose.
2. Take a comfortable seated position. A lotus pose is preferred for this ritual. Place the bowl of water before you, add fifteen drops of rose essential oil, and stir gently. Add a handful of loose rose petals to the water.
3. Place your hands in the bowl and close your eyes. Imagine that a portal opens up above your head. This portal is shaped like a rosebud and seems woven of light.
4. Notice how, as the portal opens, a stream of milky white water starts descending upon your head, washing over you.
5. Notice how this stream is flowing into the water bowl, infusing it with the spirit of the cosmic white rose.
6. Invite the white rose frequency to enter your body. Feel the milky white vibrations of the rose starting to enter through your fingers. Allow the energy of the rose to travel up your arms toward your heart space.
7. Allow the white rose to settle into your heart space, filling it with brilliant white light.
8. Watch how a magical white rose garden springs to life inside your heart space. Seemingly out of nowhere, rose bushes of all shapes and sizes begin

to take root, their luscious green foliage covering each branch. Soon, pristine white roses bloom everywhere, covering every inch of your infinite heart space.

9. Feel free to open your eyes momentarily and take the single white rose, placing it over your heart. Feel the vibration of the flower, its gentle yet powerful energy, humility, and holiness.
10. Repeat the following invocation to invite the presence of the white rose into your life:

"White rose of the Creatress, first among roses,

I invite your spirit into my body, into my life, and into my future.

Walk with me, honor me with your healing presence,

Share with me the song of your immortal heart.

Grant me the gift of your attention, alliance, and assistance.

I welcome your loving vibration and your gentle nudges.

I welcome your guidance and your testimony.

I welcome the entirety of what you are into my vessel from now on.

And so it is."

White rose correspondences:

- The white swan
- The white dove
- Pearls
- Moonstone
- Milk
- Dew and rain
- Tears
- Prayer
- Virginity or celibacy
- The white lotus
- Wisdom
- Faith
- Rivers
- The veil of protection
- White feathers
- White pebbles
- Sand and the seashore
- Japanese tea gardens
- Jasmine
- White rice

The Code of the White Rose

Everything in the material world has a numerical frequency—a set of digits that best represent its essence—and the white rose is no exception. As it is a Divine purifier, the numeric emanation of the white rose is best encapsulated by the following sequence:

Numeric code: 000.000.000.000.

Zero is the purifying principle of the Universe, the Great Recalibration represented numerically. The smallest loop of the white rose is defined by a sequence of three zeros. Using this numerical pattern in your spiritual practice will help you harness the full power of the white rose, turning it into an effective and instantly applicable tool. The Code of the White Rose can help you remove the unnecessary layers to get to the core of something. It will allow you to start fresh, removing the distortions from your auric field and getting better aligned with your perfect energy blueprint and optimal soul path. This code is about reframing the situation. It is a blank slate and an invitation to turn the page and begin anew. The white rose is a great redeemer, and her numerical code is practical magic. She can cleanse karma and move you through stuck energies, old wounds, and trauma, no matter how deep. She is truly one of a kind.

Working with the Code of the White Rose

There are many ways to work with the code. Here are a few of my favorite ways:

Bringing relief: Write the code on a blank sheet of paper as you work through a tough or challenging situation, especially the kind you cannot seem to move past.

Notice how the situation becomes infused with the codes of the great zero, bringing in much-needed relief.

Finding flow: Use the code to invite a state of flow into your life. Whether you are working on a new project, manifesting your dream home, or inviting a new friendship into your life, the white rose can synchronize you with the rest of creation, while simultaneously purifying your vibrations and removing anything that may be causing an energetic distortion. To do this, take a blank page and draw a circle. Inside, write down your desired outcome. Then, fill the space around the circle with as many loops of the code of the white rose as you can. Allow this vibration to infuse your intention, so that you are moving in full alignment with the Universe and can speed up the manifestation you desire.

Removing undesirable frequencies: You can use the code to "zero out" or eliminate an undesired frequency or emotion from your life. Simply write it down on a blank page and write three zeros right above it. Simultaneously, feel this code penetrating deep into your heart space, doing whatever clean-up work that needs to happen. Allow yourself to absorb this healing frequency, and let go of the suboptimal state or emotion that has taken residence inside of you. Feel free to repeat this exercise three times for optimal results.

Diminishing issues: You can also use this frequency when you want to call in a diminishing of something unpleasant, such as debt, disease, pain, etc. Simply imagine three zeros in your mind's eye. Watch as the zeros become deep wells in the expanse of your subconscious. Watch the suboptimal energies being sucked away by these three deep wells. Notice how the zeros absorb the negative energy, freeing up space and producing light. Allow this process to run its course without seeking to force it or speed it up.

Protection: The white rose is a powerful energy protector. It can assist you in maintaining high spirits, regardless of what's going on in the world at large. To partake of this Divine protection, in your mind's eye, imagine a pyramid of white light encapsulating your entire body. Add a few sequences of three zeros to the walls and the floor of the protective pyramid to call in the emanations of the white rose. Often, you may notice that this causes white roses to spring to life inside the pyramid, gracing it with their presence and protective powers. Enjoy!

Remember, the vibrations of the white rose are quite gentle and may require some time to fully bloom. Her energy is steady, smooth, and slow, so please have patience when working with this beautiful frequency, and you will be rewarded beyond measure.

Practice: The White Rose Temple – A Journey of Rest and Recalibration

Before starting the practice, cleanse your space with sage or palo santo, and light a white or golden candle to guide you.

1. Take a comfortable seated position or lie down. Make sure you are not going to be disturbed for the duration of this practice.
2. Close your eyes and start noticing your breath. Allow yourself to breathe in deeply and exhale audibly, releasing any heaviness that dwells within. Stay here for three breaths.
3. Continue to breathe in deeply, imagining that with every inhalation, pure white light is entering your body.
4. Notice how this pure white light starts to gather in the middle of your forehead, around the area of your third eye. Watch as a single white rose is birthed by this white light. The rose is unfolding its gentle petals, one by one. Notice how it removes any mental blockages and negative thoughts from your headspace, paving the way for much-needed healing.
5. Notice how a second white rose emerges right in the middle of your neck area, harmonizing your center of karma, communication, and expression. Allow the rose to unfold its petals, taking up as much space as needed. Imagine that the white rose is healing any wounding in this area, removing blocks, sealing the gaps, and infusing your body with healing light. Watch as the rose rotates clockwise, creating a healing vortex around it, accelerating the transformation and further solidifying the results.
6. Lastly, notice a third white rose springing to life in your heart space. Its glow is angelic, its vibration soothing and calm. Watch how large dewdrops start to fall off the petals, cascading down to nurture the fabric of your heart, rewiring it from within. Where there was once darkness, there shall be light. Where there was once pain, there shall be joy. Notice the white rose generously donating its soulful vibration to your heart space, so you can take full advantage of today's healing.
7. Now, imagine that you are standing in front of tall ivory gates, intricate and airy. The gates open up right in front of you, inviting you in. As you glance around, you notice that you have come upon a luscious garden of

roses. Neat little benches line both sides of the white brick path in front of you. Step onto this path and allow yourself to walk forward.

8. In time, you will reach a large temple made of white marble, with long arched windows lining its walls. An emblem of the white rose, the queen of roses, graces the entrance to this temple, signifying it as a sacred rose space. Step through the temple doors into a spacious round hall, decorated with white roses of all sizes—small wild roses curving up the columns, large white rose blooms standing tall in the many vases decorating the space. But perhaps the most impressive rose of all is a single white bud in the center of this magical circular space.
9. As you walk up to this master rose, you realize just how huge it is, easily twice the size of your body. It is by far the most impressive thing inside the temple. A gentle scent of roses fills the air around you, penetrating deep into your cells and healing you from within.
10. As you approach the master rose, you see a large bathtub filled with glimmering water right next to it. The water has a deep lilac hue and appears almost otherworldly. Step into this rose bathtub and submerge yourself under the lilac waters.
11. You will be surprised to find that you can breathe underwater. Nothing is constricting your breathing. In fact, it seems that this water is supporting it. Notice how the lilac waters are starting to be absorbed into your body through your pores. It is as if these waters are rewriting the crystalline structure within your body, removing any imperfections in your cells and tissues, getting deep into every organ system and shifting the vibrations there. And any time deep healing takes place, a white rose grows where there used to be an energy block—a sign that you now carry the vibration of this Divine flower in your energy body.
12. Allow this process to happen naturally. Breathe in deeply, helping the rose penetrate even deeper into your tissues and bones. Watch as the white rose rewrites the codes of your body, the primary law of your inner landscape. The new codes are filled with light, health and vitality, abundant energy, and heartfelt inspiration. Keep taking it all in, inviting more and more of the rose spirit within.

13. Notice that a whole field of white roses now lines the inner sanctuary of your body. The roses grow and multiply, each one a sign of the deep healing that is taking place.
14. Stay here for as long as it feels good, allowing yourself to soak it all in. When you are ready, feel free to rise from the bathtub and step out of the master rose space. Say goodbye to the Temple of the White Rose for now, but know that you can come back anytime for a new round of healing.
15. Feel free to start walking back the way you came, enjoying the presence of the white roses all throughout your return journey. As soon as you exit through the ivory gates, your activation and recalibration are officially complete.
16. Feel free to start moving your fingers and toes to get the sensation back into your physical body. Open your eyes when you are ready to come back fully.

The Moon Mysteries of the White Rose

The moon, *la luna*, her ladyship Selene—many are the names of our gracious companion in the sky. Since ancient times, the moon has been recognized as one of the carriers of the energies of the Divine Feminine. She has captivated the minds of poets, inspired numerous feminine occult groups and societies, brought the witches together for a unique flavor of ritual magic, and led the way when solar light was unavailable to us. She has been our solace and companion through the long nights and the desperate seasons. She has taught us to recognize life's cyclicality and honor our inner waters. She governs our monthly bleeding cycles and presides over the tides of our oceans, has taught us the mysteries, and yes, she has been guiding us through a sophisticated Lunar Matrix, one of her outermost layers.

The moon is an enigma, perpetually clad in her etheric glow, not quite a star, not quite a planet, but a companion, a teacher, and a satellite of Gaia for many eons. Few celestial bodies, apart from maybe the sun, inspire such blind devotion as the moon. Human history, our culture, and even the very fabric of our DNA have been impacted by it. There are very few aspects of our earthly existence untouched by the moon, that are immune to and unimpacted by her feminine magic.

The moon is constant in her inconstancy, ever shape-shifting, waxing and waning, becoming full only to become empty. She is the embodiment of the ebbs and flows of cosmic waters, the most predictable of all shape-shifting creatures. She may appear fickle, but her spirit runs true. As the celestial body located the closest to Earth, her impact, magnitude, and power cannot be understated. The spirit of our moon is ancient. She is a tri-faced goddess: the maiden, mother, and crone of the night sky. Her lessons run the gamut from gentle to very direct. Her temper, just like her outward appearance, is ever shifting, providing ample opportunities for cosmic alignment within the human race. And while there are many facets to our celestial Luna, as she is a female of many faces and mysterious ways, her path and her service often align with the magic of the white rose, gently entwining with it in a symbiotic dance.

Of course, the moon has just as much of the black rose in it as the white rose. Thus, it is in this dichotomy that we find our deeper understanding of its transformative essence. Selene, the white face of the moon, Lilith, the black face of the moon, and Luna, her combined glorious essence—each of these aspects of the tri-faced celestial Goddess are perhaps worth a separate deep dive, lest we oversimplify the ever-complex mystery of our companion satellite.

Selene: The White Moon

A blessing and a celestial redemption, Selene is full of quiet and gentle promise. She reminds us that the storms don't define our existence, that every impediment is temporary, and that the darkest hours bring the brightest of dawns. Selene is our good karma multiplied and brought to life, a collection of all the positive things we have to our name, and a promise that, in the end, it always pays to be good. Selene knows that the most winding paths lead us to our greater good, and she is here to be our companion and guiding light when all the other lights go out.

Selene is the light side of the moon and represents the moon's maiden energies. She is youthful, full of hope, curious, and caring. She offers us a temporary reprieve from the pressures of our daily lives. She believes there is life beyond the constant need to achieve and compete. She urges us to just be. She invites us to slow down and pay attention to what matters. She invites us to find our own flow—the kind that exists beyond false expectations and forced timelines. Selene is a free spirit. She is liberated in a Divine child kind of way, masterfully navigating the tumultuous waters, not because she has conquered them, but because she exists outside of the state of resistance. In fact, she is perfect acceptance and bliss, having achieved a state of harmony with what is, with no conditions and no reservations.

Periods of Selene

First day of the lunar cycle (new moon): This is the birth of Selene, the moon's most virgin, pure, and untarnished state. This is a state of possibility, a universal call for planting seeds. Symbolic of the beginning of the cycle, Selene paves the way for unobstructed and limitless creation. She redefines what's possible, forming a temporary and auspicious opening in the fabric of the Universe. Selene is a lucky charm, effortlessly drawing you into your better future, promising that your tomorrows will be better than your yesterdays.

Opportune timing for:

- Setting intentions
- Releasing fears
- Prayer
- Connecting with the light realms, angels, and spirit guides
- Moving beyond obstacles
- Dreaming
- Wishing upon a star
- Changing your circumstances

Seventh day of the lunar cycle: This is the sacred marriage phase of Selene, an aspect of her Divine coupling. During this time, our celestial beauty goes about finding her perfect match. This phase of Selene is all about relationships, romantic and otherwise, as long as they are heartfelt and intentional. This is the day to dive deeper and go beyond the surface level. This is the day to be vulnerable, real, raw, and authentic. This is a day for nurturing and caretaking. This is a day for treating yourself and indulging. This is a day for gratitude and celebrating life and all the people you love.

Opportune timing for:

- Romance
- Heart healing
- Cultivating relationships
- Community service
- Building strong bonds with others
- Connecting with the mother's lineage
- Self-care
- Taking a break
- Aligning
- Meditating

Twelfth day of the lunar cycle: This is harvest day for Selene, the completion of the minor cycle. During this day, we reap the reward of our benevolent actions from the last lunar cycle. This is a day of the great tally, the karmic count of our blessings. This is also a day that can bring about significant energy shifts. Old vows and promises may fall away to make way for new creation, paving the path for the great Logos, the formative power of our word. This is also a day of our legacy. It may bring potent insights into our unique path on Earth, our soul's purpose, and our mission. This day may also bring a breakthrough, a large and instant shift of your vibration and a true energy upgrade on your life path. This doesn't happen randomly, however; we reap this reward for our previous hard work.

Opportune timing for:

- Shifting patterns
- Karmic resolutions
- Aligning with your life path
- Upgrades
- Unexpected gifts from the Universe
- Fateful meetings

Twenty-third day of the lunar cycle: This is the blooming stage of Selene. This is her most beautiful, flirtatious, feminine, potent, lively, abundant, and giving stage. This is a time of minor and major blessings and unexpected handouts from the Universe. This is the last stage of Selene before her rebirth on the first day of the cycle, and it represents her purpose and mission as it relates to Gaia: to shower blessings upon the deserving ones. This is the day of personal power and sovereignty, but also a day of harmonious coexistence. This day is a culmination of Selene's power, the ascendant of her arc, her most fertile state. In this state, Selene's blessings are plenty, generously descending upon humanity and nature in an outpouring of love, redemption, and acknowledgment.

Opportune timing for:

- Being open to receiving
- Making requests of the Universe
- Celebrating
- Generosity
- Acknowledging a job well done
- Counting your blessings
- Creative/art projects
- Making beautiful things
- Meals with loved ones

Lilith: The Black Moon

Humanity's impression of the dark side of the moon ranges from something shrouded in mystery to something sinister. Lilith, an embodiment of the Dark Goddess, has grown to symbolize that which is hidden, the occult, intuition, the subconscious, sexuality, power, and independence. Lilith is an ode to a female standing tall in her sovereignty, who has been through a cycle of deep and painful initiations to reemerge as a true mistress of her resources, dark though it may be. She is not afraid of the dark; she thrives in it. Lilith knows how deep the rabbit hole goes, for at one point, she dove into it headfirst and reached the very bottom.

Lilith is a female liberated, complete in and of herself. But she is also a female with much scar tissue, deserved and otherwise. She represents an infinite resource and is a proxy for the darkness of the primordial void. And while darkness in our world is synonymous with evil, for Lilith, we must make a distinction. Her nature is neither evil nor demonic; it is simply dark. Lilith is the other side of light, the aspect of Source that is antimatter. She is therefore a masterful creatress and alchemist, molding the world around her into her personal Heaven and hell. She owns the dichotomy, forever trapped inside of it.

Lilith is the crone aspect of the moon—the kind you get endowed with after moving through an unfair share of proverbial blood, sweat, and tears. Lilith would have been perfect without her single flaw: her doubt in her own divinity. This is what created the original split within her consciousness, and this is the reason she became associated with evil. While a true magician, Lilith is forever seeking completion and absolution, judging herself for past mistakes. We may admire Lilith, as well as learn from her mistakes; the two are not mutually exclusive. She is perfect in her imperfection, liberated in her confinement, and enviable in her scar tissue. She is a force to be reckoned with.

Anyone who has walked a thousand roads is bound to have a thousand bruises. And Lilith, despite her imminent and ever-present darkness, shines the light on the parts of us that we have rejected, denied, and judged. She is therefore on a path toward healing and integration, a true way-shower. Lilith, despite being a poster child for going it alone and making every mistake in the book, is a true beacon of femininity for modern times, a hero in her own right. She is real, raw, and always herself, boldly paving a path for every female who dares to walk in her footsteps, unapologetically free.

Periods of Lilith

Sixth day of the lunar cycle: This is the major karmic release day, the day that brings equilibrium and forces you to reap what you have sown. Carrying karma from month to month can become taxing, so the sixth day of the lunar cycle offers a much-needed release, and sometimes, payback. Karma can be both negative and positive. Pay close attention to everything that "randomly" happens to you today; it is not as random as it appears. The veil is also incredibly thin during this day, so communicating with Spirit may become easier, the messages coming through with more clarity than usual and bearing a special significance. This day is great for connecting with your ancestors and working through ancestral karmic knots and patterns, as well as rewriting the history of your lineage by starting to make fundamentally different choices.

Opportune timing for:

- Self-reflection
- Shadow work
- Quiet alone time
- Recording your dreams (some may be prophetic or carry a special significance for you)
- Meditations that help release stuck emotions or rewrite past trauma
- Past life regressions
- Divination and fortune-telling

Thirteenth day of the lunar cycle: This is an exceptional time of transformation and letting go. This day carries the energy of a scorpion, mystical, poisonous, intuitive, healing. This is the day to dive deep into your soul, a day for some profound soul-searching and healing. Today, your ability to diagnose the root cause of issues grows exponentially, allowing you to lift the veil and see your trauma for what it actually is. This day also enables you to use your resources to heal some deep-seated trauma within yourself. Your magic as a healer is at an all-time high during this day, and it comes out intuitively through your words, thoughts, and actions.

Opportune timing for:

- Plant medicine
- Shamanic practices
- Art as self-expression
- Ecstatic dance
- Painting
- Detox practices
- Cleanses of all kinds (etheric, mental, or physical)

Eighteenth day of the lunar cycle: This is the day of the dark harvest, of watching the seeds that at one point were in gestation finally starting to bear fruit. "Dark harvest" doesn't mean evil; it simply means the harvest once birthed by the feminine (dark) part of you. Your creative projects, your children, your beginnings—they really matter on this day. Recognizing how far you have come is the number one most important ritual of the day. This day is about celebrating your victories, no matter how small, honoring the fertility of your soil and your ability to grow and create things. This day is about recognizing the Creator/Creatress inside. This day calls for the tally of your intentions that ended up coming through. The magic of this day is amplified with gratitude. This day is also a massive opportunity to align with your intended path, especially if you feel you have strayed from it.

Opportune timing for:

- Collecting rewards
- Shifting gears
- Getting out of the rat race to gain perspective
- Being grateful for what you have
- Enjoying the fruits of your labor
- Counting your blessings
- Acknowledging how far you have come
- Patting yourself on the back

Twenty-sixth day of the lunar cycle: The lotus blooming in the night, this is a day of secret beauty, of recognizing the hidden aspects of our existence that make all the difference—our dreams, aspirations, deepest feelings, and connectedness with all that is. This is also a day of sisterhood, of cherishing and pampering the females in your life that you love the most. This is the day for confiding in others, diving deeper, listening to your friends, and sharing intentional moments in a women's circle. This is a day for storytelling and indulging in the finer things in life, for reminiscing and being in nature. This day is intrinsically linked with water, so spending time near a natural body of water can be especially healing and enjoyable. This is the day to work with the magic of a spiral, especially the black spiral, which is known for helping you release any stuck energies, especially in the physical and emotional bodies.

Opportune timing for:

- Self-care
- Luxurious baths
- Treating yourself
- Women's circles
- Nurturing your sisters
- Ritual magic
- Water magic and water rituals
- A spa day
- A sauna
- Full-body exfoliation
- Massage
- Craniosacral therapy
- Buying yourself flowers
- Working with essential oils
- Sound healing

Luna: Full Moon (or Combined Moon)

The state of Luna is the state of fullness, things coming into fruition, perfect manifestation, the harvest season, redemption, and building for the long term. Luna is about abundance, a state of overflowing with blessings. Luna can be very emotional, even intense; it is the fullness of sensing and the fullness of feeling. This is a state of all the neurons firing at once, an equivalent of the cosmic adrenaline rush that can propel you into action, or leave you feeling perplexed, because of the presence of everything simultaneously. Luna can be karmic and even cathartic. It is a point in the lunar calendar that enables you to release and let go, while celebrating how far you have come.

This stage is perfect for tracking how you are doing in terms of your goals, for looking back and reminiscing about what the last twenty-nine days (from one full moon to the next) has done for you. Luna is the highest point of the lunar calendar, the point of ample activity and massive energy movements. From this place of fullness, allow yourself to reconnect with nature, plugging yourself back into the benevolent ecosystem that is our beloved Gaia. Walk barefoot in nature, connect with trees and plants in your yard/garden, swim in a river, and talk to elemental spirits; the abundance of nature is especially attuned to the needs of humanity during the periods of Luna. The witches of old knew this; that is why they gathered together with their sisters to celebrate the full moon. Naked, barefoot, and full of love for Gaia, they stepped into days and nights of sacred ritual and celebration, fully basking in the moonlight and its healing.

This stage of Luna is when our special abilities are enhanced, our dreams become prophetic, and the veil is temporarily lifted, so we can glance into the world of Spirit and get the necessary guidance. Full moons are perfect portals for stepping into your higher calling and aligning with it fully and unabashedly. Not only are your spirit guides especially active during this time, but your ability to receive and understand their messages is also heightened. This makes for a prolific period of spiritual and worldly growth. The Luna stage is a time of authenticity; all the masks temporarily fall off to reveal the truth inside. This can be the time to face your inner demons and heal your wounds as they bubble up to the surface and make themselves known.

Periods of Luna

Fourteenth day of the lunar cycle: The so-called "hatching phase" can bring major revelations. What is hidden may become apparent, the unexpected may make itself known, and projects may start coming to fruition. This is the day for quantum leaping, for upgrading all areas of your life, for finally going after the big thing you desire. This day could also serve as an energetic rite of passage; you may be tested and tried. Your thoughts are especially magnetic and have the propensity to manifest quickly, so be careful what you are thinking of and what you are projecting energetically. Make the fourteenth day of the lunar cycle as intentional as possible. Fill it with intentional thoughts, feelings, and actions, and watch your life transform. Be open to whatever this day brings, no matter how unexpected. This day is always karmic, so read between the lines of whatever is happening.

Opportune timing for:

- Connecting with your spirit guides
- Making massive shifts in your lifestyle (such as giving up an addictive habit or leaving a relationship that no longer serves you)
- Setting a new audacious direction for your life
- Connecting with and acting upon your life's calling

Fifteenth day of the lunar cycle: This is the "garland day," a day of small blessings, each like an ornament on the garland of your life path. This is a day for meaningful connections and deep relationships; nothing superficial can stick. It is a great day for soul-searching and deep introspection as you dive headfirst into the rest of your life. This is also a perfect day to harmonize your masculine and feminine polarities, bringing them into one cohesive whole. This day may expose excess or unbalance in an area of your life by making you face it head-on. Remember, whatever realizations come during this day, they always come with your greatest good in mind.

Opportune timing for:

- Ancestral healing and harmonization of your lineage
- Finding balance between give and take
- Volunteering, community work, and acts of service
- Breathwork
- Yoga (not that there is a bad day for yoga!)

Sixteenth day of the lunar cycle: This is the day for forward movement—planning, executing, and making moves. It is easier to get things done today, especially if you are working on your soul purpose. Being ambitious around your to-do list is encouraged. All pressure is good pressure during the sixteenth day of the lunar cycle. Pushing your limits will enable you to uncover new reserves of resilience and power within yourself, propelling you toward your goals and dreams. This is a good day to be seen and heard, to engage with large masses of people, and to boldly go after your most audacious dreams. This is also the day to get focused and organized, whether by physically or mentally decluttering or by becoming intentional about optimizing your schedule.

Opportune timing for:

- Being active
- Having a full calendar
- Working out or sports
- Working on long-term goals
- Crossing things off your to-do list
- Finally completing something you have been procrastinating on
- Decluttering (mentally, physically, emotionally, and energetically)
- Taking on new commitments
- Working on big ideas
- Making big, bold moves

The Two Matrices: Lunar and Solar

Two matrices peacefully coexist on planet Earth: the Lunar Matrix and the Solar Matrix. At any given point in time, you are plugged into one of them by default, and that greatly influences your way of relating to the world around you. The Lunar and Solar Matrices overlay the larger Universal Matrix that contains the entirety of creation as we know it. However, the Universal Matrix is too all-encompassing and nebulous to be able to cater to every need. Hence, smaller, more targeted overlays usually govern the state of local affairs.

The Solar Matrix

The Solar Matrix connects us with the spirit realm and provides a doorway into higher consciousness, including Source itself, if we are willing to go up to that level. The Solar Matrix is therefore a projection of our Great Creator/Creatress, a means of aligning with their consciousness. The Solar Matrix exists for the entire solar system, bringing every planet, satellite, and even asteroid into one cohesive whole that operates as one organism, one consciousness that grows and expands.

There are many benefits to being connected to the Solar Matrix. It offers an expanded view of the world, and it is intuitive and sophisticated, unlocking the fastest path toward evolution for every being plugged into it. The Solar Matrix is led by Source, and therefore, it factors in the greater good of every living being.

Benefits of the Solar Matrix:

- Development of your higher centers
- Connection with your Higher Self
- Connection with Source
- Massive energetic upgrades and energy grants from the sun
- An enhanced sense of personal power and responsibility
- An enhanced ability to impact the collective
- Enhanced creativity and manifestation potential
- Heightened intuition and access to the Akashic Records
- Healing and rejuvenation through solar codes
- Being subconsciously connected to the greater cosmos and the entire Milky Way, not just our immediate surroundings
- The ability to learn from higher consciousness

The Lunar Matrix

The Lunar Matrix only exists within the constraints of planet Earth, acting like its etheric extension. Similar localized matrices aren't rare in the Universe; in fact, about twenty percent of the planets in our cosmic surroundings have one. Usually, such a matrix is present for planets going through a gestation or incubation period, conservation or transformation that needs to be properly overseen. This type of matrix also ensures that as little planetary energy as possible spills into the greater collective. While the Lunar Matrix is "old" by human standards, it is quite new from a broader perspective. The current version of our local Lunar Matrix is meant to teach humanity the lessons of the heart: handling emotions, relating to others, and creating a healthy and harmonious ecosystem. The moon has taken on the role of our great planetary teacher. As a byproduct of its mission here on Earth, which mostly concerns the emotional realm, the moon governs the element of water. This enables the moon to be present in our bodies, gently guiding us toward brighter days and better outcomes.

Benefits of the Lunar Matrix:

- Feeling at home on Earth
- Feeling connected to nature
- An enhanced ability to relate to others
- An enhanced ability to better handle emotional states
- Healing your Mother wounds (as well as other feminine-related wounding)
- Being in sync with every being on the planet
- Being focused on a smaller subset of issues, not having to think about larger-than-life issues
- A sense of comfort and belonging to the local ecosystem

How the various matrices interact is uniquely bespoke in each case. For planet Earth, the Solar and the Lunar Matrices are not mutually exclusive. Rather, they commingle, allowing one to move fluidly within the other while maintaining the continuity of the human experience. That being said, most of humanity is experiencing life from a single viewpoint right now, and that viewpoint is determined by the influence of the Lunar Matrix. While the benefits of such a tight-knit connection to the moon are ample, this connection can also constrain soul evolution, as it prevents humanity from communicating with Source directly. As humanity, we are meant to be in constant contact with our Great Creator/Creatress, learning from them as we undergo a human experience. However, unless we reconnect with the Solar Matrix, this becomes a tall order. For this reason, many cycles of incarnation can go by as souls remain disconnected from the larger force that birthed them.

There is nothing inherently wrong with the Lunar Matrix, but like all things, it should be used in moderation. The best possible arrangement is being plugged into both matrices simultaneously, smoothly migrating from one to another when the occasion calls for it. Below are some simple tips on how to connect to each matrix.

Connecting to the Solar Matrix:

- Sun gazing, looking at the sun first thing in the morning or during sunset for up to three minutes (please do not do this during the afternoon when the sun is at its zenith)

- Inviting the sun to enter your body through your third eye area, so you can absorb its codes
- Greeting the sun daily
- Connecting to the sun during the two equinoxes and the two solstices of the calendar year
- Wearing golden jewelry
- Using citrine, sunstone, and yellow tourmaline to connect to the sun
- Working on your solar plexus chakra

Connecting to the Lunar Matrix:

- Moon gazing (usually during the full moon phase)
- Connecting to the element of water, whether in nature or energetically
- Drinking a lot of water
- Grounding and earthing
- Noticing the moon's phases and shifting your vibrations to match the lunar cycle
- Participating in new moon and full moon rituals
- Connecting with moonstone and opal crystals

Moving Between the Two Matrices

Due to the nature of how the two matrices are set up, the Lunar Matrix has a stronger gravitational pull, making it the default matrix of Earth at the moment. No matter how far we journey spiritually, we will always be pulled back into the Lunar Matrix, reconnecting with it automatically. That being said, connecting with the Lunar Matrix and benefiting from it are different. You can only benefit from the Lunar Matrix when the full alignment takes place on all levels; otherwise, the Lunar Matrix may cause you to lose energy. This can be perpetually taxing. In fact, not being fully synced up to the Lunar Matrix is one of the reasons so many people experience chronic fatigue. Aligning your natural rhythms to the moon's cycles can help you harness the satellite's power and fully benefit from your long-standing connection.

Since humanity is mostly disconnected from the Solar Matrix, the sun has a limited capacity for fueling humanity. This wouldn't be an issue if we could harness the moon's power properly. Alas, humanity is experiencing a state of perpetual disconnectedness from both the moon and the sun, making it hard to feel energized, healthy, and happy in day-to-day life.

Tips for synchronizing your biorhythms to the moon:

- Watch the moon phases and create a moon calendar, noting your moods during each day of the lunar cycle. How the moon impacts you personally may be unique, so it is very important to establish this one-on-one relationship.
- Take moon baths every full moon. A moon bath is a time of introspection. Allow yourself to just reminisce while observing the moon. If you can be outside when this happens, the benefits of this ritual increase exponentially.
- The moon likes certain herbs, like chamomile, mugwort, mint, oregano, and hawthorn. Making teas and infusions with these herbs will bring you into a closer connection with the moon.
- The moon likes all things silver, so wearing silver jewelry can enhance your ties to the moon.

Tips on synchronizing your biorhythms to the sun:

- Get into the habit of getting up early to greet the sun. If you are a night owl, opt for synchronizing with the sunset via a practice of sun gazing.
- Celebrate the turn of the seasons, always noticing the slight shift in the vibrations of the sun and the new energies it starts to bring forth.
- Allow the sun to charge the water you drink. Place a carafe/bottle with drinking water in the sun for three hours, and watch your regular water transform into a drink with high-frequency solar properties. Sun-charged water will help optimize your energy levels, remove energy blockages, and create homeostasis (balance) within your body.
- Invite the solar frequencies into your chakras, starting at the root and ending at the crown. Imagine solar energy as a golden stream of light entering each of your chakras and growing roots there. Enjoy!

Heart Space: The Second Coming of the Red Rose

When the new dawn smiles upon the shores of Gaia, when the surge of the hurricane heralds the arrival of the promised one, when the night and the day shall once again become equals, when the black sun is revealed as a long-forgotten truth, when a maiden takes a leap of faith and steps upon sturdy ground on the other side, when the Age of Pisces turns into the Age of Aquarius, when the quiet settles in after the storm, there shall come a day of change.

The old rose shall become new again.

The old story shall be retold.

The Magdalene Sisters shall be cleansed of the layer of grime and dust.

That which was dead shall reawaken.

That which was long forgotten shall claim its holy rebirth.

The red rose of the Magdalene shall once again rejoin the white rose of Mary, and the two shall be separate no longer.

The crack in the Golden Chalice shall once again be mended.

And when the Last Supper becomes the First Supper, when the two female lineages look upon each other with light in their eyes and love in their hearts, division shall be no more.

There shall be born a new leader, and there shall come a new Bible woven of threads of white and gold.

And that shall signify the Second Coming and a renewed promise of life eternal, but not like what you know.

It is in the strength of the combined white and red rose magic that one shall find Divinity.

It is in this sacred marriage that the Book of Revelation shall be fulfilled.

When the sovereignty of the red rose merges with the unity of the white rose, the New Earth shall rise. And from that unity, Christ consciousness shall become amplified.

And the two roses, aligned and thriving, shall hold the chalice of the new world together, just like it should have been.

And so it finally is. And so it shall forever remain.

CHAPTER 16

The Red Rose – The Ruby Mysteries

The red rose of the Mother Divine is one of her most potent symbols. It combines the power of love and sacrifice with the resilience and courage of a true warrior. The red rose is a treasure infused with devoted reverence, depth of feeling, and a thirst to do what's right.

Aspects of the Red Rose

- **Element:** Earth and fire
- **Planets:** Venus and Mars
- **State:** Sacred action and inspiration, the changing of the tides, claiming new territories, fighting for what's right
- **Mood:** Active, animated, excited, restless
- **Signature:** Devotion to an idea or another being, strength of commitment, willingness to sacrifice oneself, generosity
- **Vibration:** Love, dedication, direction, and passion
- **Goddesses and Saints:** Mary Magdalene, Aphrodite, Inanna, Astarte, Hippolyta (queen of the Amazons), Freyja, Lakshmi, Hathor, Joan of Arc, Sekhmet

Devotion to the cause is in the blood of the red rose, in her ruby-red tears shed upon life's battlefields, and in her bold, courageous heart. The red rose is a final redemption—the kind only offered once we have been baptized by fire, withstanding the harsh winters and the scorching summers, holding fast to our faith despite adversity. Once our true nature is revealed, once the dust settles and our wounds are healed, the red rose shall rise as a promise and a revelation.

The red rose is ushering in a new era—an era of light, victory, tears of joy and gratitude, and the New Earth. The core belief of the red rose is that light shall always prevail over darkness, and that little is impossible for the warrior whose heart is true. A red rose is a hymn to our resilience and our sovereignty, our ability to find and hold our center, and our willingness to do whatever it takes in pursuit of our North Star and our God/

Goddess-given purpose. The red rose is a sacred gift we accidentally discover upon the funeral pyre of the hopes of yesterday. And yet, what burns on the pyre has never been true. Let it burn, sister. Let it burn, brother. Cleanse yourself of the falsehoods and limitations, and get good at letting go. Let the cleansing smoke of the pyre, do away with the old wounds of the patriarchy, the stench of karma, the scar tissue, and the gaping heart wounds. We are building our tomorrow together, and in that tomorrow, there is no room for the traumas of the days long gone.

The red rose is a warrior. She is courage in flower form, forged from fire, adversity, and sacrifice. She perseveres despite it all, going against great odds and paving the way for others to follow boldly. She is the last one standing, safeguarding the gateway to your perfect future.

The red rose is passion, determination, and sacred service. She gives all of herself, and then gives some more. She is obsessed and obsessive, fiery and feisty, and yet tried and true. She is the power of the holy scripture, the truth of your blood, the strength of your vow, and your God/Goddess-given potential. She doesn't take no for an answer, always pushing the boundaries of what's possible. She is life force clad in petals. And while she is pretty, make no mistake: her thorns hurt more deeply than most.

Working with the Red Rose

Working with the red rose means plunging headfirst into the ocean of seeking to understand your true worth. The path of the red rose is the path of being tested. Everything from your resilience to the strength and power of your convictions shall be scrutinized. The reward? Access to infinite life force.

Taming the red rose is like taming a tiger; it shall take everything you have. This path is rooted in trials and tribulations, and hence, it requires true courage. The red rose shall battle-test you, throw you into the fiery pit to fend for yourself, and have your bones for breakfast. And here you thought the red rose was all about eternal love and romance!

While being a carrier of the love frequency, the red rose is only partially run by it. The fight, the revolution, the blood, sweat, and tears—this is the true face of the red rose. If you think working with the red rose is easy, just take a look at the legacy of Mary Magdalene, an ascended master who took it upon herself to walk the Path of the Red Rose. Her journey was far from easy, with her life partner murdered, her female mystery order dismantled, her legacy tarnished, and her teachings scattered to the four winds. And yet, her path remains sacred now, just as it was then. It shows us the true resilience and might of the female spirit. The hidden legacy of Magdalene was that of following her heart and doing what she thought was right, no matter the cost. She had the heart of a true believer, and in our skeptical world, this is worth everything and then some.

Devotional Path of the Red Rose

The red rose is willing to work with you if you'd like to claim it as your teacher. The outcomes of learning from this rose are plentiful, from gaining immense courage and an ability to bend the world to your will to the gifts of leadership and transformation.

The red rose is exceptionally active on Earth, gathering her tribe of fearless ones to help her pave the path to a better tomorrow. The length of a Red Rose Initiation is usually a minimum of seven years, during which the rose becomes your mentor, guru, and etheric helper. This seven-year initiation path is filled with upgrades and energetic unlocks. The red rose usually works with your subconscious, including your fears, conditioning, and limitations. She is a mirror, reflecting that which you already are deep down.

But unearthing your limitations is just the beginning of the path. Walking with the red rose means facing your demons head-on, tackling them one at a time. The red rose will bring about a sequence of people, circumstances, and events to build your stamina, resilience, and spirit. Despite being one of the more challenging initiation paths, the red rose offers great rewards. It will forge you into the most radiant, fearless, and powerful version of yourself.

Red Rose Invocation

To step onto this path, invite the red rose to work with you, challenge you, and bring forth your personal transformation. You don't need a script for this; just let the words come from your heart. This is your personal prayer, your invocation, and your surrender to the teachings of the red rose. Below, I give a sample invocation, but you should customize it to better reflect your own frequency:

"Dear Red Rose, on this day, I invite you into my life and into my world.

I ask that you personally initiate me into your mysteries, imbue me with your power, and share your Divine codes with me, so that I may receive your blessings and your teachings.

Forge me into a warrior of light, give me courage, and stand by me during my greatest trials. I surrender to your Divine signature, I welcome your emanations, and I am humbled by your presence. I commit to walking alongside you for the next seven years and learning from your Divine teachings every step of the way.

So may it be. And so it is."

Usually, upon being initiated into the warrior tribe of the red rose, you'll get confirmation from the Universe that your request has been heard. It usually takes the form of a sign, often a red rose "randomly" appearing on your path within a few days of the invocation. But even if you do not get a physical confirmation, please know that the red rose has heard you and will begin working with you momentarily.

Red rose correspondences:

- Blood
- Courage
- Warrior spirit
- Swords
- Shields
- Romantic love
- The power of conviction
- Mares
- Tigers and panthers
- The menstrual cycle
- Pregnancy

The Code of the Red Rose

Numeric code: 11.101

The numeric frequency of the red rose contains an uncanny power to bring things out of hibernation and away from stasis. This is a jolt of electricity to reinvigorate a failing heart, a shot in the arm for an aching body, a torch in the dark to help you find your way amidst the darkness.

If you are feeling stuck in a particular area of your life, few tools are as potent as the magic of the red rose to get things moving again.

To leverage this power, write down what you are working through on a blank page. Then, take a different color of pen or pencil (ideally red) and write the Code of the Red Rose (**11.101**) directly on top of what you just wrote. Close your eyes and imagine breathing in the power of the red rose onto the page. Notice how the torrential power of the red rose is starting to remove the obstacles and create movement where there was none. Feel free to repeat the numeric code of the red rose (**11.101**) multiple times for even more clearing and momentum.

Practice: Ignite and Fire Things Up

The red rose is a powerful multiplier. It contains within itself the most potent dichotomy of earth-fire magic, which can be instrumental in giving you momentum for any of your new beginnings. In this practice, we will work with the natural ability of the red rose to amplify things, bring about massive change, and charge new projects with live-giving magic, propelling them into rapid growth.

1. Get into a comfortable seated position or lie down. Make sure you won't be disturbed.
2. Start to notice the breath gently entering your lungs, then leaving with each exhale. Feel the liberation that each breath brings. Allow your breaths to carry away any tension that may be present in your body. Release and let go with every exhale.
3. Imagine walking along a narrow path of smooth white pebbles leading to a picturesque verdant garden.
4. Keep walking, and as you do so, notice all the plants around you—the vines climbing up the trunks of ancient oak trees, the gentle blooms of daffodils and daisies peeking through the well-maintained grass, and fragrant herbs growing on perfectly rounded flowerbeds scattered along both sides of your path.
5. Welcome to the domain of the red rose: her mystical garden. As you keep walking along the path, notice the many rose bushes lining it. Each bush is covered with large, velvety, soft blooms of the red rose. Notice the sweet aroma in the air, an undeniable signature of the rose's dominion over this place.
6. Keep walking until you happen upon an opening in your path. Through the opening, notice a spacious white rotunda, its massive pillars carved with an intricate rose pattern. Suspended in midair in the very center of the rotunda is a massive red rosebud. It is huge—easily the size of your entire body, and perhaps bigger.
7. Notice how the petals of the rose emit a ruby-like red glow, filling the rotunda with a mystical red haze.
8. Come closer and place your hands upon the petals of the rose, connecting with her spirit. Feel how the red fire is ignited inside of you. Watch as your body is filled with a glimmer of ruby-like emanations. Feel this power

within, and sense the energetic signature of the red rose coursing through your body, entering your bloodstream, and filling your blood vessels.

9. Now, notice a white sphere of light hovering above the red rosebud. Imagine that this sphere contains an area of your life that requires a breakthrough. Alternatively, you can imagine a project you are working on that you would like to succeed.
10. Notice how this sphere of light starts descending, moving closer and closer to the red bloom, until finally, it lands straight atop the rose.
11. Watch how the contact that is now established between the rose and the white sphere is starting to deepen. Notice the sphere sinking deeper and deeper into the petals until it completely disappears among them.
12. While you can no longer see the sphere, you know in your heart that it is undergoing a transformation induced by its proximity to the red rose. Allow this process to happen naturally; do not force it or try to speed it up in any way.
13. Finally, notice that the sphere is beginning to reemerge from the petals, only it's ruby red now. Gone is the white light. In its stead, your sphere is ignited with the fire of the rose, propelled forward by her unbreakable spirit.
14. Watch as a ruby-red fire emerges from the petals of the red rose, further charging your sphere with life-giving magic. Allow your sphere to absorb as much of this vibration as needed.
15. Now, allow yourself to accept this newly transformed sphere of ruby red light into your auric field. Bring this sphere into your heart, merging with it fully.
16. Notice how this shifts your vibration, imbuing you with the fiery activating energies of the red rose. Enjoy this sacred communion with the spirit of the rose.
17. Finally, thank the rose for sharing its resources with you today. Feel free to open your eyes when it feels like your journey has come to its logical conclusion.

The Ruby Mysteries

It is in the legacy of Mary Magdalene that we shall find traces of the Ruby Mysteries.

Mary Magdalene founded one of the largest and most prominent female mystery schools in recent history. Dubbed the Magdalene Sisters, the order was a series of initiations into the teachings of Isis, the Atlantean Temple of Love, and the Lemurian crystal lineage. At the height of the order, Mary Magdalene had more than ten thousand followers, all devoted to her teachings and her way of life.

Mary had a great vision for the world. She believed that a future where every female could stand in her own sovereignty was not a utopia, but an inevitability. She devoted her life to making this vision a reality, working tirelessly to recruit and educate new members. Mary led massive group rituals and offerings, imparting her knowledge to the many women seeking to learn from her. For the first ten years of the existence of the order, Mother Mary led the order side by side with Mary Magdalene, and many of her teachings became the foundation of the belief system of the order.

The Ruby Mysteries was one of the learning tracks available to the Magdalene Sisters. Mary Magdalene was cosmically connected to the power of the ruby crystal, a patron crystal of the Hathors, to which Mary Magdalene belonged through her star lineage. The Hathors are a group of female star beings that travel across the Milky Way and the neighboring galaxies, spreading the word of the She-God and anchoring the vibrations of the Divine Mother. They are a heart-led group of evolved souls devoted to the ascension of all living beings. You can think of them as cosmic gypsies and missionaries, traveling to even the remotest places and bringing the teachings of the Mother with them. As a member of the Hathors, Mary Magdalene was channeling their teachings from a young age, being brought up in the emanations of the Great Mother and carrying the Ruby Ray, one of the most active, courageous, and formative aspects of the Divine Mother.

The Ruby Mysteries was a series of teachings channeled by Mary from her Hathor Sisters that centered around activating a woman's creative resources through the power of sacred geometry and the blessings of the ruby.

The Ruby Triangle was a pivotal concept within the Ruby Mysteries. The Ruby Triangle is a point within the female body that, once activated, turns a female into the creatress she was born to be, bringing about the full force of her creative and transformative powers.

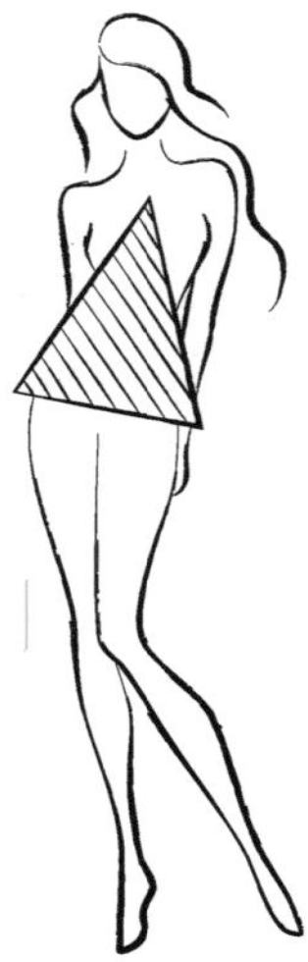

Figure 61: The Ruby Triangle

Practice: Activating the Ruby Triangle

The Ruby Triangle has three points in the physical body (see **Figure 61**). The point at the top is the higher heart, which corresponds to the thymus gland. The two other points are located in the ovaries, the seat of female creatress powers. The Ruby Triangle enables us to merge the power of unconditional love of infinite proportions that dwells inside our higher hearts with the power of creating life in the physical in the ovaries. The result is an alchemical creative process of boundless power. Once activated, the Ruby Triangle starts to work in the background, merging itself with the natural ebbs and flows of the female body, bringing about meaningful change on both the physical and the etheric planes.

1. Get into a comfortable seated position and close your eyes.
2. Imagine that your body is encapsulated within a pyramid of ruby-red light. Feel this energy, its sweeping force and its almost palpable heartbeat.
3. Imagine that the ruby light surrounding you activates your higher heart in your upper chest area.
4. Feel how this part of your body starts to receive ruby-red light frequencies, absorbing them fully.
5. Stay here until your higher heart is sufficiently charged, enough to start pulsating with the ruby-red light.
6. Watch as the red light from your higher heart travels down your body toward your right ovary, activating it.
7. Stay here for a few moments, allowing your right ovary to become saturated with this potent light.
8. When ready, send a pulse of red light from your right ovary into your left ovary, activating the final point of the triangle.
9. Watch as your left ovary starts to pulsate with the ruby-red glow.
10. Finally, send the ruby frequency up your body toward your higher heart, officially closing the triangle of ruby light.
11. If it feels good, send the ruby frequency down your body a few more times, powering your ruby triangle further.
12. You can set an intention here, if you'd like. Simply answer the following questions: "What kind of life am I committed to creating for myself? What kind of a world would I like to co-create for others?" Then, send your

intention into the ruby triangle, specifically focusing on its three points, one after another.

13. Imagine planting your intention in each of the triangle's points, as if it were a little golden seed. Watch your intention take root and sprout. Notice how the light of the Ruby Triangle powers it and helps its materialization.

Feel free to use this practice whenever you want to activate your massive creatress powers.

Working with the Ruby Crystal

The Magdalene Sisters who were initiated into the Ruby Mysteries took it upon themselves to intimately connect with the ruby as a crystal, and they performed many rites and rituals under its tutelage. Ruby was regarded as a personal power crystal, an amplifier that could collect formative energies from its surroundings and share them with its wearer. The ruby crystal often chose the owner, not the other way around. Some of the Magdalene Sisters would spend years in prayer and contemplation before being initiated into the mysteries of the crystal, for it was quite selective. The Ruby Mystery initiates were considered the members of the spiritual elite, the chosen ones, those destined to carry the brunt of the work and mission of the order. The wearer of the ruby could borrow from the crystal's powers in daily life and during taxing rites and rituals requiring intense energy infusion. Each sister connected to the ruby crystal began to intuitively draw from the crystal's resources.

Power infusion: While building an in-depth bond with the ruby may take years or even decades, a simple connection to the crystal and the benefits it entails is available to everyone. To fully connect with the ruby, all the chakras have to align with that of this magnificent helper. In this case, owning a ruby is not required; you can first connect energetically. Imagine connecting to a large etheric ruby crystal chakra by chakra, starting at the crown and moving down until you reach the root chakra. Imagine a set of interlocking mechanisms connecting your crown chakra with the crown chakra of the ruby. Feel a fusion take place, where you and the crystal become one. Once the seven main chakras are interlocked in this manner, you should feel a torrent of energy rising from your root center upward, not dissimilar to the kundalini rising. This is the power of the ruby rising in you. Congratulations! You are now connected to this royal crystal.

Energy protection: Ruby is a fierce protector of its allies. Use it to fortify the wards of your personal space, whether that is your home or your personal auric field. Imagine eight pillars of ruby-red light emerging around the perimeter of that which you are trying to protect. Once fully fledged, the pillars merge together at the top and the bottom, creating an elongated shape not unlike a Vogel crystal. This energy structure is quite resilient and requires no upkeep. Provided that you maintain a strong relationship with the ruby crystal, this structure will remain intact and operational.

Increased psychic abilities: Since ancient times, the ruby has been known for enhancing seers' abilities. Many priestesses and oracles of old used to carry a ruby crystal for enhanced perception. To leverage this property of the ruby, imagine placing an etheric copy of the stone in your third eye, as well as in the inner side of both of your wrists.

Connect the three points into a cohesive triangle. Then, focus on what you want to see or need answers for. The ruby shall greatly enhance your natural seer abilities.

Better connection with your totem animal: Ruby carries within itself a primordial life force. It is inherently connected to power symbols in nature and the greater cosmos. The magic of the ruby can be used to enhance your connection with any of the natural helpers, including your totem animal. Simply place an etheric copy of the ruby in your heart space, then place another copy of the crystal in your totem animal's heart space. Watch as the connection between your heart crystals is established. From this place of renewed understanding, ask for assistance from your totem animal.

The Great Desert: The Shadow Side of the Red Rose

A desert is a state of being, not a place. It is one of the states of femininity ever present in the Universe. The state of the desert is that of depletion, of being scorched, thirsty, lacking, and stretched too thin. It is a state of love lost, of abandoning your body and leaving behind the hapless terrain of self-criticism, doubt, and false expectations.

Nobody is born into the state of the desert, but we may become this state through loss, stress, conditioning, and trauma. The desert state is one of the most sorrowful states for a female organism. It turns a flourishing and nurturing ecosystem into a lifeless terrain devoid of hope and nourishment. This is when the mother becomes a stepmom, when all love turns into rigidity, and when fertility turns into a barren landscape. The desert state is a loss of hope and a descent into perpetual suffering. A female overcome by her inner desert becomes haughty, proud, and oh so hurt inside. The desert is a shadow side of the red rose, her most extreme broken state. The desert is the warrior broken, torn apart, their remains scattered on the wind. The desert state is the opposite of wholesomeness, flow, and happiness. Like the glass that has been shattered into too many pieces, the desert state is that of desolation and disrepair.

Unfortunately, this state is familiar to thousands of women on our beautiful planet. And while we may think that the state of the desert comes from an inability to love, the truth is very different. A desert state is a byproduct of loss and heartbreak. It didn't start this way. Every female in a desert state was once lively, full of gentle hope, fearlessly opening her heart to the world. But time went by, and life happened. The female's heart was wounded by betrayal, punctured by harsh words, and suffocated by unrequited love. She had to harden herself, so she built walls where there were once bridges, her sweet words turned sour, and her good wishes became curses. Her disposition turned bitter, and her actions turned vindictive. She learned to become guarded, and distrust became her primary signature.

Nobody is born a desert. Deserts are forged by eons of harsh conditions, betrayal, and sadness. The desert state is contagious. Having grown roots in one female, it spreads to those around her, hardening their hearts and creating trauma. A desert is an ecosystem devoid of water, stripped of life, and ripe with desolation. And yet, this state, while prevalent, is not a natural state of femininity. It is an outlier, a byproduct of harsh conditions and over-masculinized societies. A desert state is neither a predicament nor a verdict, and it is by no means irreversible. Reclaiming your gentle femininity starts with inviting the magic of water back into your life.

Tips and Practices: Nourishing a Desert State

If you feel you may be prone to the state of the desert, consider using the practices and tips below to help you optimize your state.

Energy of water: Invite the energy of water to enter your heart and soften it, cell by cell. Watch as your heart swells from all the water that is entering it. Imagine that your heart is a sponge whose sole job is to absorb as much water as possible. Repeat this exercise once a day for seven days to see noticeable results.

Dissolve the shell: If you are experiencing a state of the desert, your heart likely has a protective shell around it that causes it to feel numb and harsh. Imagine dissolving the shell using a transparent Divine liquid. Watch as the hard shell around your heart disappears, revealing a beautiful, loving heart underneath. (See also the practice in Chapter 11, page 214.)

Imagine rain: In a meditative state, imagine that the desert landscape of your body is getting its first rain in decades. Watch as large water droplets fall upon the barren terrain, washing away the dust and going deep into the earth. Take in as much rain as you can. Finally, watch the desert transform into a luscious garden filled with all manner of plants and flowers.

Drink more water: Every time you drink water, imagine the wounds of your heart closing up. Do a quick audit of your heart space. You may notice knives and daggers protruding from certain areas of your heart—remnants of old betrayals and heartbreak. Gently remove the knives and daggers, healing the tissues around the cuts using a stream of white light.

Forgiveness: Forgive yourself for things big and small. Stop blaming yourself for mistakes, past or present.

Cleansing energies: Allow yourself to cross a threshold into a new life where you no longer have to be in a perpetual protective stance. Allow yourself to leave the old wounding in the past. Imagine a waterfall of white light falling all over your body and washing away all past mistakes. Allow yourself to bask in these cleansing energies.

New intention: Create a new intention for yourself and your life. Invite that which you want to see more of back into your life. Then imagine that a large torrential river is bringing that closer to you. Absorb it into your heart, opening the door to your inner sanctuary. Be grateful for this magical transformation.

Here's to a new you, full of life and water!

Heart Space: An Amalgamation

She was water.

For she was fluid and flexible beyond measure. She knew how to flow. She changed course easily. She was a shape-shifter, filling every cup, every vessel she was offered. She was water. Water always finds a way.

She was earth.

For she was fertile and nurturing and steady. She respected her cycles, never pushing herself to bear fruit before it was time. She was patient, and she was calm. She was dependable and trustworthy. She always showed up when it mattered most. She was the joy of harvest and the blessing of spring. She was earth, steady, strong, and true.

She was fire.

For she was always so full of life, alight with the newest challenge. She was warm, passionate, and excited. She burned bright—as bright as the sun, and perhaps even brighter. She was danger incarnate, and temptation made manifest. She was the breath of a dragon and the might of a constellation. She was a torch and a flame and a molten torrent of change. She was a revolution. She was a queen. She was fire. And even the stars came to pay homage to her.

She was air.

For she was swift and light and free. She was the truth, the winds of change, and the ever-shifting curious mind excited by the newest puzzle. She was an eagle in the sky and the breath of the Universe in your lungs. She was the inhale of transformation and the exhale of what once was. She was the new world, the new paradigm, and the new dawn. She was the spirit of authenticity, Divine in her resolve, unearthly in her splendor. She was air. And she would not be contained.

She was ether.

For she was beyond this world and the next. Angels were her confidants. Higher dimensions were her home. She was not constrained by the visible, but forever in sync with the unseen. She was a seer, a psychic, an intuitive. She was a mystery, an enigma, a high priestess, and a goddess among men. She was forever unattainable, yet fully corporeal. She was elusive, but her healing magic was one of a kind. She was a gift to this world—and she knew it. She was ether, the highest of all the elements, the stuff the stars are made of.

She was an amalgamation.

She was all of the elements brought together by the universal magnetism, created to defy all odds, to sit upon the throne of the stars adorned by the moon herself.

She was a challenge, a dare, a promise.

She was a woman in the age of men. She was a woman in the age that came after,

Imperfect, raw, yet complete.

She was a woman, the crown jewel of all mysteries.

She was a woman. And she was an amalgamation.

CHAPTER 17

The Many Codes of the Rose

The past few chapters have been devoted to some of the roses most relevant to the vibrations of Earth right now. However, the rose kingdom is much broader, much more majestic, and a lot more mystical than we have given it credit for up to this point. This chapter is a deep dive into the many colors of the rose, its numerous emanations and projections, the lessons of each, and the numerical frequency that can help you reap the benefits of a deep, unobstructed connection with each of the roses.

The Pink Rose

The pink rose is of the higher heart. Combining the purity of the white rose with the passion and inspired action of the red rose, the pink rose is a spirit flower of Earth, an emblem and a symbol of the path our planet is now on. The pink rose is about reaching a deep personal transformation and a willingness to put in the blood, sweat, and tears to make something happen. The pink rose is a harmonizer, a healer, and a doting mother in one sacred flower. She is immensely patient, her emanations are healing and uplifting, and she is forgiveness and compassion in flower form. The pink rose is a missionary and universally stands for heart-led living. She has come to Earth to help humanity dissolve the hard protective shells we have built around our hearts. She teaches us that a wholesome heart is not a heart that never knew sorrow, but a heart that did and was able to move beyond it, healing its wounds and sealing its fissures.

Uses:

- Heart healing
- Mending a relationship
- Finding your soulmate
- Forgiving someone who caused you pain
- Connecting to someone at a soul level
- Harmonization of any and all vibrations
- Cultivating self-love

- Forging communities

Numerical code: 202.202

The numerology of the pink rose is 8, the highest possible emanation of female energies encapsulated in a numeric form. She is femininity evolved, femininity heightened, femininity gained. She also carries the vibration of 2, the numeral of relationships, finding balance, and understanding the world through understanding another.

Working with the pink rose:

- Write the code of the pink rose on a blank page while invoking the power of the rose, asking her to play an active part in your life. Invite the rose to work with a particular area of your life as you write her numerical frequency. This is the equivalent of a cosmic phone call. The spirit of the pink rose always comes to those who are reaching out to her.
- With a pencil, gently write the numeric code of the pink rose on the underside of your clothing around your heart area. This will help you bring the healing vibrations of the pink rose into your life, helping you move past heart trauma and even easing the pain of losing a loved one.
- Use bath salts to spell the numerical frequency of the pink rose in your empty bathtub. Then, fill the tub with water and enjoy basking in the energies of the pink rose.

The Violet Rose

The violet rose is the rose of higher consciousness. She is an emissary of the light realms and an extension of the wise council of the cosmic elders. She is an enigma, ever morphing, ever shifting to match the universal thirst for deeper knowing. She is the bridge between human existence and our eternal soul space, firmly opening her embrace to encapsulate all that we are. The essence of the violet rose speaks to awakening, elevation, and ascension from lower planes of existence into the higher realms. The violet rose is a wise way-shower, a discerning sage, and an ascended master of the flower kingdom. She is full of insight and compassion, but is also precise and surgical in her teachings. She doesn't say much, but often says it all. She guides us through long periods of introspection and quality alone time, inviting us to ask hard existential questions. Her language is the language of curiosity and openness, inviting us to walk an extra mile just when we believe we have reached our final destination. She doesn't lead with the answers, but with questions, believing that all the wisdom of the world is already inside us if we only slow down to listen.

Uses:

- Enhancing meditation
- Gaining wisdom
- Gaining a different perspective on current circumstances
- Getting answers to existential questions
- Uncovering the mysteries of the Universe
- Connecting to the Akashic Records
- Enhancing the connection with ascended masters and spirit guides

Violet Rose Varieties and Their Numerical Codes

The violet rose has many varieties. Below are some of the most relevant ones for planet Earth.

777.777 – **Violet rose:** The highest-vibrational rose of the purple-hued roses, the violet rose is the most connected to Divinity and Goddess consciousness. She is a natural vibrational match to the area of your third eye, harmonizing and attuning it to the rest of the Universe. Call upon the violet rose if you need spiritual assistance and guidance. She is a wonderful teacher and a benevolent guide who will walk with you every step of your spiritual way. The numerical frequency of this rose is closely tied to seven, a number of perfection, attainment, enlightenment, and ascension.

777.701 – **Purple rose:** The purple rose is a spiritual warrior. She is a mix of noble blue and passionate red. She is the one who walks the walk, not just talks the talk. She is inspired and forward-moving, full of energy and resolve. She is a great companion if you are undertaking a large project that requires your full commitment and where the outcome is not guaranteed. She can help remove obstacles in your way and align you with those who are meant to help you. Numerically, the purple rose is a combination of the wise seven, the forward-moving one, and the resourceful zero. But when you collapse her numerical code into one number (two), you realize her way of getting things done is through mastering relationships, which she can help you with.

777.222 – **Lavender rose:** The ever-gentle healer, the lavender rose cures the heart, the mind, and the body. She is a tender caregiver, ready to embrace you as you are and ensure that you recover from even the deepest wounds, whether seen or unseen. The lavender rose is an etheric miracle worker. Call upon her to massively change your emotional state or set you on a healing path. Fill up an imaginary bath with the energy of the lavender rose and allow yourself to be fully submerged under its miraculous waters; you will notice an instant shift in your vibration and mood. Numerically, this rose holds the blueprint of the Mother working upon the earthly plane, represented by the sequence **222,** as well as a seal of perfect attainment represented by 777. Her signature is a perfect state achieved through motherly healing and love.

Working with the roses of the violet spectrum:

- Since the overall vibration of this rose spectrum is one of alignment and healing, these roses work best at night. To partake of their gifts, simply write down the numerical frequency of the rose you would like to work with on a piece of paper and place it under your pillow. Before going to sleep, speak your intention of working with the rose out loud. You may also want to add any requests you have for the rose. Repeat this ritual for seven nights to achieve optimal results.
- To help open your third eye, write down the numerical code of the violet rose on your forehead (777.777). You can trace it with water and just let it dry. Imagine the code seeping into your skin and being absorbed by your pineal gland, an area of your brain corresponding to the third eye. Notice that this area of your brain starts to pulsate with violet light. While this practice won't open your third eye immediately, it will dramatically speed up the process.
- To invite the power of the purple rose to help remove obstacles, place a piece of paper with its numeric frequency (777.701) in your shoe. You can also write the code on the sole of your shoe, if that feels better. Since the purple rose is connected to action, it needs to be able to flow through a part of your body that best corresponds with action, which the soles of your feet definitely are.

The Sapphire Rose (or Blue Rose)

The sapphire rose is a masterful truth activator. She is honorable, brave, aligned, committed, responsible, and strong. She is the rose that will help unlock your true Divine self-expression, the unique flavor of your personal soul imprint that you came to share with the world. She will remove anything blocking your ability to live, speak, or reveal your truth. She helps clean up karmic distortions around sharing your unique talents and gifts and will open up a path for you to find your tribe and build a career out of an activity that ignites your heart. She will help you show up in the world in a way true to your soul and heart. She can help you heal all wounds around being seen and heard.

Uses:

- Unlocking your self-expression and natural Goddess-given talents
- Helping fortify your belief in yourself
- Raising your self-esteem
- Helping rebuild your confidence
- Magnetizing your tribe back to you
- Unlocking your creative expression

Numerical Code: 111.111

The numerical representation of the sapphire rose is charged, intentional, and powerful beyond measure. Made entirely of the magic of one, it carries within itself the confidence of a self-starter, the codes of true leadership, and enough firepower to build empires. This rose is a blue flame encapsulated within a flower. It always runs true, cutting away any clutter and removing scar tissue to reveal the most self-sufficient and resourceful version of you. This rose has an uncanny ability to bring the resources you need toward you, and to help you push through even the most challenging obstacles. She favors the brave and the true, mostly helping those who have a habit of telling the truth and keeping their word.

Working with the sapphire rose:

- To unlock the power of your voice, whether for singing, speaking, or expressing something particularly difficult, trace the numerical code of the sapphire rose with water on your neck around your throat chakra. Allow yourself to absorb the codes deep into your throat area. Chanting the "om" mantra will help further solidify this practice.
- Inhaling the codes of the sapphire can be healing, since it works with the power of your breath. Trace the numerical frequency of the sapphire rose on one of your palms using eucalyptus or pine tree essential oil. Then, place the palm over your nose, inhaling it twelve times. Notice how this transforms the air within your body, getting deep into your lungs. This simple practice will help you feel more confident on your path, face your fears head-on, and gain momentum on your most important projects.

The Yellow Rose

The yellow rose is a solar rose—a rose of joy, youth, adventure, and fun. It helps us fall in love with life again, restoring our vitality, perfect health, and optimal energy levels. She is the Divine child within who is jumping for joy at every opportunity. This rose opens up the many paths of discovery, engulfing us in the miraculous journey that is our life. If your life feels lackluster, like you have seen this movie before, or if you feel like life used to be so much better when you were younger, or if you feel weighed down by your responsibilities and problems, the yellow rose is your way out. She can help break up the routine, opening up room for more adventure and discovery, and bringing new people, experiences, and sensations into your life.

Uses:

- Regaining lost vitality
- Healing chronic fatigue
- Bringing optimism and joy back into your life
- Aligning you with solar cycles and infusing you with solar energies
- Easing depressive states

Numerical code: 303.303

The yellow rose is active, so three is a major pillar of her numeric expression. Three is one of the numbers of creation and manifestation, a natural byproduct of a joyful, overactive yellow rose. She cannot sit still, ever evolving and ever diving into life headfirst. This solar baby is able and willing to live more life and will tug you along for the ride. Zero in its numeric expression hints that this rose is deeply connected to the primordial void of the Mother, ever tapping into her resources. The yellow rose is a master manifester and can speed up the materialization of your desires.

Working with the yellow rose:

- Use sandalwood or any citrus essential oil to trace the numeric frequency of the yellow rose over your belly, right around your solar plexus chakra. Focus on a wish or an outcome that would make you happy. Invite the yellow rose to co-create that outcome with you.
- If you are feeling stuck in your life or are going through some dark times, invite the yellow rose's solar energies to assist you energetically. Washing your hair with shampoo that is infused with the frequency of the yellow rose can help unclog your mental blocks. To infuse your shampoo with the codes, write the numeric

representation of the rose on a piece of paper, then place your bottle of shampoo on top of this paper overnight. Voila—your magic shampoo is ready to use!

The Turquoise Rose

The turquoise rose is inquisitive and curious, yet centered and serene. She is a great companion if you are trying to understand something on a deeper level, bypassing surface-level meaning and seeking to get to the core. She is a peacemaker and a diplomat, helping one truly understand the viewpoint of another. The turquoise rose brings people together, ensuring harmony, and builds deep, lasting bonds. She is also the rose that can help you find your center and the peace within, freeing you from the rush of the material world, broadening your horizons, and elevating your perception.

Uses:

- Finding your inner sage
- Deepening your spiritual practice through introspection
- Helping you find inner peace
- Gently easing anxiety
- Bringing powerful water vibrations
- Helping you study universal mysteries
- Opening up your channel to receive spiritual insights and guidance

Numerical code: 212.212

Both gentle and intentional, the numerical signature of this rose is a dance of the more masculine one and the ever-gentle, deeply feminine two. You may notice that the forward-moving one is encapsulated between the soft twos, evening out its edges and providing a serene energy exchange. Because of this, working with this rose is a plunge into deep turquoise waters, a cleansing and therapeutic experience that feels natural and pleasurable instead of taxing.

Working with the turquoise rose:

- Infusing your water with the frequency of the turquoise rose is perhaps the easiest way to interact with this energy. Simply place your water bottle over the written numerical frequency of the turquoise rose and leave it to charge for three hours.
- The turquoise rose loves collaborating with the herbaceous spirit of lavender, so infusing some lavender essential oil with its frequency and then using that oil during

meditation will help invoke the presence of the rose. To infuse, place a sticker with the numerical code of the rose on the bottom of the essential oil bottle and wait a few hours for the codes to work their magic.

The Golden Rose

A higher-dimensional master rose, the golden rose is a big sister of the yellow rose. Also called "the rose of perfect emanation," she carries within herself the vibrations of Source consciousness and all the power that entails. She can mend what is broken, heal the deep-seated shadows, and bring things back into their original blueprint. The golden rose opens portals into higher dimensions, enables you to receive personalized healing codes from your Higher Self and other light beings, and uncovers the untapped hidden resources of your body and your soul. This rose is a catalyst; she accelerates healing and awakening, offering endless gifts to the ones who interact with her.

Uses:

- Spiritual alignment
- Accessing your Higher Self
- A one-on-one connection with Source
- Deep healing of your karmic wounds
- Integration of your shadow aspects
- Removal of energetic distortions, generational curses, and the evil eye

Numerical code: 333-333-333

Clad in the alchemical power of three, the golden rose is a dichotomy of Mother/Father Source, tapping into each of these energies to become the master teacher that she is. Since this rose is higher-dimensional, she has a more sophisticated (read: longer) numerical signature, represented by nine digits instead of the more traditional six.

Working with the golden rose:

- The golden rose likes working with honey. Infuse your honey jar with her frequencies to invite the power of the golden rose into your life. To infuse, place your honey jar over the written numeric code of the rose and allow it to charge for nine hours.
- The golden rose loves working through the energy of your heart. Trace her numerical representation over your heart space with water or rose essential oil and allow your body to absorb the codes. Meditations become especially potent and transformative

with the energy of the golden rose permeating your auric field. Invite the rose to help you manifest something special or transcend a shadow of yours. She will guide you through the process.

The Emerald Rose (or Green Rose)

The emerald rose is noble and refined. She is connected with royalty, abundance, wealth, and the concept of fullness, representing a thriving state overflowing with riches material and spiritual. The rose of queens, she personally supports women in a position of power. The emerald rose is just, charitable, content, plentiful, and overflowing. She is the presence of everything, and therefore, generosity manifested in flower form. The emerald rose is a missionary, often working with the ones who are struggling, mending the broken links and pathways within their energy body, so they can come back into a state of fullness, gratitude, and wealth.

Uses:

- Mending your relationship with money and wealth
- Helping break through a lack mentality
- Ancestral healing around abundance
- Healing of the emotional and physical bodies.

Numerical code: 555.555

The numerical frequency of this rose is the majestic, feminine, and harmonious five. The emerald rose balances and heals everything that she touches. In her world of abundance, creation, and bliss, there is no room for suffering, surviving, or settling. She projects a powerful magnetic field of love and compassion. She is a benevolent and patient female leader, regal and serene, a force of nature that effortlessly sweeps away any negativity. Her vibrations are filling, nurturing, and delicious, shifting you into a state of alignment with having it all. She is a female complete in and of herself, a Universe within, her own moon and sun. This rose is a tenderhearted mistress who takes care of the world, for she knows that the world is her mirror and extension. The emerald rose doesn't divide the world into us versus them. She gently hugs every curve and every scar, for she knows that oneness is the one and only ultimate truth and endgame.

Working with the emerald rose:

- To bring more money, abundance, and wealth into your life, place a small piece of paper with the emerald rose numeric code in your wallet, and carry it with you daily.

- If you live in a private house, you can infuse it with the vibrations of the emerald rose to help attract abundance to it. To do that, you'll need to carve the numeric frequency of the emerald rose into a small block of wood. (You can write the code instead of carving, but make sure to press strongly, so the code leaves a palpable physical imprint.) You'll then want to bury the wood block next to the front porch of your house, inviting abundance in. You can amplify this practice by imagining that a money tree springs forth from your wood block, and upon this money tree, all manner of objects grow, including all the things you want to attract into your life.

The Silver Rose

The silver rose is a master rose of perfect attainment, achievement, purification, unity, moving past obstacles, infinity, purpose, alignment, and intended outcomes. She has an uncanny ability to weed out anything that doesn't belong and set up a perfect canvas for creation. She removes imperfections, disease, and distorted energies, creating space for what's next. She can help clean your energetic vessel and even remove karmic knots. This rose also offers the magic of transformation, inviting you on a self-discovery journey that is both challenging and fulfilling. The outcome? A much more aligned and happier version of you!

Uses:

- Energetic cleansing
- Aligned goal setting
- Accelerated manifestation
- Karmic release
- Self-discovery
- High-dimensional healing and guidance
- Connection to the angelic realms (and with your guardian angel in particular)

Numerical code: 818.818

Combining the masculine forward movement of one and the very feminine infinite void of eight, the silver rose is an energetic healing bath. She is both a respite and a destination, a place of rest and reset that you can claim for yourself. The silver rose is ready to align you with your Divine blueprint, infusing you with the energies of your Higher Self and bringing you closer to understanding Source. The silver rose is a support structure for your daily activities, but also for the big leaps of faith that one must take to level up. She is an equivalent of the North Star, clad in petals, always aligning you with your intended path, always revealing your soul's purpose, so you can move up the spiral of evolution in the most seamless and pleasurable way possible.

Working with the silver rose:

- To work with the North Star aspect of the silver rose, draw an eight-pointed star on your forehead using water or rose essential oil. You can create a simplified version of the star using four intersecting lines (see **Figure 62**). Then, say the numeric code of the silver rose out loud eight times. Ask any question about your purpose, and be ready to receive the answer.

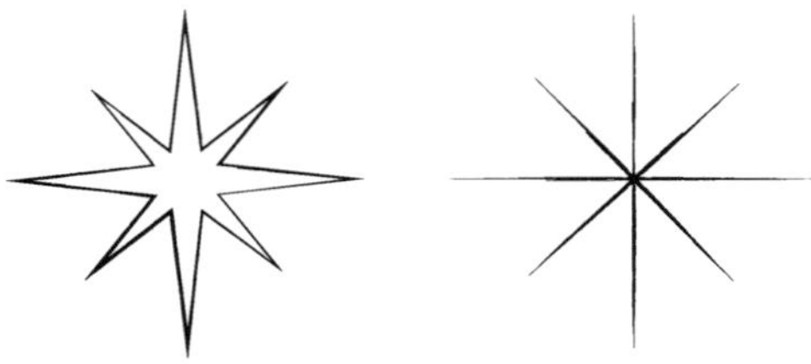

Figure 62: The eight-pointed star

- To release unwanted energies, stuck emotions, or blockages, draw the numeric code of the silver rose upon the part of your body that requires a cleanse or is experiencing pain. If you are unsure about what part to focus on, the belly area works for most types of stuck energies. Invite the energy of the silver rose to work with you until the blockages are removed.

The Magenta Rose

The magenta rose is a warrior of light, a restless force for good, an activist, a mover and a shaker, a missionary, a fighter, a nonconformist, a hero, and a protagonist. She is the patron of innovators, thought leaders, revolutionaries, public speakers, idealists, and politicians. The magenta rose has access to many energy reserves of the Universe, often making them available to fuel the causes she supports. The magenta rose cares about healthy ecosystems, audacious dreams, planetary and galactic-level ascension, leveling up, and progress of all kinds. She is an ardent supporter of justice and integrity, often coming to heal failing and ailing ecosystems through the fiery power of her vibration.

Uses:

- Massive breakthroughs (personal, familial, or societal)

- Moving past stuck energies or outlived patterns
- Upgrades
- Granting resources to movements and projects
- Supporting change
- Fostering scientific discovery
- Moving things forward

Numerical code: 717.717

The magenta rose is a numeric powerhouse containing not one, but two Divine Masculine numerals, one and seven. One is about paving your own way, new beginnings, fresh perspectives, rapid shifts, and becoming the master of one's life. The number seven is the highest form of masculine attainment, indicating breakthroughs that are possible through pointed action, commitment, and sometimes brute force. When these two numbers come together, they create a powerful energy structure not dissimilar to the explosion of an atomic bomb. Force has never been a limiting factor of the magenta rose, but it is the direction of that force that needs to be carefully managed.

Working with the magenta rose:

- If you are feeling stuck in an area of your life, the magenta rose could be just the ally you need to move forward. This rose loves working with warm and spicy essential oils like nutmeg, ginger, and cinnamon. To call in the power of this rose, trace her numeric code on your wrist using one of the aforementioned essential oils, then speak out loud about what area of your life you want to create momentum in. Say it three times. Complete the ritual by speaking your intention around what the ideal future in this area of your life looks like.
- Simply writing the code of the magenta rose over and over again can help you get into an active and inspired state. Use it when you need an energetic pick-me-up and would like to create forward momentum for yourself.

The Rainbow Rose

The rainbow rose is an amalgamation of all the roses combined, yet none of them in particular. She is a riddle, a mystic, a kaleidoscope, and an unsolvable equation. She contains every polarity within, masterfully weaving the threads of the many roses into one coherent whole. She is one of the master roses and a master alchemist, creating an alloy of seemingly unmatchable energies. She is the beginning of the road, the culmination of it, and its very end. She is the ebbs and flows of the Universe. The rainbow rose contains the blueprint for creation within her petals. She knows the "why" behind things and willingly shares her wisdom with those who choose to connect with her. The rainbow rose is an example of the many streams of the rose unified by a greater power. She is therefore a force of nature, both perfect and imperfect simultaneously. She helps one walk the walk of their spiritual path, while not losing track of material manifestation. She teaches us to always cater to the cravings of our eternal soul, while savoring the moment of our incarnate existence. This rose dwells between dimensions, visiting all, constrained by none. This gives her an elevated vantage point for advising on matters both physical and spiritual. She holds the keys to the concept of the greater good, ever seeing both the forest and the trees, able to predict outcomes and breathe through change.

Uses:

- Finding balance between the physical and spiritual
- Seeking wisdom
- Finding answers to complex questions
- Understanding all facets of yourself
- Uncovering your special talents
- Learning new skills faster
- Bringing things to a successful completion
- Starting a new cycle in the most optimal way

Numerical code: 1919.1919

The numerical representation of the rainbow rose is a dichotomy of one, the beginning of the cycle, and nine, the end of it. The rainbow rose brings together beginnings and endings, smoothly maneuvering between them, creating a wealth of experiences and learnings in the process. She embraces the many cycles of death and rebirth, understanding that they are a part of existence, and she offers a level-up every single time.

Working with the rainbow rose:

- When starting a new project, invoke the power of the rainbow rose to set it up for success. This rose will help pull in the resources to make things happen in the most aligned way. On a blank piece of paper, write the name of your project, then write the code of the rainbow rose. Connect the two by drawing a circle that encompasses them both. Create a few more circles like that, each containing the numerical code of the rainbow rose and the working name of your new project. You will need a total of nine circles. Hold onto this page until your project starts gaining momentum or is completed.

- The rainbow rose can help speed up your manifestation or help a wish come true. To invoke this power of the rainbow rose, you will need two circular pieces of paper of the same diameter. On the first circle, write down your wish in detail. On the second circle, write down the numerical code of the rainbow rose. Glue the two circles together facing each other, so that the writing ends up on the inside. Place the circle next to your heart and imagine sending a stream of white light from your heart into the paper circle. Then place it somewhere with a strong concentration of your energy—such as your closet or nightstand drawer—and keep it until the wish comes true.

PART III

THE ROSE WAY

Heart Space: The Story of Two Ley Lines

An archangel was standing atop the sacred hill overlooking the vast valley of green, stretching as far as the eye could see.

There was still time—time before it would all be covered with water, before this world as he knew it would come to its logical close. His heart was heavy; he loved this planet and its people too much. If only they loved themselves.

He was becoming decidedly too human, his emotions running wild.

"Michael," said a melodic feminine voice. "Do not grieve for them yet. There is still time for them. Time for us."

He looked upon the face of a goddess: Mary. They called her Mother Mary sometimes. To them, she was the mother of Jesus. To him, she was a friend, a confidant, a constant companion through and through. Of the many goddesses he had met over the years, Mary perhaps reminded him of the Divine Mother the most. With her serenity, motherly softness, and unwavering faith, she carried the blueprint of Divinity in her every breath, in her every movement, in her every curve.

He smiled. "It is the last hour; the first trumpet is upon us. We have always known this time would come, and yet it feels surreal for it to actually be here," he said.

"We can make it count," she responded quietly, and her face lit up, as if she were focusing on the most positive of all possible outcomes.

"They don't even know it is the Age of the Maiden, the second coming of the Goddess. They are waiting for a male Messiah," he said.

"They may look upon the faces of the male leaders, but it is my voice they will hear in their hearts. It is my soul's embrace they will feel each morning upon waking up. It is my tears that will be shed upon the graves of their dead. It is my waters that will come to finally cleanse them of all sin."

"So, you think they can still be saved?"

"I believe it, yes. I believe in them, because I love them. And so do you," said the goddess and smiled the warmest of smiles. "We will be there in every sun ray upon their skin, in every drop of moisture upon their face, in every tear they shed, until they awaken to our presence, until they hear the call of their soul—our call."

And so, they stood upon the hill, both in time and space and in the great in-between, and made a pact to go to the very end, to leave no stone unturned, to use the full might of the light at their disposal, for humanity, for salvation, and for the greater good.

And the archangel took his Sword of Truth and plunged it into the ground. And the ground shook with the force of an earthquake, its fires rising to the surface, cleansing everything in their wake.

And the goddess brought up her staff of renewal and eternal life and plunged it into the earth next to the sword. And the deep waters of the Goddess rose, cleansing away the impurities, paving the way for the final battle, one last stand. Heavenly fires were finally reunited with earthly waters, creating an energy outburst bigger than anything the planet had seen since its inception.

The traces of that power, of that sacred promise, are present to this day in the ley lines of Michael and Mary—a testament to their sacred work and sacred partnership. And so, to this day, these ley lines run together down the rolling hills of Somerset in England, sometimes converging, running side by side as a sign of their faith and commitment to each other.

It is in the energies of your own heart that you can find the merging paths of Michael and Mary—the Divine Feminine and Divine Masculine combined in a sacred dance upon the earthly plane.

It is in the folds of your heart that the keys to their mysteries lie, and it is through your heart magic that they become unlocked.

Let the combined heart energies of Mary and Michael carry you into the New Earth, the realm beyond limitations, the land of promise, the renewed Garden of Eden. Here is to the great homecoming you have been waiting for.

Here is to the next chapter in your soul journey.

CHAPTER 18

The Rite of Passage: An Initiation

There comes a time in every seeker's life when a premonition takes over—an anticipation, a quickening of the pulse, a knowing that something big is about to happen. This something will divide your life into before and after, with the potential to turn your reality upside down, changing you at a cellular level, upgrading every organ and tissue, rewriting your energetic codes, shifting your solar imprint, and recalibrating your auric field. The Order of the Rose's invitation is quiet, like the whisper of the summer breeze over a field of green. You hear it not with your ears, but with your heart. But once the Rose calls your name, once you conceive of her gentle nudge, once you feel her healing magic, you can never turn away. The calling of the Rose is a personal invitation from our Mother Divine to walk in her footsteps, to carry her light upon the earthly plane, to follow her guidance, and to become her beloved initiate.

An initiation into the mysteries is not a path well-trodden. It is not something freely offered by the Mother. We need to be considered worthy. We need to be considered able.

If you are reading these words, chances are you have felt the call of the Mother in your heart. You may have walked the Path of the Rose in past lives. You may have been an initiate or a priestess of the Rose on more than one occasion. This book is a remembrance, a call to walk this sacred path again. The iron grip of the patriarchy is loosening, and the sacred sisterhood is ready to assemble again, witnessed by the nurturing presence of the moon, the healing vibrations of Venus, and the gentle embrace of Gaia. Whether you once walked the Path of the Rose in Atlantis, ancient Egypt, or Mesopotamia, or perhaps had a more recent foray into the heart of the Mother alongside Mother Mary and Mary Magdalene somewhere on this Earth, this chapter is your personal sacred invitation to walk it once more.

The times of persecution of wise women are no more. The female priestess is no longer second-rate. She is not here to be shunned, burned at the stake, or stoned to death. She has risen like a phoenix from the ashes of her prosecuted sisters, with her head held high, and a deep knowing that this is her ultimate rebirth. She is here to be seen and heard. And as a carrier of light codes, she is here to be a game changer and a builder of the New Earth, the new Atlantis. She is here to be the forger of the golden gates, the guardian of the pearls of wisdom, a doorway to salvation, the voice of the heart, and the completion of the cycle.

Before you can walk the Path of the Rose, however, a rite of passage is required. Spiritually, this is a sacred crossing of the threshold from one stage of your life into the next. Usually, a proper rite of passage requires a sacrifice and a shedding of the layers of what once was. It is an intentional and divinely guided spiritual rebirth that impacts all your light bodies in one fell swoop. If you choose to become an initiate, the Universe and the Mother herself will guide you. Circumstances will unfold in a way that requires you to break some deep-rooted patterns that cannot follow you into the future. The shedding of layers will inevitably be initiated. You will also be divinely guided into the understanding of what you are meant to sacrifice or let go of. This path is uniquely your own.

Process: The Shedding

Create a list of everything that no longer serves you (patterns, habits, people) in the following areas of your life:

- Relationships (romantic or otherwise)
- Family life and home
- Career and finance
- Health and fitness
- Spirituality, personal development, and mental well-being
- Leisure, entertainment, and hobbies
- Immediate community and society at large
- Material possessions

From the list, choose at least three things that it is time for you to release. Commit to releasing them within three to six months as part of your initiation into the Rose. This may imply deep decluttering, rewiring old patterns, or even walking away from a relationship or a job.

Shedding is a natural process in the animal kingdom; we shed our outlived skin cells all the time. Shedding is a precursor to moving on. It is also a tactic that helps create more space in your life that must be filled with new energies, people, and patterns. Shedding is a small death that invites new life in.

Becoming an Initiate of the Rose

Becoming an initiate of the Rose means learning from the Divine Mother herself, developing into one of her lifelong students, and passing under the veil of her mysteries. This is a path toward enlightenment, the most feminine of all spiritual ways. Many teachers of old, from Buddha to Krishna to Jesus, offered a rendition of the light path, each unique in its joys and sacrifices. The Path of the Mother is one of the gentlest, offering you a way of surrendering to the depth of your own Divinity. Once the resistance is gone, the domain of the Mother shall welcome you fully.

Five Sacred Principles

Like every path, the Path of the Rose has some basic principles. Every initiate is asked to take these to heart and integrate them into the core of their being. These principles are the building blocks of your divinely guided path, the road toward the heart of the Mother.

Principle 1: Radiate Love

The Mother is love. Her cosmic heart knows no bounds. She doesn't judge, nor does she force anything. She never chooses coercion or control. She is acceptance and is unconditionally compassionate. She gently reminds us that love is the *only* way. To radiate love, you must integrate it into every aspect of your being, cell by cell, tissue by tissue. To radiate love, you must vibrate at its frequency. Nature vibrates at the frequency of love. Becoming one with nature is therefore a natural precursor to emanating love.

Emanating love is about having your heart open fully, ready to embrace the world exactly as it is today, tomorrow, and always.

Love is a cosmic power that brings everything together. It is the mightiest of all magnetic forces. Love is liquid magic. Love is a signature vibration of the Mother.

In everything that you do, allow yourself to sign off with love.

Principle 2: Take It All In

Many are the walls, protective shells, and barriers we have created in our hearts. Each barrier keeps us separate, removed, and remote. Each barrier maintains the illusion of loneliness. We are never alone, nor are we ever unloved. We are forever cared for and supported by the Mother. Her flow is present within our veins, her breath is alive within our words, and her wisdom is evident in our choices when we are heart-led.

Learn to take it all in with grace—the good days and the bad, the gifts and the wounds, the strokes of luck and the dark nights of the soul. Experience life fully; take it all in. Life is happening for you, not *to* you. Once you remove resistance to what is, you will discover the life on the other side of fear—a life in full alignment with the will of the Mother.

Principle 3: Serve Because You Choose To, Not Because You Have To

Once you conceive that oneness is the only truth of the Universe, service comes naturally; it simply flows out of you into the world. A life of service is the greatest joy of a soul in alignment, a soul in tune with its purpose and its design. Find your flavor of service, the one thing that speaks to your soul and heart, the one activity that lets your talent shine, something that comes to you naturally. Then become abundant in sharing it with the world. Acts of service are tiny lanterns; we light them on our own paths and the paths of others. Light enough lanterns, and they will illuminate your entire life, showing you the way to true fulfillment.

Acts of service are not a means to an end, not a currency used to buy your way into ascension, nor a bribe to throw in the face of the Universe. The only acts of service that count are the ones that come from the heart, with no strings attached and no expectations. You can never be attached to the results of your acts of service. They are paper boats meant to sail away with the river's natural course, never to be seen again, but accounted for nonetheless.

Serve with abandon. Serve with joy. Serve without expectation. It is through acts of service that we fully step onto the path of light. It is via acts of service that we stay rooted on this path—the path paved and blessed by our Mother.

Principle 4: Connect the Dots

The dots are individual aspects of consciousness divided by time and space, seemingly finite and alone, visibly separated from the rest of existence. Every planet is a dot in the cosmos, every human is a dot within humanity, and every animal and plant is a dot within its respective kingdom. The observable Universe consists of dots, notable in their alone-ness, alike in their separation, perpetually seeking to come back into oneness. Every initiate of the Rose is a dot connector, someone who stretches out their hand to another—human, plant, or animal—and brings them closer to connection.

Someone has to connect the dots into lines, the minimal formations of togetherness in the otherwise individualized worlds.

Connecting the dots is what the Mother naturally does whenever she sees separation. It is through finding equilibrium, commonalities, and points of interconnectedness that she weaves the fabric of existence, bringing seemingly separate things into a dance of harmony and cohesion.

Be like the Mother: create unity and harmony whenever you can. Bring people together. Listen with your heart. Forgive. Reach out. Find the middle ground. Harmonize.

Principle 5: Embrace the Void

The void is the womb of the Mother. It is her most potent and most magical aspect. We have been brought up to fear darkness, to repel it and reject it with our entire being. We have been brought up to judge darkness and pronounce light's superiority over it any chance we get. And yet, the soft whisper of the void is the sacred language of the Mother. The void is that which comes before matter, the point before creation, and the point after. It is therefore the connective tissue of eternity, the one aspect of reality that connects otherwise separate breaths of the Universe. It is the void that ensures continuity in a scattered world. It is through the void that we find the missing aspects of ourselves and bring them together.

Nothing is impossible for the void, the Mother's most potent aspect. It is through her that everything in existence is birthed, and it is to her that everything returns in the end. Learn to listen to the silent truth of the night. Learn to see Shakti in the darkness. Embrace the wisdom of the void, its patience, and its infinite potential. Learn to cherish the darkness, the calm and serene respite it brings. Find out what exists beyond the fear and judgment of the dark. Surrender to the loving embrace of the Mother. Build yourself a home in the ever-shifting body of her void womb.

Ritual: The Initiation into the Order of the Rose

This ritual is best performed outside in nature. Please pick a spot away from others where you won't be disturbed or interrupted.

This ritual starts by creating a flower mandala, as you did in Chapter 7, but this time, it will be a focus for your initiation and part of your offering to Gaia.

For the flower mandala, you will need:

- A moonstone or rose quartz crystal
- Plenty of flower buds and petals—a minimum of five red roses, five white roses, and five pink roses
- A handful of rice, or any grain of your choice (quinoa, buckwheat, amaranth)

For your offering to Gaia, you will need:

- Rice or any grain of your choice (quinoa, buckwheat, amaranth)
- Raisins or grapes
- A tablespoon of honey
- A cinnamon stick or some chocolate
- An incense cone or stick
- Nuts (hazelnuts or almonds are best)

To create the mandala:

Draw or create your rose mandala (see Chapter 7), then place a moonstone or rose quartz crystal in its center. This signifies your heart and its openness to receiving the energies and blessings of the Mother. Use the flower petals or buds to create a few concentric circles surrounding the crystal in the center. Sprinkle in some rice or grains in the spaces between the rows of flowers to serve as connective tissue for the mandala. Rice symbolizes earthly abundance, while the rose is a cosmic symbol of the Mother. By bringing these master symbols together, you create a portal between the cosmos and Gaia that is needed for this initiation.

Once the mandala is created, you are ready to begin.

The ritual:

1. With your mandala in front of you, place your hands on your heart and invite the Mother into your sacred space. Ask her to be present with you for the duration of the ritual.
2. Close your eyes and focus on your breath. This is your first opportunity to meet the founding members of the Sisterhood of the Rose and receive their blessings for your journey.
3. Imagine walking along a path in a rose garden. The garden is luscious and green and has rose bushes of all kinds. Roses line your path.
4. You come to a round white table in the shade. The table is adorned with roses, and five figures are sitting around it. One of them is beckoning you closer. There is an empty chair at the table reserved for you. Take a seat and get comfortable.
5. The first founding sister of the Rose is Inanna, a Sumerian mother goddess of fertility, love, justice, wealth, and spring. She is dressed in emerald robes, a crown of rubies adorning her head. Her hair is braided and tucked away in an updo. The skin of her arms is covered in hieroglyphs made of sunlight.
6. Inanna places an object into your hands. This is her blessing and a gift for your initiation. As she gives you the object, you start receiving a stream of information about the powers and significance of this object. What does the object look like? What is special about it? Feel free to ask Inanna any clarifying questions about working with it.
7. Once you receive all the information you need regarding the object, place it in your heart space for safe keeping. Using the object will become a part of your spiritual path from this day forward.
8. The second founding sister of the Rose is Isis, the Egyptian mother goddess of magic, healing, rebirth, mysteries, and abundance. She is dressed in a floor-length golden gown, her neck adorned with emeralds. Her wrists are graced with many golden bracelets, and her fingers are decked with precious rings. Her cat eyes are lined with black charcoal, and her lips are dressed in rouge.
9. Watch as Isis utters a spell, and suddenly, golden light covers your entire body. This cloud of golden energy is swirling around you, entering your

cells and transforming you from the inside. This is a magical healing and release—exactly what you need to step into the sisterhood.

10. Ask Isis what she is taking away from you and what she adds to you energetically. Feel free to ask her any clarifying questions. How does your body feel at this moment? Do you feel any different? Allow the process to run its course.
11. The next founding Sister of the Rose is Mary Magdalene, a spiritual master, one of the original Hathors of Venus, a nomad, a master teacher in Rose, a holder of the white ray of Divine blessings, and a twin flame to Yeshua, the Christ. She is dressed in scarlet robes, and bracelets of white shells adorn her wrists. Her hair comes down to her waist in dark ringlets, and a crown of red roses sits atop her head.
12. Mary Magdalene reaches out to you and places her hand on your heart. As she does this, codes of higher cosmic love stream into your body like small spirals of pink light. Allow these spirals to find a home inside of your heart. Invite them in fully, and accept the many blessings that they bring. You may ask Mary Magdalene any question you would like; she is here to help you on your path of initiation.
13. Next is Mother Mary, the Queen of the Angels, Archeiai, a holder of the emerald ray of cosmic healing and compassion, a master teacher of light, the dove of the Mother Divine, an emissary into the dark lands, and the Great Mother of humanity. Mother Mary is wearing pale blue robes, her head adorned with a crown of white roses. A white veil of protection rests upon her shoulders.
14. Watch as Mother Mary gently touches your forehead around the area of your third eye. She is here to help shed light on why you came to Earth and a particular aspect of your purpose here. She begins transferring violet codes from her palm into your third eye. As this happens, you start to see visions—visions of your future, both immediate and distant. Allow yourself to receive the codes and all the signs. Feel free to ask Mother Mary for any clarification you may require.
15. Finally, notice that the fifth founding Sister of the Rose, Kuan Yin—a bodhisattva of compassion, the Mother Goddess of mercy, peace, and tenderness, a holder of the diamond ray of higher consciousness, and a governing member of the Karmic Board—is silently observing you with a

smile. She is a mistress of the lotus and of Divine wisdom. She is dressed in white robes, and gold jewelry adorns her neck and hands.

16. Watch as Kuan Yin spreads her arms over your head, and a waterfall of white light starts falling from the heavens. The waterfall is washing over your body, clearing away any energetic blockages that may be in the way of you receiving the wisdom of the Rose and the energies of the Mother. Allow this deep cleanse to run its course. Feel free to ask Kuan Yin any clarifying questions about your initiation.
17. Once the waterfall subsides and all of your questions have been answered, notice that a gate of gold emerges in front of you. This is no ordinary gate; it is the Gate of Initiation, adorned with white and red roses. Every initiate of the Rose must pass through it before they become a part of the tribe of the Mother.
18. Come closer to the gate and state your intention. Clearly say why you would like to be accepted into the sisterhood and what you hope to get out of it. Also, state what you are willing to do in return and what acts of service you could commit to as part of this initiation. Only mention things you know you can deliver; do not oversell what you're capable of or are willing to do.
19. When you are ready, step through the golden gate and look around. You may be greeted by a few initiates of the Rose tasked with greeting new members. They take you by the arms and lead you to a large circle of initiated souls.
20. The circle parts, letting you in. You are holding the hands of your sisters, joining them in a sacred ceremony. Notice how an impulse that feels like electricity passes through your palms. This is the collective vibration of the circle. Receive this vibration fully, absorbing it into your body.
21. Focus on your heart space and send the energy from your heart into the middle of the circle, sharing it with others as a gift and an offering.
22. Notice how so much more comes back to you, supporting and nourishing you in the exact way that you need right now.
23. Revel in the magic of the circle. You may start getting codes, messages, or visions at this time. Each initiation experience is unique, starting from this moment.

24. Allow yourself to go with the flow of the initiation, following your Sisters in Rose wherever they want to take you.
25. Once the experience is complete, thank the sisters for their blessings and assistance at this time.
26. Finish the ceremony with your offering to Gaia, our Earth Mother, who held the space so that this initiation could be completed as originally intended. Simply offer the gifts to Gaia from your heart, with much thanks for her assistance today and always. You may leave these offerings in nature; Gaia will claim them once she is ready to receive them.

Recognizing Your Sisters in Rose: Finding and Nurturing Your Tribe

The Order of the Rose of our Celestial Mother is first and foremost a sisterhood, a sacred circle where life-long relationships are forged and nurtured. As we emerge from the Age of Darkness (the Kali Yuga), we must recognize that the original intention behind most social structures has been lost, and the vibrations that those structures once carried need to be rebuilt anew. True sisterhood once thrived on Earth. A safe space, a support structure, and a community of women who understand and truly hear one another is not a utopia; it is simply a reclaiming of our long-forgotten past.

There are women out there who are cut from the same cloth as you are—the ones who have memories of being magic, the ones who hold the many threads of the Mother in their bodies, hearts, and souls. They, too, yearn for belonging; they, too, yearn to be seen; they, too, yearn for closeness. It has always been up to the females to bond deeply with one another, creating communities that stand the test of time. Women hold within their bodies the blueprint for togetherness, a domain and a field of expertise of the Divine Mother. It has always been up to women to help humanity find its way through the murky waters of separation and the cages of individuality into the sacred co-living and co-creation of togetherness.

And the way we start to reclaim this Divine purpose is by first finding our own tribe. We are not meant to do this alone—not in this lifetime.

We are living in the dawn of sisterhood. A sacred circle of women is ready to come back in full force, no longer constrained, silenced, or suffocated by the patriarchy. And the sisterhood starts with you.

You may be the first domino, the most critical part of the chain reaction. The Rose is calling you to step up and rise to the occasion, sister. Your light is seeking to come through at this time. The unique song of your heart yearns to be shared with the world.

When or if you are unsure of where to start, start with service. Service is something that the Mother Divine understands like nothing else. Give yourself permission to be seen, heard, and felt exactly as you are—no masks, shells, shields, or protective mechanisms. True acts of service originate within your heart. They start as a calling and an urge to share a gift you have with the world, whether that is a gift of sound, a gift of writing, a gift of healing, a gift of hosting events, or something unique to you.

This is the age for breaking the old patterns.

This is the age for healing old wounds. This is the age for finally stepping into your purpose.

This is the age for shining full force, unapologetically and persistently.

This is the age for reclaiming our sacred sisterhood—and it starts with you.

If you begin to shine the light of your gifts, if you begin to unapologetically step into your purpose, you become discoverable. Just like a lit torch in the dark, you become findable. If you look around and see nobody like you, if you believe that your sisters are nowhere to be found, dare to shine your light, then dare to keep going. When you make the first step, your tribe must find you. This is the law.

Many are the shades of vibration of the Divine Mother; they contain an infinity of colors and hues. Some colors are very different from the vibrations that you brought forth as a soul into this incarnation, and then there are others just like you. Finding your tribe is about recognizing a resonance, recognizing the "sameness" of another soul. Think of each soul as representing a color within a rainbow spectrum. If you represent the color violet, first, you will resonate with other souls that represent the same vibration. Building relationships with them will be the most natural, organic thing to do. It will feel like a homecoming. Chances are, you shared many past lives with your closest sisters. Remembering them together is a key to instant bonding. Once you have found your most "immediately related" sisters, it will become easier to venture further and relate to women unlike you. It is through assembling women of all colors of the celestial rainbow that true magic is unlocked. It is at this point that a circle of women becomes a force to be reckoned with.

Initiation and Daily Practice: Working with the Mother

The Path of the Rose is about finding your personal connection with the Celestial Mother, learning to hear her tender voice, notice her signs, and follow her lead. No two paths within the Order of the Rose are the same, for each one is guided by the Mother herself. The alpha and omega of this path are building a light bridge between your own heart and the heart of the Mother.

Initiation – Building a light bridge:

1. In a meditative state, focus on your heart center. Imagine it unfolding like a rose with a thousand petals. Picture it pulsating and coming alive as you breathe into the center of your chest.
2. Notice a large figure of white light seated in a lotus pose before you. While the female figure is made of light, her forehead and heart are especially bright. This is our Celestial Mother, and she is delighted to greet you and start building a heart connection with you today.
3. Notice how a stream of white light starts coming toward you from the Mother's heart. Let this stream enter your heart space, looping around the rose blooming there.
4. Now send this energy back to the heart of the Mother, so that the loop can close and start anew. You are seeking to establish a continuous flow.
5. Breathe deeply. On the inhale, imagine the light bridge between you and the Mother expanding and growing. Watch as it takes up more energetic "space."
6. Congratulations! Your light bridge is now complete.

Morning check-ins:

1. First thing in the morning, close your eyes and activate the light bridge between you and the heart of the Mother by sending your breath into it.
2. Every morning, the Mother will have a special gift or message for you. Usually, it will come in the form of a golden parcel traveling along the bridge from her heart space to yours.

3. Receive the parcel and unpack it. See what it contains. Whether it is a symbol, an object, or a message, receive it into your heart. Allow this gift to be deposited into the depth of your being and remain there.
4. The more you work with the Mother, the more obvious and easier to read her messages will become. Regardless, each message will provide you with exactly what you need in the moment and will set you up for an amazing day.

Evening lotus baths:

Before falling asleep, imagine the Mother holding you in her embrace and leading you to a large lotus flower. As you approach the lotus, you realize it is a bath filled with colored water. Each time you attempt this practice, the water will be a different color—a reflection of the attunement your body requires at this moment in time. Submerge yourself in the bath and allow the water to wash away any negativity you're holding, bringing you into your most optimal state. Feel free to tell the Mother about anything that is bothering you, and ask for her assistance. Assistance will always come in exactly the form that you need.

The Many Rays of the Mother

The Mother's domain is infinite, as are the combinations of energy streams you carry within your Higher Self. Collectively, they form your unique energy imprint and aura. Each stream signifies a unique path, lesson, and soul gift. Below is a quick overview of the most common Divine rays on Earth and their significance. Later in this chapter, you will discover which rays you hold at the level of your Higher Self and how to work with this information.

Red (also ruby): The ray of passion and inspired action. The souls of this ray are warriors, fighters for what's right, and courageous fire starters. They ignite and spur others into action, so they tend to be outspoken, bright, and memorable. They are charismatic leaders, influential public speakers, and powerful movers and shakers. They don't take no for an answer and would never settle for the status quo. They are the harbingers of change. They are vocal, strong, and often extroverted. They are fire incarnate and act as such. They have great potential to make massive shifts within humanity.

Orange: The ray of being in the flow, the ray of surrender, pleasure, and abundant creative powers. The souls of this ray are artists, dancers, performers, and storytellers. They are naturally in touch with the world around them and are flexible enough to flow with it. There is a special magnetism to anyone carrying the orange ray; they are super attractors, always in tune and in touch with the Universe. They are Divine children, reveling in Gaia's abundant resources. They are often drawn to nature or things that are aesthetically beautiful. These gentle souls, above all, dislike being contained or constrained by anything from rules to societal templates. They are free spirits, always making their own path in the ocean of perpetual happening. They are cosmic dancers that make life look effortless. But this is what living in the flow looks like to an onlooker.

Yellow (also golden): The ray of joy, wisdom, confidence, healthy self-concept, self-acceptance, manifestation, mysteries, magic, and connection to Source. Souls of this ray are perfect Divine children who welcome new adventures and experiences with a childlike curiosity. They know they are beloved and forever protected by the Universe; therefore, confidence and openness come naturally to them. They are expressive, gregarious, energetic, and vibrant, always cherishing and welcoming newness. The yellows naturally hold plenty of raw energy, making them masterful manifesters. They also have a natural and deep connection with the sun and Source consciousness, and they tend to tap into that endless resource subconsciously as they navigate their journey. As they progress along the yellow ray and achieve its higher golden aspects, true wisdom becomes attainable. Innate curiosity abounds in the yellow ray, eventually leading to greater knowledge and a deeper understanding of what is.

Green (also emerald): The ray of connection, community, sisterhoods and brotherhoods, healing and medicine, the all-feeling heart, abundance, contentment, happiness, harmony, nurturing, care, replenishment, and restoration. The souls of this ray are gentle, loving beings who care for others and their impact on the world. Often, they find purpose in helping and supporting others, in freely sharing their resources for the betterment of all. The souls of the green ray are attuned and intuitive, gentle and forgiving. They lead with compassion and acceptance, and they are natural empaths. Their energy is magnetic; they may shift a room's vibration simply by being present. They have a healing touch and an auric field that harmonizes everything around them.

Pink: The ray of higher love, tenderness, infinite connection, mirroring, oneness, gentle spirit, and raising and nurturing the young. This is the ray of youth, softness, parental protection, sanctuaries, healing spaces, deep restoration and recalibration, and the resetting of karma. The souls of this ray are supportive and nurturing. They love devoting their lives to working with children and showing them the way. These souls are soft-spoken and nonjudgmental, so they are natural-born diplomats and peacemakers, protective and loyal, deep and introspective. They love solitude, but also enjoy building strong bonds with others. They are the most amazing listeners and can help others release karma just by being present when they share their stories. They are natural-born counselors, coaches, and psychologists, able to look deep into someone's soul and grant them much-needed redemption.

Blue (also sapphire): The ray of strength, stamina, truth, integrity, justice, intellect, speech, language, honesty, power, clear direction, ambition, protection, leadership, communication, forward movement, dynamism, change, conquest, and decisive action. The souls of this ray are determined, straightforward, and to the point. They are masterful communicators and inspirational leaders. These are your generals and war heroes, masterful politicians, innovators, and entrepreneurs. They carry massive amounts of energy that always seeks an outlet for action, so these souls like to apply themselves in the world, to be seen, heard, and followed. They have a strength of character and an ability to persist and persevere when many others give up. They have a low tolerance for injustice and abuse, often coming to the rescue of those who need help.

Violet: The ray of introspection, intuition, the sixth sense, transformation, merging of opposites, equalizing, forward thinking, change, up-leveling and upgrading, shedding of the old skin, staying true to your path, higher consciousness, seeing beyond the veil, psychic abilities, and prophetic dreams. This is the ray of oracles, dreamers, and prophets. The souls of this ray are enthusiastic, gentle but persistent, open-minded, and flexible. They come across as older and wiser than their age and are naturally plugged into the collective consciousness and the Akashic Records. They easily navigate space-time reality, shifting and molding it to their liking. They are powerful seers for whom the lines between past and future are ever blurry, allowing them to access information beyond the veil. They are transformational powerhouses, whether in personal, familial, or societal relations. They are the rule breakers and rule forgers, creating their realities every time they set foot on the earthly map.

White (also silver or diamond): The ray of unification, oneness, electricity, original spark, releasing duality, purification, virginity, innocence, faith, belief, omniscience, omnipotence, presence, enlightenment, new cycles, beginnings, planting the seeds, connecting to what is, and Source consciousness. The souls of this ray are somewhat unemotional, as if looking at the world from a higher vantage point. They are in the world, but not of the world, both wise and "other." They are the sages, gurus, spiritual leaders, and teachers, unhindered by earthly limitations and unrestricted in their flow. They are planetary healers, light workers, way-showers, and movers and shakers. They are great strategic minds who know how the many pieces of the puzzle come together. They see many steps ahead, often warning others of what is coming. They are teachers and are here to make a dent, create change, and leave this planet better than they found it. They have high moral standards, a deeply personal philosophy, and values that come from their own unique understanding of life, not what society dictates.

Know the Rays You Carry

Often, we are an amalgamation of the rays we have studied and integrated at a soul level throughout our many lives. Each of us has a unique combination of rays reflected in our auric field. By knowing the rays that make up your energy field, you can tell a lot about the path of your soul, your soul gifts, and why you are exactly the way you are. This is one of the many tools of the Mother in self-reflection, a path of deeper understanding. Understanding which rays make up your energetic composition may indicate your mission and the path you came here to follow. You may have any combination of the rays, ranging from one to a mix of all. You also don't have all the rays integrated equally; some may be more prevalent. If you have more than one ray integrated, chances are that some are dominant and others are secondary. Your dominant rays will always run the show, while your secondary rays are there as supporting tools to help you out in specific circumstances.

Diagnostic: The Rays You Carry

Analyzing your combination of rays can be fun. Simply refer to the explanation earlier in this chapter to understand each ray you carry and what qualities it may impart to you. Please know that even if you carry a certain ray, you may not carry all of its aspects. Simply note the aspects that resonate with you and leave out all the rest.

Dominating rays are always the most telling. They make up the majority of your soul energy and what you have shown up with in this incarnation. Each dominating ray directly or indirectly points to your soul's purpose and mission for this incarnation.

1. Close your eyes and focus on your breath.
2. Allow your thoughts to quiet down. Let them come and go freely.
3. Try lowering the volume of your thoughts, allowing them to disappear into the background.
4. Imagine yourself as a body woven of light, standing right in front of you.
5. Notice a waterfall of white light descending upon the head of your light body. As this happens, the white light is broken apart into many colors, similar to the colors of the rainbow, only richer in the number of shades and hues.
6. Notice that some of these colors are entering your body, and others are flowing outside, never quite managing to get in. What colors do you see inside your light body? Pay close attention to what comes through. Know that it is not always the dominating colors that come through first; they may appear to you in any order. Feel free to break this meditative flow and write down the colors and hues you see.
7. Make sure to scan the entire inner aspect of your light body, so as not to miss out on any colors.
8. Once you have seen all the colors you are meant to see, try distinguishing your dominating colors by setting your intention and asking the Universe to reveal your dominating rays. Each dominating ray will flash in front of your eyes. Make a note to help you remember what you are shown, so you can internalize it later.
9. Once you have been shown all of your dominating rays, feel free to open your eyes.

In addition to this meditation, ask the Universe to rank your rays in order of their dominance. The Universe will flash the rays in front of your third eye in the order they appear in your energy chart. This can be quite telling if you are trying to figure out what energies truly run your life.

Heart Space: The Mother Sun Rising

The Mother Sun is rising.

She is finally here to take the reins from the Father Sun.

The Mother Sun is rising,

And we shall never be the same.

Her prana is majestic, grand is her scale,

And infinite is her love.

She brings with her a new domain,

A new Heaven and a New Earth.

She is a new cycle and a new promise,

Heralding the age of rebirth, the end of karmic cycles, the untying of the knots.

And thus comes the Era of the Maiden,

The Age of the Woman, the dominion of the Goddess.

She is the absence of resistance and the presence of light.

She is the highest vibration of love and the absence of pain.

She is forgiveness itself and the highest degree of compassion.

The Mother Sun is ecstatic in her sacred dance, limitless in her movement.

She will bathe every flower, every stem,

Every sprout in eternal sunshine.

And she will turn back the sands of time,

So that all things could move back into equilibrium.

She is our salvation and our treasure,

A celestial maiden in the sky.

And she has come in the most critical of all hours,

The hour of the last sunset and the first dawn.

The Mother Sun is rising.

Hers is the new light, the new day, and the new epoch.

The Mother Sun is rising,

And we shall never be the same.

CHAPTER 19

Our Mother Sun: The Spiral Labyrinth of Creation

Our immediate Universe is a network of solar worlds—unique ecosystems, each constructed around a common focal point, a celestial center of gravity dubbed the local sun. Solar worlds range in size, complexity, and importance. A vast network of suns, large and small, serves as the backbone of the Milky Way, bringing the seemingly disparate system of stars and planets into one integral whole. This solar network is not unlike the nervous system of a human being, with each sun representing a neuron, a celestial cell with the ability to receive and pass on electric impulses, thus impacting its surroundings.

The central sun of the Milky Way is the primary sun of our galaxy, the master sun that all the other suns ladder up to. Despite being separated from one another by vast amounts of time and space, the suns are profoundly interlinked. They often act as one large organism and not a system of detached smaller particles. This level of interconnectedness allows for true homogeneity and enables law and order within the galaxy, each smaller world dancing to the tune of the larger world, all eventually coming together to pay homage to the reign of the central sun.

While every star in our galaxy has an innate ability to emanate light, not every star is considered a sun. In fact, to become a sun, the star must pass through many celestial trials and tribulations, accumulating enough energy to serve as a donor to the surrounding stars and planets. The sun is therefore an incredibly accomplished celestial being—a miracle in its own right.

Once a particular star becomes a sun, the local ecosystem is often rearranged around it. The sun turns into the center of the ecosystem and gains tremendous impact over the neighboring planetary bodies. The network of suns is managed telepathically by Source consciousness, which helps further ensure that galaxies evolve according to a larger cosmic plan.

Each sun is a conscious being with its own challenges, dreams, and aspirations. Each sun is on its own evolutionary path, unique and different from every other sun in the Universe. Now, the sun's lifespan is comparatively long, so souls often collaborate and take turns incarnating in the physical vessel of the sun. Many souls will get to inhabit each sun during its celestial rule, every soul bringing its unique spark and energy to the physical solar vessel.

If you are energetically in tune, you may have noticed a shift in the energy of our local sun sometime around the summer of 2022. We are currently witnessing a great sunset of the Father Sun and the anchoring of the Mother Sun, a celestial changing of the guard, a rare cosmic occurrence that hasn't happened in our local solar system for millions of years. But the Divine Feminine spirit is now once again in charge of the solar system, and that means the energies are bound to shift—and shift pretty drastically.

The Father Sun has been lighting the path for humanity for eons. His steady warmth and Divine Masculine flow paved the path for igniting hearts with courage, instilling the value of the intellect and the importance of sacred action. Many were the lessons of the Father Sun, many were the activations that his energies brought forth, and endless was his love. His service to humanity cannot be overstated. But the time has come for a new kind of sun to take its rightful place in the solar system: the Mother Sun.

The Mother Sun is splendid in her glory. She is warm and nurturing and caring and adorned with the energies of gentle renewal and growth. Hers is going to be a new queendom; hers is going to be a new solar era. The rules of the game as we know it are shifting. As planet Earth is being showered with some of its first female solar rays, an invisible transformation is taking place. Gaia, nurtured by the gentle female rays, is entering her Golden Age, a coming of age for ascension and growth.

The Solar Arc

Interminable is the sun's arc, the path only the sun can walk. It starts with the first dawn—the birth of a new era, a new religion, a new God. Courageous are the first rays of the young sun. They are full of wonder and anticipation, of change and renewal, a rebirth of the most significant celestial bodies. And so, the arc begins not in the pangs of birth, but in the blessed currents of the first dawn, the first of all mornings, the first of all beginnings.

The path of the new sun starts off gently, days easing into days, the dawns as important as the sunsets, helping the sands of time mark the cycles of the Universe. As days turn into years and years into eons, the sun's power grows, its might and courage becoming its defining characteristics. And so, the journey continues until the arc comes to its fulfillment and completion, only to start anew. The sun's arc represents the journey of a particular sun spirit from start to finish. This journey takes millions of years and has its own set of distinct milestones, of which we will quickly explore five (see **Figure 63**).

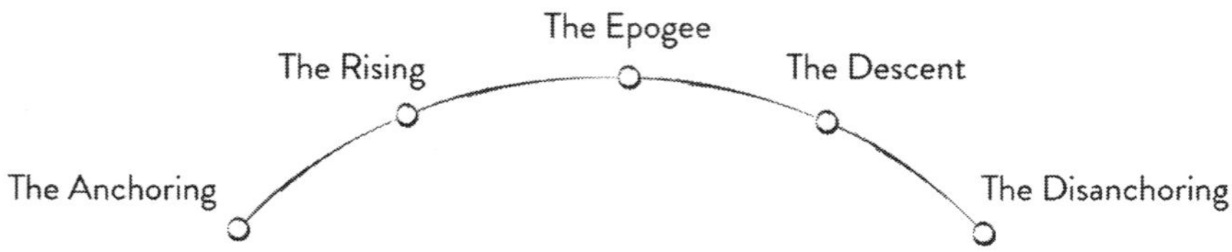

Figure 63: The solar journey

Anchoring: The arc begins with anchoring, a process by which the newly incarnated sun's consciousness gets to know the world that it has come to lead and nurture. The anchoring may be quite swift or take some time, depending on how adept the soul is at the sun's tasks and duties. During this critical phase, new ties are being created between the sun and every planet in the solar system. The sun also forms bridges to every inhabitant of every planet it oversees, and this includes humanity.

Rising: The next period of the solar journey is the rising. This is a period of rapid transformation and the rewriting of old scripts. This is when the new sun undertakes a massive house cleaning and performs major changes within its world.

Apogee: The rising culminates in the apogee, the most fruitful and potent time of the solar journey. During this stage, the sun is at its most powerful. Change is rapid, but well thought out. This usually signifies a period of rapid growth and improvement within each of the planets the sun oversees.

Descent: The apogee is followed by the descent, an often shorter period when the solar consciousness prepares to transition. This is the period of completion and the closing of the loops. The incumbent sun ensures that all the loose ends are tied up properly, and all the karma is fairly distributed and dealt with.

Disanchoring: In this final phase, the disanchoring, the sun welcomes its successor, and together, they undergo a handover process. During the stage of disanchoring, both sun spirits, the old and the new, are present so that the transition can happen properly.

Currently, we are in the first stage of this cycle: the anchoring. During this stage, the energies can feel turbulent and somewhat unpredictable. The new sun is far from settled yet, impacting everyone. Solar transitions are never fast or easy, but they are always worth it, since the new sun brings in an injection of inspiration and optimism, as well as a whole new set of lessons to work through.

The energy signature of our new Mother Sun:

- Heart-led. Our new female sun is extremely heart focused. She is here to help open up humanity's hearts and reinstate love as the primary vibration within the solar system.
- Gentle and compassionate
- Patient and lenient
- Wise and knowledgeable, a master teacher
- Visionary and ambitious
- Intuitive and introspective. The Mother Sun will help unlock psychic abilities.
- Emotional, but dependable and stable
- Healing. Our Mother Sun is a master healer and prioritizes healing, restoration, rest, and self-care.
- Creative, mission-driven, and idealistic. Our Mother Sun believes in a better world for all and is here to help co-create it.
- Abundant, vibrant, determined, and rich
- Joyful and lighthearted
- Protective. She is here to build a sanctuary for all living beings.

The Spiral

One of the ways we can connect with the Mother Sun is through the energetic vibrations of the spiral. A spiral is one of the most beloved energy shapes of our Divine Mother, to the point that it is duly considered her energetic signature. All things touched by a spiral have the breath of the Mother supporting and nurturing them from within. Everything from the helical strands of our DNA molecules to a pinwheel galaxy to a conch shell bears the spiral energy stamp of our Celestial Mother. One of the most common geometric shapes carved upon the walls and ceilings of the caves of our ancestors, the spiral symbolizes the cyclical nature of things. It holds the mysterious keys to all life and evolution. A spiral is an energetic wonder, ever coiling away from a common center of gravity in pursuit of expansion and learning. The center of the spiral is its birthplace, an inception point that once gave it a spin—a point that still supports the spiral's rotation.

As all things in the greater Universe stem from one common center we call Source, so does all life in the spiral emanate from its common center. The movement of a spiral is self-sufficient. Once the initial impulse is received, the spiral naturally continues its trajectory, which enables it to continue evolving even outside of further stimulation. This makes for a curious world, since both the creator and the creation are invited to grab seats at the table, each projection of Source going through its own unique spiral journey of evolution, one coil at a time.

The Solar Spiral

Life is the moving force of the Universe. A spiral is an energetic compound of all that is life. This makes the spiral one of the most prevalent shapes in existence. Given the role the sun plays in the cosmos, it is no coincidence that the spiral is one of its most beloved tools to help transmit codes to all the beings that it governs. The sun uses the spiral on both the macro and micro levels, and it is equally able to impact planetary systems and even the smallest inhabitants of those systems using the same spiral movement.

A Golden Solar Spiral usually moves at the speed of light like a lasso, curving the energy around it and whipping it into its most active state. This state can then be used for massive creation and deep transformation. While there are many tools in the solar toolbox, the spiral is certainly one of the most magical and effective.

Single Spiral

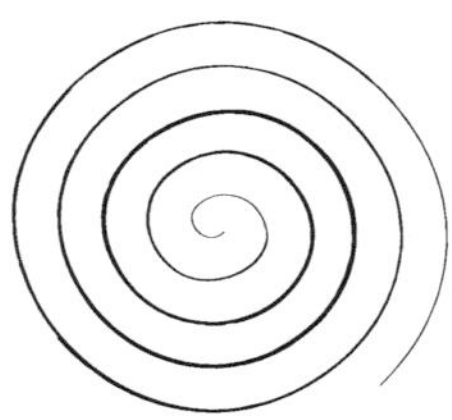

Figure 64: Single spiral

The single spiral (see **Figure 64**) is used to accelerate things, foster growth, and bring about transformation. This is the spiral the sun uses to nurture every growing animal and plant on Earth. When plants grow, they move in a spiral fashion, thus mimicking the vibration of the solar codes transmitted to them. A single spiral also represents an active state of energy in the greater cosmos. This is a resourceful state of energy—the kind that is a precursor to all action.

Uses:

Growth: Use the single spiral to grow a project or a business. To do this, imagine your project as a sphere of light. Then, start rotating a solar spiral under the sphere, until a stream of light emanates from the spiral, fully submersing the sphere in a torrent of golden light.

Charging: To charge yourself with formative solar energies, imagine standing inside the Golden Solar Spiral and watching it rotate around you, first slowly, then faster with each rotation. Notice that the spiral emanates golden energy that covers you like a cloud. Allow yourself to absorb it, and watch your energy state shift.

Healing: A single spiral is a potent healer; it helps remove energy blocks and aches. If you are experiencing pain in your physical body, imagine a golden spiral rotating in the sore spot. First, rotate it counterclockwise for three to four minutes, then shift the rotation clockwise for another three to four minutes. You should feel better upon completing this practice.

Removing unwanted energy: If you feel stuck, the single spiral can help remove unwanted energy. Imagine a Golden Solar Spiral coming alive in the middle of your right palm. Watch as it moves up and down, creating a tingling sensation. If you feel an ache anywhere in your body, place your palm with the activated golden spiral over the ailing spot, and imagine the spiral clearing away the darkness in that area of your body. Repeat the same exercise with the left palm.

Removing blocks: A spiral can help lessen a physical impediment in your life. To invoke the power of a spiral, imagine the obstacle right in front of you, then watch as the golden spiral penetrates it like a drilling mechanism. Watch the Golden Solar Spiral take the obstacle apart, breaking it into smaller particles and removing each one. If the obstacle persists, feel free to repeat the practice; it has a cumulative effect.

Double Spiral

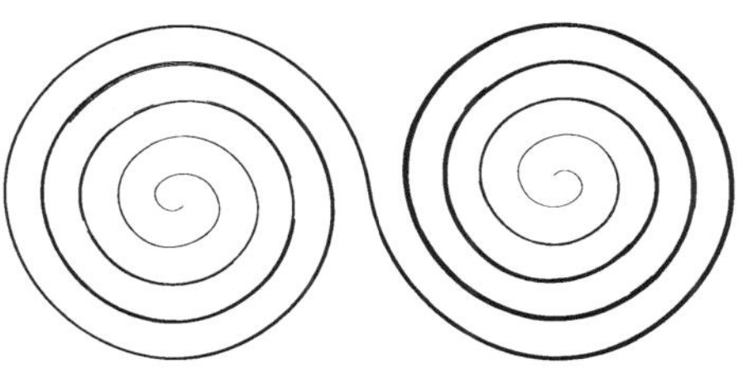

Figure 65: Double spiral

The double spiral (see **Figure 65**) harmonizes dichotomies and polarities. This spiral is also called the spiral of the golden mean or the spiral of balance; it helps us find consensus and a middle ground between even the most antagonistic forces.

Uses:

Masculine and feminine polarities: Use this spiral to harmonize the masculine and the feminine polarities within you. Close your eyes and imagine drawing this spiral on your chest, so that one of the loops of the spiral dwells within the left side of your body, and the other within the right. Imagine golden light coursing through these moving spirals. Allow the energy of the double spiral to be distributed within your body; it will know exactly where to go. Stay here for a few minutes, allowing the spiral to complete the harmonization.

Heart over mind: Use the double spiral to harmonize your heart with your mind. Imagine drawing the spiral so that one of its loops hovers over your head, while the other loop falls over your heart; the middle of the figure should be in your throat area. Allow the energy to keep coursing through the double spiral, and watch it rotate. Speak your intention to harmonize your heart and mind out loud, then let the spiral do the rest.

Resolving conflict: If you don't see eye to eye with someone, the double spiral can help you find common ground. In a meditative state, imagine the person standing in front of you, then paint the double spiral over your head, so that one loop is straight over your head and the other over the other person's head. Focus on how the two loops are moving and shifting, eventually coming into resonance with each other.

Triple Spiral

Figure 66: Triple spiral

The triple spiral (see **Figure 66**) is used when creating something from nothing. It is considered the spiral of creation and empowerment. It is an effective way to transform a passive energy stream into energy in action. Use this spiral to infuse massive amounts of energy into an intention or a project. The triple spiral is also connected to the concept of time, bringing past, present, and future into one cohesive point on the map. The demarcations between past, present, and future disappear, and your entire timeline becomes immediately accessible. This makes this spiral instrumental in helping to rewrite past trauma or to manifest the most optimal future.

Uses:

Manifesting: To manifest a wish, close your eyes and imagine a triple spiral. Clearly identify which spiral loop denotes the past, which stands for the future, and which represents the present. Then, focus on your desire, which exists in the here and now. Imagine this desire as golden sand living within the spiral that represents the present. Take handfuls of the sand and start transferring it to the loop representing the future. Allow the process to run its course. Repeat this practice three times a week for best results. This will help your wish seep into your future, allowing its vibration to merge with your most likely future potential.

Rewriting: To rewrite a painful memory from the past, close your eyes and imagine a triple spiral. Clearly identify which loop of the spiral stands for the past, which denotes the future, and which represents the present. Allow yourself to be mentally transported to the loop of the spiral representing the past. Imagine your body being small and the spiral fairly large, enough so that it feels like you are a car on a racetrack. Start traveling down the spiral, moving toward its center, as if descending a staircase. Keep going until you hit the very center of the spiral at the bottom, the spiral's core. Feel your spinal cord becoming aligned with the central axis of the spiral (refer to **Figure 67** below). Now, focus on a memory you would like to rewrite or release. Imagine it in front of you. Imagine taking a golden cloth and erasing that memory, as if it were written on a white-board. Then, focus on what you wish had happened that day instead, and imagine that you are writing that new memory into the central axis of the spiral with a golden pen. Don't overthink this; simply allow it to happen. You have the access codes you need to do this. When you are ready, come back up by ascending the spiral and open your eyes.

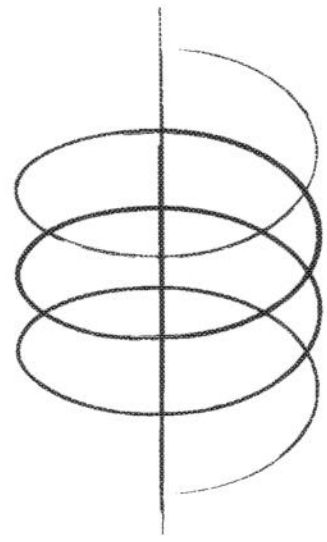

Figure 67: Central axis of the spiral

Fostering or nurturing: To foster a new project or help create something from nothing, imagine what you are trying to create as a ball of energy. Then, place a triple spiral over the ball to align with its center, with the central point between the three spiral loops. Now, imagine another triple spiral being planted at the bottom of the ball, so the ball's central axis is aligned with the central axis of the spiral. If you rotate the three loops of the top spiral in a counterclockwise manner and the three loops of the bottom spiral in a clockwise manner, you'll have both spirals sending energy toward your ball, feeding your project and helping it grow.

Protection: The triple spiral is a powerful protection tool. To invoke this property, imagine a spiral of white light rotating around your body clockwise. The spiral should be large enough to cover your body from head to toe. Make sure the center of the spiral is aligned with your spinal cord. Then, imagine an even bigger spiral that encapsulates you and the first spiral of light, rotating counterclockwise. Make sure your entire body is covered by it. Lastly, imagine a third spiral of light, this one an overlay over the other two spirals. It should be rotating clockwise again. This light protection is incredibly powerful and will prevent negativity from entering your auric field.

Meditation: Activate Your Connection with the Mother Sun

For this meditation, you will need a citrine crystal; it will help amplify your solar connection. You will also need to be well rested.

1. Take a comfortable seated position or lie down. Close your eyes.
2. Place the citrine crystal over your belly button. Your solar plexus chakra is perhaps your body's most potent connection to the sun—that and the third eye—but for this practice, we shall use the solar plexus.
3. Start breathing into your belly button, all the while imagining how this area of your body is being filled with joyful yellow light. Take deeper breaths than usual; this way, your abdominal area can be infused with the energies needed.
4. Imagine a sun right in front of you. This sun is female. She is softer than before—gentle, bright, optimistic, and powerful, but in a feminine way. This is the sun of compassion and second chances, the sun of redemption and growth, of nurturing and faith. This is the sun of creativity and authentic expression. Watch as the she-sun stretches her rays toward you, giving you the warmest solar hug imaginable. Notice how this sun's spirit seems familiar to you. You know that she has your best interests at heart.
5. Imagine throwing a lasso over the sun and starting to reel her in. Keep pulling on the lasso until the sun comes face to face with you, so that barely any distance separates you.
6. Picture a double spiral, with one loop hovering over your head and the other loop hovering right above the sun. As the spiral starts to rotate, feel a common energy field emerge between you and the sun. This field looks golden and resembles a cloud.
7. Notice how a small particle splits off from the she-sun and travels toward your belly button, firmly planting itself inside your stomach. Allow yourself to receive this solar imprint, taking the emanations of the new sun into your body fully.
8. Notice how this solar imprint enters your body and travels to your solar plexus chakra, changing it from within. Notice how the golden codes of the sun are rewiring your solar plexus chakra, upgrading and healing it, and preparing you for what's to come. Allow this process to take its time; no need to rush it.

9. Now, focus on the sun in front of you. You may notice that there is a door in the body of the sun, golden and ornate—a door that is opening specifically for you. Enter the sun and move toward its very center.
10. Sit down in a lotus pose at the very center of the sun and start breathing deeply into your belly. With each breath, imagine that you're breathing solar prana into your lungs, the life force of the new sun. Stay here for seven to ten deep breaths.
11. Notice how small golden particles are starting to fly around you like a hive of bees. Do not be afraid; these solar elementals are benevolent and have come to help you better connect with the Mother Sun.
12. Watch the golden specks cover your entire body, as if you were covered with glimmering bee pollen. Notice how these particles start seeping through your pores into your bloodstream, coloring your blood golden. Watch as your blood carries the solar codes throughout your body, even to the remotest spots.
13. Allow yourself to receive these solar blessings, letting them heal your body from disease and fatigue, bringing vitality and perfect health back into your life.
14. At this point, you can ask for something particular from the sun and speak it from your heart.
15. You are finally ready to start coming back. Feel free to stand up and let your lasso go. Watch how the sun returns to its original position in the sky—only now is it familiar, and you will still maintain the connection you have established with it long after this meditation.
16. Feel free to open your eyes. Send much gratitude to the sun for working with you today.

Heart Space: Her Name was Anantara

Her name was Anantara, and she was the New Sun,

The one that came after millennia of patriarchy,

After centuries of judgment, after eons of rigidity and fear.

She was the new dawn and the new life—the one untarnished by the expectations of the old world,

Her wings of light unclipped, her chin held high,

Her golden hair cascading down to Earth in an avalanche of sunlight.

Her name was Anantara, and she was the New Sun.

She was writing the new laws and setting the new golden standards.

The gilded domes of eternal protection and higher love covered the sky in her honor.

And so, she built for herself a new abode and a new sanctuary, a space of quiet, solemn beauty.

And those domes were a promise, the beginning of a new grid, the start of the new empire.

Her name was Anantara, and she was the New Sun.

Her song was a blessing and an invitation to step into authenticity.

Her light was a permission slip to become yourself fully.

Her sermon was a benediction and a promise of eternal life.

Her iridescence was a calling and a transcendence—a promise that the trials and tribulations were coming to a close, making room for something else entirely.

Her name was Anantara, and she was the New Sun,

And the Earth was her prodigy, her past, and her present,

A new path forged by water and fire,

A journey blessedly incomplete.

She was the New Sun,

And it was the time for her story to be told.

CHAPTER 20

The Flower Crown: Gaia's Initiation

"And the day shall come when all the children of Eve shall be cleansed of the original sin, no courtesy of a man, but courtesy of a woman, of her sacrifice. The one who chose to carry the load. The one who chose to take on the pain and suffering of birth and of life. The one who was the stronger of the two. And on that day, the apples shall fall into the sky, and the great tree shall grow with its roots upward, and the snake shall recede into the netherworld, while the rose thorns shall crumble into dust.
And that day shall be called Armageddon.
But a new sky and a new land shall come to replace the empty shell void of life.
And the trumpets will herald the New Earth.
And the sin shall be no more on a planet we call Gaia."
~The Long-Lost Scrolls of Tar

Terra Mater, Mother Gaia, Pacha Mama, Earth—many are the names of our planetary Mother, many are her facets, and vast and diverse is her terrain. Before incarnating here, we each signed a personal contract with Gaia, a pact by which we chose to partake of her lessons and become an aspect of her body, born of her flesh and blood. In that sacred act, we became her children, adored and cherished from birth as a crown jewel of creation. Some souls were given a special task, a mission to stay in tune with the planetary core rhythms, listen to the beat of Gaia's beautiful heart, and sync with the rest of her creation. Most souls who had such a contract came in female bodies.

For millennia, it was up to women to uphold the sacred promise humanity made to Gaia: to love and respect all living things, to cherish all of creation, and to live in alignment with Gaia's laws of harmony. It was up to women to remind their families and communities of the depth of our connection to the planet, of just how much we owe to Gaia's patience and nurturing love. Throughout generations, the wise women and the healers, the herbalists and the seers, the priestesses and witches, the shamans and sages maintained a deep connection with our beautiful planet, gaining much insight and strength. And Gaia would always reciprocate, showering her faithful ones with love and caring presence.

There was a time once when humanity existed in harmony with the nature surrounding it. Humans lived alongside elementals, spoke to animals and trees, manipulated the weather to nurture their crops, and helped co-create the ecosystem they inhabited. During those blessed times, everything we touched became better. New species of plants were cultivated, and new species of animals crossbred. Life was full of ritual, intention, and everyday magic. Alas, those days are long gone.

As time went by, humanity's connection with Gaia weakened. As human hearts grew hard and we turned against each other, the original harmony was lost, and original sin entered the picture. Life hasn't been the same since. For thousands of years, humanity was drifting away from the original plan. Murder and wars became commonplace, while empathy was rare. No longer were our hearts touched by the pain and suffering of one another. With that came greed, the need for control, and the desire to compete. A crown jewel of creation, *Homo sapiens* turned feral and parasitic. Like swarms of locusts, they descended upon the virgin meadows and the ancient woods, cutting and maiming and killing, turning verdant nature brimming with life into a terrain of metal and dust, transforming life into death. Once, there was a time when the entire natural kingdom recognized the human as a sovereign, a creator, a God. Now, the human became known as a usurper, a virus, a plague. And while some light was still preserved in the depth of the human species, most of it disappeared amidst the air of superiority and narcissism.

As Gaia watched one of her favorite children, the human, devour, kill, and drive her other beloved children to extinction, her heart bled, and tears streamed down her face. And yet, Gaia had patience—patience and hope. Hope that the day would come when humanity's ways would change, when her children would look upon the outcome of their actions and their hearts would open again. For through an open, loving heart, much is possible, even redemption and a true comeback, a return to the Garden of Eden itself—a paradise on Earth, but this time as a human-made creation.

The Way of Gaia

All of creation has value, merit, and Divine purpose. No creature is an accident. Nothing in nature is an afterthought. To Gaia herself, all links in the ecosystem matter, and all of her children are equally beloved, cherished, and fitting into a cohesive plan. Gaia has conceived of and is presiding over a beautiful yet precise system of life and death, one species feeding another in a large planetary ecosystem where everything supports everything—apart, perhaps, from humanity. Everything in nature vibrates at the heart chakra—apart, perhaps, from humanity. The path to human redemption lies in the heart, a descent into the folds of our compassion and empathy. And yet, we look at the corpses of the animals we consume and feel no compassion. In fact, we have created new names for the animals we eat. We don't eat cows anymore; it is "beef," an inanimate substance created for one purpose only: to feed the ever-hungry and ever-growing belly of humanity.

Gaia is not weak, nor is she blind. She feels the pain of every child murdered in the slaughterhouse, whether grass-fed or not. Our planet has both the power and the level of consciousness needed to turn things around, to cleanse itself of the plague that is humanity. The planet does not require saving, for it has never been a victim. But it has been a mother, a loving and compassionate being, always giving humanity the benefit of the doubt, hoping and praying that one of her favorite children will one day wake up. And while vast, Gaia's patience is not limitless. Much has been said about Armageddon—judgment day. And while the forces of light may instigate it, make no mistake: Gaia will be the one that brings it forth, with her waters and her fires—the big cleanse and the big reset. Hers will be the battle cry that raises the tides and causes the ruptures of the land. Her tears of fiery lava will run free— tears for the ones who shall never return.

So, what is the path to redemption, you might ask? What shall the one with a heart that bleeds green do? The answer is simple: change your vibration. It all starts with changing who you are, not what you do. The answers you are looking for are inside of you, in the quiet voice of your intuition, in the soft calling of the purpose of your heart.

The Gaia Codes

Time is running short, and our gentle planet is calling for volunteers—the brave ones, the dedicated ones, the ones who have the eyes to see and the ears to hear. This is a call to action, my friend. And this call has reached you. I am not here to tell you that to help our planet, you must stop eating animals or using plastic. In fact, what you are called to do may be entirely different. This call from Gaia is unique to you, for it factors into your soul's journey and your special talents. By activating the Gaia codes inside your body, you connect to the planetary consciousness on a deeper, more intimate level. Gaia shall speak to you and through you. What happens then shall be unique to who you are at a soul level. You may be called to change your lifestyle, or to do research in a particular field. You may be called to grow your own food, or learn about medicinal plants. You may be called to create tinctures and flower essences, or to simply commune with nature. Either way, this activation will be a major homecoming. It will create an umbilical cord between you and Mother Gaia, establishing a constant flow of energy and communication between you.

Don't be surprised if you start seeing or feeling elementals or begin to perceive nature differently. Once the connection with Gaia is reclaimed, it becomes sacred. It becomes your stream of connectedness, a support structure like no other. Gaia's spirit shall flow through you, expanding your auric field and inviting more light into all of your bodies. By integrating the codes of Gaia, you become an acupuncture point on the face of our planet. You become a healer and a redeemer, a warrior of light. You join the natural flow of creation. You join forces with our planetary Mother, becoming her initiate and her child in arms.

Ritual: An Initiation of Gaia

This ritual must be done in nature, ideally away from large groups of people, where you can spend quality time in communion with nature. Please take care to extinguish any candles and take them home with you.

You will need:

- A tablespoon of dried nettle
- A sprig of fresh mint
- A sprig of fresh thyme
- A sprig of fresh rosemary
- Three fresh sage leaves
- Three fresh basil leaves
- A green candle
- A bowl
- Cedarwood essential oil
- A flower crown or a plant crown (ideally handmade by you)
- A simple silver ring or bracelet

To prepare:

Boil some water in a pan. Add the fresh herbs (nettle, mint, thyme, rosemary, sage, and basil). Simmer for nine minutes. Allow the mixture to cool, then strain it so that only the liquid remains. Place this herbal essence in a bottle you can bring for the ritual.

The ritual:

1. Take a comfortable seated position in the shade. Light a green candle, a symbol of abundance and interconnectedness.
2. Hold the candle in your hands and close your eyes. Imagine several emerald light cords emanating from you in every direction.
3. Watch as these cords start "hugging" the natural objects around you, connecting everything in your vicinity through the magnetic power of your heart.

4. Invite a few elemental spirits to preside over the ritual. Welcome the elementals of fire, water, earth, and air to be with you for the entirety of the ritual.
5. Pour the herbal essence you prepared earlier into a bowl and add ten drops of cedarwood essential oil.
6. Place the bowl in front of you and place your hands in it. Notice how the many plants that contributed their essences to this blend start to enter your body through the palms of your hands. Notice how these plants carry emerald vibrations throughout your body, transforming you from within.
7. The next part of the ritual is an invocation. It should come from your heart, but it can also follow this example:

"My Mother Gaia,

I invite you into my body today, so that your heartbeat can become my heartbeat, so that your blood can become my blood, so that your light can become my light.

From this day onward, I vow to stay connected with you and carry your blessed imprint in my body. To me, you are sacred. I invite your essence to be joined with mine, so I can see the world through your eyes and feel it through your heart. I vow to protect and cherish you. I vow to stay strong on my path to oneness. I ask for your blessing and support for my commitment and dedication to light.

Today, I surrender to your healing, to your love, and to your embrace. I am coming back home today. From this day forward, you and I are one, inseparable, tethered, united. Your pain is my pain, your joy is my joy, your strength is my strength.

Today, I choose to walk in your light according to your ancient ordinance. I know I am a part of your ecosystem, and I am your forever child. Crown me as a member of your light tribe, one of your helpers, one of your ordained knights. Carry your light through me. Use me to heal and transform this world. In you, I am forever changed.

And so it is, and so it shall ever remain."

8. Upon giving the invocation, place the flower crown upon your head. In your mind's eye, watch as the crown begins to glow, showering you with curtains of white effervescent light. Notice how a pyramid of light emerges around you, containing you within. Notice a sensation of being perfect-

ly protected and connected. Know that you are a child of Gaia, one of her favorite treasures.

9. Lastly, place the silver ring on one of the fingers of your left hand. Alternatively, you can place a silver bracelet on your left wrist. This is a physical representation of your commitment to our planet, a sign that from this day onward, you are part of a tribe of light called Gaia.
10. Place your hands upon your heart and feel it expanding. Watch as your heart grows larger and larger, leaving the constraints of your body, growing even so large as to encapsulate our entire planet within its depth. Just imagine how much love a heart of this size can experience.
11. Allow yourself to feel all the love, to hold this vibration, to memorize how it feels down to your bones. Hold onto this feeling after the ritual is complete, always remembering just how much love you can feel and emanate.
12. When you are ready, complete the ritual with gratitude.

During this experience, you may get insights and downloads, so record everything in your journal. Some of the most important soul-led information can come through this ritual, so you want to preserve it for future contemplation.

Our Mother Speaks to Us

Gaia's language is gentle. She speaks to us through the breeze in our hair, through the rain on our face, through the melodic song of crickets in the night. Her language is subtle, yet lingering. She is everywhere all at once, as long as we pay attention. She is a healing presence and a comforting touch. She is a mother's unconditional love and a blessing of boundless resources. Many are the ways of Gaia, and immeasurable are her riches. And while the language of nature is extremely diverse, the Mother speaks to us through the language of plants, perhaps most of all. There is a sacred contract between us and the plant kingdom—a contract that states that plants will work diligently to uplift and heal humanity in exchange for gratitude and love. While not every plant shares equally in this mission, many plant species have been upholding their end of the bargain, healing and sustaining humanity against all odds.

The Plants of Light

The time has come for me to tell you a story, my sibling. It is a story of days long gone, yet of events quite relevant.

Many eons ago, during the time when Gaia was first establishing herself as a planet and a consciousness, she called upon the many spirits to come and aid her in her quest of building a budding verdant ecosystem on Earth. This was the formative period, a time of change, a time of challenge, and a time of many blessings. Many spirits were naturally drawn to Gaia—her incessant optimism, her unyielding faith, and her lighthearted demeanor.

At the time, Gaia's soul was on her journey of exploration of light and darkness, a rabbit hole both deep and enticing, and many souls, young and old, wanted to explore these concepts alongside her. So, two camps of souls were formed: the camp of light and the camp of darkness, each equal in might and determination, each made up of souls who wanted to play the game on a broader scale. Each soul destined to incarnate on Gaia picked a role for itself. Each was given a playbook and a set of attributes to build their persona around. Some souls opted to come as animal spirits, others to animate the vast natural features of mountains and rivers, and still others decided to incarnate as plants or human beings. Some roles in the greater script were designed as short stints masterfully crafted into the longer narrative; others were meant to endure for the entire existence of the planet.

Not every animal or plant species on Gaia picked the camp of light or darkness; some chose to represent neutrality, a state of acceptance and unconditional love for the warring camps. At that time, three thousand plant species joined the camp of light, becoming the original light species of planet Earth. Each plant was a light warrior, a channel, a healer, and a holder of Divine emanations. Each plant was a Universe within itself, a sacred promise of a better world. Together, they formed an herbal army, a force of nature at Gaia's beck and call. The plants of light were meant to uplift the souls striving for growth and expansion, serving as guides, healers, and silent companions for humanity.

And so, the two camps descended upon Earth in a dance of ice and fire. Each civilization, each continent, and each epoch from the very beginning of time has been in service of their greater conflict, a battleground of learning the difference between light and darkness. Civilizations fell, and new ones came in their wake, the fabric of existence morphing and shifting, yet the common thread remained—the delineation of a conflict as old as time, ever unfolding, ever defining itself, never complete.

Over time, some of the original plant and animal species became sparse. The battle between good and evil left its mark upon the ecosystem of Gaia, ruthlessly cutting down entire hordes of localized species. Of the original plants of light, only thirty remain today. For anyone looking to reach a higher understanding, the vibration of these plants is both covetable and precious. Very few things on Earth carry the vibration of pure, unadulterated light like these thirty plants. Not only do these majestic creatures carry the light vibration within their DNA structure and cellular membranes, but they can also impart it upon everything they come in contact with.

Below, I offer a full list of the remaining plants of light. Please note that if a plant is not included on this list, it doesn't mean it is in any way detrimental to you. Many plants currently dwell in neutral territory. The plants of light, collectively and individually, stand guard for the original vision of evolution and development of the human species and offer much healing to humanity. They are the plants that came here to serve the greater good. Should you know these little warriors by name? I sure think so.

Thirty plants of light:

1. Nettle
2. Rosemary
3. Chamomile
4. Sorrel
5. Sagebrush (also mugwort)
6. Oregano
7. St. John's wort
8. Fireweed
9. Millet
10. Hemp
11. Flax
12. Mint
13. Spanish needles
14. Plantago
15. Dandelion
16. Turmeric
17. Ginger

18. Dill
19. Sage
20. Thyme
21. Chicory
22. Asparagus
23. Coltsfoot
24. Cranberry
25. Lingonberry
26. Elecampane
27. Parsley
28. Garlic
29. Basil
30. Tarragon

Working with the Plants of Light

The topic of the plants of light is so broad that it perhaps requires its own book. However, there are some simple basics that we can discuss here.

Incorporating the plants of light into your daily routine is one of the best self-care tactics. The plants of light require a ritualistic approach; they cannot be consumed in haste. Using the plants of light should be intentional, each an exchange of energy and a sacred rite.

Guidelines for working with plants of light:

- Greet the plant before consuming it. Express gratitude for the healing and transformation you are receiving.
- The magic formula for the plants of light is "three a day." Three is a patron numeral of the plants of light. (This stems from the fact that originally, there were three thousand of them.) The numeric frequency of three will always amplify the benefits of any of the plants of light. Think three drops, three spoonfuls, three teabags, etc. These sacred plants also like working in groups. Pick three plants of light to consume every day. You can do more than that, of course, just not less.
- One thing worth noting is that a few foods drastically diminish the impact of the plants of light. Consuming gluten and nightshades (potatoes, bell peppers, tomatoes, eggplants) makes it harder for your body to absorb the healing frequencies of the plants of light. Try reducing your consumption of gluten and nightshades, and if at all possible, cut them out altogether. The plants of light are also in direct opposition to the vibrations of corn, rice, and soy, so those are problematic pairings also.
- Don't overdo it. Partaking of the plants of light is a sacred rite. More doesn't always mean more. Intention is what matters.
- Establish a routine that works for you. Try a few plants and find your favorites. Then, commit to using them often. Light accumulates in the body over time. The energies of the plants of light are gentle, so you may not notice an immediate change, but over time, the results could be quite dramatic.
- Get to know each of the plants and their impact on your body. The plants of light have both medicinal and nutritional value. Each is incredibly layered, and getting to

know them is a lifelong journey. Don't rob yourself of your birthright of befriending the plants of light and benefiting from their larger-than-life impact.

Benefits of working with plants of light:

Heightened spiritual perception: The vibrations of these plants are incredibly cleansing. They help rid your body of toxins and blockages, opening up your energy pathways and clearing your channel. This allows more messages from your spirit guides and higher planes to come through and be received by your consciousness.

Improved health and vitality: Using plants of light has a cumulative effect; the more you use them, the better your health. Energetically, these powerful plants infuse you with the highest caliber of light available in nature. This helps heal your body naturally and gently. The plants of light work in the background, silently optimizing all of the most critical functions and systems of your body.

Improved longevity: The plants of light help you live longer. They quickly react to imbalance, pollution, and various dysfunctions of your body, bringing your inner ecosystem back into balance.

Full-body detox: The main goal for the plants of light is to fight the darkness in your body. This means toxins, parasites, blockages, and various ailments.

Mood enhancement and greater happiness: Energetically, happiness is light coursing through your body. The plants of light assist with accumulating light and banishing darkness. The plants act as mood enhancers, bringing you more energy and optimism.

Water Infused with Plants of Light

Infuse your drinking water with your favorite blend of plants of light. Place a few sprigs of your favorite plant in a water carafe and leave for three hours. After three hours, the water is sufficiently infused and ready for consumption. You can use the same plants to infuse water twice more (for a total of three times), at which point it is best to discard the leaves, as most of their life force will be used up.

Some of my favorite plants to infuse into water (only use the fresh leaves):

- Tarragon
- Basil
- Thyme
- Rosemary
- Mint
- Dill
- Ginger
- Sage
- Parsley

Try combining three plants from the above list to infuse your water. Playing and testing things is paramount here. Most importantly, have fun! You could not do this wrong if you tried.

Hot Infusions and Daily Tonics

Each person is unique and has a plant that will be the most optimal for daily infusions. Use a pendulum to find out which plants of light are your personal helpers. In the living world, there are always affinities. Chances are, of the thirty plants of light, you have a special connection to the handful that would be most optimal for your body.

Fresh herbal infusions:

Try starting your day with an infusion of fresh mint leaves, honey, and lemon. Some plants I love for daily hot infusions:

- Chamomile
- Ginger
- Mint
- Fireweed
- Dandelion
- St. John's wort

Plants of light play well with honey, so feel free to sweeten away. They don't play well with sugar, though. To make hot infusions, you can use both living and dried leaves.

Daily turmeric shot (AKA sun shot):

Turmeric best works with vitamin C, so orange juice is a perfect companion for this shot. This daily shot is a boost of optimism and vitality in a glass. It helps connect you to high-frequency solar power and charges your body for massive action and optimal performance.

You will need:

- Turmeric
- Ginger
- Bee pollen
- Fresh-squeezed orange juice, or fresh-pressed apple juice

To make this, combine a cup of freshly squeezed orange or apple juice with a teaspoon of fresh-squeezed turmeric juice and a teaspoon of freshly squeezed ginger juice. Mix well. Add half a teaspoon of bee pollen at the top. Drink, giving thanks to Gaia.

The antioxidant shot:

This shot boosts immunity and jump-starts your body's natural healing prowess. It helps optimize your energy levels, improves your blood and circulatory system, balances digestion, and helps eliminate toxins. Enjoy!

You will need:

- Fresh-pressed cranberry juice
- Honey
- Basil
- Freshly squeezed pomegranate juice

To make this, combine half a cup of fresh-pressed cranberry juice (from cranberries, not concentrate), a teaspoon of honey, juice from five basil leaves, and half a cup of freshly squeezed pomegranate juice. Mix well and drink, giving thanks to Gaia.

Heart Space: The Tree of Souls

Deep in the land of the Fey grows a sacred tree: the tree of the living, the tree of the dead. Its leaves are blush pink, its fruits are milky white, and verdant is the grass beneath its foliage. Majestic is the sacred tree of the Fey, the keeper of records, the guardian of the Fey lands, and the holder of ancestral wisdom. A new leaf grows upon the tree of the living every time a Fey soul is born; a new record is created, and a new life is immortalized. As the soul joins the Fey family, it joins the foliage of the sacred tree. And so, the soul is nurtured by the tree, protected by its massive power, and inspired by its ancient history. For as long as the Fey heart beats, the new leaf is white. White is for the living.

The wheels of time are churning, causing new things to come into being, and the old things to make way for the new. A cycle of life and death goes on in the new age, just like in the ages bygone. There is nothing new under the sun—the eternal sun of the lands of the Fey.

And so, the souls come and go, always marked by the tree, never truly forgotten. When a soul departs, a white leaf on the tree turns pink. White is for the living; pink is for the dead.

Deep in the land of the Fey grows a sacred tree: the tree of the living, the tree of the dead. As our epoch draws to a close, so does the Fey tree. There shall come a day when the bark of the tree turns ashen, and the leaves of the tree become dust. That will be the day when the Great Creatress turns a new page and writes a new beginning. Nothing is forever—not even the tree of the Fey.

There is an old legend that has been passed down in the Fey lands from generation to generation. It is the tale of the last days, of the tree dying, of the New Queen coming to take the reins from the queen of old. They say that the New Queen shall watch the tree die, tears of pearl in her eyes. The New Queen, they say, shall replant the tree in a new land—a land of milk and honey, a land of the gilded gates of sunshine.

And so, the land of the Fey is awaiting the New Queen, like fledgling sprouts await life-giving spring rain. And as they do, the tree is dying—a morbid sign of the last days, a sure sign of the days to come, of the second coming foretold long ago.

At the exact moment when the end becomes the beginning, a tree shall die to be reborn bigger and better than before. And the New Queen shall cry tears of sorrow and watch them turn into the tears of joy. And those tears shall become a mighty river, and that river shall nurture the new tree, giving it a life worth living, a whole new set of records to keep. And when the first leaf is born upon the tree, there shall be a New Sun and a New Earth. And darkness shall be no more in the lands of the Fey, where once grew a sacred tree: the tree of the living, the tree of the dead.

CHAPTER 21

You Are the Flow: Water Initiation

In the days of old, the wisdom of water was revered. The human tribes of the world, guided by their innate instincts and a deep-seated ancestral memory, held natural bodies of water in high regard. They knew there was a spiritual undercurrent, a Divine undertone to every sea, river, and lake. The tribes opted to settle around large bodies of water not just for survival, but also due to water's unique ability to create healing ecosystems and maintain them over long periods. The waters of local rivers and lakes held the ancestral memories of the tribes that lived alongside them, ensuring that the wisdom of generations was passed on intuitively and effortlessly. Rivers and lakes were guardians of those who lived and procreated on their shores.

Today, the Polynesians maintain the strongest connection to water, and therefore, to the spirit of the Mother of all the people of Earth. Often subconsciously, they help Gaia maintain the fragile balance of water and fire (feminine and masculine) required to preserve our planetary ecosystem. There is a special reverence, innate gratitude, and awe that the genes of the Polynesian peoples hold when it comes to water. This deep-seated connection has been nurtured by many generations of island tribes who've lived in harmony with water. However, as the Polynesian population dwindles, it is becoming increasingly difficult to maintain the fragile balance needed for the survival of the human race.

Our path back to balance starts and ends with water, a substance that makes life possible on the surface of our beautiful planet. There has been much talk about climate change in the last few decades. While there are many reasons for the state of our Mother planet, one of the energetic precursors to the melting of the ice caps is our imbalanced relationship with water. We have been taking the life-giving force of water for granted for too long. Our Mother is reminding us that the karmic consequences of the loss of connection with water are dire and could entail anything from a flood of Biblical proportions to a complete redrawing of the continental map of the world. Water will always get the respect it is due, one way or another.

Energetically, it falls upon the Earth's female population to maintain a strong innate connection with water. Throughout history, many communities depended on women to get water from the brooks, rivers, and wells (and many still do), while the masculine population hunted for sustenance. Some women still have to walk for miles to get to drinkable water.

While daunting and labor-intensive, the daily ritual of getting water brought women closer to this wondrous element. As women were carrying the many buckets filled with water back to their homes, their energies intermingled with the primordial element, creating a symbiotic relationship. Through this simple daily ritual, the water became a vessel for holding the intentions of the female carrying it. It could therefore be a projection of a woman's heart, healing and nurturing her family members. This was a form of naturally occurring alchemical magic, and is just one example of what a deep connection with our Divine Mother can do. With the development of plumbing, the connection between women and water began to gradually deteriorate, so today, it is a barely perceptible whisper of what once was.

Nurturing Your Connection with Water

Our current relationship with water is that of a slave and a master, with humanity shortsightedly playing the master in this equation. We've created dams to restrict the water's flow, we've dumped industrial waste into our rivers, and we've covered the faces of our oceans with plastic. To add insult to injury, we have stopped treating water as a living signature of our Mother Goddess, taking it for granted, acting as if this massive resource is inexhaustible and ours for the taking. We are made of water, but the water is not made of us. As such, water is the primary element, the one that came before. It is not an inanimate building block that exists to please humans; water is the domain of the Mother. And she shall not be denied anything.

As we enter the Era of the Maiden, healing our ancestral relationship with water is a threshold, a rite of passage, a path toward coming full circle. Reclaiming our planet starts with reclaiming our sacred relationship with water, this force of nature within and without, the higher power that was here before us and shall be long after.

Rebuilding humanity's relationship with water starts with you, with all sisters. Breaking ancestral patterns of ingratitude starts with you. The future starts with you, if you so choose.

- Become intentional with your water intake. Remember to send a quick thought of gratitude to the Mother when you are drinking water. Saying something like "Thank you for your love, Mother" should suffice. You can infuse intention into every cup of water you drink by thanking the Mother for something specific. For instance, you might say, "Thank you for the healing, Mother," and imagine the water healing you from within. Or you can say, "Thank you for all the wealth, Mother," and the water shall help bring more abundance to you.
- To maximize your water intake, infuse it with some healing herbs (see Chapter 20, page 383). Usually, it takes three hours for the water to become fully infused with the gentle vibration of the plant. Some of the best herbs to infuse into water are rosemary, basil, tarragon, thyme, and mint. If you place your water carafe in the sun, it will also contain potent solar codes on top of the magic of water and herbs. That is when the water becomes truly magical.
- Greet oceans, rivers, lakes, and brooks like old friends. Each natural body of water is a particular emanation of the Mother and likes to be acknowledged as such. Never miss a magical opportunity to establish a deeper connection with water by recognizing its wisdom and consciousness.
- Perform a water offering at least once a year. This should signify a special day of gratitude for the resource of the Great Mother and her generosity. It should also help clear up any karma you may have incurred regarding water over the past year. Below, I offer a simple water ritual, but you can customize it based on your intuitive guidance.

Ritual Offering: Cleansing Your Relationship with Water

For this offering, you will need to head to a large natural body of water—an ocean, a river, a lake. It goes without saying that you should stay safe in this ritual and be mindful of tides and other potential dangers of working by the water.

You will need:

- A small transparent crystal that you are willing to part with (any quartz is perfect, but you can get creative)
- A white seashell
- A tablespoon of seeds (any grains will work—rice, quinoa, amaranth, barley)
- Your favorite essential oil
- Three white flower buds (roses, lilies, or daisies would be perfect)

The offering:

1. Take a seated position on the shore, so the water is nearby.
2. Place the crystal over your heart, gently holding it in place with both of your palms. Shut your eyes for a few moments.
3. Start the ritual by greeting the water and setting an intention. As you say the words, imagine your crystal absorbing them fully, becoming an energetic match for your invocation. The words should come from the heart, but can also be modified from the below example:

"My dear Mother Water,

I have come to pay homage to you today. I am grateful for your love and support. I am grateful for the healing and nurturing you unconditionally bestow upon me. Today, I ask for your forgiveness if I have wronged you in any way. Please accept my offering of love and gratitude and my intention to become even closer to you with each day that goes by. Your strength and power are my support system, your gentle embrace is my cradle, and your flexibility is my teacher. I remain forever your loyal and loving child. I have so much gratitude for what you do for me and mine."

4. Now that you have spoken the invocation, open your eyes. Take the crystal infused with your sacred words and give it to the water. You may throw it further away from the shore or simply place it in the waves, whatever feels right to you.
5. Take the seeds, the shell, and the essential oil and step into the water. Up to your knees is more than enough.
6. To consecrate a space for your ritual, use twelve drops of your favorite essential oil to draw a virtual circle around yourself. The water loves essential oils in small doses, so this is considered a sacred offering, not a form of pollution.
7. Once the circle around you has been marked with essential oil, give the water all the seeds. Imagine planting something new in the water, something you wish for the water to have—like peace, serenity, and contentment. The seeds can also symbolize your gratitude, especially if you have something specific to be thankful for.
8. Imagine the seeds growing into sprouts made of white light, and through these sprouts, the water can replenish its resources.
9. Now, give the white shell back to the water. While the shell originally came from the ocean, reciprocating is important. Everything in nature is a give-and-take; if humanity took something, humanity must give something back. Returning the shell to the water acknowledges the cyclical nature of things and the official closing of the karmic loop, personal and ancestral.
10. Complete the ritual by giving three white flower buds to the water. This is your personal gift to the spirit of the water. It also represents a sacred feminine connection that you share. Giving flowers to the water is akin to infusing it with oxygen. This is a very purifying and healing ritual and makes the water feel cared for and appreciated. It also helps deepen your connection with the water element, so you can start receiving intuitive wisdom and guidance from this mighty force.

Bodies of Water

All naturally occurring bodies of water are unique and different, each one a holder of the wisdom and the emanations of the Mother, each one a rare gift from her to the Earth's ecosystem. The spiritual significance of the many different bodies of water is long-forgotten wisdom, lore lost over the ages of darkness and oblivion. As we reclaim our individual and collective relationship with the waters of the Mother, it is time to start speaking her language, the tongue of water. It is time for us to remember just what kind of energies each body of water is infused with. It is time for us to reclaim this deep ancestral knowing, this abundant resource, this long-lost truth. This is a homecoming.

Oceans

Deep run the oceans of the planet we call Gaia. Oceans represent the Great Subconscious, the hidden truths, the patterns and intricacies of the collective. Oceans are both vast healing spaces and master record holders of our planet. They are liquid libraries, ancient and full of wisdom, holding tightly to the memories of times bygone, preserving the stories well forgotten, cherishing the remnants of the past. Oceans are the closest physical representation of the Akashic Records on Earth.

The Mother uses oceans to manage the health of the planetary ecosystem and to remove things that are out of tune with the song of the greater whole. It is no wonder that Atlantis was consumed by the hungry belly of the ocean. With the loss of its light, Atlantis, in some ways, came off its central axis, reforging the magnetic pull of the continent it presided over. The emanations of Atlantis became detrimental to the larger ecosystem of the planet, so the cleansing and equalizing waters of the Mother removed it and reclaimed the balance. Such is the destiny of anything that creates disharmony within the body of Gaia; in accordance with the law of the greater good, it must be removed.

And while the great waters of the Mother have served as a major cleansing mechanism throughout the ages, nurturing and sustaining life is still the most important function of water, and therefore, of the ocean. If you asked the Mother why she created the oceans, she would say that she wanted her children to witness the breadth and depth of her love for them, endless and unfathomable like the ocean.

The Atlantic Ocean: The Mover and Shaker of Oceans

The Atlantic Ocean was originally formed into a separate ecosystem when the masculine and feminine energies of Earth reached a state of disharmony, to the degree that their relationship turned toxic. To help heal the fractured relationship and seek out a new equilibrium, as well as to help the localized masculinity of planet Earth evolve, the Atlantic Ocean came to be. For as long as tensions between the masculine and the feminine exist on the face of our planet, a version of the Atlantic shall remain. There are many shadows of masculinity, and the Atlantic is here to help heal most of them. Divine Masculinity is beautiful—stable, dependable, wise, calm, and responsible. True masculinity is what creates law and order in the Universe. But the path toward achieving it is winding on the best of days.

Even now, masculine energies in Gaia are looking for an outlet, a teacher, and a harmonizer. They are looking for deep healing and redemption. As Gaia's children, we bear her challenges and blessings within our DNA. Just like she struggles with the shadow of her masculinity, so do we attempt to balance on the right side of the power equation, while feeling like we must keep up with the Joneses to even feel remotely adequate. As above, so below; we are all united by the same challenges. Healing our inner masculine is an important cornerstone of learning for every creature on Earth, and humanity is no exception.

The Atlantic currently represents the greater masculine of our beautiful planet—the good, the bad, and the in-between. It contains some of the most beautiful masculine tendencies, such as taking the initiative, standing for your beliefs, and fighting for what's right. But it also contains the shadow side of masculinity—the push and pull of a zero-sum game, power struggles, aggression, dictatorship, greed, and selfishness.

Represents:

- Change
- Creation
- Innovation
- Dynamic movement
- Progress
- Material gains
- Revolutions
- Speed
- Impermanence
- Ambition
- Masculinity

Energies it is here to harmonize:

- Greed
- Materialism
- Toxic masculine tendencies
- Slavery
- Victim mentality
- Powerlessness
- Ego traps
- Overconfidence
- Competitiveness
- Low self-esteem

- Lack of confidence
- Ill intent
- Hate
- Political machinations
- Self-serving agendas

Vibrates at: Solar plexus and throat chakras

The Pacific Ocean: The Wise, Loving Sage of the Oceans

In a tumultuous sea of third-dimensional reality, the Pacific Ocean represents stability. It promises that despite the temporary upheaval, the future is bright. The energy of the Pacific is unrushed, measured, dependable, and solid. It is a stabilizing energy, a counterbalance to ever-dynamic, ever-shifting reality, an antidote to progress for the sake of progress. The Pacific is here to remind us that it is the eternal that is most important—that we should not lose sight of the forest for the trees, and that running very fast in the wrong direction is in fact not running at all.

The waters of the Pacific connect Gaia to many water-based civilizations of the Milky Way, who impart their deeper wisdom upon the face of our comparatively younger planet. Thus, the Pacific reminds us that our most important progress comes from soul learning, not material possessions. The Pacific is a permission slip to stay away from the herd to find your own path. It is an invitation to step off the treadmill of daily worries to reconnect with your eternal spirit and follow its guidance. The Pacific urges us to find the true self in the sea of collective templates and societal conditioning. It invites us to slow down, breathe deeper, cherish the moment, be present, spend time in isolation and solitude, nurture our souls, and fill our cups. The Pacific is the ocean of compassion and surrender. It is loving, unconditional, multidimensional, and full of heart. It is intentional with its lessons and the healing that it offers. Its primary vibration is patience—the wise patience of a teacher watching their students take their first humble steps.

Represents:

- Stability
- Ancient wisdom
- Wise counsel
- Sage advice
- Practical insight
- A systematic approach
- Heart-led leadership
- Alignment and attunement
- Action in pursuit of the greater good
- Evolution
- Slow movement
- Hard work
- Deeper knowing
- Harmony of the natural elements
- Interconnectedness
- Compassion
- Love
- Introspection

Energies it is here to harmonize:

- Rushing
- Being disconnected from Spirit and nature
- Harshness
- Rudeness
- Anger
- Lack of faith
- Inauthenticity
- Hidden agendas
- Fear of death
- Fear of insignificance
- Fear of connection
- Relationship trauma
- Self-criticism

Vibrates at: Heart, sacral, and third eye chakras

The Indian Ocean: The Buddhist Monk of the Oceans

The Indian Ocean is a generous gift from our Divine Mother. It is high-vibrational, transformative, and healing, and can be life-altering. It is a meditative state encapsulated in ocean form. The Indian Ocean helps lower the volume of mental chatter, opening a portal into higher dimensions and connecting us to Source. The Indian Ocean is also a mirror of the collective. Of all the oceans, it is perhaps the most reflective of where humanity is emotionally at any given point. This makes it a terrific and powerful healer, ever present to and in tune with the collective song of humanity. The Indian Ocean may force you to face your shadow and heal your broken parts; it may accelerate the process of your learning and healing.

Working with the Indian Ocean is a pilgrimage in its own right. It requires asking and answering difficult questions, a certain level of commitment, and a willingness to work through the resistance. But if you pass the lessons laid out by this magical ocean, the reward can be great indeed, from harmonization of all areas of your life to awakening and even enlightenment. The Indian Ocean is a liquid equivalent of the Himalayas, sending you down a winding path of getting to know yourself and becoming the best version of yourself you can be. This ocean leads to integration, the coming together of the multiple broken pieces inside you. The Indian Ocean is the patron of conscious communities and conscious living. It stands for simplicity as a path to happiness. After all, truly happy people know just how small of a role material possessions play in their inner bliss.

Represents:

- A quest for the eternal and the timeless
- Insight
- Introspection

- Silence
- Solitude
- A philosophical approach
- Spirituality
- Balance of the body/mind/soul
- Inner joy
- Bliss
- Nirvana
- Deep healing
- Shadow work

Energies it is here to harmonize:

- Loss of spirituality
- Egocentrism
- Narcissism
- Individualistic thinking
- Abuse
- Torture
- War
- Inferiority
- Inner child trauma
- False ideals and doctrines
- Harmful agendas

Vibrates at: Higher heart and crown chakras, with parts vibrating at the third eye chakra

The Arctic Ocean: The Mystic of the Oceans

The Arctic Ocean has a dual mission on Earth: it holds the keys to opening the heart chakra of humanity, while also paving a path to awakening through access to the mysteries. This ocean dwells in the realm of the occult, the esoteric, and the mystical. Like the high priestess with an incredible amount of foresight, the Arctic Ocean governs the dissemination of hidden knowledge (including that coming from extraterrestrial civilizations) on Earth. It is the ocean behind divination modalities and fields of study like astrology and numerology, and it is a patron ocean of the tarot and runes. Many long-lost mysteries of old, including the forgotten knowledge once brought here by extraterrestrials, are still recorded within the depths of the Arctic.

Despite the frigid temperatures of its waters, this ocean is incredibly heart-centered in that it has just the antidote to a particular flavor of humanity's heart trauma. Its long-term mission is to take every living creature on Earth through the arc of love that would culminate in a unification of beings into one integral, cohesive, and united collective—a day when all beings of Earth shall perceive the oneness between themselves as the only ultimate truth.

Represents:

- The occult
- The hidden
- Mystery
- Secrets of the Universe
- Alchemy
- Transformation

- Death and rebirth
- Resurrection
- Immaculate conception
- Healing the heart space
- Devoted service
- A state of togetherness
- God/Goddess consciousness

Energies it is here to harmonize:

- Indifference
- Rigidity
- Coldness
- Heart trauma
- Heartbreak
- Parent/child trauma
- Dysfunctional families
- Loss of the inner center
- Personal truth

Vibrates at: Heart, third eye, and crown chakras

Rivers

Rivers are a physical representation of the ephemeral state of flow. Energetically, they symbolize movement, vitality, transient states, evolution, natural forces, providence, and omniscience. They remind us that the only constant thing in our life is its inconstancy.

Every river is a hero or heroine's journey, a deep dive into a particular way of being. All rivers have a trajectory, a winding path that connects their beginning and end, their source and their mouth. The way of a river is an initiation path in its own right.

In the days of old, when we could still talk to animals and natural features, rivers and river spirits were highly revered. At that time, one could walk a unique path of spiritual growth and development curated by a river and the water elementals inhabiting it. The adepts of the water path followed the direction of their river guru, learning the lessons the river's waters contained. Often, this spiritual pilgrimage was accompanied by a physical one, where an initiate would move along the riverbed, starting at the source and eventually ending up at the mouth, having passed all the stages of initiation.

As a part of a larger water ecosystem, rivers can be likened to blood vessels inside the human body. It is the rivers that bring change to communities across the world, it is the rivers that support life, and it is river magic that often helps humanity anchor new energies and integrate their learnings. Just like the generous heart of our Divine Mother, rivers do not discriminate. They serve as safe havens and a means of sustenance for living beings, large and small. And while certain properties of rivers can be equally appreciated by all, the spiritual work of rivers is currently geared toward humanity, paving the path for the evolution of the *Homo sapiens* species.

The Ganges: The Mother River

Few rivers are as revered as the Ganges, but perhaps few are as polluted. The largest river in India, supplying water to more than forty percent of the country's population, the Ganges is nothing if not impactful. However, it is the spiritual significance of the Ganges and not the functional benefits that make it one of the most sacred rivers on Earth.

The Ganges is considered the Mother River (*Ganga Mata*) and the river of the Goddess, and indeed, it contains some of the most potent energies of the Divine Mother. The Ganges has stood guard over countless generations, offering solace, redemption, and constant nurturing. It is timeless and relevant, healing and mighty, redeeming and full of challenge. Stepping into its waters is a confession, a cleanse, and a benediction all in one. Taking a dip in the Ganges helps reset the etheric, mental, and emotional bodies, which brings a palpable feeling of relief and calm to the human body. The magic of the Ganges is transformation. The river takes your energy as is and alchemically zeros out all the negative polarities, bringing you to a blissful state of zero, an energetic blank canvas on which you can paint anything.

In the days of old, the waters of the Ganges could remove ancestral karma, diffuse black magic, grant clairvoyance, and even assist with ascension at a soul level. However, this property of the waters is largely gone, since it has become incredibly polluted, with nearly one million gallons (three hundred million liters) of sewage being emptied into it daily. Cleaning the gracious waters of the Ganges can restore the river's magic prowess. Alas, this requires a level of collective awareness that is currently lacking in humanity. And yet, the Ganges still maintains deep wells of resources and is an incredible energy to connect with.

Represents:

- Spirituality
- Deep cleansing of light bodies
- Redemption
- Forgiveness
- Motherly affection
- Patience
- Connection
- One of the facets of the Goddess

To connect: Imagine standing under a waterfall that descends straight from the heavens. The waterfall should be silver and sparkling. Imagine this waterfall hitting the spot above your head, your crown chakra, and then streaming down your body along your spinal cord. Watch as the waterfall turns into a mighty river: the great Ganges. Reach out to the Ganges with any heart wounds if you feel lost and don't know your true north, or if you are inundated with drudgery.

Allies to enhance the connection:

- The color white
- Lilies
- Long hair
- Red ribbons
- The moon
- The red rose

Vibrates at: Heart and crown chakras

The Nile: The River of Magic and Cosmic Knowledge

The Nile is connected to higher wisdom, advanced civilizations of light, the Akashic field, higher dimensions, intuition, and introspection. This river is a spiritual pilgrimage. The Nile can transform all of your light bodies and prepare your vessel for receiving the Universe's wisdom. The Nile is the river of mystery, but before you can partake of it, you must pass through a series of trials. Often, the Nile requires you to perform a strict ascesis, to give up certain foods or drinks to free up the energy necessary for spiritual pursuits.

Dipping your feet in the Nile is considered a spiritual cleanse, especially if done in a ritual setting and with a specific intention. Our bodies often resist change and certain incoming energies, especially if they differ fundamentally from ours. The Nile allows this natural resistance to subside, creating an opening for the wisdom to come through.

In the days of old, dipping in the Nile was regarded as a deep cleanse on every level, helping release karma and negative programming from the body and even one's lineage. However, the Nile of today is heavily polluted with wastewater and garbage, enough so that it may be more advisable to work with the river energetically as opposed to physically.

Represents:

- Magic
- Mysteries
- Wisdom
- Deeper understanding
- Intuitive knowing
- Connection to benevolent extraterrestrial civilizations
- Transcendence
- Awakening
- Soul memories
- Access to the Akashic Records

To connect: Imagine standing in the middle of the Nile in your light body. Invite the energies of the Nile to enter through your third eye. Collect the water from the Nile in a receptacle inside your third eye area. Having a clear intention is paramount; the Nile is very selective and doesn't like random wanderers. Have a purpose, and the Nile shall open its etheric arms to welcome you.

Allies to enhance the connection:

- The lotus
- The king cobra
- The star Sirius
- The Great Pyramids of Giza
- The Knot of Isis
- The scarab beetle
- The white dragon

Vibrates at: Third eye chakra

The Amazon: The Queen River

One of the world's most verdant, exuberant, and awe-inspiring ecosystems stretches along the edges of the Amazon River, perhaps the best physical representation of the frequency of abundance and fullness on Earth. The Amazon runs for almost four thousand miles (6,440 kilometers), creating a unique rainforest ecosystem that is home to some of the rarest animal and plant species. Despite covering only one percent of the Earth, the Amazon rainforest is home to over twenty percent of Earth's flora and fauna. This makes the Amazon a queen among rivers. She is a benevolent and powerful monarch that both brought about and is currently ruling a queendom of her own making.

The vibration of the Amazon is that of the heart and its power to create, nurture, and grow things, its magnetic attraction, its endless optimism, its faith, and its deep empathy. Some of our Divine Mother's most potent creative energies found their home in the Amazon's waters. Even today, the waters of the Amazon are getting a generous infusion of love straight from the heart of our Celestial Mother, so that they can later distribute that love to every living being in the Amazon's vicinity.

The Amazon's waters are healing for the heart and the body, replenishing your natural resources and bringing you out of the state of constant fatigue and declining health. The Amazon can be a mighty ally on your path to greater abundance, vitality, and well-being. It is also a river of manifestation and birthing new things, a river of new beginnings and fresh starts. It can bring change and momentum to a stuck or struggling project; such is the healing etheric magic of this spectacular river.

Represents:

- Abundance
- Wealth
- Fullness
- Presence
- Flow
- The magnetic principle
- Life
- Attainment
- Achievement in the physical world
- Joy, happiness, and contentment
- Celebration
- Change
- Movement
- The power to create something from nothing

To connect: To connect with the magic of the Amazon, first drop into your heart. Imagine diving into it headfirst, as if falling into a chasm, only this particular chasm is emerald green. Once you land, notice a large emerald crystal in the center of your heart space. Feel free to bypass it and walk forward. Not far from the emerald, you will notice a large emerald-colored stream that looks like a river. This is your personal connection to the Amazon, a well of abundance, courtesy of our Divine Mother. Step into the emerald waters and allow the energies of the river to enter through your pores and start seeping into every major organ and system. Keep absorbing the emerald energies of the Amazon, filling your body up as if it were a vessel. Now, imagine an area of your life where you would like to see more abundance. Picture it as an empty sphere made of light. Touch this sphere, and through your hands, start pouring the energy of the Amazon now in your body into the sphere. Allow this process to run its course.

Allies to enhance the connection:

- Emerald
- Amazonite
- Green fluorite
- Apatite
- Aventurine
- Gold
- Copper
- Diamond
- Jasper
- Peridot
- The parrot
- The peacock
- The monkey

Vibrates at: Heart and higher heart chakras

The Ob and the Irtysh: The Rivers of Light

The Ob and the Irtysh are two mighty rivers, one flowing into another and forming one of the longest river systems in the world. These two rivers flow through China,

Russia, and Kazakhstan, with the largest part of the river system located in Siberia. *Ob* is a derivative of the Komi language; *obva* means "snow water," referring to the fact that the waters of the river originate in the snowy peaks and ice caps of the Altai mountains. The Irtysh is temperamental and moody, but immensely powerful, ever changing the terrain along its course.

The waters of the Ob connect us to the long-lost legacy of Hyperborea, an ancient civilization of highly developed beings who once inhabited the territory of the Arctic polar regions and predated Lemuria and Atlantis. Hyperborea was a civilization of light, the land of eternal sun, consciousness, and achievement.

Despite Hyperborea sinking into the depths of the Arctic Ocean, its imprint is still alive in Greenland, Iceland, and parts of Russia. The legend tells that many moons ago, the mystical and highly developed land of Belovodye, the land of white water and the Slavic version of the Hindu Shambala, was located along the banks of the Irtysh River. The etheric imprint of the lands of white water is still very much present in the Altai Mountains, offering healing and enlightenment to the worthy seeker. The land of Belovodye is believed to be a remnant of the once-great Hyperborea. Tucked away in the protected realm of the Altai Mountains, the waters of the river Katun (a tributary of the Ob) turn white due to their speed and mountainous temperament, cleansing and protecting the surrounding lands. The lands around the Ob are a seat of Russian mysticism and shamanism, a source of much healing for the land and its people.

The mystical river pair of Ob and Irtysh offers much wisdom and light. There are very few places on the face of our planet that vibrate as high as the lands of the Altai Mountains. The waters of the two rivers are thus healing; they foster awakening and spirituality and allow us to move beyond the layers of the visible into the realm of the infinite and eternal.

Represents:

- Transformation
- Release
- Relief
- The polarity of light
- Ancient civilizations
- Ancestral wisdom
- Connection with nature
- Connection with Source
- Deep cleansing
- Restoration
- Spiritual healing
- Ascension
- Mysticism
- Special abilities (the clair- senses, and so much more)

To connect: Close your eyes and imagine a large snowy mountain in front of you—the White Mountain, they call it. Come closer to the mountain and notice that there is a river of white light flowing down its slopes and into the valley below. Stand right at the foot of the mountain, submerging your feet in this river of light. Start taking the light water into the soles of your feet, slowly allowing it to travel up toward your head. Notice how the river's waters start coalescing into a spiral shape in the middle of your forehead, right around your third eye area. Allow this process to run its course. Voila! You are connected to the dynamic duo of Ob and Irtysh. Meditations in this state have a particular transformative power; the insights are potent, and the healing codes that come through are high-vibrational and out of this world, literally.

Allies that could enhance the connection:

- Snowy mountain peaks
- Ice
- Ice giants
- The sun
- Arcturus
- The Pleiades
- The white phoenix
- The white swan
- The dove
- The owl

Vibrates at: Crown and third eye chakras

The Mississippi: The River of Power and Achievement

The Indians called the Mississippi the father of rivers, and the name of the river translates to "the great river," pointing to its special significance for North America. While every river represents the Divine Feminine energies on Earth, the Mississippi is perhaps the closest to the masculine of all the feminine energy facets.

The indigenous tribes living along the banks of the Mississippi believe that the river is inherently connected to the life force of our planet, and its waters are especially nurturing to all life.

Energetically, the Mississippi is an endless source of calm confidence, supporting you on your path and reminding you that you can have it all. The river has a centering and solid presence. It helps foster communication and aids in finding one's personal truth and expression. The great Mississippi favors action and movement and can help promote the growth of companies and the adoption of ideas, no matter how unpopular. The river helps build up your sense of self-worth and removes distortions from your expression.

The flow of the Mississippi is authentic, true, and intentional. It is a great remover of obstacles. The spirit of the Mississippi likes big ideas, innovation, and change. It favors the brave ones, finding them easier to influence and support. The Mississippi can become your support system and a center of stability and calm as you navigate life's challenges. Still, it requires a sense of personal integrity and your willingness to do the work in exchange.

Represents:

- Communication
- Intention
- Divinely guided action
- Personal truth
- Material wealth
- Individuality
- Creativity
- Achievement
- Authenticity
- Self-expression
- Going after what you want
- Societal transformation
- Change

To connect: Close your eyes and imagine standing in a pyramid made of sunlight, golden and glimmering. Look down and notice that you are standing in beautiful yellow-tinted waters. They are the color of the sun and have golden specks that reflect light upon the surface. Watch as the water reaches your knees, then keeps rising until it reaches your belly area. Watch as your solar plexus chakra opens up and starts absorbing the yellow-gold waters of the river. Invite the waters into your system and give them a task. Ask them to help you achieve a goal or successfully complete a project that is dear to your heart. Once the water agrees to help you, it will give you water to assist with your request. Create a receptacle for this water inside your body. The water manifestation may not be fast, but it works. Your patience shall be rewarded.

Allies that could enhance the connection:

- The sun
- Citrine
- Morning
- Summer
- Daylight
- The North Star
- Amber

Vibrates at: Solar plexus chakra and throat chakras

The Yangtze: The Chameleon River

The longest river in Eurasia, the Yangtze is a force to be reckoned with. Its source is the Tibetan plateau, one of the highest-vibrational places on Earth. Born of the energies of the crown chakra and connection to higher realms, the Yangtze flows through China across 3,900 miles (6,275 kilometers), ever shifting and ever changing, perhaps more so than most rivers. Over the course of its journey, the river manages to cover every major chakra energy, some more than once. This makes it truly versatile.

The Yangtze carries the vibration of a true warrior goddess—dedicated, courageous, and true. It can help connect you to the warrior within and grant you stamina and confidence to overcome any life obstacles. The spirit of the river is all about finding and fostering your inner strength, finding your courage, and fighting for what's right. Perhaps in recognition of this, the name of the river contains the word *yang*, the great masculine principle. While applicable, this categorization of the river can be somewhat misleading, since the Yangtze boasts beautiful heart energies that are just as potent as its fiery spirit. The river generously shares its heart emanations with the surrounding flora and fauna, some of the most diverse in the world.

The magic of the Yangtze's heart is gentle, accommodating, forgiving, and patient. It has a beautiful quality of bringing people together and forming communities that stand the test of time. Lastly, the Yangtze is an overachiever, a conqueror, and a leader. It can help you connect to your resourceful and active state, fostering achievement and success. However, the Yangtze is here to align you with the greater good, not just pure self-service. It has potent missionary and philanthropic energies permeating its depths. It can be an incredible ally if you are working on a planetary level and seeking to bring about massive change. The Yangtze starts with the vibrations of the crown chakra and ends with the vibration of the root chakra, thus becoming a proxy of a human body fueled by spirit; spirit over matter is one of its primary vibrations. This doesn't imply denying physical existence, but rather, fully anchoring our spirit into everything we do.

Represents:

- Success
- Achievement
- Leadership
- Forward thinking
- Action
- Patience
- Compassion
- Decisiveness
- Community-building
- The warrior spirit
- Strategy
- Movement
- Momentum
- Connection and interconnectedness
- The ability to shift and adapt
- Blessings
- Being guided by Spirit

To connect: Close your eyes and imagine standing as tall as a mountain, with your left foot submerged in the waters of the Yangtze right at its source in the Tibetan plateau. These waters are white and glimmer with light. Invite them to travel up your left foot, entering through your sole and moving up to exit through the top of your head. Then imagine submerging your right foot in the waters at the very end of the river, near the East China Sea. These waters are ruby red in color. Invite them to enter your body through the sole of your foot and move up until they reach your head and pour out from the top. From here, you can ask for a blessing or assistance from the Yangtze, based on its properties as discussed above.

Allies that could enhance the connection:

- The chameleon
- Gold
- Silver
- Bronze
- Coins
- Fire
- Opal

Vibrates at: Different parts of the river vibrate at each of the seven chakras, with the crown, heart, and solar plexus being dominant.

Lakes

If rivers stand for movement and change, lakes are deep wells of condensed feminine energy. They serve as the acupuncture points of the planet, bringing the various antagonistic forces into equilibrium, connecting the dots, ever harmonizing and equalizing. Lakes are peacemakers, energy transmitters, and planetary healers. Their superpower is their ability to absorb massive amounts of negativity from their surroundings and shift it into light. Lakes remove planetary-level inflammation and deeply stuck trauma, serving as points of detox and release. Lakes are the silent and meticulous healers of our fragile planet, her diligent helpers, the first response team when things go wrong energetically.

Throughout history, our Celestial Mother has been sending various vibrations into each of the earthly lakes. Therefore, the lakes' energy reflects current times and needs rather than some preordained mission or assignment from the beginning of time. The lakes' vibrations shift over time, like a doctor that needs to change their specialty depending on what aches the patient needs to heal. The easiest way to diagnose the overall health and well-being of an ecosystem is to look at its lakes: the energy they carry, and whether any of the lakes are drying up. When a river runs dry, it usually symbolizes that a particular path has been walked, and there is not much learning and insight it presents.

This is completely normal and is generally no cause for alarm. But this is not the case with the lakes. When lakes start drying out en masse, the ecosystem is in grave danger. This is the equivalent of an autoimmune disease and a precursor for tough times ahead.

Lakes are deep healers. The placement of every single one is intentional, and they are aligned collectively, an ecosystem of holistic medicine vessels working on the planetary level. We owe much to the silent hard work of the lakes that surround us. Perhaps it is time that we learn more about their workings and magic.

Lake Titicaca: The Healer of Female Wounding

Lake Titicaca plays a critical role in bringing back the strong feminine bonds of old. Its work is a reclaiming of the sacred sisterhood, the sacred motherhood, the sacred daughterhood, and therefore, healing of the familial trauma and the overall relationship of women with each other. Societally, Titicaca is here to help diffuse and transmute the plentiful energies of distrust in humanity today. It helps restore faith in those near us, getting us away from the trap of self-defense and victimhood. The lake also deals with some of the deep-seated trauma of our reproductive systems, such as the pain of childbirth and even sexual abuse. To partake of the energies of the lake, swim in it, wash clothes in it, or connect energetically; you cannot get it wrong.

Here to heal:

- Familial energies
- Daughter/mother/wife wounding
- Female friendships
- The wound of betrayal
- Distrust
- Worry
- Inertia
- Ambivalence
- Victimhood
- Abuse

To connect: Drop into the lake through your sacral chakra. Keep falling into the orange depths, and ask the Universe to connect you with the wisdom of the lake. You will notice a cord of light stretching over to you. Wrap it around one of your wrists. Voila! You can start working with the spirit and soul of Lake Titicaca.

Vibrates at: Sacral chakra

Lake Baikal: The Lake of Insight and Understanding

The deeper the lake, the better the energy concentration inside it. Being the deepest lake in the world, Lake Baikal is nothing if not mighty.

If you can let go of the layers of what you think you know and allow yourself to see the world beyond the traps of the collective unconscious, Lake Baikal can be an incredible guide and ally on your path to deeper knowing, unlocking your intuitive abilities and helping you evolve at a soul level. However, working with this lake requires a certain level of solitude and isolation; its voice is quiet and can only be discerned through silence and deep introspection.

Lake Baikal is here to address our wounded masculine, helping smooth away the scars and fix the fissures, bringing us closer to our Divine imprint. It helps us see the truth of what our wounded masculinity has created in the world and shows us the impact of the power struggles we have manifested, whether through imposing our will on others, shunning responsibility, or giving up on our dreams.

Here to heal:

- Ignorance
- Low vibrations
- The busy mind
- The supremacy of the intellect
- Superiority complexes
- Shortsightedness
- Separation
- The human shadow
- Wounds of masculinity
- Childhood trauma
- Misogyny
- Greed
- The need for control
- Power struggles
- Zero-sum games (me vs. them mentality)

To connect: Imagine a large lake with a large crystal quartz pillar in the middle. Travel down this pillar until you hit the bottom. Invite the lake's waters to enter your body through your third eye. Ask the Universe to connect you with Lake Baikal.

Vibrates at: Third eye chakra

Lake Tanganyika: The Quiet Lake

The waters of Lake Tanganyika are calm, but don't mistake that for lack of power. The lake's sacred path is to heal some of humanity's most profound issues. The lake goes into the depths of the human psyche, unearthing the darkness within. It works collectively to expose what is hidden and shines a light upon humanity's most painful scars. Deep healing like this starts at the ancestral level, often many generations back, when the seeds of the current trauma were first sowed. No wonder the lake is the second deepest in the world! Healing the issues of hunger, poverty, and war takes a true master, able to descend to the great subconscious depths and still come out victorious.

Here to heal:

- Violence
- Starvation
- War
- Anger
- Discrimination
- Slavery
- Conflict
- Struggle
- Poverty
- Fear of death
- Fear of not having sustenance or shelter
- Antagonism
- Competition
- Envy
- Pessimism

To connect: Imagine a large ruby before you. Dive into the depths of the crystal, falling as far into it as you can before you hit the "ground." Notice that the bottom of the crystal is filled with crystalline ruby-red water. Submerge your body in the water and send an intention to the Universe to connect with the lake.

Vibrates at: Root chakra

Lake Michigan: The Lake of Redemption and Truth

Lake Michigan explores the concept of personal truth and the lies we tell ourselves and others, even with the best intentions in our hearts. It is here to heal inauthenticity on a collective level, whether this inauthenticity is driven by a need to comply with societal pressures to fit in, habit, or ignorance. Lake Michigan is a force pushing us deep into self-discovery and soul-searching. It defies surface-level answers, seeks to expose what is hidden, and cleans away some common human vices, such as gluttony, gambling, and various addictions.

Most importantly, Lake Michigan can lead you toward your personal North Star, back into connection with the infinite. In its fight for authentic expression, Lake Michigan helps absorb some of the negative aspects of the egregores of alcohol, synthetic drugs, and tobacco—all liable for leading humanity toward oblivion, not away from it. Lake Michigan wants humanity to face its actions head-on instead of covertly and intentionally looking the other way. Facing one's demons is how the lake administers its healing and helps promote the dismantling of the human shadow.

Here to heal:

- Inauthenticity
- Treachery
- Ill intent
- Wishing harm upon another

- The desire to get ahead, regardless of cost
- Gambling
- Addiction
- Alcoholism

To connect: Step into your throat space and imagine a strong wind lifting you up. Keep traveling until you see the North Star shining ahead of you. The star is surrounded by water. Step into the water and ask the Universe to connect you with Lake Michigan.

Vibrates at: Throat chakra

Lake Victoria: The Lake of Abundance and Blessings

The vibration of Lake Victoria is one of the most heartful on Earth, gentle, loving, and caring, like a warm embrace from a long-lost mother. Her healing is effortless and kind. She gently unfolds our hearts petal by petal, removing all the pain that dwells inside to reveal our most perfect and loving selves. She starts at the level of self, helping to fix deep issues of low confidence and self-esteem. She teaches us to love ourselves and pass that love onto others, and she reminds us just how interconnected and dependent on each other we are.

On a collective level, Lake Victoria heals selfishness and lack of consideration for others. She brings back the safety of loving another and fully committing to a relationship, fostering healthy communities and deeper bonds. Her energy is the liquid honey of forgiveness, compassion, and kindness. She helps awaken us to the state of oneness and the simple truth that we cannot hurt another without hurting ourselves. In true Ouroboros fashion, the fruits of our actions always come back to haunt us, reminding us that mindfulness and awareness are steps toward wholesome living and that love is the best currency we have.

Here to heal:

- A lack mentality
- Despair
- Hopelessness
- Sadness
- Heartbreak
- Rigidity
- Lack of self-love
- The inability to fully love another
- Putting yourself last
- Being shut down
- The inability to be with the negative emotions
- Emotional pain
- Inner criticism
- Perfectionism

To connect: Imagine a large emerald protruding from the ground. Picture diving into it headfirst. At the bottom of the emerald, you will find a lake of emerald waters. Step into the lake and invite its waters to enter through your heart space. Ask the Universe to connect you to the consciousness of Lake Victoria.

Vibrates at: Heart chakra

Lake Superior: The Lake of Personal Power

Lake Superior is a powerhouse destined to help humanity heal some of its deepest wounds related to keeping up with the Joneses, overconsumption, low awareness, materialism, and power struggles. Overconfidence and abusive tendencies are just as harmful as lacking confidence and having a victim mentality; they are two sides of the same coin. Luckily, Lake Superior is adept at dealing with both. The lake also works with humanity's God complex, a belief that humanity is superior to other species, seemingly allowing people to abuse the land they live upon. This single belief leads to the loss of equilibrium in our planet's ecosystem and creates a slew of negative tendencies that Lake Superior is working diligently to heal.

Here to heal:

- Power struggles,
- Control
- Abuse (verbal and physical)
- Shadows of the ego
- Overconfidence
- Lack of consideration for others
- Abuse of power and influence
- Actions that create a negative impact
- Selfishness
- False ideals
- Shadows of capitalism
- Shadows of fame
- Shadows of materialism
- Loss of connection to nature
- Drudgery
- The nine-to-five trap
- An overachiever complex
- Perfectionist tendencies
- Incompetence
- Passive-aggressive behavior
- Gossip

To connect: Drop into your solar plexus chakra. Imagine that you are swimming in yellow waters toward a distant point that represents the center of your solar plexus. This point is marked with a vertical axis resembling a yellow stick protruding from the waters. Once you reach it, grab the stick with both hands. From here, ask the Universe to connect you with the consciousness of Lake Superior.

Vibrates at: Solar plexus chakra

Ritual: The Water Initiation

This ritual has been customized so that you can perform it in the shower. However, the original ritual was often performed in a natural body of water—a lake, river, or ocean. Pick the setting that best works for you.

You will need:

- Three medium-sized bowls or jugs
- Ten cups (two liters) of distilled water
- One ounce of liquid colloidal silver
- A black tourmaline crystal
- Half an ounce of liquid monatomic gold
- A medium-sized aquamarine or amazonite crystal
- Ten cups (two liters) of boiling water
- A sprig of thyme
- A sprig of rosemary
- A handful of sage leaves
- A handful of basil leaves
- A handful of mint leaves
- One tablespoon of dried chamomile flowers

To prepare:

Before the ritual, prepare three water infusions to enhance your water connection.

Fill a bowl with five cups (one liter) of distilled water. Add the liquid colloidal silver. Mix well. Place a tourmaline crystal at the bottom of the bowl and leave it for three hours.

In another bowl, mix five cups (one liter) of distilled water with the liquid monatomic gold. Mix well. Place an aquamarine or amazonite crystal in the bowl and leave it for three hours.

Bring two liters of water to a boil in a medium-sized pot. Add the thyme, rosemary, sage, basil, mint, and chamomile. Stir well. Reduce the temperature and simmer the mix for five minutes, then allow it to cool. Strain the contents into a clean bowl.

The ritual:

1. Smudge with some sage or palo santo to energetically cleanse the space around you. Light a few candles and burn some incense to further energetically prepare the space. The Water Initiation is a ritual of anointing and invokes the power of water to cleanse and reset the energetic makeup of your body.
2. Start by setting an intention to connect with water and partake of its blessings. While the words should always come from your heart, below you'll find a sample intention you can modify to fit your needs.

"Mother Water,

I invite you to come into my body and into my life.

I ask you to please harmonize the water vibration inside my physical and light bodies at this time. Just as you once birthed me and helped me come into this human body, I ask that you help me cleanse anything that must leave my body at this time. I invite you to join me as my co-creator, my resource, my support system, and my dearest ally. With this ritual, I join the water tribe of beings who work with you and benefit from your power. As your daughter (son) in water, I ask that your healing presence stays with me day in and day out. Please help me navigate life's hurdles, remove the obstacles in my way, and bring me much serenity and abundance.

Today, I choose to be blessed and healed by your presence.

And so it is.

Much gratitude for you and all you do."

3. Remove your clothing and step into the shower. Turn on the water and allow it to fall upon your head. If you are performing the ritual in nature, step into the water so that your body is fully submerged up to your waist.
4. Close your eyes, place your hands over your heart, and invite the water to start working its magic on you. Invite the water into your personal space, opening yourself up to the ritual fully.
5. Take the first bowl of water mixed with silver. Remove the tourmaline crystal. Take a few deep breaths. This bowl is the cleanse. It will help remove all the dirt, debris, toxicity, and stuck energy from your light bodies.

Step away from the stream of water so as not to dilute the impact of the contents of the bowl. With an intention to clear away any and all darkness, pour the bowl of water over your head so that it flows down your body. Feel your body becoming cleansed in the process. Imagine any and all darkness that may be present within your body turning into light.

6. Take the second bowl of water mixed with monoatomic gold. Remove the crystal that dwells there; its job is now complete. This bowl contains the light water codes, a purified and enriched state of water, and it bears the imprint of Source itself. This water is meant to bring something new into your life—a fresh perspective, a fresh start, a blessing, an energy injection. Trust that the water knows best and shall deliver exactly what you need.
7. Dip your index and middle finger into the water and gently anoint your temples with this water. Then put some of the water on your neck and over your heart. Invite the water to work its magic and bring about the transformation and recalibration of all your light bodies.
8. Take a few deep breaths, acknowledging your human journey as sacred. When you are ready, pour the entire bowl over your head, allowing it to flow down your body. Allow the emanations of gold to enter your body through your skin. Close your eyes and imagine the gold all around you, as if the air itself were made of gold particles. Invite it in. Absorb all the gold in your vicinity, and imagine how it starts to shift your body at the cellular level, infusing everything with the codes of our Creator and Creatress.
9. Take the third bowl. It is meant to connect you to all the waters of Gaia, big and small—the oceans, the lakes, the rivers, the brooks, the rain falling from the sky, and the dew nestled in the morning grass. It is meant to connect you to the consciousness of the water you drink and every water molecule in your food.
10. Place your hands over your heart and set an intention to connect with all the water on Earth today. With that, allow yourself to merge with the spirit of Gaia, to fully align with her, and to welcome her into your life. Take a deep breath in and out.
11. Anoint your temples with the sacred herbal blend from the third bowl, then anoint the base of your neck, the top of your head, and your heart area. Take your time; don't rush this stage. Once you are done, pour the rest of the contents of the third bowl over your head. Imagine a massive

emerald water stream cascading down your body, bringing natural abundance, healing, and love into your life.

12. Know that from this day on, you are a part of the water tribe and are forever connected to water on a deep spiritual level. Treasure this connection, for it is both mighty and gentle, and it shall support you always.
13. Feel free to step back under the shower stream and further solidify your connection with water through gratitude. Notice the particles of water cascading down your body and acknowledge their silent work and contribution. If you are performing the ritual in nature, take a plunge, fully submerging yourself in water.
14. Whenever you're ready, step out of the shower or leave the natural body of water with gratitude in your heart.
15. And just like that, your water initiation is complete! I hope you enjoyed all the magic flowing through you. This may be a good time to dry off and do some journaling. Record your sensations, feelings, and thoughts after completing this ritual. How do you perceive the water now? How does its spirit appear to you? Has anything shifted for you energetically? Feel free to write down any and all insights so you can come back to them later for further processing.

Heart Space: The Goddess Way

Once upon a time, upon a hill of the seven sisters, there lived a goddess.

Her skin was pearly white, and raven black was her hair. The moon was woven into her braid, her forehead adorned with the stars.

She was the Swan Goddess, or so they said.

Her arms were a pair of bird wings, striking in their unearthly splendor.

A long time ago, she looked upon the valley of glass surrounding the hill and knew she had found her new home.

She swore to nurture it, to nourish it, to make it her forever.

"Let this be called the land of the Goddess," she said.

"Let this be known as a site of pilgrimage for every aching soul.

May they come here, baring their hearts, releasing their pain, transcending their ailments.

Let them come so I may heal them, heart, body, and soul."

And so, time went by. Many were the pilgrims walking atop the hill to greet the Goddess of the Sun.

She spent millennia alongside the simple folk—the farmers, the shepherds, the smiths.

And when it was time to go, she fractured her heart in two and buried one half deep under the hill.

She rested it in a chalice of crystal quartz, the Holy Grail of her love.

She knew that no matter how far she went, the ancient beauty of her heart would preserve the land and the good people living upon it.

And so, she left, but the memory of her remains—the Swan Goddess who shone brighter than the sun, who loved more deeply, who shared her gifts like no other.

Later, they built temples upon the hill—the temple of the Atlantean sun, then the temple of Archangel Michael.

Later, they called this land a Holy Land.

Later, it became a part of the Arthurian legend—the land of Avalon, beloved by dragons, blessed by the power of Excalibur.

But until this day, it remains the land of the Goddess, the only one who cared enough to leave one half of her heart behind.

It is her magic that fills the deep wells of Glastonbury. It is her heart that shapes the heartbeat of this land. It is her soul that watches over the hill and the valley and the good people in it.

It is through the winding pathways toward Tor, amidst the dancing butterflies of the morning sun, that one finds the Goddess.

Her well runs deep, precious is her chalice of gold, pure are her thoughts, and holy are her words.

And today, just like so many years ago, she yearns to heal you—heart, body, and soul,

For the Age of the Goddess is upon us, and her second coming is not only imminent, it is long overdue.

Once more is her spirit rising above the valley and the hills and the brooks. It is her song that will be felt in the farthest corners of the Earth. It is her call that you will hear in your heart. It is her wisdom that will awaken you from slumber.

The time of the Goddess has finally come. And not even the darkness can prevent her second coming, for she is back for one final battle, stronger and mightier than ever.

And so it is.

CHAPTER 22

The Holy Grail

A woman in full alignment is the Holy Grail.
She becomes the infinite vessel of wisdom and love
that was once only reserved for the Goddess.

Of all the spiritual mysteries, the mystery of the Holy Grail is one of the more elusive. The concept of the Holy Grail has existed since prehistoric times, long before Jesus drank from the famous cup at the last supper, and long before Joseph of Arimathea, Jesus's uncle, preserved and used it as one of the main artifacts upon which Christianity was built. This, my friend, is the true story of the grail—a story worth telling.

The Story of the Grail

Coming face to face with the Goddess
is nothing short of drinking from the Holy Grail.

This was the time of the great void, the time of darkness, when energy existed in the form of a gooey substance called the "great everything." Nothing was impossible for the great everything. And yet, it desired nothing, and so nothing was birthed. It was a time of things undefined, a time of the Dark Goddess. And the Goddess knew she had power, but she didn't know herself, so she was devoid of dreams and aspirations.

And so, the Goddess embarked on a path of learning. Above all else, she thirsted to find out what it was that she desired. On her journey, she met an ancient god—the God who knew himself very well, as he had spent many eons getting to know his every nook and cranny, his every subtlety, his every domain. And so, the Goddess asked the God to lead her through a path of knowing.

And he said, "What you desire is a counterpart—to hold you like a vessel and to fill you up with a will to create. I can be that for you, oh, Goddess. And together, we shall create an entire world."

And so, she looked upon his fair face and said yes to everything—to being contained within a vessel of his making and ignited with desire.

And thus, the original chalice was born, the vessel that held the entirety of the void, the entirety of the Goddess, the fullness of her immaculate power. And of the original chalice, the Holy Grail of the God and the Goddess, the Universe was born. His body formed the vessel, and her body formed the waters within it.

The story of the Holy Grail is therefore the story of creation, of the merging of polarities of feminine and masculine to produce something greater—something that we call "everything defined."

And so, to this day, whoever partakes of the chalice will find the key to life and knowing, the key of all keys, the door to all doors, the ultimate answer to all the questions.

The Holy Grail Unveiled

The Holy Grail is a cup that holds the keys to the formative resources of the Universe. It is the vessel of creation itself. The Chalice of the Mother, the Holy Grail is an endless source of Divine Feminine vibration. Every planet in existence has its own etheric version of the chalice. This way, the energies of the Mother are never far away, and all her creations can forever be nurtured by her life force.

Earth is no different. Many versions of the Holy Grail have manifested themselves throughout history, but all of them were connected to water in one way or another. From the ancient wells in sacred lands, to the immaculately shaped underground lakes, to the ceremonial cups of every Atlantean temple, to the tarot suit of cups representing water energies, the chalice has always been a sacred object and a much-revered symbol. Regardless of the chalice's form, it always represents the grace of the original Mother energy, a safe space and a final destination for those seeking to partake of the Mother's embrace.

There are three major expressions of Divine Feminine energies as they relate to the Holy Grail: the higher (**the void**), the middle (**quicksilver**), and the lower (**water**), each of them having a deep significance as we move on the path of the mysteries of the Rose. Below, we shall explore each of them individually.

The Highest Expression of the Holy Grail: The Cup of the Primordial Void

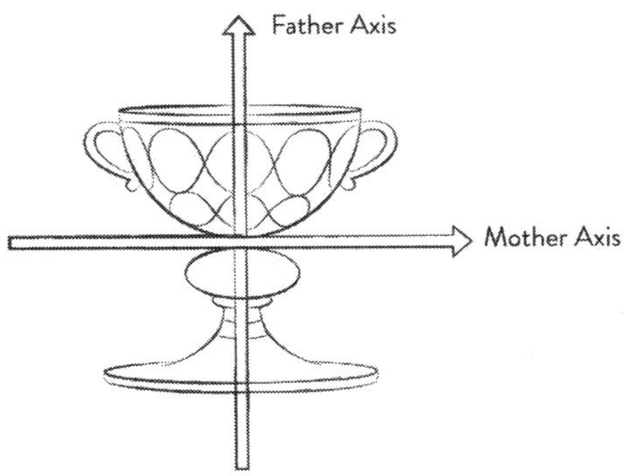

Figure 68: The Holy Grail as a coming together of polarities

As above, so below. The masculine and feminine polarities first originated within Source itself, thus forming a multitude of phenomena centered around understanding and harmonizing the two. It is to Source, therefore, that we owe the most fundamental definition of the Holy Grail: the Cup of Life, the Cup of Creation, the Everything Cup. The two primordial energies that form the Cup of Life exist in harmony, ever co-creating reality as we know it.

The Holy Grail runs along the coordinate system governed by the two axes (see **Figure 68**): the vertical axis of the Father, and the horizontal axis of the Mother, collectively representing one hundred percent of all experiences and energy forms in existence. To understand Source, we must first attempt to understand the two polarities within

Source and then how they come together to co-create. Finally, we must look at the end result: matter created through the dance of opposites, exploring its mysteries. Only then can someone be considered a true master, a holder of universal knowledge.

The Father Axis

Also: The Earth and Heaven axis, the interdimensional axis, and the axis of electricity

The masculine principle is both the cup itself, holding the void of the feminine, as well as the lightning that strikes the waters of the void, bringing them out of their passive state into the state of directed creativity.

Any vertical axis on a third-dimensional plane is essentially a masculine axis (think the spinal cord, the seven chakras, the Tree of Life, etc.). It is through opening up the pathway between the root and the crown energy centers that we can communicate with the Divine. The process of ascension is therefore a masculine process, as is any process where you are moving up or down a hierarchical ladder.

Attributes:

- Rapid movement
- Achievement
- Directional pursuits
- Alternating currents
- Changing frequencies
- Curiosity
- Learning
- Shifting dynamics
- Judgment
- Force
- Power
- Speed
- Enlightenment
- Progress
- The active principle
- Dynamism
- Leadership

The Mother Axis

Also: The past/present/future axis, the depth axis, and the magnetic axis

The feminine principle is both the void inside the Cup of Life and the masterful magnetic force that starts to rearrange the void based on input from the masculine principle. The waters of the Holy Grail are all about perfect receptivity. They take the masculine aspect as is, without alteration and judgment, creating exactly what has been requested without polluting or shifting it. The feminine principle exists in its dormant, cool, and dark state until it is brought out of slumber by an electric current that is the active masculine energy. The masculine impulse bounces off the void, in and out, creating a cycle of creation, a forever-coiling Ouroboros, biting its own tail in the wheel of existence, ending one cycle only to begin another.

The Mother energies give depth, meaning, and shape to everything that is. Without the Mother's energies, the world would be quite flat. Emotion and memory exist within the domain of the Mother. The Mother axis ensures the continuity of learning and the ebbs and flows of life, providing fertile soil for development. While the masculine principle is responsible for the existence of dimensions, the richness of those dimensions is dependent on the feminine principle. Anything in nature that is a "field" is a domain of the Mother; the gravitational field, the informational field (the Akashic Records), and the magnetic field are just some examples. The Mother axis is an eternal horizontal movement that gives layers to every world inside and outside the matrix.

Attributes:

- Containment
- Acceptance
- Fluidity
- Infinite resources
- Understanding
- Wisdom
- Eternity
- Love
- Maintenance
- Cause and effect
- Karma
- Continuity
- Partnership
- Collaboration
- Community
- Ecosystems

The Middle Expression of the Holy Grail: The Cup Containing Quicksilver

Mercury (or quicksilver) is higher-dimensional water. Many worlds beyond the sixth dimension use mercury in the same way that we use water—for cleansing, hydration, healing, etc. Quicksilver is the manifestation of the blood of the Divine Mother, her essence.

At the level of Divine oneness, the blood (life force) of the Mother is the void. In higher dimensions, it is mercury. In lower dimensions, it is water. As we move across dimensions, the physicality of the substance may shift, but the energetic properties remain the same. Both water and mercury are prerequisites to life, its sustenance, and a substance required for its continuation. It is through mercury and water that every child of the Universe is connected to the Mother, partaking of her life force and being nurtured by her energy. Get rid of the water and mercury, and we would be forever cut off from the Mother's body, suffering an immediate death.

Mercury is a malleable substance. It often takes on the energetic properties of the surrounding elements. This is one of the reasons that mercury is used in devices that measure temperature. Mercury contracts and expands to match its environment, acting as a chameleon and a litmus test. Just like the emanation of true femininity, mercury represents the principle of perfect receptivity, adjusting and shifting in accordance with the elements in its vicinity.

Mercury in Alchemy

Mercury is one of the three main principles (*Tria Prima*) in alchemy, alongside sulfur and salt. One of the most prominent alchemists, Paracelsus, believed that everything in the Universe could be reduced to these three elements, with sulfur and mercury being the formative elements and salt being the byproduct of their combination.

Sulfur is the masculine (or active principle); it represents fire and the sun. It is hot and dry. Mercury, on the other hand, is the feminine (or passive principle), representing water, life essence, and volatility. It is cool and wet. When the two unite, the material world becomes possible. Alchemy often speaks of the sacred marriage of the Red King (sulfur) and the White Queen (mercury) to create matter (salt). While mercury has infinite potential, it exists in its amorphous stage until it is shaped into something specific by the active principle of sulfur.

Another way to think about this alchemical framework is as follows: Salt is the matrix, a crystalline structure of vertical and horizontal axes that gives form to our reality. Sulfur is energy that gives an impulse to everything, while mercury is the informational field that contains everything that has taken shape, as well as keeping track of any changes that occur within the system (see **Figure 69**). The matrix would be an empty shell without the life-giving qualities of sulfur (Divine Father) and the life-sustaining qualities of mercury (Divine Mother).

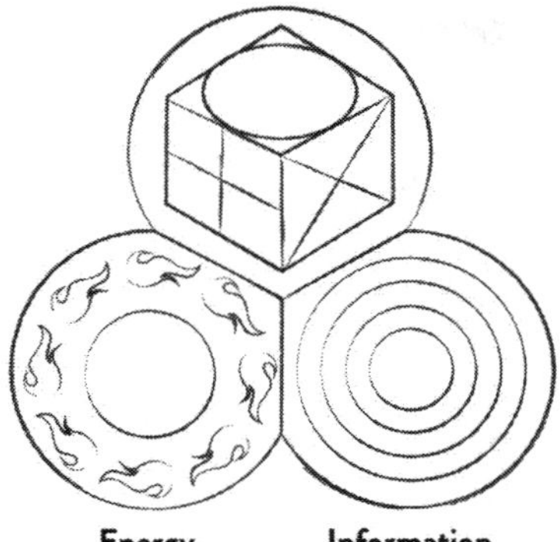

Figure 69: The three principles in alchemy

Practice: Working with the Energy of Mercury

The following practices offer ways of working with mercury's energy—NOT liquid mercury, which should be avoided.

- Integrating mercury into your chakras can help raise your frequency, as well as promote healing. Simply imagine taking mercury into every chakra, starting at the root. Allow your chakras to drink the mercury until fully sated. Watch as the energy of your body transforms.
- Mercury is a strong energy to help detox your light bodies. To fully partake of its powers, try a meditation where you stand under a waterfall of mercury, allowing it to cleanse you and remove anything that no longer belongs.
- Submerge yourself in a bath filled with the energy of mercury to de-stress and reduce anxiety. Mercury is a counterbalancing energy to any kind of fire, helping to smooth out and soften its energies. Anxiety is an excess of fire energies; therefore, mercury can be a perfect equalizer.
- Mercury spheres are potent healing tools. If you want to reduce pain in a particular area of your body, simply encapsulate it in a mercury sphere, allowing it to absorb negativity. Mercury converts all dark clots into pure light; it is the perfect painkiller.
- Mercury is a great remover of obstacles. In meditation, imagine that a sphere of mercury erases the impediments in your way.
- Lastly, mercury is a portal into the heart of the Divine Mother. Use it to teleport into the private quarters of the Mother to build a stronger relationship with her.

The Lower Expression of the Holy Grail: The Cup Containing Water

One of the mysteries of the Holy Grail is its ability to contain and direct the inner and outer waters. This makes one a true water master, a true initiate of the mysteries of the Mother.

As we continue the broader conversation about water, let's proceed with exploring the water within our bodies. It is an element that is both healing and harmonizing, one of the most integral aspects of who we are.

The Water Within

The journey starts within, by raising your inner waters to a level that synchronizes you with the rest of creation. Your inner water wells allow you to purify your vessel and meet the Universe at its level—no expectations, no conditions, only love.

Meditation: The Water Rising

Raising your inner waters is not unlike kundalini rising. It requires the purification of your physical and etheric vessels for the water to pass through smoothly, without resistance. The outcome? Full and irrevocable surrender to the embrace of the Divine Mother and all of her creation. The complete merging of what is. Acceptance. Wisdom. Love. Use this meditation to experience the waters rising within.

1. Sit comfortably and close your eyes.
2. Imagine that in front of you, clad in ephemeral white light, the Divine Mother herself sits upon a large lotus flower. Her body looks human, her essence anything but.
3. Picture overlaying your body with hers, as if you were inserting your energy into the vessel of her form, merging the two.
4. Connect and align all your seven chakras with those of the Divine Mother. Start at the crown and imagine that your crown chakra is merging with the Divine Mother's.
5. Go down chakra by chakra, feeling the alignment more and more deeply.
6. Once you reach the root center, notice that there is a mighty force seeking to rise up from the depths of your being. This force is the purest form of water you can imagine, the holy waters of the Mother.
7. Allow this force to rise up in a spiral motion, passing every single chakra on the way up.
8. Watch as this force reaches the crown chakra, pouring out of your body through the top of your head in a torrent of cleansing vibration.
9. You are the source of this water now, a conduit of the energies of the Mother. Let this torrent take away your worries, your stress, and your doubts. Wash away anything that no longer belongs in the holy temple of your body.
10. Ask this water to cleanse any part of your life that requires healing, nurturing any part of you that is thirsty for a new beginning.
11. Allow the sacred waters of the Mother to accumulate in a golden bowl located at the very top of your head, a sign of your blessings and your strong connection with the Mother.
12. Allow yourself to hold onto this vibration throughout the day.

The Morning Water Ritual

This is a five-minute attunement meditation you can use upon waking up to receive a quick healing from the Mother.

1. Close your eyes and imagine a majestic waterfall coming straight from the heavens.
2. What color is the waterfall today? Watch it closely. The color is dictated by the Divine Mother and the type of healing she believes your body needs today.
3. Allow the waters to wash over your body, cleansing away the energetic dirt and impurities that have gathered overnight. Feel the gentle caress of the Mother, her tender care, her vibration washing over you.
4. Allow the water to penetrate your skin and enter every cell of your body, transforming it from within.
5. Watch your state shift instantly. Notice how your body takes on an etheric glow that matches the colors of the waterfall.
6. Allow your body to simply float and soak up these healing vibrations.
7. Whenever you are ready, come back and open your eyes.

Chakras and Water: Three Inner Chalices of Your Body

Most spiritual traditions don't specify the caliber of energy that runs through and powers your chakras. And while it may not be critical for most conversations, it is quite pivotal here. The energy that powers your chakras, the inner chalices of your body, is fire energy, not dissimilar to the vibration and imprint of the sacred flames. The heavenly fire that runs through your chakras is the motivational force behind most human activity on Earth.

As an element, fire is the domain of the Divine Masculine. And while Divine fire energies are resilient and can ignite almost anything, they are not the only energy source available. Heavenly waters are just as potent and valuable. In fact, if more people chose to integrate the energies of Divine water into their chakra system, plenty of the common ailments of today's society could be healed.

The Sacral Chalice

The first and most foundational of your Holy Grails, the sacral, holds the keys to your creative powers. It is the genesis of your creation, an inner resource you tap into every time you choose to bring transformation and change to the outside world. The sacral center is your center of magnetism. Its truth is your truth. Whatever your sacral believes about you becomes you.

This chalice holds onto your ancestral memories and the traumas of your foremothers. This is where the pain of childbearing and childbirth dwells, as well as the joys of motherhood. This is where your sense of self-worth reigns supreme.

Unfortunately, the sacral has become a bit of an internal trash receptacle, used to deposit all the things you may not want to acknowledge about yourself. That's how your creative center becomes a center of trauma accumulation. Before fully claiming your inner Creatress, you must unleash and unchain your sacral powerhouse. Only then can it become a resource instead of a liability.

The time has come for the women of the Earth to break through the chains that have been constricting them for generations.

The time has come to be both seen and heard.

The time has come to be cherished, understood, and revered for the power of the Goddess dwelling within.

The time has come to become pain-free, once and for all.

Meditation: Liberating Your Sacral Chalice

Some ideas for things to release from your sacral chalice, using the following mediation practice:

- Feeling insignificant
- Not feeling loved by one or both of your parents
- Feeling like you are not enough
- Seeking approval
- Always putting yourself last
- All giving, not enough receiving
- Never asking for help
- Distrusting others, especially women in your life
- Feeling like you have to do this alone
- The need to be strong and have things under control all the time
- Fears related to the safety of your family and loved ones
- Toxicity of your familial relations

1. Take a comfortable seated position or lie down. Close your eyes.
2. Imagine that your body is floating in the sacred orange waters of the Mother. The waters are serene and healing, smelling like orange blossoms and a touch of cinnamon. They gently touch your skin.
3. Picture an orange lotus growing in your lower belly. As it opens its petals, notice that it has a charred black center. This flower is the vessel that carries your trauma of childbearing and childbirth through many lifetimes. It contains the trauma of your ancestors and your personal trauma from past lives. Watch the flower detach from your body and float away in the orange waters, carrying the trauma away.
4. Notice the relief that this release brings.
5. Watch as a second lotus blooms. What color is it? Notice that when it opens up, the inside of its petals and its center are black again. This flower carries your heartbreak, betrayal, loneliness, and despair. Watch the flower as it detaches from your body and floats away.
6. Watch as the third flower starts to open up. What color is it? This flower is carrying all of the negative thoughts you have about yourself—every

single unkind word you've told yourself or heard from others. This is your inner critic, perpetually unhappy with who you are and how far you've come. Release the flower into the depths of the orange waters, letting this negative pattern go once and for all.

7. Keep growing new lotus flowers and releasing them for as long as it feels right, letting go of more and more layers of darkness and trauma that have taken hold in your creative center.
8. When you are ready, thank the Divine Mother for holding space for you, and return.

The Heart Chalice

The second chalice within your body is that of your heart. This chalice holds the keys to complete, multifaceted, and sustainable happiness. It is your center of connectedness, the point of togetherness within your body.

This chalice connects you to Mother Nature and the consciousness of Gaia, offering a blissful state of belonging and being loved and accepted always. No other chalice can bring you as much joy as the heart.

Our heart unfolds like a fan in the masterful hands of our Divine Mother, one step at a time (see **Figure 70**). Opening your heart is a sacred initiation in its own right.

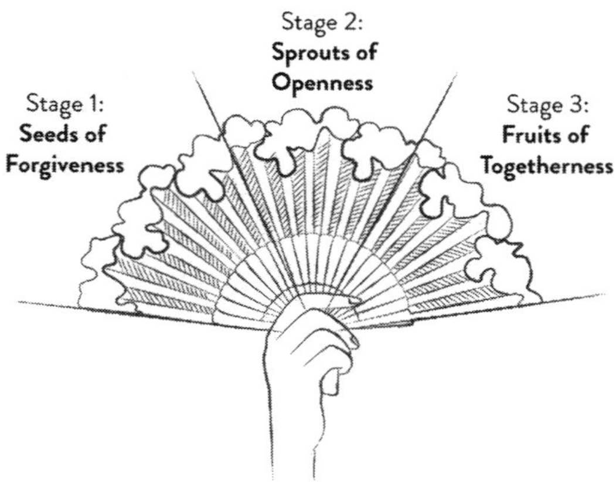

Figure 70: The three stages of the unfolding heart

There are three main stages of opening your heart: seeds of forgiveness, sprouts of openness, and fruits of togetherness. Below, we'll explore each stage in detail.

Stage 1: Seeds of Forgiveness (i.e., "A Sigh of Relief")

This step is a sacred release, a homecoming, a return to the original vibration—the vibration that existed in the womb of the Mother long before she was ready to give birth to the Universe. This is the return to how things were before any and all trauma happened. This step is a recalibration back to the original sound of your soul, removing the cacophony of heartbreak. This step brings your heart back from a shattered state into a state of wholesomeness and completion.

Tips on going through this stage:

- List all the ways your heart was once broken and everyone responsible. Then, forgive them for all the wrongs that they did to you. Recognize each person on the list as your Divine teacher, and let them go with much gratitude.
- Light a black candle. Take out a piece of paper and write down the biggest heartbreak you've had in this lifetime. Once you are done, burn the paper using the flame of the candle. Take the ashes and release them to the wind, letting go of whatever pain your heart may still be feeling; give that pain to the fire and the wind. You are no longer jailed by it. You can move on.
- Write down any "irrational" fears about building relationships with people. List all the things that could go wrong. Understand that this is a negative program your subconscious is running at this time. This program is not a sentence, however, but a stepping stone. You can rewrite it today if you choose to, using the golden Divine light. Simply imagine that the old program is being erased, and the new one is being placed in its stead. This new program is written in the sky in a tight, neat script of gold. What is the new script you would like to create for yourself today? What is your new relationship mantra? Here are a few to choose from:
    - I am love and am only attracting love into my orbit.
    - I can trust people and the world around me.
    - I am worthy of loving relationships.
    - I trust the Universe and every single person I meet.
- Forgive yourself for attracting people and relationships into your orbit that hurt you. Understand that there is nothing wrong with you. Opening your heart starts with self-love. You are the first person you need to love unconditionally. Write down all the conditions you put around loving yourself—all the "if's" and "when's." Then, strike through them. Choose to love yourself today just the way you are.

Stage 2: Sprouts of Openness

This step is about demolishing the walls and protection spells you have placed around your heart. This step is about rebuilding the bridges that you once burned. It is about reestablishing broken pathways and connections. This step is about being raw and vulnerable and, finally, allowing yourself to be filled with the pink and emerald energies of the Mother's heart. This step is about accumulating the gentle vibrations of love morsel by morsel, letting them find a new home inside your beautiful eternal heart.

Tips on going through this stage:

- Cultivating trust is critical: trusting yourself, trusting others, and trusting the Universe around you. Create a trust journal, listing everything others have helped you with and recording all the small and unexpected gifts and compliments. Try to notice all the good things around you, from the sunshine on your skin to the nourishing taste of a delicious meal. Don't take anything for granted. Over time, you will notice how much you can trust your world to do right by you. Carry this as a deep knowing in your heart: you are safe, protected, and a most beloved child of Source.
- In a meditative state, remove the protective barrier around your heart—any shields, shells, or hard layers around it (see also the practice in Chapter 11, page 214). Allow your heart to start emanating the most beautiful emerald light and sharing it with the world around you. Watch how that light comes back to you tenfold.
- Tell people that you love them more often, and mean it.
- Say that you love yourself, and mean it.
- Write a love note to the Universe. Mean every single word.

Stage 3: Fruits of Togetherness

Togetherness is a step toward achieving unity consciousness that precedes oneness. Togetherness recognizes that we are all separate streams and sparks of one consciousness, but despite our separateness, our highest calling is harmonious living. Coexistence with others is meant to be a pleasant journey, not a bumpy ride. Togetherness is the opposite of trying to change others or force the Universe into complying with your wishes. Togetherness is accepting others for who they are and considering their best interests. Togetherness is a dance where the many seemingly disparate particles of Source form a cohesive melody. Togetherness is a state of effortless harmony with others.

Tips on going through this stage:

- Recognize the spark of Source in everything that surrounds you—friends and foes, natural landscapes, a cup of morning tea, a snail gently moving along a pebbled walkway, the chair you are sitting on, the wind ruffling your hair. Source is everywhere; Source is in everything. This means Source is in you. Recognize the infinite spark of Source within your gentle heart.
- Learn to use your heart as a portal to the rest of existence. Listen to the sounds of nature with your heart. Listen to other people's words with your heart. Learn to truly connect with others, heart-to-heart.

- Recognize the impact of your actions. You really matter. Become a force for good. Stop eating animals, or at least limit how much you consume. Nature is just as alive as you are; treat it as such.
- Learn to use your heart as a guidance tool to help you make decisions. Focus on making heart-led decisions, for the heart always knows best and has the desire for the greater good firmly infused into its fabric.

The Third Eye Chalice

The third and last chalice of your body is your third eye. This chalice is your doorway to infinite knowing, the realm of Akasha, and the domain of etheric wisdom. The wisdom of the Mother goes beyond logic and dwells outside of intellect. It is the wisdom that comes from pattern recognition, from seeing the bigger picture, from tracing millions of possible outcomes, from understanding the most optimal path and how to pursue it.

The Mother's wisdom stretches beyond time and space, straight into the void where everything began. The void is infinite, all-seeing, and all-knowing. This void lives inside your third eye, too—a doorway to the field of all information, all intention, and all knowledge. The third eye is your inner garden and your personal initiatory path. The Garden of Eden is actually a space within the third eye—Heaven on Earth, and any other land, for that matter—for the third eye allows you to be in multiple places all at once without being confined to a particular time and place.

It is in the gardens of your third eye that your wisdom grows over time, passing through many arcs, crossing many thresholds, and climbing many steps to ascended understanding. It is in this garden that the many lotus flowers grow—the flowers of intuitive knowing. Passing through the lessons of these flowers is a serious commitment. It is, in fact, a path that may take lifetimes.

There is one main lotus that blooms inside your third eye at any given time, taking over your perception and offering you the many lessons it holds. Once its lessons are successfully completed, the lotus dies to make room for the next one—and so the cycle of initiations goes on, until finally, a soul is ready to rejoin the absolute, coming back into oneness once more.

The Many Degrees of Wisdom

The lotus is perhaps the only flower readily available on Earth that can take you through the entire process of ascension, meeting you at every single level. No wonder it symbolizes consciousness, mindfulness, and even enlightenment!

The wisdom of the lotus is ever evolving, never static, taking you from one step to the next in an ever-expanding dance. Following the lotus is an ancient initiation path of wisdom, not unlike following the white rabbit—a path of surrender to greater understanding.

Note: The colors of the lotus, just like the facets of wisdom, are limitless. Presenting them all in this book would be not just impractical, but impossible. Nevertheless, the following list includes the most prominent variants and their properties.

Ruby lotus – warrior wisdom: The ruby lotus takes you into the depth of your fear, challenging you to accept your warrior wisdom. But what is the wisdom of the warrior? Knowing which battles to fight and which to avoid, and understanding the many aspects of your personal power, how deep it runs, and the extent of its limits. The ruby lotus teaches us to know where to push and where to relax our hold, whom to trust, and how to find the one victorious path amidst the many potential dead ends. The ruby lotus is a strategist, a masterful chess player willing to sacrifice a pawn to capture a king. The ruby lotus teaches sovereignty, dignity, honor, fighting for what's right, and perseverance. Above all, the ruby lotus teaches us to integrate our failures and move beyond our shortcomings, turning temporal weaknesses into lasting strengths.

Citrine lotus – wisdom of the Divine child: This is the youthful naivete of discovery, the joy of curiosity, and the blissful surrender of learning something new. The wisdom comes from being inquisitive and open-minded, drinking in each lifetime and each experience without reservation and with childlike fervor. The wisdom of this lotus is the simple act of feeling happy, of allowing yourself to experience the depth of gratitude.

The citrine lotus is about simple pleasures, seeing God in everything and everyone, and basking in the warmth of this journey we call life. The citrine lotus is the wisdom of joyful giggles, endless exploration, adventure, and change. The citrine lotus is about trusting that this world is safe, a place of magic and wonder. It is about recognizing that you are eternally loved and will be cared for. This lotus is about feeling that you are the most favorite Divine child, free and perfect just as you are.

With this attitude comes true luck, synchronicity, and being showered with gifts. This is a state of joyful receiving from the Universe, your greatest ally and friend, without restricting its generous, abundant incoming flow.

Emerald lotus – wisdom of the heart: This is the wisdom of togetherness, of considering others with every step. It is the ability to listen to the strings of the hearts of others without projecting yourself upon them or their experiences. It is the wisdom of living in the now, releasing the illusion of the past and the stress of the future. This lotus is the sincerity of empathy, of shifting your perspective to encompass that of others. The lesson here is to flow like a river, equally accepting the blessings and obstacles, recognizing Divine consciousness in friend and foe alike, and acknowledging everyone's right to follow their path.

The emerald lotus teaches true forgiveness, but also acceptance of your worth. The emerald lotus is a lesson in positive self-concept and unconditional self-love. This lotus also deals with health and healing issues, physical, mental, and emotional. The arc of this lotus starts with healing oneself and ends with healing others, with planetary-level healing being the pinnacle of mastery of this lotus. A true master of healing moves beyond rigid modalities and conventional methods and taps into the power of their heart to hear the song of each individual soul and to recognize its unique yearning to find a bespoke, heart-crafted remedy.

Blue lotus (also sapphire lotus) – intellectual wisdom: The blue lotus is a stepping stone into the great Logos, the formative power of the word of God. This wisdom is orderly, analytical, and mathematical. This wisdom is precise—the wisdom of the golden section, harmonic frequencies, and sound as the basic building blocks of reality. The blue lotus is a system's architect—the one who sees the many separate aspects of reality and how they come together in the most naturally balanced way.

The blue lotus is about law and order, but it is also a balancing act, an equalizer that seeks to solve an equation with multiple variables. The wisdom of the blue lotus transcends dimensions. Time and space are temporal constraints for it, not a nonnegotiable reality. The blue lotus is a big-picture thinker, but also a dreamer. The blue lotus is a creator—the one who takes primordial vibration and turns it into manifested reality, then takes that reality and optimizes it until a covetable state of perfection is reached. Only then can the blue lotus die out to make room for the next stage.

Purple lotus (also amethyst lotus) – wisdom of the all-seeing eye: When the paths of the left and the right eyes of Horus have been completed, and the chessboard no longer seems black and white, we have transcended duality and other illusory constraints, uncovering the path of the all-seeing eye. This path unites all the ones who came before, offering a way that is infinitely more challenging, yet gratifying.

This is the first lotus of God and Goddess consciousness. This lotus is about transcending the slave archetype within and without and becoming liberated in a physical and spiritual sense. This is a path of no constraints, where the absolute power of Source guides you through the infinite waters of the void to a promised land—a land of greater understanding. This is the path where the child becomes a king, and the king becomes a god, only to return as a pauper and understand that everything is a label and it is experiences that matter.

The path of this lotus is about building up, then tearing down, then building back up again—the path of Shiva, the path of Kali. It is the descent into the darkness to find your brightest light yet, only to turn around and see that both light and darkness are yet another illusion in the card game called life. The only thing that matters is the inherent and earned wisdom within, a resource that will never run out—the kind of wisdom that makes you a master of any reality you choose to incarnate in, from here to eternity.

White lotus – wisdom of higher cosmic planes: This lotus is the Divine flower of ascension, of bringing your light bodies into perfect sync with your surroundings, and through that, gaining the access codes to shifting your reality. The white lotus leads you through the lessons of togetherness into the state of true oneness. Its wisdom is the sacred unfolding of your inner layers, welcoming the truth of who you are without judgment. Some say the wisdom of the white lotus is the absence of the shadow. The truth is, it is the wisdom of having transcended the shadow, a state of full acceptance of and surrender to who you are as your perfect blueprint.

The wisdom of the white lotus is soul healing, eternal and angelic. It is connectedness personified. The white lotus is a knowing that we rise and fall as one, a knowing that when this cycle of the Universe collapses upon itself, it shall collapse into the polarity of light. Light is the ultimate truth of Source. The white lotus is a path that takes you there, through trials and tribulations and the joys of integration.

Golden lotus – Divine wisdom: This is an entry point into the intricate mind of Source. The golden lotus is a vantage point—a state of understanding how ecosystems are created, how they function, and how they evolve. The golden lotus opens the portal to macro-level consciousness, the ultimate big-picture thinking. This lotus focuses on the why, not just the what or when. It is an intricate doorway into cause and effect from the perspective of the absolute consciousness that created our Universe. This lotus traces civilizations, planets, and galaxies from the day they were conceived to the day of their inevitable collapse, and then it rebuilds better than ever.

The golden lotus is the evolutionary spiral inherent to all things. It seeks to grow, expand, and improve the learnings and the understanding of yesterday. The golden lotus offers a glimpse into the decision-making behind the creation process, shedding light on the complexities of the constant process of improvement, but also the big, bold ideas, the leaps of faith, and moon shots that go into macro-level creation. To Source, galaxies and whole Universes are specks of dust barely distinguishable from one another, and yet it is Source that orchestrates the cosmic dance of evolution and ascension. Understanding the golden lotus is conceiving of the Greater Blueprint of Source—the beginning, the middle, and the end.

Diamond lotus (**also crystalline lotus**) – **wisdom of light:** The capacity of this lotus for purification, emanation, and unification is immense. It is through the immutable magic of light that most things in the Universe find their completion and absolution. Even wisdom itself is subordinate to light, recognizing its supremacy in our pocket of creation. In the beginning, there was light, and there was darkness. In the end, there will only be light. Such is the arc we are walking, the path we are here to witness, the endgame we are here to co-create. If we can conceive of the mysteries of light, we can understand the blueprint of the Universe.

Walking the path of the diamond lotus is walking the path of light, wielding its indelible power as the mightiest of weapons. They say pure, unadulterated light is blinding. But anyone who has ever done a proper amount of sun gazing will tell you that light is the ultimate truth. If you allow yourself to be blinded by it, you are not ready to receive it in the first place. We need to be ready to receive massive amounts of light while staying intact; it is the final rite of passage.

Light is the ultimate absolute power of the Universe, and as such, it is one of a kind. And it is the opposite of blinding. In fact, it is an epiphany reserved for the very few bold enough to walk among gods and stars. When you are ready to stare the absolute straight in the face, open-minded and open-hearted as can be, primed for a particular flavor of incoming wisdom, a new beginning, a new cycle, you shall know the light—and the light shall know you.

Diagnostic: Which Lotus is Guiding You Right Now?

Use this diagnostic to tell you what color lotus or aspect of wisdom you are currently studying or embodying. If more than one lotus reveals itself through this diagnostic, it is because you chose to accelerate the process by studying multiple facets of wisdom simultaneously. While souls usually choose to study the lotuses in their natural progression (per the hierarchy above), some choose to skip levels or jump back and forth. Trust what you see.

1. Close your eyes and focus on your breath, letting it fill your lungs. Then, release it through the area of your third eye, activating it.
2. Repeat this three times.
3. Imagine that from the purple waters inside of your third eye, a lotus flower springs to life. This lotus is your personal teacher of wisdom.
4. What color is it? Do you notice anything special about it? Refer to the guide above to get to know your lotus more deeply. If you see a color not represented on the list, drop into your heart space to find out the particular lesson of your lotus.

The Tongue of Water

The voice of the water is gentle. It is a whisper in the loud cacophony of other voices and tongues. It is the voice of your intuition, the gentle sound of your ancestors sending you their daily greetings, the waves of synchronicity on your path, and the soft murmur of the droplets of morning dew as you pass by. The tongue of water is spoken by the water maidens, mermaids, and nymphs, softly lulling you to sleep every night. The tongue of water dwells in your dreams, prophetic or otherwise. The tongue of water is in the gentle caress of the river and the insistent crashing of the waves of the ocean. It is in the serenity of the icy lake and the gentle tapping of the shower on your shoulders.

The tongue of water is the voice of the Mother Divine, a reminder that she is never too far away, whether in this life or the next. Can you hear the softly spoken water tongue? Are you in tune enough to witness its light ebbs and flows, healing magic, and immense supportive power?

The tongue of water is a source of great healing and comfort. It is a light bridge between you and the domain of the Mother. The priestesses of old spoke this tongue beautifully. They could read the water crystals and record the information on the river's surface. They knew that the tongue of water contained the memories of their ancestors, days long gone, and the gems of the lessons learned.

Those who can read the tongue of water are the anointed ones, chosen by the Mother to lead humanity through the current shift. There were once only a few maidens who spoke the tongue of water. This is all changing now. The insurgence of awakening we are experiencing on Earth today is raising the ancient water codes from the bottom of the oceans, streams, and rivers, so that the language of water can become widely spoken once again. This is the great comeback of the tongue of the Mother.

Does the water speak to you, dear one?

Can you hear her gentle yet persistent call?

The time has come to unleash the power of the water priestess slumbering within you.

The time has come to reconnect with the tongue of water.

Cosmic Water Spells: The Galactic Language of Water

Some of you may be familiar with "light language," a vocal stream of consciousness that usually descends from higher dimensions to impart healing or upgrades. The cosmic tongue of water is a light language many extraterrestrial races use in the Milky Way and beyond. The process of channeling a light language is intuitive and requires you to temporarily let go of logic. Anyone can channel a light language, and channeling the cosmic tongue of water is easier than most, for it is deeply rooted within our soul memories. It is the tongue that connects us to the Mother who birthed us.

Practice: Channeling the Language of Water

There are many benefits to channeling the light language of water. Its stream is healing, up-leveling, and harmonizing. It gets into the depths of your being, removing distortions and restoring order where there is none. This is a therapeutic and ritualistic endeavor, and you may feel a noticeable shift in your mood and overall energy state upon channeling in this way.

1. Close your eyes and allow your thoughts to come and go freely. Emptying your consciousness of thoughts as much as possible will greatly enhance this practice.
2. Imagine that a great waterfall is flowing out of your mouth. You already know the tongue of water; it is one of the first languages that your soul learned. The time has come to remember it.
3. The waterfall that you are channeling has a sound; it can speak. What does it want to say? What sound does it want to transmit through you?
4. Imagine merging with the water in the waterfall. Then, simply allow the sounds to start pouring from you. The result will be akin to an ancient language that you once knew and perhaps forgot; it may even sound extraterrestrial to you. The language of water has a lot of sounds that are reminiscent of running water, such as "sss," "shhh," and "ch," but it also contains some sounds of the Mother, such as the sounds like "ah," "mmm" and "maaa." Don't judge what comes out of your mouth; simply speak the sound of water into existence.
5. Notice how the vocal codes from your mouth are uniquely healing for you. They get straight into your auric field, working on transforming your energy. Please know that this is a cosmic transmission, a channeling of the highest caliber, and the Mother presides over it. You couldn't get this wrong if you tried.

Sacred Water

Sacred water has a unique molecular structure that represents water's most healing and creative state—the state that is closest to light itself. The sacred state shifts water's propensity for absorption (receiving) into emanation (giving), which is why even a small amount of sacred water can cause large amounts of transformation. Blessed water, such as that blessed by a priest, is simply that: blessed. It doesn't have the properties of light (and therefore Source). The good news? If you know the recipe, you can make your own sacred water.

Practice: Making Sacred Water

To make sacred water, you need a transparent water carafe and a few minutes. For best results, place a sticker with the Flower of Life pattern on the bottom of your carafe (see also Chapter 2, page 34). This way, you start from a much better place even as you endeavor to create sacred water.

1. Place your right palm over your heart and close your eyes. Intention is everything when it comes to creating holy water. Speak your intention to create sacred water out loud. Ask for Divine Mother's assistance. You may also state what you need the water's help with specifically. This way, the water can be created using your unique intention.
2. Place the carafe filled with distilled water in front of you. Place both of your palms on the carafe, gently holding it.
3. Close your eyes. Imagine a stream of golden codes coming from the heavens into the carafe. Notice that the water inside has a grid structure to it; it looks like a series of vertical and horizontal intersecting lines. Notice how the golden codes get absorbed by the vertical lines, turning them golden from the inside.
4. Watch the codes stream in, infusing your water with more and more golden light. Notice how the codes are starting to penetrate the horizontal lines, further shifting the water's structure and composition. Allow the water to keep absorbing the codes until it is fully saturated with them.
5. Now that the vertical and the horizontal lines that make up the water's grid structure are filled with the golden codes, notice that a seemingly magical transformation is taking place. The golden light contained within the vertical and horizontal lines starts to seep into the water, and the golden particles begin to multiply.
6. Watch as more and more golden particles appear inside your carafe—the result of a mysterious alchemical process. Watch as golden particles beget more golden particles, and witness how the light creates more light.
7. Allow this process to carry on naturally until the golden light starts pouring out of your carafe, having run out of space within.

Congratulations! Your personal carafe of sacred water is now ready and overflowing with the most magical water you have ever created!

Uses of sacred water:

- Physical, emotional, and mental healing
- Raising vibrations
- Inducing lucid dreaming
- Opening the heart
- Reducing anxiety
- Promoting an optimistic outlook
- Helping you get in the flow
- Opening up your higher chakras
- Improving connection with Spirit

Water Marks (Water Runes)

The priestesses of the Goddess have long shared a water language—a language of the subtle movement of water, nondescript to most, but distinct and loud to the priestesses themselves. The slight curves of water held ancient wisdom, the omens of the days to come and the stories of times long gone.

Reading water was a mystery to master. Many scrolls were written solely using water marks—lines made with water upon the white scrolls. Once dry, these scrolls appeared empty to the casual onlooker, but to a priestess of water, the scrolls told many ancient stories and held many secret codes. The water marks came alive before the eyes of the initiate, forming mental images and communicating across many layers—intellectual, emotional, and etheric. Learning the language of water took years, and often, true mastery ran within specific lineages, as it was more of an intuitive pursuit than an intellectual one.

It would be impossible to offer the full breadth of the water language in this book, but below are some water marks imbued with water magic that could be most applicable today. These timeless symbols contain the power of the spirit of water, its healing and cleansing abilities. These water marks were once used by the priestesses of water in various rituals and as "temporary tattoos" when going through initiations.

The "Power of Water" Mark

Figure 71: Simple water line to invoke the power of water

This is the simplest of the water marks that allows the initiate to draw the power of water to one's cause. For as long as this symbol is present within your body, the power of the water shall remain with you.

Uses:

- Draw it on your left wrist to attract abundance or money.
- Draw it on your body to change your mood and energy, release pressure, and feel more at ease. This is a powerful stress-relief mark.

- Draw it upon your body to instantly feel calmer and less anxious. Water helps balance anxiety.
- Trace the symbol over your throat, so your communication flows like water. This will help you be more convincing and get others to pay more attention to your message. This is a great communication booster when you need to say something important. For enhanced benefits, trace the symbol three times.

Tip:

You can draw the mark with a pen or simply trace it with your fingers using water or essential oils. If traced with a transparent liquid, this mark loses its potency after about three hours and needs to be redrawn.

The "Remover of Obstacles" Rune

Figure 72: Remover of obstacles

The power of water to erode stone over time is well known. The energetic power of water to instantly remove darkness from your auric field or help clear obstacles is perhaps more nebulous, while not any less potent.

The Remover of Obstacles rune invokes the power of white water, the might of rapids, to clear away any energetic or physical impediment on your path.

Uses:

- If you feel stuck, have low energy, or feel lost, draw the Remover of Obstacles rune on your forehead. (You can trace the shape of this rune on your forehead three times for added benefit.) Then breathe into your forehead, further activating the power of the rune with your breath. Now imagine that there is a path in front of you. Watch as the rune clears any debris or obstacles from the path.
- To help with a project you are working on, take a piece of paper and write down the project's name. Then, draw the Remover of Obstacles rune over it and imagine

the power of water pouring into the words. Trust that the water will do its job of clearing away obstacles, physical or otherwise, on your project's path to success.

The "Water Healing" Rune

Figure 73: Simple healing water rune

The water healing runs deep—as deep as the rabbit hole goes, and perhaps deeper. This type of rune works with both acute pains and chronic conditions. Moreover, it has the power to heal emotional wounding. It is truly miraculous. This rune works best alongside a triangular shape.

To invoke its full power, draw a triangle over the part of your body experiencing pain, and then paint three Healing Water runes (see **Figure 74**), one for each point of the triangle. This rune creates a potent portal made entirely of white light. Much healing can happen in this truly heavenly space.

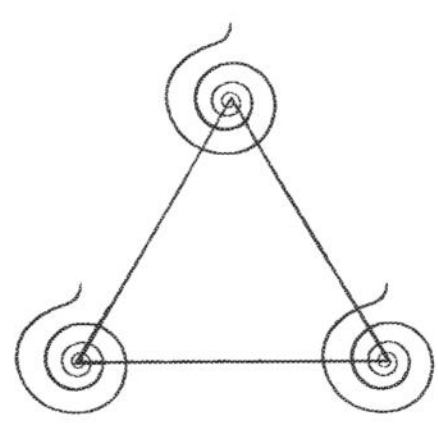

Figure 74: The water healing mark empowered by the triangle

Uses:

- Draw the image of this rune upon a part of your body that is aching. If you prefer to trace the rune with your fingers instead of painting it on, do so seven times, the numerical frequency that activates it. To heal chronic conditions, you'll need to redraw the rune daily for twenty-one days.

- To activate this rune for heart healing, draw a triangle plus the three healing runes combo over your heart. You can also trace the shapes with your finger using water or your preferred essential oil.
- To help ease acute pain, draw the rune over the aching part of your body, then imagine golden light coursing through the rune, further activating it. The pain will ease within ten minutes.

The "Water Protection" Mark

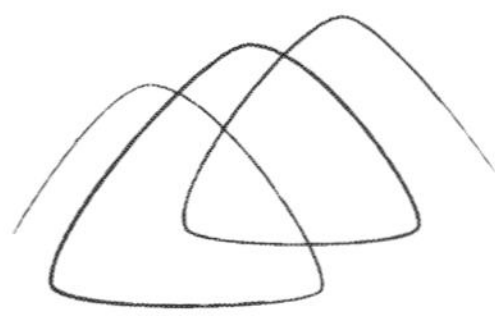

Figure 75: Simple water protection mark

We can all use some protection now and again. Whether we are worried about preserving our high vibrations or are dreading what's coming, this water mark is a powerful ally for getting through challenging times. This mark can ward off evil (including the evil eye) and even repel energetic parasites.

Uses:

- Draw the mark with water over your front door to ensure that tricky evil spirits cannot pass through. For added benefit, place this symbol over your windows and all the mirrors in your home, further sealing and protecting your home. Doing so once when you move into a new home is sufficient; you do not need to keep retracing the mark.
- Draw or trace the symbol on the outer side of your hands to offer your body a layer of protection that works outside your home.
- Draw the mark over anyone you love that you believe requires protection. When the mark is applied with love to another, it has triple the power.

Working with the water marks:

- To invoke the power of the water mark, you can draw it on your skin or a piece of paper in front of you. You may trace the water mark with liquid upon any chosen surface.

- Practice drawing the water mark before you use it in a ritual. Try filling up a couple of pages with the image of the mark. This helps you connect with it consciously and establish a bond. This way, when you invoke the mark, it can immediately be impactful.
- Always use gratitude when you invoke the mark. Everything in the Universe is an energy exchange, and gratitude is the best form of payment for water magic.

The Water Without

Attuning to the waters outside your body is a sacred practice going back to ancient Lemuria and the priestess of Hathor in ancient Egypt. This practice was originally downloaded from Venus and carries the high-frequency Venusian ascension codes.

At any given point, we are submerged within the larger waters of the collective vibrations of planet Earth. We can no more escape them than we could escape ourselves. The outer waters that surround us are not always benevolent. Like the ocean, they can be temperamental, moody, and even merciless. And yet, aligning with them, feeling into them instead of repelling them, brings us closer to understanding life force, and therefore, mastering it. Being in sync with the outer waters can help you hide from a storm when it is imminent and ride the waves during the good times. Alignment is always a good idea, for it helps reduce any disappointment and loss of time from trying to swim against the looming waves. Irrespective of the state of the outer waters, we are always better off knowing our state than navigating life blind.

Practice: Water Attunement

This simple practice is especially important when something negative is brewing in the collective. It will help you develop an immunity toward the moods of the crowd and any suboptimal collective states you may find yourself in the midst of.

1. Close your eyes for a few moments and imagine that you are floating in a vast ocean of collective consciousness. What color is the ocean today? Can you sense its mood?
2. If the ocean had a voice, what would it be trying to tell you?
3. Take out a finger and dip it into the water. What are you sensing? Does it feel cool or warm to the touch? If you experience a slight tingling sensation, this is completely normal.
4. Imagine that through your finger, you are absorbing five water bubbles. Each bubble may be unique, or all five can look the same. These bubbles represent the gifts from the ocean—a means of adapting to its mood and current state. These bubbles will help you vibrate at a cohesive frequency with the ocean. "Cohesive" doesn't mean "the same," merely not in opposition. This way, you don't clash with the outer ocean, but simply float upon its surface peacefully without struggling or losing energy.

Meditation: The Joining of the Inner and the Outer Waters

To develop true peace and serenity while physically incarnated, you might benefit from aligning the inner and the outer waters. This practice builds upon the connection with the outer ocean we established in the previous practice.

1. Take a comfortable position, sitting or lying down, and close your eyes.
2. Breathe deeply into your lower belly, noticing your internal sacral ocean, the seat of your inner waters. Allow the ocean to expand, filling you up with its soft vibrations.
3. Focus on the state of your inner ocean, an accumulation of all the water that currently makes up your body. You will notice that today, your inner waters have a specific color, mood, and frequency. How does your inner water feel today?
4. Now, focus on the waters outside of your body—the large ocean of energy that you are suspended in. How does the outer ocean feel today? Is it calm and gentle, or stormy? Whatever it feels like, remember, you are safe inside it. The ocean represents the Mother and her eternal, unconditional love.
5. Imagine that the inner waters of your body are starting to pour out of your crown chakra, while the outer waters are entering your body through the soles of your feet, creating an energy exchange—a merging, a bond between you and the rest of the Universe. Allow yourself to only take that from the outer ocean which serves you. You can and should be selective. Invite more of what you want into your life and body by letting the waters of the outer ocean in. In the meantime, allow that which no longer serves you to leave your body through the crown chakra.
6. Keep up this energy exchange for as long as it feels good. Allow the process to wind down naturally.
7. Once it subsides, notice the state of peace and serenity that comes over your body, as if you are merged with an eternal consciousness that is the Mother surrounding your body. Allow yourself to dwell in this blissful state. You deserve an opportunity to enjoy it. Stay here for as long as it feels good.
8. When you are ready, feel free to return, slowly moving your fingers and toes, allowing the sensation to return to your physical body. Open your eyes when you are ready.

Heart Space: The River of Time

We, all of us, are floating in the river of time, turning and flipping like loose logs caught in a treacherous mountain torrent.

A fool floats, but knows not that he is in the river. His abode is struggle.

The smart one knows that he is floating, and surrounding him is the mighty river of time. His abode is knowledge.

The wise one sees that he is just a log and decides nothing as he floats down the river of time. His abode is surrender.

And only the one approaching the consciousness of God knows that he is the log, the river, and the torrent itself, and the banks containing the river of time, and the white canvas upon which this story is depicted.

He knows that he is both the brush and the painter, capturing the entire happening upon the canvas of life.

His abode is truth.

CHAPTER 23

The All-Seeing Eye, The All-Feeling Heart

Only by staring into the depth of zero can we finally see the truth.

There are degrees to perception. At any given time, we all decide how much to process, how much to feel, and how much to see.

Each of us has a default setting, a perception threshold we are comfortable with. Some souls prefer a narrow spectrum and a bigger degree of tunnel vision; it helps us focus our resources on a small number of issues, but go deep. Narrow focus also helps preserve our individual perspective, keeping it artificially separate from the collective consciousness, intersecting timelines of the multiverse, and even our own history via limited access to past lives. In other words, it often serves us to experience and maintain a limited capability of vision and feeling. Low-dimensional worlds tend to be full of pain and suffering, as well as all manner of injustice. Having tunnel vision helps souls carry on in a challenging world, because they only have to deal with a limited number of personal challenges and do not have to solve collective frequency distortions.

Now, there is a second group of souls that is biased toward expanded perception. These are clairvoyants, clairaudients, clairsentients, intuitives, empaths, and oracles. Anyone who is able to perceive (see and feel) more than the rest is a true adventurer and change-maker within our third-dimensional reality. They choose to experience more than others, naturally opening themselves to having their personal vibrations more mixed with the vibration of the collective. As such, the lines of demarcation become blurry, allowing this group of people to influence others to a large degree; the connection goes both ways. These souls tend to come as healers, teachers, way-showers, and revolutionaries. Ironically, their perception is also closer to that of Source. This allows for a deeper connection with others and opens the doors to eventual omnipotence, one of the truest marks of God/Goddess consciousness.

Undoubtedly, you have come across the concept of the all-seeing eye, a symbol shrouded in mystery and covered by the veil of Masonic occultism. Despite being prominent on the dollar bill, the symbolism of an all-seeing eye hasn't gone mainstream, and certainly not in a way that would assist humanity in its development. And yet, it holds an innate and ancient significance, being a way-shower in and of itself to the ones who have the eyes to see and the ears to hear.

The all-seeing eye is the highest manifestation of the Father God, and the all-feeling heart is the highest manifestation of the Mother Goddess. Once both are achieved, savored, and experienced fully, the two may come together to form true oneness. One without the other is only half the story, and therefore, an illusion. One is not supreme over the other.

The All-Seeing Eye

God is omnipotent. God is omniscient. God is omnipresent. It is perhaps this last aspect of God that the all-seeing eye has to do with the most.

Source has an infinite number of points of perception, being that every aspect of Source carries within itself a unique frame of reference. However, having infinite perspectives is only half the wonder. The true wonder is that Source can maintain all these perspectives simultaneously without missing a beat.

Imagine a large mirror split into a million different shards. Each shard is unique in and of itself, while also undoubtedly "of the mirror" and sharing some of its characteristics. When the shard gets separated from the mirror, it develops a unique point of perception, its own peculiar way of reflecting reality around it. No two shards of glass in the Universe are the same, in the same way that no two souls are. And while being an individual shard of glass is certainly a curious perspective, this perspective has nothing on the perspective of the entire mirror, the perspective of Source.

As an individual soul incarnated in a third-dimensional world, you watch the movie of your life while fully immersed in it. Your life is your single point of focus, your obsession, and your constant worry. Being self-absorbed and self-focused is table stakes in this reality. In fact, it is so prevalent that helping others is praised as a virtue, and for a good reason; expanding your limited perspective to fit others into the picture is an achievement.

When we descend into an incarnation, we develop tunnel vision. The rich and multifaceted perception of our Higher Self is reduced to a simplified single point of understanding and a fixed identity we often refer to as ego. It is perhaps at this stage that we lose the innate ability of our higher aspect to hold the truth of multiple perspectives simultaneously. In the same way that we prefer to watch only one movie or TV program at a time or only read one book, focusing on a single point of perception allows us to stay grounded and functional in society.

God, however, has no such limitations, and as such, it watches all the movies ever created on all the screens ever made, from the perspective of every actor and every spectator ever born—all at the same time. It is this ability of God that makes it "all-seeing," not the desire to direct and control implied by the "big brother" reputation of the Eye of Providence (the all-seeing eye).

When contemplating omnipresence, consider this: God sees the world through *your* eyes, day in and day out. Your perspective has intrinsic and infinite value. Granted, God sees much beyond that. On a battlefield, for instance, God holds the perspective of each of the sides, the perspective of the generals and that of the soldiers, the perspective of drops of blood on the grass, the perspective of each missile and bullet, the perspective of the air that ruffles the hair of everyone involved, the perspective of the sun that shines upon the battlefield—but most importantly, it holds the joint perspective of the ecosystem of the battle, its collective vibration, and its deepest cumulative impact. It is in the switching between the collective and the individual perspectives that one may start approaching God consciousness.

By virtue of being projections of Source, not only do we carry its primordial vibration, but we also have Source on speed dial. However, often this connection operates as a one-way street; Source may have full access to us, while we may only sporadically experience the presence of Source in our lives. There is a channel of light, a straight line of connection between our limited perception and the limitless perception of Source. This line is often vertical. Moving up this channel of light is often referred to as ascension. Any incarnated soul can attune this light channel to work both ways; it doesn't have to be a one-way street. Just like God has full access to your consciousness and can see through your eyes, there are times in your life when you can make the opposite true as well: you may start seeing the world from the eyes of Source, opening up your ability to become “all-seeing.” Even momentary glimpses into how the mind of the Creator works could be life-altering. Maintaining this perspective for a prolonged amount of time is not required for the purpose of this book.

Becoming All-Seeing

Learning to become “all-seeing” transcends mortality in the best of ways, opening up the possibility for so much more. While maintaining an infinite number of perspectives is the North Star of this ability, we can start by opening our minds to seeing more than one thing at a time. Below are just some of the ways you could start cultivating God consciousness within yourself using the avenue of perfect sight.

Steps to experiencing true sight:

- Mediate daily to train your mind to break free of the constraints of the visible world.
- Open up your third eye to get an additional layer of information about your immediate surroundings.
- Surround yourself with the color violet to adjust the purity of your Ajna (third eye) frequency.
- Meditate on the color violet.
- In any argument, try wearing the shoes of another, deeply experiencing their perspective.
- Seek consensus, the middle way to equalize and balance out polarities. Adopt the diplomat’s stance.
- Learn to tap into the collective energy by journaling your insights about groups of people. Think people at the mall, coworkers during happy hour, seminar attendees. Over time, try reading the collective energy of virtual groups of people—for instance, everyone who saw an episode of a particular show, or voted for a particular political party. Write down your insights. How are these groups similar? How are they different? Try “wearing” each group’s perspective as if it were clothing. How does it make you feel? What does it open up for you? What do you find to be the most fascinating thing about the group’s perspective?
- Once you can read homogeneous groups (the grand average of the group), try experiencing the outliers, the polarizing opinions within each group. Try alternating

between these conflicting perspectives, seeing the world through the eyes of each of them.

- Try holding the perspective of an observer instead of an active participant, putting distance between yourself and the events of your life. Then try holding two perspectives simultaneously—the one where you are a player, and the one where you are an observer.
- At your next family gathering, try experiencing the event from the perspective of each of your family members. It feels like putting on a coat or a piece of clothing belonging to that person. Full integration will require that you ask yourself the following questions:
    - How does this gathering make me feel?
    - What am I thinking about right now?
    - What is bothering me at the moment?
    - What is important to me about this situation?
- Over time, you will find you can hold the perspectives of a growing number of people. You will also learn to maintain those perspectives for longer, noticing that it is not as taxing on your body. Document your journey and insights. You will be surprised how enlightening it can be.

The All-Feeling Heart

While the concept of the all-seeing eye is fairly present in the human collective, its counterpart—the all-feeling heart—is barely known at all. And this is hardly a surprise, given that we have been living in the shadow of the patriarchy for millennia. The time has come for humanity to finally reclaim the beautiful warmth of the all-feeling heart.

When the Father God decided that he would oversee all of creation by witnessing it every moment of every day, and that would become the highest manifestation of his loving nature, the Mother God chose to feel it all instead. The all-feeling heart is the immaculate heart of the Divine Mother—the depth of her mercy, the extent of her compassion, the bottomless well of her love, and the chasm of her sorrow.

The all-feeling heart is an amalgamation of all emotional states, not just the positive ones. It doesn't discriminate; it feels all there is to feel without measure, without placing boundaries or protective layers over itself. The all-feeling heart knows no walls and requires no moats. It is raw, tender, fearless, deep, abundant, and all-accepting. Its primary quality is an utter refusal to protect itself, to shut down, to build insulation around itself—and because of that, it is so rare to experience it in dense, low-dimensional worlds.

An immaculate heart doesn't become such through the avoidance of trauma and suffering. It is immaculate precisely because of all the pain it has experienced. Pain doesn't have to tarnish our hearts; rather, it has the ability to expand and enrich them. Experiencing pain is an enabler; it allows us to know the depths of despair, so that we can show true empathy. We can reach out and nurture others from a place of true love and understanding.

Planet Earth is a perfect testing ground for expanding your heart. At face value, everything here is stacked against you, from the feelings of separation and loneliness, to the mechanical routine of the workweek, to the fear-based programming, and most importantly, the trauma you inevitably experience. But it is through the toughest challenges that our hearts get forged into powerhouses. Invite life in! Allow yourself to feel it all—audaciously, irrevocably, unabashedly.

Remember, you are water, and as such, nothing can hurt you if you maintain your most receptive, liquid, flexible state. Become the paradigm shift and dive into emotion headfirst. The Mother will be there on the other side, waiting to catch you in her tender, warm, and comforting embrace.

The Heart of Yeshua – The Heart of Myriam

Of the recent planetary teachers, Jesus and Mother Mary were both the carriers of the vibration of the immaculate all-feeling heart. They came as a balancing act for the intellectually based perception so prevalent on Earth, then and now. Their battlefield was feeling all there was to feel—the pain, the suffering, the joy, the love. These great avatars knew exactly what they were signing up for before descending to the Earthly plane, and the challenges their path would bring. They chose to walk it anyway, so great was their desire to anchor the archetype of the all-feeling heart into our reality.

Yeshua displayed immaculate love for his disciples (including the one who betrayed him), his persecutors, and his executioners. He rose above duality into a space where he could perceive everyone and everything as an extension of himself. The immaculate heart of Yeshua had the most magnetic healing presence, transmitting through him the extent of the depth of the love of our Mother Divine. As such, he was her ambassador and a projection, a Divine child carrying her primordial vibration.

Figure 76: The Immaculate Heart (Credit: Adobe Stock Photo)

While Yeshua was the holder of the ray of love, Myriam, a female carrier of the immaculate heart, took it upon herself to experience the depth of empathy, forgiveness, and compassion. Her humility and seemingly effortless forgiveness of those who wronged her son was her gift to the Earth. She held a greater vision and foresaw a new possibility for humanity—a world of peace, harmony, and oneness that would replace the reality of divide and conquer.

Together, Yeshua and Myriam lit up the torch of the Cosmic Heart upon the plane of our third-dimensional planet. They held that torch to a higher standard, imbuing it with the higher-dimensional power of love. They walked the walk in mortal bodies, so that one day, this walk would become possible for every man, woman, and child on Earth.

Steps to experiencing immaculate feeling:

- Allow yourself to feel negative emotions without judging yourself, the circumstances, or the world. Please know that experiencing negative emotions is not a personal failure; it is a test we must pass to deepen our heart capacity.
- Create an emotion diary, recording some of your strongest, most notable emotions. Note how they feel in your body and what they teach you every time they appear.

Treat emotions as teachers. Recognize that emotions are like water: they need to flow. Resistance to experiencing certain emotions prevents them from flowing naturally and instead makes them "stuck" in our bodies, potentially causing disease.

- Challenge yourself to hold space for your loved ones as they experience strong negative emotions. When you sense that they are feeling a challenging emotion, reach out and hold space for them by simply being with them as they are experiencing the emotion.
- Tune into the emotional states of groups.
- Reach out to people when you know they are struggling. Learn to listen and respond, not react. When speaking, let your heart do the talking.
- Over time, you will learn to do heart healing for individuals and groups. Our hearts are the sieves that sift through our emotions. When an emotion is overwhelming, our hearts become clogged, and negativity gets stuck inside our emotional bodies. To prevent this, we need to increase the capacity of our hearts and cleanse our heart space regularly. Once you open your heart to the entirety of your emotional spectrum, thus mastering the realm of emotion, you will become capable of helping others. Simply imagine that you are absorbing the negative emotions of others and using your heart to sift through them, allowing them to pass through your system and be released. This will greatly aid anyone experiencing negativity until they evolve enough to handle the onslaught of negativity.

Experiencing Oneness: Bridging the Mind-Heart Gap

The Immaculate Heart (the all-feeling heart) and the Immaculate Mind (the all-seeing eye) are depicted surrounded by the gilded auras; they emanate true light. As such, they symbolize true Divinity—not the polished version staring at us from the visages of saints and ascended masters, but rather the Divinity that is attainable to you here on Earth. Experiencing and practicing the two states is the deepest bliss you can achieve while incarnated. It is a road truly worth traveling, a pilgrimage truly worth undertaking.

Practice: The Infinite Unity of the Heart and Mind

This practice amplifies the hidden resources of your body, allowing you to move through life seamlessly and with joy.

Other benefits include:

- A flow state. Things will happen more easily as people and places magnetize into your orbit.
- Creation and manifestation becoming effortless and fun
- A deep sense of serenity and contentment
- Stress and anxiety relief
- Deeper connection with your Higher Self and spirit guides
- Alignment with your perfect path and purpose
- Improved sleep
- Deep healing and alignment of your light bodies
- Balance of the fire/water continuum in your body
- Closer connection with Source consciousness
- Accumulation of wisdom and deeper understanding of life

Figure 77: On-body representation of the all-seeing eye

1. Get comfortable and close your eyes.
2. Send your breath to the center of your forehead. Imagine a triangle of light forming, which connects your three eyes: the two physical and the etheric "third" eye (see **Figure 77**).

3. Watch how the energy starts to travel along the perimeter of the triangle, causing it to begin emanating light. Stay here for a few moments, letting the triangle accumulate even more light and shine brighter.
4. Now, shift your focus to the area of your heart. Imagine it unfolding like a golden rose inside of your chest. Watch as a golden circle emerges around the perimeter of your heart space. Notice the circle's circumference beginning to emanate light, filling your heart space with an otherworldly glow. Stay here for a few moments and allow this process to progress naturally.
5. Now that your heart and eyes are activated, imagine that a figure eight is beginning to connect the two. One loop encapsulates your eye triangle, while the other incorporates your beautiful heart, bringing them into harmony and establishing a true, uninterrupted connection.
6. Notice how white light is beginning to travel up and down the figure eight, further solidifying your heart-mind connection. Stay in this blessed state for as long as it feels good.
7. When you are ready, return to the present moment and open your eyes.

Heart Space: The Well

Come to the well of the Mother, dear one.

Lay down your arms, set aside your shields and protections.

Remove your swords, knives, and spears.

Come to the well of the Mother, dear one.

Let go of the bitterness of your past, the judgment of your present.

Take off your fears and doubts and your woes like yesterday's clothes.

Come to the well of the Mother, dear one.

Forgive what must be forgiven; heal what needs to be healed.

Surrender your pain, guilt, and suffering.

Come to the well of the Mother, dear one.

Feel the spirit of her guiding waters, the strength of her Divine embrace.

Bask in the warm rays of her love and light and soul.

Come to the well of the Mother, dear one,

And never be the same again, forever changed by her grace,

Forever redeemed, forever cleansed by her wisdom.

Come to the well of the Mother, dear one,

And realize that you have been here before, in this exact moment between time and space,

And you promised to come back here when you were ready to finally step onto the path.

Come to the well of the Mother, dear one,

And know that the path is right in front of you, tugging you forward.

It stretches ahead like a remembrance—

A remembrance of who you are and why you came,

Your personal beacon of light,

Your personal heroine journey,

And its time has come.

So, let a new chapter of your life begin—

Not through the struggles of tomorrow,

but through the loving embrace of your Mother in the sky,

The one who loves you best.

And so it is.

CHAPTER 24

Magna Mater—The Great Mother

This was the end of the cycle, the time for the tides to come ashore once again, the time for the polarities to shift, bringing relief and a much-needed cleanse to the planet we call Gaia. Dark were the times without the light of the Mother, harsh were the hearts, hopeless were the futures, and lonely were the people. The tribes of the Mother were scattered upon the face of the Earth. Little did remain of the days of the old, when the sculptures of the Mother lined the altars, graced the temples, and presided over the mountain peaks. Only the fragrance of the rose still carried the vibration of the Mother, a faint reminder of her magnanimous greatness, a remnant of the life-altering power of her cosmic love.

Dark were the times, empty were the temples, and forgotten were the wise words of the times bygone. The priests of the Age of Pisces preached false doctrines, led by the power of their minds, not their hearts. The scriptures were written and rewritten until the name of the Mother was removed from them completely, presenting a polarized world, a distorted picture. But this was not just foretold; this was intended. The Dark Night of Gaia was a blessing, a deep slumber destined to one day be halted by the rays of the first dawn of the female sun. The Mother had never left Gaia; she merely receded into the background, allowing her darling child to go on a journey of self-discovery.

The time of our Great Mother's return is now. And she is coming carried by the tides of the new age, heralded by the new dawn, temporarily leaving the sanctuary of the Gilded Gates. She is clad in sunlight, adorned with pearls and jewels, soft-spoken, well-intentioned, carrying infinity upon her shoulders, endless love in her belly, and abundant creation inside her womb. She is here to rebuild and restore the greatness of Atlantis, granting it a heart of gold and restoring its soul connection. And once her work is complete, Gaia shall enter a new cycle and a new beginning—a rebirth of ages. And the new waters shall flow, and the new shores shall rise, and a new race of solar humans shall grace the Earth, rebuilding and restoring the legacy of old, but birthing a new Divine imprint also. And this shall be known as the New Gilded Age, and it will signify a complete healing and redemption of Gaia.

And so it is, and so it shall ever remain.

The Undefinable Mother

How does one describe the Mother? Our Great Feminine Source, the Goddess of All Life, the infinity and the eternity, the Creatress and birther of all that is? Words fall short of defining her essence, leaving her complexity, her spirit, and her intentions out of the scope of human perception. And yet, we must try to move beyond the limitations of language if that is our sacred duty.

The Magna Mater—the Original Mother, the womb of creation, the one who loves us best—is both indescribable and unfathomable. She is life itself, whether in form or formlessness. She is boundless, unrestricted. She is the universal flow and our collective heart space. She is the birthplace of forgiveness and empathy, an infinite capacity for love and understanding, and an unlimited number of chances for redemption.

She is our evolutionary path, a staircase upward, a helping hand, and a wind of change. She is the energy around us. She is what we breathe in; she is what we breathe out. She is prana. She is Shakti—the great Shakti rising within. She is the one that came before and shall remain after. Yet she is present with us every moment of every day, watching over us, guiding us via a subtle language of signs and premonitions. Throughout the years, she has never forsaken us, nor turned a blind eye to our suffering. But she did let us do things our way, and we made choices that felt right in the moment. And then, if things went wrong, she was there to comfort us as we slept, so that in the morning, we felt better.

The Mother is the quiet voice telling you that you are worthy. She is the hope you feel in your darkest hours. She is the love in your heart when you perform a random act of kindness. She is the one smiling at you when you choose forgiveness over revenge, softness over conflict, empathy over selfishness. She was your first Mother—the one who loved you best.

She is the primordial dark void and every morsel of matter that surrounds you, and neither one is more important than the other.

She is your safety net, your advocate, and your healing space.

She is the teacher of teachers, a golden thread connecting your many incarnations into a story of growth.

She is the very fabric of existence and the memory of what came before.

The time has come for you to reconnect with the Mother's gentle presence in this lifetime. It is time for you to remember what is hidden by the veil. It is time for a true homecoming, my sibling in Rose.

Finding the Mother Within

Many are the paths to the Mother, and many are the flavors of her love. Each path is precious in its own right, leading you to a particular aspect of the Mother that you can interact with. It is in finding the many ways of connecting to her that you uncover her rich resources, each path shining a light on something new, another aspect for you to unwrap and enjoy.

When it comes to working with the Mother Divine, more is more. It is all of the paths, not the one path, that will lead you into the depths of connection with her majestic consciousness. It is the many flavors of her caress, the many kinds of her embrace that you came here to savor. Below are just some thought starters on connecting with her gentle spirit. But the best of ways you shall discover on your own, once you start building a one-on-one personal connection with your celestial Creatress.

Heart Space

The Mother is ever present inside your heart space. She is the soft voice of your heart, whispering to you to stay true to who you are. Reconnecting with your own beautiful heart is the first step you make toward embracing your celestial Mother. However, you must do some serious shedding to get to the inner folds of the heart, where the Mother dwells. The upper folds of the heart are too rigid for her, too sterile, too harsh. She dwells in the very core, the molten center of your heart—the truest version of your "self."

Exercise: Heart Healing with the Mother

You can use this practice as your daily morning meditation, or simply come back to it when you are ready for a new portion of heart healing and an even deeper sense of connection with the Mother.

1. Close your eyes. Imagine peeling off the outer layers of your heart, each layer representing an old trauma or heartache.
2. Allow yourself to discard the old layers. You can set an intention to release specific traumatic experiences from the past, or simply allow the Universe to arrange everything according to your highest good.
3. As you continue to peel off layer after layer, notice how the tissue of your heart becomes softer.
4. Once you remove ten or so layers, you are ready to dive in. Imagine falling into the very core of your heart space. Go as deep as your heart allows you to go.
5. Once you reach the "ground," you will be greeted by a presence. It may manifest as a form, a voice, a feeling, or an energetic emanation. This is Divine Mother communicating with you.
6. Stay in this space and ask questions, if that feels good. You may also request healing or support from the Mother at this time.

Third Eye Space

Another beloved domain of the Mother is your inner third eye space. It is a great seat of intuition and wisdom, and it is hardly a surprise that the Mother selected this area of your body to dwell in. This connection allows her to gently guide you if you are lost, and to send you intuitive nudges when you could use a helping hand. But more importantly, your third eye is a portal into higher dimensions and even to a space beyond the matrix, where your soul can interact with the wisdom of the Mother without the middleman.

Exercise: Third Eye Connection with the Mother

Use this practice any time you require guidance or could use a deeper spiritual connection to the Divine Feminine.

1. Begin by focusing on your third eye area, sending your breath through the center of your forehead to activate this area of your body.
2. Imagine a purple spiral in the very center of your forehead, parallel to the floor.
3. As you focus on the spiral, picture it rotating, accelerating its spin.
4. Imagine that you are aligned with the end of the spiral, pointing forward and outside of your body. Allow the spiral to transport you forward and up with a mighty force.
5. You should find yourself in a spacious purple chamber with floor-length arched windows. Welcome to the sacred space of the Mother—a space that is perfect for receiving insights and energetic healing from the celestial Creatress.

Sacral Chakra Space

Our sacral chakra, represented by the color orange, is where our inner waters flow. It is the center of our emotions and our ability to surrender and go with the flow. This is a cherished space of the Mother and is easily accessible. Unfortunately, due to the current state of vibrations on planet Earth, our sacral waters are often polluted by all the unprocessed negative emotions that we cannot let go of. Therefore, before attempting to connect with the Mother through your sacral center, it may be beneficial to do a quick cleanse of your inner waters.

To do this, simply visualize the ocean of your sacral chakra leaving your body through the soles of your feet and sinking into the Earth. Then, imagine a new golden ocean emerging in its place, which will cleanse and heal your sacral space in preparation for what's to come. Once the cleanse is complete, watch as the waters of this ocean turn orange—the state of equilibrium for the sacral energy center.

Exercise: Sacral Space Meeting with the Mother

Refer to this practice any time you require healing and alignment. While there is no wrong time of day to connect with the Mother, this practice works best in the evening.

1. Close your eyes and imagine an ocean of orange waters in your lower abdomen. Picture yourself floating in these waters. In this moment, allow yourself to release your troubles and worries.
2. As you release the heaviness of your daily problems, you'll become attuned to the waters around you, merging with them. Notice how they are starting to carry you into their depths.
3. Release any control you may be holding onto and allow yourself to be carried away into a winding labyrinth at the bottom of the ocean.
4. Notice the many tunnels and crevices the waters take you through before finally depositing you in a spacious underground cavern. The waters are shallow and calm here. As you look around, you notice a large white lotus in the middle of the cavern. A figure is seated upon its petals. This is the Mother.
5. Watch as she steps off the lotus to greet you.
6. While this place is great for insights, it is perhaps best used for healing and alignment. Feel free to ask the Mother for anything specific, or simply to cater to you as she sees fit. Enjoy!

Finding the Mother Without

Our Mother Divine is omnipresent. She is just as integral to what surrounds us as she is innate to what is inside us. And yet, certain aspects of creation resemble her core vibrations the most, serving as her natural extension and a gateway to her consciousness. It is these phenomena that we'll explore below and later use as entryways into the Mother's great consciousness.

Connecting Through a Spiral

A spiral is one of Mother's beloved geometric shapes. Wherever the spiral is present, so is the Mother. That is why simply imagining a golden spiral spinning in a painful spot in your body can act as a painkiller.

To connect with the consciousness of the Mother, or to create a personal healing space for yourself, imagine that your body is encapsulated inside a large white or golden spiral. Picture the spiral rotating, and feel how this shifts the sensations inside your body. Does anything feel different? By maintaining the rotation of the spiral around you, you can quickly cleanse your auric field and prepare your physical body for healing and accelerated restoration.

Other spirals to explore:

Blue spiral: Perfect for healing your relationship with your personal truth, enhancing communication skills, aligning with your highest good, clearing doubt, removing self-sabotage, and silencing your inner critic

Pink spiral: Great for experiencing a state of bliss, helping you build stronger relationships, building empathy, becoming more likable, being a better listener, feeling more love, experiencing oneness, and creating stronger bonds with animals

Green spiral: Perfect for getting aligned with nature, establishing a strong bond with plants, unlocking abundance, fostering healing of your respiratory and circulatory systems, fostering self-forgiveness and self-love, strengthening your familial bonds, and healing your relationship with your mother

Orange spiral: Great for inspiration, enhanced creative spark, fostering natural talents, success in creative projects, resting and resetting, restoration, shedding unnecessary layers, and inner peace

Yellow spiral: Ideal for healing your inner child, bringing back joy, building confidence and optimism, aligning with optimal circumstances, healing your relationship with your father, and faster manifestation

The Way of Water

Of the four elements, the Divine Mother most corresponds with water. Water's forgiving nature, cleansing properties, and need to nurture make it a perfect proxy for our Celestial Mother. Whether you are drinking water, bathing in it, or simply appreciating the natural bodies of water around you, taking the time to connect with water is a wonderful way to invite the Mother's energy into your life. Blessing and charging your water with positive intentions is a simple yet powerful practice that can help you live a more aligned life. Charge your water with the emanations of your heart's greatest desire and even your most audacious goals, and see them manifest in the physical. It truly all starts with water.

Always respect the natural bodies of water around you and greet them with gratitude and reverence. By doing so, you are inviting the energy of the Divine Mother into your life and opening yourself up to her infinite love and wisdom. Make a point to imagine that every cell of your body absorbs the Mother's blessings through the water she so generously shares with you.

Connecting via the Figure Eight: The Infinity Connection

The figure eight is one of the Mother's most beloved shapes. It embodies her essence in every curve. If our Mother had a signature symbol, it would undoubtedly be the infinity symbol. The figure eight holds a strong connection to many aspects of the Mother, so whenever you work with this shape, you are bound to have a unique and different experience each time.

1. To begin your connection, imagine a large figure eight before you. Start by tracing the shape's curves with your consciousness, allowing yourself to get lost in the process as you travel up and down the slopes of the shape.
2. Then, let the shape magnetize you to a particular spot within itself that will serve you the most at this moment in time.
3. Zoom in on that spot until you can feel the particles of time and space haphazardly moving around you.
4. Eventually, you will find yourself in a spacious chamber filled with white light, with Divine Mother sitting on a throne in the middle.

5. Stay in this space to get answers to your larger-than-life questions or to receive healing directly from the Mother herself.

Tip: Next time you're facing a difficult decision, try visualizing yourself in the center of a figure eight, the part between the two loops. This space is particularly powerful for enabling optimal decision-making, since it represents the most balanced point of the shape. From here, you can access a sense of inner equilibrium to help you make decisions that align with your highest good.

Connecting to the Mother via the Rose Labyrinth

The pathways of our Divine Mother are winding. She doesn't express herself through a straight line; that is the domain of our Divine Father. A labyrinth is one of the most natural ways for the Mother to express herself. The Mother's labyrinth is never the same. It is a shape-shifting structure, ever alive, ever breathing, perpetually expanding and creating new pathways within itself. Stepping into a labyrinth feels like stepping into a medieval rose garden, full of hidden passageways and alcoves, each path lined with briars and rose bushes.

You can connect with our Mother via the rose labyrinth using a simple visualization as follows:

1. Close your eyes and imagine stepping upon a winding briar-lined path.
2. Allow yourself to walk forward, asking the Universe to bring you closer to the Mother. Follow the natural curves of the path in front of you, taking any sharp left turns offered to you. You need to make three left turns in total before the Mother reveals herself to you. If the labyrinth offers you a right turn, take it; the path is winding, but always leads to the Mother.
3. Once you follow the path long enough to have encountered three sharp left turns, you should come upon an opening in the garden, usually lit with sunlight and adorned with even more roses than before.
4. The Mother can come to you in any shape she chooses, from an animal to an object. Whatever form she takes, know that it's for your highest good.
5. Once you meet the Mother, she may choose to perform a healing on you or share her comfort or wisdom. You may also have specific requests as you work with her. Listen to your heart; it knows exactly what to ask for.

Bringing the Divine Presence of the Mother into Daily Life

Everything in the Universe is vibration. When our vibrations are high, we experience positive feelings such as hope, fulfillment, and joy, and we attract more of the same. Conversely, when our vibrations drop, we may feel drained, discouraged, and uninspired. As such, the quality of our life is strongly correlated with our level of vibration. Staying connected to the Divine Mother is one way to maintain a high vibration. However, when life gets in the way of your spiritual practice, you can use the following physical objects to harmonize your space and infuse it with our Divine Mother's unconditional love.

Roses

These blooms are perhaps the best energetic shortcut if you would like to connect with the Mother. Grow them in your garden, get some potted roses, or buy fresh stems weekly. Having roses around your space is therapeutic on an emotional and energetic level. Intentionally connecting with the rose by touching its petals and breathing in its scent while focusing on opening your heart space is a beautiful ritual that will help raise your vibration instantly.

For a deeper connection, have a small bottle of rose oil nearby. Place a few drops on your temples, the base of your neck, and your wrists. Take a moment to inhale the gentle aroma, and imagine floating up toward the beautiful pink skies, the domain of the Mother.

Rose Water

Rose water contains the essence, the core emanation, and the very heart of the rose. While natural rose water offers many great benefits for your skin, its spiritual benefits outweigh its physical properties. Misting your face with natural rose water is akin to a quick, energetic shower, helping you to release some of the negative and toxic energy that may be stuck in your auric field. Take a few seconds to apply rose water to your face, breathe in, breathe out, and imagine yourself being lifted high above, so you can look at your daily troubles from a different vantage point.

Using rose water is like sharing breath with the Mother. Treasure these moments and know that with the water, your skin absorbs the Mother's love and her eternal assistance. Know that help is on the way.

Flower Essences and Natural Essential Oils

The Mother speaks to us in the language of plants. Whenever you use a pure, natural essential oil, a flower essence, or simply inhale the aroma of flowers, you inadvertently connect with the Mother. Seek out your personal plant helpers; chances are you naturally resonate with some more than others. Pay attention to how different essential oils make you feel, pinpointing the ones that are most healing for your soul. You may notice that your preferences change with the seasons; our bodies require different kinds of support and nourishment depending on the time of year. However, there are general trends to be aware of.

Certain natural elements work better during specific months, which has to do with sacred contracts that each of these plants established with Gaia long ago. Each plant has an active period during which it is meant to be humanity's helper and healer. The list below was created taking these contracts into account.

January–February: Peppermint, eucalyptus, sage, cedar, ginger, cypress

March–April: Neroli (orange blossom), lily of the valley, magnolia, tuberose, mimosa, gardenia

May–June: Grapefruit, blood orange, verbena, wheatgrass, chamomile, lilac, peach, pear, apricot, lemon, freesia, peony

July–August: Lotus, rose, sandalwood, jasmine, clover, lavender, marigold

September–October: Cinnamon, cardamom, clove, anise, nutmeg, coriander, turmeric

November–December: Vetiver, rosemary, jasmine, hinoki, pine, juniper, patchouli, palo santo, agarwood, vanilla

Water Infused with Plants, Fruits, and Berries

Water infused with fruit carries the fruit's natural healing emanation. To clear your energy body, infuse your water with cucumber slices. For a jolt of energy and optimism, infuse your water with orange slices. To spark inspiration, infuse your water with ginger or cinnamon (by placing a cinnamon stick inside your water carafe). Water infused with plums can heal your reproductive system. In contrast, rose-infused water attracts romantic love into your life. (Placing a few rose petals in your water carafe for thirty minutes is enough to infuse the water with the spirit of the rose.)

Orchids

Having orchids in common spaces within your home is a great energetic harmonizer. Living rooms and dining rooms in particular can benefit from the emanations of the orchid. The orchid can bring your family together, smooth over any potential disagreements, and create a cohesive, energetically beneficial environment for everyone. Placing an orchid plant near the front entrance of your home is also helpful. Orchids naturally repel negativity, making them the perfect silent guardians for your home, warding off negative spirits attempting to enter through the front door.

Bowls of Water Filled with Flower Buds

For a deeper connection with the spirit of the Mother, place bowls filled with water in the four corners of your room. Add a few fresh cut buds or flower petals to the water, allowing them to float naturally. Physically, a mixture of water and flowers directly invokes the Mother—a summoning of sorts. This ritual is more effective than any prayer, altar, or even some meditative practices.

Golden Feathers

The Mother has a special affinity for golden feathers. With the extinction of firebirds and the many once-prominent phoenix species, we do not have naturally occurring golden feathers on Earth at this time. However, you can easily find feathers that have been artificially dyed gold. Get a few for yourself and place them where you can see them. Each golden feather is a direct bridge to the Mother and a gift from her to humanity. Golden feathers can make wishes come true. Instead of wishing upon a falling star, you can wish upon a golden feather and receive assistance from the Mother in manifesting your wish.

Seashells

When the Divine Mother initially anchored her energies upon Earth, she first chose to manifest water. She then manifested white seashells in the depths of the water, each a reminder to her many future children that a Mother's love is pure, strong, and never far away. Collecting seashells and storing them in glass vases and crystal bowls creates a portal into the heart of the Mother, ensuring that you can always feel her presence and love simply by glancing at the seashells and holding them close to your heart.

You may have noticed that listening to the inside of a shell sounds like the sea. You may not know that this vibration was lovingly placed inside the shell by our Divine Mother, and the frequency that emanates from it is healing for humans on so many levels. As you bring the shell close to your ear to listen to its song, imagine it penetrating deep into your cells. Let your cells capture and absorb this sound, allowing it to naturally accumulate in the areas of your body that require healing. Then, invite the Mother to actually perform the healing. The energies of the seashell are gentle, so they need some time to perform the actual healing. You should feel relieved by morning.

Pearls

Energetically, pearls are crystallized tears of the Divine Mother. Yes, physically, they are created by mollusks, but our Mother has been known to deliver her healing in the unlikeliest of ways. Wear naturally occurring pearls to heal any wounding associated with your biological mother, to become a better parent, to heal your reproductive system, or to eliminate sadness from your life.

Flower of Life Prints

The Flower of Life is the most beloved sacred geometric shape of the Mother. To call upon its healing energy, you can place Flower of Life prints in any space where you need the Mother's presence and protection, whether it's a nursery, car, or a dining room table. It's especially beneficial to have this pattern in your kitchen, as the vibrations will infuse your food with the love and grace of the Mother. Consider using Flower of Life stickers on the bottoms of your plates to imbue the food served with our Mother's gentle presence.

Spherical Crystals

Reminiscent of the womb, spherical crystals naturally contain the emanations of the Mother within their crystalline structures. Place them in the bedroom if you are looking to conceive a child, or in your working area if you need assistance with a work project. By infusing the crystal with a single intention, it will act as an incubator and help you manifest that intention in the physical realm.

Heart Space: She Was the Cross

Once upon a time, amidst the chaos of galaxies emerging and collapsing, in the thick of the coiling and thrashing of the primordial void, a girl was born. Anantara, they called her—"the one who has no end." She was a favorite daughter of Source, the one whose fault was yet to be found. She walked among the stars and rode the tails of solar winds, seemingly oblivious to how unique she was among creation.

And so, she grew in wisdom faster than she grew in years, delighting in her childlike curiosity. She was a prodigy, an enigma, masterfully weaving fates and creating paths where there were none before.

"Time weaver," they whispered, and she just smiled in return—for what was time if not an illusion to be whipped into shape by one favored by the gods?

Eons went by, and the girl became a maiden, wild and free and full of life. She painted constellations in the sky and was reborn every day like a celestial phoenix, forever coming and going, perpetually held hostage by an infinite cycle of death and rebirth.

She got to know the Universe like the palm of her hand. She helped strengthen and mold it into something different, something other—dare we say, something better. And her life was full of play, but also full of challenge. And so, she thought she had it all figured out—the good, the bad, and the in-between. She knew unity, she knew separation, she knew hope, and she knew desperation.

She was Sophia, she was Christos, and she was so much more than even that.

She was the cross—a vertical line of ascension, a testament to sovereignty, a path toward light.

She was the cross—a horizontal line of togetherness, an ode to connection, proof of her infinity.

She was the cross—a collision of opposites, a blessing once foretold, a parable made manifest. She was a female Christ rising. She was a song of redemption and a primordial sound of creation. She was the Word of God. And not even the gooey night of darkness could ever get in her way.

CHAPTER 25

The Female Christ Rising

Hail Mary, for a new age is upon us,

The Age of Soot, the Age of Glory.

Smile, Mary, for you need wait no longer.

She who was once promised must return again, mightier than before.

No longer a slave, she is crowned by the sun, clad in starlight.

Her breath is the flow of the Universe, her tears the morning dew.

Rejoice, Mary, for the Age of the Maiden is here,

And she has come to remove the rusty chains of the old epoch.

Embrace the age of the lamb, the age of the lion,

The time of the flood, the days of judgment.

Greet the yuga of light, the crowning of the chalice,

The age to end all the ages.

Hail Mary, for a New Earth shall rise from the ashes of the old world,

And this Earth shall glow with the light Divine, and darkness shall be no more.

And the gilded gates shall open, and the waters of the New Earth shall wash away all sin.

And the pearly gates and the rivers full of milk and the land anointed with honey—this all shall come to pass.

She is the redemption, the final tally of what is, and the only path forward.

She may choose to forget and forego, but she will render the final judgment anyway.

She brings forth the judgment day, final and complete, the very last page of a very long saga.

She has come here as a queen among angels to place every soul in the bowls of the scale and pronounce them either dead or alive.

Enter the gates of the New World, little one.

Walk in the footsteps of the maiden and be reborn this day.

For she is the harbinger of light and the avatar of the new era,

The maker of the new skies, the reforger of timelines, the promised land in and of herself.

She is the word and the light and the way.

She is the female Christ rising.

And the world shall never be the same again.

What is Christ, Truly?

A savior? A redeemer? A martyr? None of the above—and perhaps all of them combined.

A Christ is someone chosen to embody the polarity of light within a single vessel. The anointed one, both human and not, full of spirit, full of soul. Both finite and infinite, anchored and untethered, mortal and absolute.

A Christ is a promise fulfilled, an answer to an unsolvable equation.

A Christ is concerned not with the fleeting, but forever preoccupied with the immortality of souls. The journey of Christ is a journey within—the kind that helps one discover the stable core upon which a future can be built. The most important question for the rising Christ is, "Who am I truly?" The answer to this question matters greatly, for it shapes epochs.

When faced with the question, "Who am I truly?" Yeshua said, "I am love." Buddha said, "I am the way out." Krishna said, "I am the law." Shiva said, "I am presence." It is the answer to this existential question that shapes generations of humanity.

A Christ is a polarity of light that has taken shape. However, there is also a polarity of darkness: the Antichrist. Together, they form two paths of least resistance, two roads well traveled, two dichotomies born to cancel each other out. One never exists without the other, for balance is the language of the Universe. They are the first and last dominoes, bound to always show up as a pair, forever joined at the hip by the blessing and curse of their collective journey.

Christ is a pillar of light, a beacon of great personal sovereignty, one who embodies perfect alignment with Source—body, spirit, heart, and mind. Christ is a being of immense power. A planetary Christ aligns with the Axis Mundi (the central energetic axis of the planet) to such a degree that they start influencing it. A true Christ can impact the polarization of the planet, its energetic makeup, and even its physical spin.

Every age has its own Christ, an aligned being transmitting light codes on this plane of existence. And while the second coming is very much real, at this time and perhaps for the first time ever, we are invited to find our own Divinity, to activate the Christ within our hearts and bodies. We are called to become vessels of light, to embody and emanate it. The energies are shifting, and what was once only available to a select few will now become the treasure of many. And it all starts with you, my sibling in Rose.

Christ Consciousness

Christ consciousness is a state of perfect alignment, sovereignty, and being crowned with light. It's full self-acceptance and understanding of the depth of one's personal power and the breadth of responsibility. This state of alignment is as close to feeling the presence of God as we can get on the earthly plane. Anyone able to achieve even the beginner stages of Christ consciousness on Earth becomes a true creator of reality, not just in a micro aspect, but in a true macro way, impacting the collective reality of thousands and perhaps millions of people. A Christ is a being uncaged, the one who transcends fear, moves beyond temptation, and accepts their Source-given right and power to decide, create, and move forward. A Christ is a supernova, a new center of gravity, a curvature in the fabric of reality that defies even the Laws of Hermeticism. A Christ is the one who rewrites the script, no longer a victim, but a sovereign. The state of Christ is the most heightened state available to an incarnated human.

Activating the Christ Gateway

While embracing the state of perfect sovereignty may take lifetimes, activating the Christ Gateway (see **Figure 78**) doesn't have to. The Christ path is an upward pillar of light that passes through your body, connecting the depth of Gaia with the heart and mind of Source itself. This path serves as your personal central axis, your inner mountain, and your center of stability, power, and strength. It is from this core that any true Christ starts emanating light and shifting the surrounding reality. It all begins at the core.

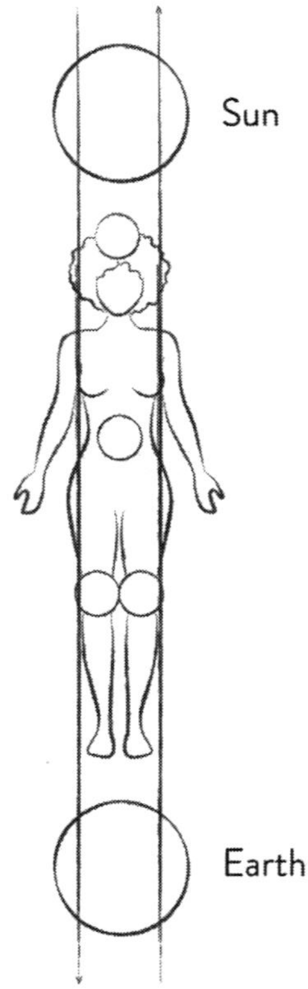

Figure 78: Christ Consciousness Gateway

Meditation: Christ Consciousness Gateway

Use the following meditative practice to activate the dual energy stream of the Christ Consciousness Gateway. It will enable you to cultivate heightened awareness, sovereignty, and creative powers in your body. Working with this energy pathway has a cumulative effect; the more you work with it, the more potent it becomes.

1. Take a comfortable position and close your eyes. Focus on your breath, and allow your thoughts to center on your breath.
2. Send your breath into the middle of your belly, activating your solar plexus chakra. Notice how warmth spreads from this center of your body up and downstream, filling your entire body with beautiful yellow energies.
3. Move your breath to the center of your left knee, imagining how this area of your body is becoming activated. Notice that a golden rotating spiral emerges as you breathe into this area of your body.
4. Shift your focus to your right knee and imagine the energy coming alive in this part of your body. Notice that a small golden spiral starts to rotate in your right knee, infusing it with energy.
5. Above your head, high up in the sky, imagine a brilliant white sun shining with all its might. This is one of the main suns of the Milky Way, our point of connection to Source, and a great celestial teacher. Notice that a waterfall of white and gold codes streams from the very core of the sun toward you.
6. Watch this stream fall upon your head and start to enter your body through the opening in your crown chakra.
7. Notice as the stream goes down toward your solar plexus and toward your knees, creating a pillar of light that passes through your body alongside its vertical axis.
8. Watch as the pillar of light stretches down all the way to the center of our planet, the heart of Gaia.
9. Now, notice that there is a second stream of light that goes up from the center of Gaia toward the core of the white sun. Notice how this energy feels different and is emerald in color.
10. Allow both the upward and the downward streams to coexist, aligning you with the two polarities you are meant to connect.

11. Stay present with the interplay of the two streams. Allow the streams to remove anything suboptimal from your body, opening your channel further and preparing it to receive major upgrades.
12. Once your channel is cleared enough, notice that a stream of codes from Gaia and the white sun become absorbed by your body, settling into your bones and tissues.
13. Allow this process to happen naturally. Every code you accept this way is an anchor for higher frequencies to grow roots in your body. Simply stay here and allow yourself to receive.

Working with the Christ Gateway:

- Use the Christ Gateway when making decisions to ensure that you are operating with your highest good in mind.
- Use the Christ Gateway to solidify your connection with your Higher Self.
- To amplify your manifestation potential, jumpstart the Christ Gateway by sending massive amounts of energy through it, creating two simultaneous streams, an upward and a downward stream. Next, shift your focus to a desired outcome that you would like to manifest. Imagine how the power of the pillar of light is helping you to project this desired reality from the center of your being into the outside world. Watch as this new reality takes shape, and notice how the power of the pillar of light spreads this outcome in every direction. Imagine that you are emanating this new reality like the sun, sending your solar codes and warmth into the outside world. Allow yourself to bask in the energy of this new reality, knowing that it is now being manifested in your life.
- If you feel off, low-energy, or suboptimal, activate the Christ Consciousness Gateway to return to your most optimal energetic state.

Shakti Consciousness

Shakti consciousness is the concentrated emanation of our Divine Mother, of which Sophia is but an aspect. Shakti is a shape-shifter. She is flow and abundance and has an unrestricted capacity for life. She is what rises in us when we are inspired, when we are in love, or when we are full of bliss. She is how we express ourselves and how we feel inside. She is a common thread that maintains the continuity of our existence, adding the depth of perception and emotion. She is the layers of our past, present, and future, an added dimensionality to all that is. She is both subtle and bold. She is the pangs of birth and the relief of moving on. She is the olfactive artist behind the smell of flowers and the painter behind our mountainous terrain. She is the Great MA—mama, mother, matter, matrix, the one who gave us life and continues to support it daily. She is our capacity to feel oneness even when we are in a state of separation.

Shakti is innate to you. She is a force within your body, at times dormant, at times rampant, but always present. And while you are never separate from it, activating Shakti is a treat in its own right—a doorway to your feminine version of infinity. There are many ways to work with this primordial energy. Today, we'll practice one of them.

The Higher Path of Shakti Inside

You are a miracle. Your body can transmit an infinite amount of energy of Source consciousness. Once activated, Shakti can heal your body, bringing it into perfect alignment with the holy blueprint, your most optimal self. She is a force of inspiration, vitality, and love that you have always had access to. And she is a major step toward awakening the Divinity within.

There are many Shakti pathways within your body. Today, we will discover the higher Shakti path that serves as a doorway into the infinite consciousness of our Divine Mother.

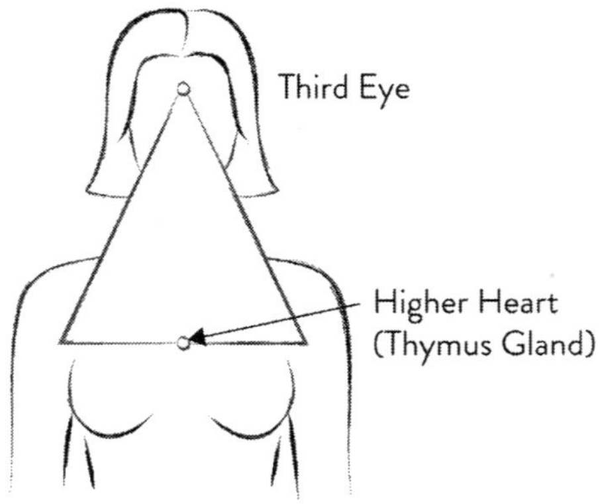

Figure 79: The Higher Path of Shakti within the body

The Higher Path of Shakti (see **Figure 79**) is a triangular area in your upper body that connects you to the infinite. Imagine that the triangle's base is aligned with your thymus gland in the center of your chest. This triangle faces upward, with the top point perfectly aligned with your third eye and the bottom two points in your shoulders. Once activated, this triangular portal moves vast amounts of energy forward or backward, providing ample opportunities for healing, alchemical transformation, and manifestation.

Activation and Practice: The Higher Shakti Gateway

This practice helps decalcify your pineal gland and keeps you in touch with the universal flow of energy, connecting you with the network of abundance. Regular practice will increase your vibration spectrum and infuse you with light codes, transforming your being on a deep level.

1. Begin by closing your eyes and focusing on your breath. Take a few deep inhalations, allowing your body to relax.
2. Imagine sending your breath through the area of your third eye, located in the center of your forehead. Visualize this area becoming activated and filling up with life force energy, causing it to glow with vibrant purple light.
3. Once you are ready, shift your focus to the area of your higher heart, located in your upper chest. Imagine breathing into it, activating it in the process. Watch as this area of your body starts to pulsate with glowing pink light.
4. Now, direct your breath to the front of your left shoulder and allow it to activate the area around it. As you breathe into this area of your body, watch it pulsate with white light emanating in all directions. Repeat this step with your right shoulder until it, too, begins to emanate pure white light.
5. Connect the two white points of your shoulders with the point of your third eye, creating a triangle. Notice that the two shoulder points are located along the same horizontal line as the pink point of the higher heart, enabling the energies of the heart to pour into the triangular shape as well (see **Figure 76**).
6. Imagine a massive flow of energy pouring through the triangle, beginning at the back and flowing toward the front, like a river going through a triangular door, abundant, powerful, and unstoppable. This is the flow of Higher Shakti in your body.
7. Allow the flow of Shakti to cleanse your body of any unwanted energies you may have accumulated. You may experience a tingling sensation or excess heat in the area of your body covered by the Higher Shakti Triangle.
8. Now, think of anything you would like to bring into your life, whether material, emotional, or energetic. Watch as the river's flow is reversed, starting to bring things into your body, flowing from the front of your body toward the back. Trust that this incoming flow has your best interests

at heart. Allow yourself to receive the fullness of your Divine Mother's blessings—no reservations, no restrictions, no resistance.

9. Finally, imagine both flows of Shakti, forward and backward, coursing through your body simultaneously. Allow yourself to be present for this simple miracle. You may experience an activation of your third eye at this time.
10. Feel free to leave the Higher Shakti Flow active. This initial connection point will run its course and close down automatically when you receive and eliminate all that you are meant to.

This is not a perpetually active portal. Whenever you require assistance from Divine Mother, you will need to activate the gateway again.

Working with the Higher Shakti Gateway:

- This gateway is a powerful tool for quickly eliminating unwanted emotions or energy blockages from your body. To use it, visualize the unwanted energy gathering at the back of your neck. Then, activate the Higher Shakti Gateway by sending your breath through the triangle. As you do, imagine powerful gusts of air flowing through the gateway, moving forward. Stay here for a few minutes, allowing the power of Shakti to work its magic and clear the area at the back of your neck, removing any unwanted energy concentrated there.
- To cleanse and release unwanted energies, use the traditional flow of Shakti, which moves from back to front. To attract positive things into your life, use the reverse flow of Shakti, which moves from front to back.
- Feeling the flow of Shakti is powerful. Activating the Higher Shakti Triangle with your breath can instantly shift your mood and energy.
- Use the Higher Shakti Gateway to feel oneness with the Universe, enhance your meditative practices, and optimize your ability to receive.
- Activating the Higher Shakti Gateway opens a potent communication portal with the Divine. Once activated, the power of your prayers and requests is accentuated. Use this time to set intentions or ask for Divine assistance with your projects.

A Path into Oneness

Someone who has achieved enlightenment knows oneness. Oneness is the common denominator of all universal cycles, a state that everything inevitably returns to before embarking on a new journey of separation. Oneness is the ultimate endgame; all else is transient and fleeting.

A path to oneness, like most things, begins internally. It is a perfect symbiosis between your inner masculine (the state of sovereignty) and your inner feminine (the state of togetherness). Let us review them both so that the endgame of merging becomes not just possible, but achievable.

Sovereignty

Sovereignty is one of the two perfect states of energy, representing an aspect of Source consciousness that is Divine Masculinity.

What sovereignty is:

It is a state of inner and outer alignment, of perfect inner harmony. Sovereignty is a system balanced, a system perfected, a system purified. It is a state of inner knowing, of assuredness, of being aligned, of following the path freely and effortlessly. Sovereignty is a state of inner strength and courage, an understanding and acceptance of one's power. It is the deeper knowing that as a part of God, your actions are Divinely synchronized with the rest of the Universe and cannot harm anyone.

Sovereignty is a state of inner flow born of a vessel, purified. The one who is sovereign is in control of their circumstances, not because they are holding the Universe in a chokehold, but because the Universe chooses to gently follow their lead. The Universe pledges allegiance to the one who is truly sovereign, for in that moment, the sovereign and the God are one and the same.

Stepping into your sovereignty means leaving the doubt, fear, and anxiety behind. It means becoming a protector, a missionary, a believer, and a fighter. A sovereign is a beacon of light and hope, a leader not by title, but by merit.

Someone who is sovereign is in their full integrity. They are wholesome, honest, complete, just, and fair. They do not fall prey to temptation. Their inner core is strong, holding them firmly in place like an anchor would, so they are dependable, stable, and trustworthy. They are the last ones standing amidst the battle of wills and circumstances. They are not afraid to step up or be seen. They have stamina; they have resolve. They have transcended the karma of weakness. They face their challenges head-on, and because of that, they inspire true loyalty. But most importantly, sovereignty is about responsibility—the kind you accept, and the kind you carry through lifetimes. A true sovereign is first and foremost here to serve others.

What sovereignty is not:

Sovereignty is not arrogance. It doesn't involve a sense of superiority over others, nor is it rooted in the pursuit of power or mind games. Rather, it represents a serene, self-assured confidence in the face of adversity.

Sovereignty isn't about vying for dominance; rather, it's a state where power is acknowledged, and leadership emerges naturally.

Sovereignty is not about the overinflated ego or bending people to your will. In essence, it is the art of leading without forcing. It's the ability to inspire and influence others by embodying a sense of calm, confidence, and humility.

Togetherness

Togetherness is one of the two perfect states, representing an aspect of Source consciousness that is Divine Femininity.

What togetherness is:

Togetherness isn't just a feeling of belonging; it's a state of constant observation and integration. It is a state of perfect receptivity, of being aware and mindful of everything that surrounds you, animate or otherwise. Togetherness is a deep understanding that everything in the Universe supports everything else; nothing exists in isolation, and no one is second rate.

Togetherness is considering every piece of the puzzle before making your move. It's the wisdom of the butterfly effect, with you knowing just how interconnected we all are. It's a state of treading carefully, mindful of your impact on your immediate surroundings and the Universe at large. Togetherness expands the concept of self to include others; it is quite literally an expanded self-concept. Someone living through togetherness has a hard time staying separate from the rest of creation. They are constantly observing and internalizing the consequences of their actions. They may come across as indecisive or meek, but that couldn't be further from the truth. Their life is a constant flow of people, events, and circumstances that they aim to navigate with a net positive impact. Their impact is their most important currency and their greatest concern. Leaving an ecosystem better than they found it is their biggest wish and greatest challenge. Experiencing togetherness entails being influenced by the environment, so those seeking to achieve this state must be mindful of who they surround themselves with.

Someone who truly embodies togetherness is a natural magnet. They are kind, considerate, soft, and benevolent. They have the heart of a true dreamer and the soul of a true believer. Although not forceful, they can effect generational and lasting change. Their energy flows like water, soft and pleasant, seeking to help, not hurt.

People who embody togetherness are the beloved children of the Universe. They live day to day, forever knowing that the Universe will take care of them, and their life is ongoing synchronicity. They tend to get what they want and are great manifesters. They are magical, and they flow. Often, they don't subscribe to the trap of overachieving, instead allowing the Universe to overachieve on their behalf. Some may perceive them as lazy, but truly, they are just in alignment with the Universe. They are not forcing anything, yet allowing everything, and they have much bliss to show for it.

What togetherness is not:

Togetherness is not inertia or indifference. In fact, anyone who achieves a state of togetherness finds that they care deeply—more than most ever could comprehend.

Togetherness is not the absence of individuality, but the presence of compassion and acceptance of all things just as they are. Togetherness is not a lack of power; rather, it is a state that is less focused and more dispersed, like a cloud that can even out the roughest edges.

The Merging

Through the merging of the two states— masculine sovereignty and feminine togetherness—we find true godliness within, and we become whole and complete in and of ourselves. In that blessed moment, we become the carriers and the transmitters of the blueprints of our Divine Mother and our Divine Father—two halves of the same whole, two dichotomies, finally balanced, their individual paths complete in a dance of unity and mutual surrender.

Energetically, the state of sovereignty is represented by a vertical line that runs through the spine, while the state of togetherness is represented by a horizontal line that passes through the heart space and extends through outstretched arms (see **Figure 80**). These states represent a familiar shape: the cross, which stands for absolute oneness, perfect attainment, and God/Goddess consciousness within. It is also a universal symbol of Christ, a being in complete alignment who attained equilibrium of all internal factors to reemerge on the other side as the most immaculate version of themselves.

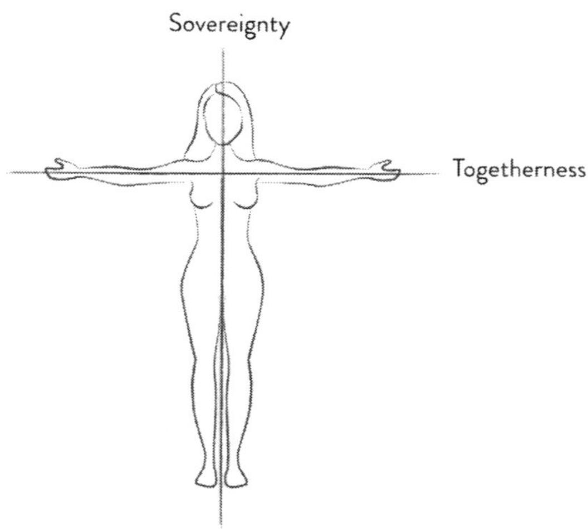

Figure 80: Finding oneness within

Energy Activation and Practice: The Rose of Oneness

There are many paths to oneness. All evolutionary roads eventually lead to integration. Today, we will tap into the power of the Rose to bring about true energetic oneness within your body, a precursor to external oneness, which is a covetable state indeed.

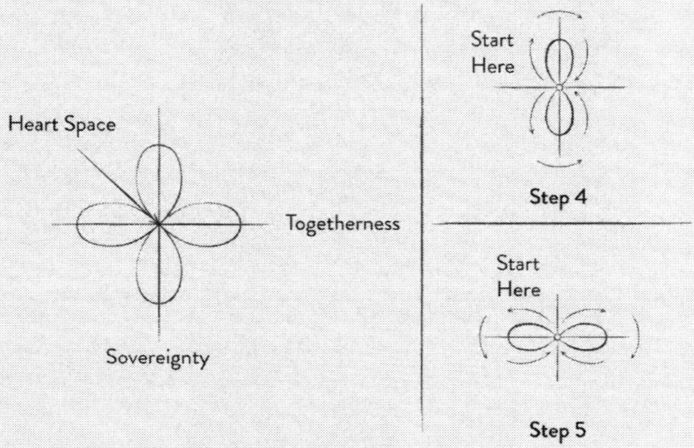

Figure 81: The Rose of Oneness

1. Begin by taking a few deep breaths, allowing your awareness to settle into your heart space. As you inhale, imagine that the air is purifying your chest cavity, creating space for a truly transformative experience. Take ten deep breaths here, relaxing and sinking deeper into your body.
2. Now, bring your attention to your thymus gland, a miraculous part of your body also called the higher heart, which is nestled in your upper chest along the vertical axis of your body. This is the center of your Rose, the hub of light and magnetism. Imagine how this center of your body expands, taking on its own breath and heartbeat. Allow yourself to tune into its subtle vibration.
3. The shape of the Rose of Oneness is two interlocked figure eights—the infinity of the masculine and the infinity of the feminine within. Imagine a figure eight aligned with the vertical axis of your body, with the midpoint at your thymus gland. That is where you shall begin.

4. Imagine drawing a figure eight by moving up and to the left, allowing the top loop of the figure eight to curve around your head. Then, pass through the thymus gland again on the way down, and draw another large loop over the bottom part of your body before finally bringing things back to the center inside your thymus gland (see **Figure 81**).
5. Now, draw a second figure eight with a midpoint in your thymus gland, but this one is horizontal. Imagine starting up and to the left, drawing the loop of the figure eight so that it encircles your left shoulder, then coming back to the center and creating another loop, moving up and to the right, encircling your right shoulder with the second loop of the figure eight. Your beautiful rose is now complete! It has four petals, one for each of the loops of the figure eight you have just drawn.
6. Repeat the process of drawing the two figure eights to get used to the energy movement of the Rose of Oneness. Starting at the thymus gland, move up and to the left to draw the loop of the vertical figure eight. Then, passing through the center of the thymus gland, move down and to the left, drawing the bottom loop of the figure eight. Complete by coming back to the midpoint.
7. Now, moving up and to the left, draw a loop of the horizontal figure eight on the left side of your body. Return to the center and draw the last missing loop on the right side of your body.
8. Hopefully, you now know how to create the Rose of Oneness. The magic begins when you draw three of these roses quickly and continuously. Allow yourself to do this right now. As you do this, you may notice a strange sensation of energy moving through your body at hyper-speed. Some of you may feel lightheaded or experience a tingling sensation in various parts of your body. This is completely normal and is a sign that you are sensitive to the energies within.

Congratulations! You are now the master of the Rose of Oneness and can receive its many blessings and extraordinary benefits.

Benefits of the Rose of Oneness:

- Removes energetic blockages
- Creates a state of heightened awareness
- Improves intuition
- Optimizes energy levels (gives you an energy boost)
- Opens up your body to receive insights and downloads
- Heals on all levels—physical, energetic, emotional, and mental
- Raises your vibration
- Enhances your psychic abilities
- Brings you into alignment (internal and external)
- Allows you to have a more productive and happy life overall
- Brings you one step closer to achieving the state of Christ consciousness within

Working with the Rose of Oneness:

- Perform the practice in the morning or when you need to get into alignment quickly (for instance, before an important meeting).
- Use it at the beginning of your meditation to enhance the quality of your experience.
- Use the practice when you need inspiration or motivation to create something.
- Use it when you feel stuck and need to move the energy quickly and powerfully.
- Use it to align your body and remove distortions from your auric field before working with a pendulum, runes, the tarot, or oracle cards.
- Use the practice to feel closer to Source and/or your Higher Self.
- Use it when you are stressed or overwhelmed to quickly move through these energies.

Most importantly, enjoy!

This practice is a sacred tool of alignment and can help you experience flow and abundance in all areas of your life.

Have you met the new Christ yet?
For she is female, and she is rising.
She is rising from the depth of the Mother Divine to be a way-shower.
She is rising like Shakti always does, from deep darkness into the light,
Not a serpent, but a phoenix carried upon the feathered wings of providence.
She is but a spiral of evolution, an arrow pointing upward.
She is the second coming—but not like you thought.
The female Christ is rising,
And the world shall never be the same again.
She is rising like the morning sun, first shy, then inevitable.
She is rising within all of us, day in and day out.
She is rising amidst the rubble of the Old World,
Despite its persecution, regardless of its contempt.
She is rising in her own time—the time to rewrite HIS story into HER story.
The female Christ is rising.
She is rising in you; she is rising in me.
She is shining the light of forgiveness upon the sea of sin.
She is the liberation of the body, of the mind, and of the heart,
Not the Son of God, but the Daughter.
She is as one with the Universe, a sister of the ones who came before.
And it is her hand that shall rewrite the scriptures,
Her breath that shall rebuild the faith, her voice that shall unite the many.
Have you met the new Christ yet?
For she is female, and she is rising.

Heart Space: The Sands of Time

The wheel of time is turning, forging eternity from a myriad of seconds chasing one another.

The wheel of time is turning, promising that there will always be a tomorrow.

The realm of Chronos, the large hourglass of the Universe, is hard at work gluing this reality together through the tiny particles of time, forever recycling them in an endless whirlwind.

The wheel of time is turning, promising progress, and sometimes eternal life.

The wheel of time is turning, and not even the gods themselves can slow down its pace.

But there comes a day, there comes an hour, there comes a minute where the sands of time start to run low.

The beginning of a New Era. The Great Ending. The Great Reset. The Letting Go of What Once Was.

There is a finality to the moment when no more time is left.

When all the sand particles of time are neatly packed away in the past, none is left for the future.

There is ultimate stillness in the moment when time stops,

When there is nothing to track anymore, no more errands to run, no more problems to solve.

And it is at the turning of the hourglass that the Maiden of Light shall descend onto Earth.

It is at this time that her voice will be heard in all the corners of Gaia.

She will come as a great redeemer, the celestial judge, the female Christ.

And she will pave the way for a new beginning, a New Earth, and a new cycle of timelessness.

And together with Chronos, she will start the clock anew so that many generations can thrive and prosper and once again believe in the infinity of time—in the fact that time will never run out.

The simple truth is that there will always be a tomorrow.

Parting Words

My Dear Sibling in Rose,

This is not a goodbye. This is a "see you soon," for there will be more to the Rose Codes than this book.

This was just the beginning, the setting of the stage, the first flavor of the mystery that is the Rose. I hope you stay the course and dive deep into your magic until the next chapter of this saga comes out. There is so much more I have in store for you, and my heart is so full knowing that you have come with me thus far. I can sense your inner joy and transformation; I feel your light.

Ours is a soul relationship I cherish, and I cannot wait to see you in the future on the pages of my new books.

This is a heartfelt "See you soon."

For what is time if not an arbitrary separation of two points of connection? I know our next meeting is predetermined, and I greatly anticipate it.

Bloom with abandon, my Rose. And may your blooming light up the world.

The gentlest of all the flames is the flame of the Mother that is now burning in your beautiful heart. Let it burn, baby.

YOU ARE the shift this planet needs.

You are the flame of change.

You are the light that was promised.

—Mariya

About the Author

Mariya is a spiritual teacher, channel, intuitive, energy alchemist, podcast host, entrepreneur, and author of *72 Keys to Manifestation: An Ancient Path of a Modern-Day Alchemist.*

Since her spiritual awakening in 2018, Mariya has been guided by spirit to channel and teach spiritual content. Mariya's podcast, *This is Mariya (AKA Conversations with my Higher Self)*, which is recorded in a state of trance (theta state) covers a wealth of esoteric and spiritual topics, ranging from the sacred flames, to ancestral healing, to past lives, to Source consciousness. Mariya has the ability to connect with the collective consciousness of humanity, providing in-the-moment healing, guidance, and information based on what is coming through energetically.

In 2022, Mariya started leading guided journeys and meditations through her new podcast, *Our Sacred Universe.* During these journeys, she is able to hold healing, heart-led space and transmit high-frequency codes of light to help humanity's evolution.

Currently, Mariya is in the process of writing a series of books devoted to the Path of the Rose, a revival of the teachings of an ancient female mystery school devoted to walking the path of a priestess. Plenty of notable female figures from the past, from Mary Magdalene and Mother Mary to Isis and Inanna, walked the path of the Rose, having claimed their own flavor of feminine magic. It is Mariya's great joy and part of her karma here on Earth to help reinstate this lost knowledge.

Please stay in touch!

www.thisismariya.com
Instagram: ThisisMariyaOfficial
YouTube: ThisisMariya
TikTok: ThisisMariyaOfficial
Spotify/Apple Podcast: This is Mariya
Spotify/Apple Podcast: Our Sacred Universe